D1595229

Women's Theatre Writing in Victorian Britain

Women's Theatre Writing in Victorian Britain

Katherine Newey

palgrave
macmillan

First published 2005 by
PALGRAVE MACMILLAN
Houndmills, Basingstoke, Hampshire RG21 6XS and
175 Fifth Avenue, New York, N.Y. 10010
Companies and representatives throughout the world

PALGRAVE MACMILLAN is the global academic imprint of the Palgrave Macmillan division of St. Martin's Press, LLC and of Palgrave Macmillan Ltd. Macmillan® is a registered trademark in the United States, United Kingdom and other countries. Palgrave is a registered trademark in the European Union and other countries.

ISBN-13: 978–1–4039–4332–3 hardback
ISBN-10: 1–4039–4332–X hardback

This book is printed on paper suitable for recycling and made from fully managed and sustained forest sources.

A catalogue record for this book is available from the British Library.

Library of Congress Cataloging-in-Publication Data
Newey, Katherine.
    Women's theatre writing in Victorian Britain / Katherine Newey.
        p.   cm.
    Includes bibliographical references and index.
    ISBN 1–4039–4332–X (cloth)
    1. English drama—Women authors—History and criticism.   2. Women in the theater—Great Britain—History—19th century.   3. Women and literature—Great Britain—History—19th century.   4. English drama—19th century—History and criticism.   I. Title.
PR734.W6N49 2005
    822'.8099287—dc22   2005047239

10   9   8   7   6   5   4   3   2   1
14   13   12   11   10   09   08   07   06   05

Printed and bound in Great Britain by
Antony Rowe Ltd, Chippenham and Eastbourne

To my teachers and colleagues, Penny Gay, Margaret Harris, and Elizabeth Webby

Contents

Acknowledgements

My scholarly debts are recorded in this book's endnotes, but a project this large needs a lot of assistance along the way and it is a delight to thank those who helped me. I am grateful to a number of libraries who have granted me permission to quote from unpublished sources: the Brotherton Collection, Leeds University Library; the Duke of Devonshire and the Chatsworth Settlement Trustees; the Fales Library, New York University; the Harry Ransom Centre for Humanities Research, University of Texas (Austin); Independent Age (holders of the Backsettown Trust); and the Harvard Theatre Collection, Houghton Library, Harvard University. Part of Chapter 5, 'Home and Nation,' is a version of '*Home Plays for Ladies*: Women's Work in Home Theatricals,' first published in *Nineteenth Century Theatre and Film* (Winter 1998), and reproduced here by permission of the editors. All quotation falls under the definition of 'fair dealing,' and every attempt has been made to contact copyright holders.

I was fortunate to receive substantial funding from the Australian Research Council, and I thank research assistants Margaret Leask, Sylvia Martin, Tiffany Donnelly, and Gillian Sykes. Grants from the Society for Theatre Research and the Australian Academy of Humanities enabled me to travel, and a Mellon Foundation Fellowship gave me a period of research at the Harry Ransom Humanities Research Centre, University of Texas (Austin). The New Literatures Research Centre at the University of Wollongong provided seed funding, and the British Academy and the Arts and Humanities Research Board (UK) have awarded me substantial time and travel to finish the book.

I am lucky to have a wonderful network of colleagues whose intellectual generosity and interest in this project have made it all worthwhile. Heartfelt thanks to Virginia Blain, Dinah Birch, Jacky Bratton, Gilli Bush-Bailey, Claire Cochrane, Tom Crochunis, Catherine Burroughs, and the 'Romantic drama gang' at NASSR, Jim Davis, Tracy Davis, Marysa Demoor, Ellen Donkin, Richard Fotheringham, Hilary Fraser, Viv Gardner, Jules Holledge, Louis James, Judith Johnston, Veronica Kelly, Emma Liggins, Gail Marshall, Andrew Maunder, David Mayer and Helen Day-Mayer, Jane Moody, Elizabeth Schafer, Richard Schoch, Joanne Shattock, Cathy Waters, Nicolas Whybrow, and Joanne Wilkes, colleagues in the Australasian Victorian Studies and the Australasian

Drama Studies Associations, participants in the Theatre Historiography working group of the International Federation of Theatre Research, the virtual common room of the VICTORIA electronic discussion list, and my patient editors at Palgrave Macmillan, Emily Rosser and Paula Kennedy. In addition, the work for this project began and ended in libraries at opposite ends of the world: Fisher Library at the University of Sydney, the British Library, the John Rylands Library at the University of Manchester, and Lancaster University Library and Rare Books Collection.

As well as my travels in the UK, the USA, and Australia, this book was written and researched in four institutions in two hemispheres, and I owe much to the intellectual and social stamina of my family, friends, and colleagues in these places. My friends and family know who they are, and the champagne is in the fridge in three continents – particularly for the sibs' international telephone support network! I would especially like to thank my colleagues at the University of Wollongong, Jim Wieland, John Senczuk, Rebecca Albury, Graham Barwell, Susan Dodds, Dorothy Jones, Carmel Pass, Anne Lear, and Paul Sharrad. At Royal Holloway College, University of London, the Drama Department hosted me for a marvellous year, and I thank them for taking on a stranger from the other side of the world. I will be forever in the debt of Liz Schafer and Vincent Jones for participating in that adventure. My colleagues at Lancaster University welcomed me and this project (which must have seemed never-ending to them), and I thank particularly Gabriella Giannachi, Alison Findlay, Karen Juers-Munby, Tess Cosslett, Mike Sanders, Alison Easton, and of course, Jeffrey Richards. Last, but by no means least, I return to the University of Sydney and my first teachers and colleagues there, particularly the three exemplary women (my 'Doktor-Mütter') to whom this book is dedicated.

Introduction: Framing the Victorian Woman Playwright

This book is about the appearances, disappearances, and reappearances of women's words in the British theatre from the late Romantic period to the beginning of the twentieth century. My principal focus is playwriting for the commercial London theatre, although I also consider the substantial work of women for amateur and home theatricals, women's work in translating and adapting for the stage, the agitprop theatre of the suffragette movement, and the para-theatrical writing – not quite closet drama, not quite stage success – which characterized dramatic writing by women in the mid- and late-Victorian periods. My aim is to make visible those previously invisible women writers, whose work has been shrouded by a combination of factors: the material practices of the London theatre industry which presented a misogynist obstacle course, Victorian gender ideology which theorized the public nature of the playwright's task to be unfeminine, a practice of theatre historiography which has consistently converted partisan aesthetic judgements into universal statements of fact, and the scholarly discipline of Victorian Studies which has consistently ignored the theatre as a significant element of nineteenth-century culture.

The woman playwright

At first sight, my task might seem straightforward: to chart the work of hundreds of women playwrights who between them produced over one thousand titles between 1800 and 1900. Yet recent critical and historical theory has questioned both parts of that description. Feminist theory has questioned the notion of such a unitary category as 'woman,'[1] and post-structural theory has turned its attention to questions of authorship as the central focus of writing history. The moves from 'woman' to 'gender,'[2] and from 'writer' to 'author-function'[3] have been both instructive and liberatory for feminist literary history, and might at first, make this book seem naïve or essentializing. But as feminist theorist Agnes Heller wrote about women writers and the death of the subject: 'Before someone is buried, they need first to be identified,'[4] and in this book I am committed to naming previously invisible women – identifying who actually wrote what and how. Recent scholars of eighteenth century and Romantic women's playwriting have argued part of my case for me. In response to concerns about segregating women writers from the 'mainstream' of theatre history, Catherine Burroughs argues for patience with what she calls 'an archaeological study focused primarily on bringing to light undiscovered or long-forgotten texts of women writers,' categorizing such work as 'first-phase scholarship.'[5] And following Burroughs, Misty Anderson defends apparently 'old fashioned' studies of women writers as still necessary while scholars still 'look only to the usual canonical suspects.'[6]

I am not, however, advocating a separation of women playwrights into an oppositional or marginalized grouping; as Tracy Davis has argued, nineteenth-century women playwrights were 'not a counterpublic but rather part of the public sphere struggling with the structures and settings of sociability leading to representation.'[7] I take my cue from Victorian women playwrights themselves who persistently resisted quarantine, although they were just as persistently forced into it. Cicely Hamilton was reported to have responded with characteristic forthrightness from the woman's point of view to the toast to 'British Dramatists' at a celebratory dinner held by the O. P. Club in 1914:

> She did not think that there was a woman's point of view in the theatre. Her point of view was the same as a man's, only man refused to recognize that it was the same.[8]

Hamilton's claim to equality, and her exasperation at male insistence on imposing difference, is representative of many women writers' thinking about the theatre as a scene of writing and professional endeavour in the nineteenth century. Augusta Webster explained this in her typically humorous (but serious) manner to Edmund Gosse:

> I don't dispute that a man's work and a woman's on the same theme differ where the theme is one they naturally approach from different points. [. . .] But I feel that (though an inquiry into the distinctive differences of men's and women's work would be a legitimate subject

for a critic), when the critic simply professes to be reviewing such and such a product, book or picture or sonata, what he has undertaken is to tell the public and the author about the *result* before him, and that it is not more reasonable in doing so to introduce a classification of authors by sex than ones by rank or bodily health or income or any other of the important material differences which, influencing personality, influence persons in all they do of every kind.[9]

And earlier in the century, in a period of acute gender panic over 'lady' playwrights, Emma Robinson wrote to James Robinson Planché regarding the banning of her play, *Richelieu in Love* in 1844, complaining, 'I am far more afraid of having too hot a champion than of wanting one.'[10]

All in all, I want to resist speaking definitively of a distinct school of women's dramatic writing in the nineteenth century or reading women's playwriting as *necessarily* different in form or content from men's play writing. Women's output was too various, and responsive to local conditions. Yet, indisputably, women's plays *were* viewed and read differently by their contemporaries, and women faced gender-specific obstacles in the achievement of professional status as playwrights. On these grounds, I am interested in what connects women's playwriting across the century and identifying the common themes and concerns which emerge from this large body of women's writing, however individually each writer deals with them. Much of the argument of this book is dedicated to examining the interplay between the gendered differences in production and reception of women's play writing, and the themes, materials, and genres of women's writing for performance. What impact did women's gender difficulties have on the content and form of their plays? And how did the theme, content, genre chosen by a woman playwright affect her reception? Approached in this way, an acknowledgement of the variety of women's writing across the nineteenth century does not preclude an awareness of a female writing tradition or traditions. And looking across the work and working conditions of a number of women playwrights, it is also possible to place issues of gender alongside those of class, to offer a corrective to the sometimes oppressive category of 'lady playwright.' What emerges when looked at in this way is a body of work which demonstrates women playwrights' abilities to exploit the very conditions which seem to restrain them, and to work from within the conventions of their profession to produce works which can be read by the twenty-first-century feminist historian against the grain of Victorian ideologies of class, race, and gender.

In examining what women wrote about and how they expressed themselves when they were given the opportunity to take to the stage with their words, I have become fascinated by what drew women to the theatre, despite the substantial obstacles in their way. In looking at this work, I find answers which are obvious perhaps, but nonetheless bear repeating. Writing for public performance gave women a powerful voice with immediate impact, and a woman playwright could deliberately organize bodies and events on the fictional stage in ways that she was not always able to in the world off-stage. As a playwright, a woman had a possibility of agency. And her voice could be a playful one, could be multiply deployed, and sceptical and subversive, while maintaining the outward decorum of generic expectations.

Nineteenth-century theatre history: Keeping on forgetting

This book will not chart the movement from dark pre-feminist days of the popular theatre in the 1820s and 1830s, to a liberated theatre of the modern woman by the end of the First World War, although this is my chronological sweep. The history of women's work as professional playwrights is not one of a smooth and triumphant progress from oppression and silence to freedom and voice, although in Chapter 3 I do argue for progress towards a grudging acceptance of some aspects of women's playwriting by the turn of the twentieth century. However, this marginal acceptance was undercut by a counterdiscourse which was critical of the so-called feminization of English culture at the *fin de siècle* and the related Modernist project which created an artificial divide between the Victorian and the modern. So 'acceptance' is a contingent term, and this instance of popular women's playwriting – stranded between the modernist avant-garde and the literary drama – is a typical example of the dialectical relationship between women's playwriting and the rest of the theatrical establishment throughout the nineteenth century.

My study starts in contemplation of an earlier rift between 'notions of female authorship [...], and play writing [...]' which Ellen Donkin identifies at the conclusion of her study of late eighteenth and early nineteenth-century women playwrights.[11] Donkin ponders, but does not explain, the reversal in women's positions as theatre professionals from much performed authors at the end of the eighteenth century to oddities and extras in the 1820s. The 1820s, it seems, was the critical period of counter-revolution for women's writing for performance. Not coincidentally, this was a period of some turbulence and change for the London theatre industry as a whole, and in my first and second chapters,

I explore the ways in which this instability caught ambitious women playwrights (or would-be playwrights) in its changes. While conditions in the theatre tightened for all playwrights in the 1820s, women were doubly affected, as increasing restrictions on feminine behaviour that we have since labelled 'Victorian' hampered their participation as fully professional writers, and disabled women writers in ways which were quite different from their fellow male playwrights. Through the study of a series of 'exceptional' women playwrights, I look at women's interventions into the apparently masculine realms of the legitimate theatre, high comedy, and historical verse tragedy, balancing the success of such raids into masculine territory against the personal professional difficulties experienced by these playwrights.

Although I have chosen not to include a study of Joanna Baillie in this book (of all nineteenth-century women playwrights her work has been the most thoroughly discussed in recent revisionist scholarship) aspects of her work and working life offer an important paradigm for my discussion of women playwrights in the 1820s. Recent reassessments of Baillie's dramatic authorship have been fundamental to the revision of theoretical and historiographical assumptions which had hitherto kept Romantic theatre at the outer edges of relevance for Romantic literary studies generally.[12] Key features of her work which are of relevance for discussing an emergent tradition of women's playwriting are the consideration of the cultural work of the closet drama, and a broadened understanding of the possible relationships between the Romantic theatre and national politics. After Elizabeth Inchbald, Joanna Baillie has always been the most consistently visible woman playwright of the late eighteenth and nineteenth centuries. However, to state this is not to say much. Despite public recognition of her work, and its usually respectful critical reception, Baillie's career contained significant contradictions and difficulties, which came to be symbolic for women playwrights following her.[13] Baillie's recognition was won in spite of considerable difficulties, both personal and public, and her career often teetered between unarguable success and an abiding sense of personal and aesthetic failure. It is this sense of failure, rather than recognition of their successes, which has marked the history of women's playwriting to this day. Part of the task of my second chapter is to rebalance this critical history, and to move carefully between women playwrights' own senses of the shapes and outcomes of their careers, and a more independent assessment of their achievements.

Countering the problematic status of the exceptional woman, and the woman playwright in the legitimate theatre, in Chapter 3 I consider women who wrote plays as part of the family theatre business. They were actresses, managers, choreographers and teachers, mothers, daughters, and wives, as well as playwrights. They wrote for the 'illegitimate' theatres and saloons of the East End and the South Bank, and the West End matinées and fashionable theatres at the end of the century, and the early film industry. In this way, I argue, they made a defining contribution to what Peter Bailey calls 'popular modernism.'[14] Unlike the uncomfortable spotlight on Hemans or Mitford, these women's work has been actively forgotten, covered over by the processes of Victorian gender ideology then, which sought to identify women by their domestic relationships, and the teleology of theatre history now, which has, until recently, valued only playwriting which contributed to the establishment of British realism and a literary drama. But it is a tenet of feminist historiography that, as Helen Day argues, 'women's theatre history [...] is inclusive rather than exclusive and without imposed hierarchies. The high and the popular co-exist and have equal status,'[15] and in Chapter 3 I am interested in the ways that women's theatre writing moved between the categories of 'high' and 'low' (or, more comfortably, 'popular') culture in what Jane Moody has called a revolution in London theatre in the nineteenth century, when illegitimate culture supplanted the legitimate and regulated theatre of the Patent houses.[16]

However, the pressures on women writers to conform to a 'high art' model of literary production can be seen in the contrasting careers of George Eliot and Augusta Webster, whose verse dramas I discuss in Chapter 4. This chapter, together with Chapter 2, looks at a range of engagements by women playwrights with the cultural capital implicit in the literary drama across the Victorian period. I trace the dialectical dance of involvement with and retreat from the Victorian stage; in the cases of Mitford and Hemans, this occurred within each career, while Eliot and Webster were much more guarded about their ambitions for the theatre (as opposed to the drama). I am interested in Eliot and Webster's turn to drama, and the conflicting pulls between public performance and private contemplation which it represented – in very different ways – for each writer. Their plays were not written primarily for performance but took up the dramatic and the theatrical in ways which solidify the tradition of dramatic verse for women playwrights. In this, I argue that they are representative writers, rather than individual geniuses, because, although I focus on Eliot and Webster, there are others who are candidates for similar examination, such as 'Michael Field' (Katherine Bradley and Edith Cooper), Katharine Hinkson

Tynan, Emily Pfeiffer, and Harriet Childe-Pemberton. Again, issues of choice and focus in scholarship are relevant here – although there has been a resurgence of interest in the work of 'Michael Field,' little work has been done on their dramatic writing, which was not inconsiderable. They had one play, *A Question of Memory*, performed by the non-commercial, avant-garde Independent Theatre Society at the Opera Comique in 1893, and 'their insistence on publishing largely unperformable verse tragedies' (as Angela Leighton puts it)[17] persisted throughout their joint writing career. E. Warwick Slinn offers a suggestive way into further theoretical work on verse drama by bringing together the aesthetic and the political through his analysis of the performativity of the dramatic monologue as the 'discursive means by which normative structures and personal subjectivities are shown to invade and constitute each other through acts of speaking,' arguing that it is the 'excesses' of poetic form which draw attention to contemporary issues, as much as such poems' 'thematic allusiveness.'[18] The attraction of the theatre as a vehicle for political work when income was not at stake is the focus of the second half of my discussion of women's theatre writing and 'art,' as I look at the investment a series of women writers made in translations of Henrik Ibsen in the late nineteenth century. With Eleanor Marx, pre-eminently, I find a new confidence in a theatre which could not only serve progressive aesthetic and intellectual ambitions, but also offer compelling public entertainment (if not commercial success) – even Clement Scott, a socially conservative anti-Ibsenite through and through, conceded that the attention of the audience was wholly gripped by Achurch's *Doll's House*.[19] I am not suggesting, however, that these three exemplars make a neat pattern of the progress of women's playwriting across the Victorian period; rather, I offer these women as examples of negotiation with the high stakes of 'art.' Even if economic capital was not at stake, the investment in cultural capital was substantial.

Women's theatre writing was not always staged in theatre buildings – a truism now after a century of avant-garde performance and particularly women's theatre fuelled by feminist experimentation – but in Chapter 5 I suggest ways in which women's writing in the Victorian period offers models for the oppositional critique of later twentieth century political theatre. The apparently conservative content of plays written for performance in the home, in schools, and by children masks the way in which the activity of theatre within the home challenged the boundaries of the public and private spheres so powerful in constraining the activities of women in the theatre industry. Writing for this niche market, as several women playwrights specialized in doing, and performing in amateur and home performance as it became increasingly fashionable, not only suggests the permeability of these gendered boundaries, but offers a corrective to the historiographical assumption that the Victorian middle-class were largely ignorant of the popular theatre of their day, and fundamentally anti-theatrical. Furthermore, a study of theatre in the home allows us to see the ways in which Victorian domestic ideology could be subverted from within: as Barbara Caine and Anne Mellor find in their separate studies of women's role in the public sphere in the nineteenth century. Hilary Fraser and Judith Johnston neatly sum up this double movement in their study of the Victorian periodical, a medium closely paralleling the theatre in this period, with their observation that '[T]he "Politics of Home" addresses both the political public domain of national government and the political private domain of domestic government.'[20] The links between the government of the home and the government of the nation are to be found in the apparently frivolous social comedies and 'silver fork' novels of Catherine Gore as well as the agitprop theatre of the suffragettes, and the patriotic melodramas of Mrs Kimberley during the First World War.

My conclusion returns to the popular theatre of the *fin de siècle* to look at another set of representative women writers who included the theatre in their professional writing careers. Again, my point is to examine the work of these women, and also to reflect on how that examination might change our assumptions about the theatre of the late Victorian period. To borrow a metaphor from the country where I started this research, I am proposing the theatre, and its dramatic writing, as the 'Antipodes' of Victorian literature, and the work of women playwrights as pioneers of that territory who can tell us much about its hinterlands. In making sense of the work of some many Victorian women play-wrights, I have been involved in the work of discovery of this land of hitherto 'invisible' women, who, like the Antipodes, were actually always already there. But like the geographical Antipodes of the popular imagi-nation, the Victorian theatre is for many scholars a far away place, full of odd things, where perhaps the natives walk on their heads? But what happens when we make that long journey to the Victorian theatre and discover that actually it is not isolated, upside down, or back to front, but really quite like the world we are used to, but with differences enough to give some fresh views of our familiar environment? Through women's theatre writing, I trace the continuing popularity of female-centred, and female-authored popular drama on the stage to the end of the nineteenth century, an understanding of which has the potential to disrupt the historiographical model of a smooth evolutionary development towards psychological realism and representational naturalism at the end of the nineteenth century – that male-centred account of the British theatre.

1
Rescuing the Stage

In a puff for Frances Burney's historical tragedy *Hubert de Vere*, the *Oracle* announced that 'Miss Burney's pen will retrieve the Stage, degraded beyond bearing by the tricking trash which our Harlequin Writers have forced upon the Public.'[1] In the latter part of her life, Hannah More justified her earlier work as a playwright by the desire to convert 'the Stage [. . .] into a school of virtue.'[2] In 1826, the *Theatrical Examiner* wrote of Mary Russell Mitford 'that this lady has in some measure rescued the stage from these moving nuisances, those puning [*sic*] pirates who infest the purlieus of the theatres, under the assumed name of authors.'[3] And about Mitford's later play, *Rienzi* (1828), the ubiquitous D.——G. wrote, 'The reception of this tragedy is a proof that, though the public have been wont to feed on garbage, they have no disinclination to wholesome food.'[4]

These comments represent one face of the critical reception of women playwrights on the London stage in the late eighteenth and early nineteenth centuries. Their positive and welcoming tenor marks a period of relative visibility for women playwrights who in this period according to Ellen Donkin achieved 'a modest momentum.'[5] Yet, this momentum could be attributed to the positioning of women writers and femininity as the guardian and guarantor of stage morality during a period of discursive and industrial crisis over the state of the theatre to 1843. This was a role as easily transgressed as fulfilled, and had problematic consequences for the status and reception of women's playwriting. In the discursive construction of the woman playwright in this period, always to be the 'rescuer' suggests a kind of alien status, implying women playwrights were not part of the profession which needed rescuing, but outsiders who could occasionally perform heroic gestures as a sort of moral housekeeping. And there were conditions attached. The welcome by largely male critics and theatre managers was conditional on women playwrights' maintenance of a feminine demeanour, policed through the discourse of respectability. Women's participation as playwrights was tolerated, and at times even welcomed, if they wrote as 'proper ladies' in Mary Poovey's terms[6] and acted as moral gatekeepers or apologists for the theatre. As a consequence, the late Romantic period saw women playwrights increasingly labouring under the necessity of participating in a set of highly gendered conventions of playwriting in content and style, and circumscribed possibilities in the development of artistic and professional *personae*. Greg Kucich comments that the reviewing of women playwrights in the Romantic period reveals the theatre as 'one of Romanticism's more charged cultural sites of gender contention marked by conflicting postures of welcome, containment, and threatened resistance.'[7] Needless to say, such moral and professional demands were never made of male playwrights, and indeed, restrictions on their freedom were regarded as inimical to their artistry, as the move to de-regulate the London stage in 1843 suggests.

So, women playwrights' 'rescue' of the stage in the first three decades of the nineteenth century was less the long-overdue public recognition of women's undisputed talents than the positioning of a minority of women playwrights as 'exceptional.' While the recognition of these women is important, their identification as exceptional is a double-edged sword for the history of women's playwriting. Every time a woman writer was spotlit in this way, the acceptance of women playwrights as normal, diverse and numerous in their presence in the theatrical profession became more tenuous. The recognition of the few exceptional women playwrights seems to have occurred alongside the general perception that there existed no other type of woman playwright. The discourse of exceptionality is part of the gendered process of uncoupling the identity of 'woman' from that of 'playwright,'[8] a process reiterated throughout the nineteenth century and accepted into the twentieth century as a given of British theatre history. In an attempt to break this vicious circle, I will be arguing for the normative identity of women playwrights in the nineteenth century. If we acquiesce in the view of women playwrights as *exceptions* to the category of playwright in the nineteenth century, then we must run the risk of wilfully persisting in a damagingly incomplete version of the past.

However, in this chapter and the next I want to pursue the consequences of exceptionality for a handful of women playwrights, who, in their various ways, set out to reform or rescue the British theatre by working within its most authoritative institution, the legitimate drama played at the Theatres Royal. In looking at these exceptions, it is possible to identify those attributes of the female pen which were thought could ease the problems of the nineteenth-century stage, but that also needed to be contained within the boundaries of exceptionality and respectability. Except for Fanny Kemble, my subjects in these chapters are women for whom playwriting was part of a wider writing career, but who did not come from theatrical families. Other characteristics of women theatre workers' exceptionality which I explore include the woman's identification (both by herself and by others) as middle-class, or respectable, or as a gentlewoman in a period of class instability; her need to survive independently because the conventional expectations of a male relative or husband as provider were not met; and the pursuit of her ambition and talent in spite of powerful social proscriptions against such desires. The saving graces of femininity which were on occasion welcomed into the theatre were necessarily underpinned by women's work – intellectual, emotional, and physical – and in the theatre, this work was often too visible. Given the hegemonic power of ideologies of respectable femininity which stressed female subservience, lack of agency, and a refusal to engage directly with material concerns of income and profession, the conditions of exceptionality – of ladies' work made visible – inevitably caused conflict. In this chapter, I look at the consequences of those conflicts for particular women writers and theatre workers – Isabel Hill and Fanny Kemble, and the winners of playwriting competitions held across the nineteenth century – arguing that this model of exceptionality has structured our histories and historiographies of British theatre and women's writing ever since.

Saving the National Drama

In 1829, Isabel Hill attempted to save the English National Drama. In August, the Theatre Royal, Covent Garden faced another of its financial crises, and was likely to be closed down, with the properties, scenery, and costumes sold to pay creditors and share-holders. Writers and actors were exhorted to give their services free to save this 'temple of the National Drama.'[9] Isabel Hill responded with her comedy, *The First of May; or, A Royal Love-Match*, which opened on 10 October 1829. On 5 October, opening this rescue season, Fanny Kemble, daughter of Charles Kemble the indebted manager of Covent Garden, and third generation of one of England's foremost theatrical families, made her public stage debut as Juliet in a season of *Romeo and Juliet*. Although

Fanny Kemble did not perform in *The First of May* – and indeed much to Benson Hill's *chagrin* Isabel's play seemed to be deliberately slighted by its selection 'for the nights that Miss Fanny Kemble did *not* appear'[10] – Kemble's and Hill's simultaneous involvement in a season expressly designed to rescue the fortunes of the proprietors of Covent Garden serves to illustrate some of the central themes of this book. More particularly, the contrasts between Hill's and Kemble's contributions to Covent Garden's 1829 autumn season open up some of the paradoxes enacted by middle-class women working in the theatre that are my concern.

What was the woman's play offered to Covent Garden at this time of crisis? Surprisingly, *The First of May* is very unlike Hill's earlier, unperformed play, *The Poet's Child* (1820), or her later unperformed verse drama *Brian the Probationer; or, The Red Hand* (1842), or descriptions of the unnamed script she produced for actor James Warde, praised by Kemble and Macready, and was also never performed.[11] It is not in the mould of the formal five-act verse tragedy generally considered the pattern of legitimate drama of this period, and which might have been thought particularly suitable for a season devoted to restoring the fortunes of a Patent theatre. Instead, it is a knowing and ephemeral piece, sub-titled 'A Petite Comedy in Two Acts,'[12] close to farce in its plot of potential sexual transgression, and designed to show off the dancers and singers of Charles Kemble's company, as well as his theatrical property in costumes. It is written in colloquial prose, and opens and closes with song and dance numbers involving a sizeable chorus and ballet company, with the playbill for its first performance listing these featured *divertissements*. *The First of May* headed the bill for Saturday, 10 October 1829, five days after the new season opened, and starred Charles Kemble as Edward IV, and Ellen Tree (who had made her Covent Garden debut four nights earlier as Lady Townly in *The Provok'd Wife*) as Lady Elizabeth Gray. The play recounts Edward IV's wooing and marriage of Elizabeth Gray (*nee* Woodville), turning an episode of English dynastic history during the Wars of the Roses into a series of comic situations where the ignoble reputations of some of the noble characters are central to the plot. Edward IV is represented quite openly as a libertine by himself and other characters – indeed, it is his reputation as a lover of beautiful young girls which is crucial to the plot, when he sets out to test the trust of his wife-to-be. Three marriage plots intertwine – Edward's wooing of the Widow Elizabeth; the attempts of Katherine, ward of city merchant Oldgrave, to marry her lover Henry Woodville (Elizabeth's brother) rather than be forced into a marriage with her elderly guardian; and the eventual marriage of her guardian to the Widow Jolly, sister of Katherine's dead mother. The play ends in the standard comic resolution of marriage, but along the way, various permutations of cross-gendered disguise, sexual impropriety, and cross-generational couplings run very close to the line of immodesty on the censored public stage at the time.

To a modern reader, the play is both perplexing and exhilarating. Exhilarating in that it is written with great verve and gusto, but perplexing in the way it seems neither to carry the weight of its occasion – the support of a National Theatre in crisis – nor to reflect Hill's more earnest aspirations as poet and woman of letters. For a woman who had written at least two poetic dramas, this looks like a missed opportunity. Yet the play is exhilarating precisely because it confounds such expectations. *The First of May* is a commercial play, an occasional piece, written with an eye to its immediate market. It shows off all the riches of the Covent Garden company to their best effect by exploiting both the physical property and abundant talent of a major theatre company in a Patent Theatre, with dancers, singers, and lavish costumes (the *Athenæum* comments that 'The dresses helped the piece considerably').[13] Indeed, the play could be read as expressly designed to exhibit all the trappings of cultural status and accumulated wealth which supporters of the theatre monopoly maintained were impossible at the minor theatres.

It is also a play which dwells on the libertine character of Edward IV, and constructs a plot around the sexual knowingness of its characters. There is an ironic fitness in the Theatre Royal staging a play about the dissipations of a monarch at a time when memories of George IV's Regency were still fresh, and Britain was in the middle of social and political reorganization reform. But most importantly, for a young woman to enter so wholeheartedly into representing the sexual foibles of a past monarch suggests an answer to one of the questions we might ask of women playwrights: why were they drawn to the theatre, despite the very real hazards participation had for them? The playfulness of the piece, its ludic possibilities, offer a powerful answer here. The character of the libertine King gives Hill an opportunity to play with the representation of male sexuality, a topic usually proscribed for respectable women. A frank acknowledgement of Edwards's licentiousness, sanctioned by historic 'fact,' sets the tone for her representations of other characters' innuendo and frank admissions of desire, including those of the juvenile heroine, Katherine, and, more predictably, the comic Widow Jolly. The reading of this dramaturgy as subversive is reinforced by Misty Anderson's concluding comments on women's comedy, as she remarks that 'women [...] have used humor as a way to speak the unspeakable. Taboo material can explode into public discourse through jokes and wordplay, bribing the hearers to assent to its wicked logic when direct speech would be ineffective or impossible.'[14]

The play of desire starts in the first scene where a conventional scenario of youthful rebellion is consistently pinned down by overt references to sexual misbehaviour and innuendo. Katherine rebels against her guardian Oldgrave's plan to marry her himself, claiming that she 'will never be sacrificed to an old trader, while I have my youth, my eyes, and a soul that makes me worthy to mix with Lords and Ladies' (f. 233). Oldgrave snaps back 'But what manner of Ladies will they be Kate? The Lady Lucy – or mistress Shore?' (f. 233) placing Katherine in the company of the King's mistresses. There is little preaching to counter the King's desire, and certainly no punishment of him for his 'sins.' On the contrary, in answer to a friend's remonstrances, the King explains his behaviour in terms of his royal position:

> I only wish that thou wert forced for one day to feel the galling weight of a crown [...] and then see how thou wouldst support such life without the aid of some kind half dozen women. (f. 237)

So Hill converts libertinism into solace and support for a lonely king, using the possibilities of comedy to reverse – if only for a moment – the moral assumptions of her audience to offer them a more pragmatic view of kingship and masculinity.

Contemporary critics were lukewarm about the quality of the play, the *Examiner* typical in calling it 'slight in every respect.'[15] Of course, after the sensation of Fanny Kemble's stage debut, the debut of an obscure 'lady' playwright could be overlooked. But critics were clear in their disapproval of the play's morality. 'The dissoluteness of the King is rather too strongly dwelt upon; and from a female pen the development of such a character is peculiarly indecorous and disagreeable.'[16] That ominous phrase, 'from a female pen,' draws the battle lines for reviewers. Quite simply, and to repeat what is now a truism of Victorian literary studies, the woman author was expected to produce more conventionally moral and decorous writing. But this 'more' was also less: the woman writer's moral gate-keeping role apparently made her unsuited for writing about a full range of lives, situations, actions, and characters. This is clear in the *Athenæum*'s opinion of Hill's portrayal of the libertine king:

> None but fools make a vaunt of their success in matters of this kind [...]. A male author would probably have kept this consideration in

view, but the ladies are ever sorry hands at portraying a libertine, although it is a favourite subject with many of the air who aspire to be authoresses.[17]

The *Athenæum* does not project moral judgements of the play onto Hill's private character (although other critics did do so). Rather, the review accuses Hill of incompetence through lack of knowledge because of her gender. Here is the vicious circle of respectable femininity. Through it, a woman writer could damage her artistry, in what Angela Leighton identifies as the 'dissociation of sensibility' which was 'one of the woman poet's most disabling inheritances.'[18] The pattern Leighton identifies in the production and reception of poetry by women in the first half of the nineteenth century was even more marked in women's theatre writing of this period. State censorship, self-censorship, and managerial and critical censure combined with the gendered ideologies of respectability and domesticity to exert extraordinary pressures on women writing for the theatre.

Isabel Hill's career to 1829 may well have prepared her for such adverse critical reception. Even as a woman barely out of her teens, she was aware of the dilemma of the 'female pen' as a marker of difference, which carried with it the dilemma of feminine exceptionality. In an introductory essay 'An Indefinite Article' to her volume of her early poems and essays, Hill observes that once a woman made public the products of her pen, she was robbed.

> The remark [...] implies that literary celebrity should be left for the lords of the creation; that *we* are sure to be disgraced and spoiled by success, and shunned even if we fail, – as if the mantle of inspiration were the poisoned shirt of Nessus; as if the poet's bays wrinkled a female brow, [...] but gave *all* the Dons a right to exclaim, 'How the d——l came a *woman* in the *press*?' Such is the lot of scribbling spinsters, which I discovered too late.[19]

This ironic introduction is typically energetic and self-aware. In it and subsequent essays, Hill displays a shrewd intelligence and pragmatic approach to earning a living by her pen, notwithstanding her gentle-womanly status. Isabel Hill is perhaps best remembered now as the first English translator of Madame de Staël's novel, *Corinne*, a novel by a cosmopolitan female author who Sherry Simon contends was central in the formulation of 'the terms of an intellectual liberalism which would be decisive for Romanticism and influential far into the twentieth century.'[20] Hill's translator's note indicates *her* independence of mind and understanding of translation as what Simon calls 'cultural mediation' (42): 'Madame de Staël's diffuse manner obliged me also to transpose pretty freely. [. . .] It may appear profanation to have altered a syllable; but, having been accustomed to consult the taste of my own country, I could not outrage it by being more literal.'[21] This novel, claimed by Ellen Moers as '*the* book of the woman of genius,'[22] might have inspired Hill by its portrait of a powerful and free-spirited woman artist; but Hill's talent and personality moved on a different track. Her brother, Earle Benson Hill, points out her 'industry, and readiness to fulfil any engagement with which she may be intrusted' to Edward Morgan, Richard Bentley's office manager, when soliciting payment on account for her Chateaubriand translation.[23] Hill maintained a stoic attitude to the knife-edge of constant penury, but Bentley's records suggest that neither Isabel nor Benson Hill – who undertook business negotiations on his sister's behalf – was very skilled at selling their literary properties to publishers or theatre managers. Benson's notes and receipts to Bentley and Morgan reveal his constant requests for monies owed to him and his sister, and his soliciting of work at a piece-rate was at a lower rate than other authors and translators were receiving.[24] It is clear from all the extant documents of Hill's life that the exchange of money for words was a central negotiation of her life, but one she found difficult to balance against her gentlewomanly status.

Given her economic circumstances, Hill's determination to be a dramatist takes on added significance. She wrote at least 6 plays, three of which were performed, but unpublished (*The First of May*, *My Own Twin Brother*, and *West-Country Wooing*),[25] an unnamed and unperformed adaptation of the Irish story,[26] and two published, but unperformed plays (*The Poet's Child*, and *Brian the Probationer*). There is evidence in her brother's 'Memoir' of at least another one, if not two, unperformed plays, but these manuscripts are not traceable. She also wrote a three-volume novel *Brother Tragedians* (1834) in which she expounds her theories of the stage as an important medium for both moral and aesthetic education, through Leopold, son of one of the title's tragedians, who argues passionately that 'The world must be amused; it may receive lessons from the stage, more readily than from the pulpit. The very consciences of men are best touched through their senses and imaginations.'[27] In this novel she also speaks directly as a female writer to her readers, writing back to the 'Dons' of her earlier essay and the critics of *The First of May*, to argue that:

> Reader! May not good lessons be inculcated – even on the subject of human frailty, by *a woman*? As long as female writers are either pathetic or terrible they may deal with what themes they please. In this case I can be neither [...]. I will write nothing that the best of men might not *write*, the best of women *read*; but it were absurd in me to mince like a Miss. (76)

Hill's protest is against the double bind of femininity in which women writers could find themselves. Women writers of the 1820s and 1830s found various ways to live within or subvert its constraints. Hill's direct address to her audience in *Brother Tragedians*, and her arrangements for the performance of her farce, *My Own Twin Brother* – another comedy which sailed close to the boundaries of gentlewomanly propriety – testify to her courage in challenging such limitations.

Nevertheless, remaining faithful to such an ambition caused Hill some strain and despair. The uncertainties of theatre managements, and the changing fortunes and status of playwrights at this time made playwriting a difficult choice for any writer. There is no record of how much Hill was paid for her performed pieces, but it can be assumed that *The First of May* was offered *gratis* to a Covent Garden management in distress. At first glance, Hill's continuing difficulties with money make her offer of a play *gratis* to Covent Garden remarkable. And yet, her action is also consistent with her ambitions as a writer and playwright. To have a play performed at one of the two Theatres Royal was a sought-after prize, and the added publicity of the crisis of Covent Garden's management, with its public meetings, threat of selling up the theatre's properties, and closure as a working theatre,[28] meant that the season which opened in October that year received more than usual publicity. However, more importantly, Hill's offer of a play *gratis* to Covent Garden indicates her own sense of participating in the activities of a significant national cultural institution; the acceptance of her play shows how, when in crisis, that institution brought in those whom it usually marginalized. When Hill offered her play, she claimed a place in the 'imagined community' of the National Drama, and a material role in the London theatre profession as one of its rescuers and protectors. And it is my contention that while she was able to do so on this occasion because of her respectability, that very status of lady playwright hampered her attempts to gain a permanent place.

As a rescuing angel (as opposed to a knight in shining armour) of the Covent Garden theatre, Isabel Hill was in a liminal position, a dialectical tension existing between her conflicting desires – for writerly success, and to remain a private gentlewoman. Catherine Burroughs argues that Joanna Baillie's theatre theory in its embrace of 'both the private closet and the public stage [...] modeled the oscillating stance that characterizes much of Romantic women's theater theory.'[29] Burroughs' notion of 'oscillation' is useful to explore Hill's ambiguous position within the material practices of the London theatre. Hill's brother Benson's career as an actor gave her some access to the profession, using him to act as go-between, negotiator, and make introductions to actors and managers. But Benson was not a star actor who could dictate his own terms, and his standing as a soldier and a gentleman caused him to hold himself aloof as much as possible from the normal intercourse of working actors. Indeed, a critical reading of Benson's autobiographical writings emphasizes how Benson Hill fetishized this *habitus* of middle-classness, and stressed it even more with regard to his sister. Yet it is clear from Benson Hill's memoirs just how fragile their class position was, and how much they both had to *perform* the conventions of middle-class standards, even while staying in poor lodging houses with damp beds in Cambray, or dealing with down-to-earth Edinburgh landladies.[30] Isabel Hill's difference from members of other theatrical families was constantly played out in physical and spatial terms. The difficulties of attending the theatre, for pleasure or business, were pronounced. Where to sit in the theatre, and with whom, for example, was a problem for Isabel from Benson's first engagement in a company in Worthing, where the manager's wife:

> politely expressed her wish for 'Miss Hill to waive ceremony, and consider a seat in the manager's private box always her own. Such a being must not go unprotected into the front. She was not of the profession, nor accustomed to theatricals, but a poet and a gentlewoman.'[31]

At Birmingham, when Benson played in Alfred Bunn's company, Bunn also offered Isabel the use of his private box, but she refused it, as there was no guarantee that she would be alone, but might come into contact with a 'fallen pillar of female virtue' or 'a column just tottering.'[32] It was not on the grounds of wealth that they kept themselves separate – Benson Hill openly admits throughout his memoirs that they were poor – it was 'Ipswich and Eton,'[33] and a set of beliefs enabled by wealth, yet never invoking wealth as their mainspring, on which the Hills acted. As a gentleman, Benson could mix in a spirit of fellowship with his acting colleagues, even if they were of an 'inferior' class. However, Isabel Hill removed herself from even this relationship with other theatre workers. In language Hill herself would never have used, she was damned if she did make money – too much success was bad for her femininity – and damned if she did not, as the unladylike exposure in the public world of the theatre was all for nothing.

Saving Covent Garden

The public identity which Isabel Hill found so irksome, yet sought via her pen, was also required of another reluctant young woman in the rescue plan for Covent Garden in 1829. And indubitably, it was Fanny Kemble's first appearance on stage as Juliet in *Romeo and Juliet* which saved the theatre and her family's business from financial ruin. Fanny Kemble's exceptionality is also riven with the contradictions of the 'proper lady' who must work in the theatre, and the ambitious young woman of strong feelings who was raised as an educated gentlewoman through her parents' comfortable income earned through the family business of the theatre. The story of Kemble's debut is well-known – Fanny told it herself in *Record of a Girlhood* – and has been retold in numerous biographies and critical studies in the twentieth century. The story that is retold is a variation of Kemble's own account of her stage career: her parents' decision that she should perform in a theatre season at Covent Garden designed to avert their bankruptcy, her first nervous recital of Juliet for her parents in their home, her solo performance on the empty stage of Covent Garden to try her voice in the space, her debut, with its heightened expectations, and her immediate and overwhelming success.[34] Kemble's own narrative is vivid: her descriptions of the intensity of preparations, the hard work and professional judgement involved, together with the recapturing of that state of acute apprehension combined with a kind of oblivion which characterizes stage nerves – all of these captivate the reader. In this account, we find her ability to communicate which made her such a memorable performer, both on the stage, and in the dramatic readings by which she made a comfortable income in her middle-age. Something, too, can be found of the power of her personality which made her a celebrity, as famous for being *herself* as for what she did.

However, the power of her writing can make us forget that Kemble was writing almost fifty years after the event. The Fanny Kemble represented in *The Record of a Girlhood* has come to be seen as a woman who hated the stage, performed reluctantly, and wished to retreat to private life and family.[35] Mary Jean Corbett makes a detailed argument about Kemble's performance of Victorian discourses of respectability, arguing that her identity was formed through 'middle-class values and standards as expressed in anti-theatrical terms,' and that her 'hatred for the stage derives from her internalization of gendered norms for public behaviour.'[36] This is part of Corbett's broader argument about the formation of the middle-class female subject in the late Victorian and Edwardian periods, and her use of actresses' autobiographies to demonstrate the cultural power of patriarchal paradigms, arguing that even these apparently independent women worked within 'naturalized, gendered conventions for theatrical and textual performance which increasingly conform to middle-class standards for domestic femininity' (108). In her reading of Kemble's autobiography, Corbett identifies Kemble's persistent return to her anxiety over the status of the actor, the respectability of the profession, and her own distaste for the profession of the stage. But Corbett's concern is with late Victorian subjectivity: what I want to explore here is the voice and experience of Kemble's younger self – as a Romantic teenager – and the contrast of her youthful ardency and ambition with the established Victorian lady of 1878.

Record of a Girlhood is not a unitary text, much as Kemble's connecting autobiographical passages try to make it so. It is a patchwork of Kemble's transcriptions of letters (mostly to her close friend Harriet St Leger), her journals, and her reflections and linking narratives written fifty years later. An examination of Kemble's autobiographical reflections in 1878, in the light of her self-writing from fifty years earlier suggests that a rather more complex reading of Kemble's career is necessary. Undoubtedly, Kemble expresses her dislike of the stage clearly; in *Record of a Girlhood*, she repeatedly returns to her misgivings about the theatrical profession. In heartfelt tones she reflects on her spectacular first performance, and its heavy fate for her:

> And so my life was determined, and I devoted myself to an avocation which I never liked or honoured, and about the very nature of which I have never been able to come to any decided opinion. [. . .] a *business* which is incessant excitement and factitious emotion seems to me unworthy of a man; a business which is public exhibition, unworthy of a woman. (Vol. 2, 60–1)

But this sense of a wasted life and misdirected talent is at odds with Kemble's earlier desires as expressed in her letters to Harriet St Leger, and Kemble's own records of her eighteen-year old self's artistic ambitions. Her older self attempts to censor and control her past, moulding it to fit a later model of middle-class propriety. Certainly, her concern for the respectability of the profession, and her repeated returns to the vexed question of the morality and fitness of the stage suggest a continuing anxiety about the conflict between the successful female performer (as Kemble was into late middle-age) and the successful middle-class woman. The divided self in Kemble's autobiography moves, often painfully as we see above, between these possible lives for women. But *Record of a Girlhood* is also stranded between late Romantic conceptions of the social behaviour and status of artists, and later high Victorian ideas of bourgeois respectability. In the late 1820s, and coming from a family of respected artists, Kemble confidently mixes with a social *élite*, she enjoys having her picture painted by Lawrence, and seeing her engravings of her performances in the shops; fifty years later, she seems torn between enjoying her memories of fashionable London life, and emphasizing her desire for the private contemplative life of a writing woman. It is as if she is anxious to camouflage the ardency of her young ambitions, to apologize for the publicity of her early life, by focussing on its difficulties, stresses, and shocks. As Corbett argues, Kemble is concerned to create herself as an autobiographical subject who carried 'the norms of middle-class private-sphere femininity to a new public role.'[37] While I do not dispute the weight of evidence, both from Fanny's letters of the period and her reflections in *Record of a Girlhood*, the blanket assumption of Fanny's dislike for the stage needs to be complicated. Kemble's linking passages in *Record of a Girlhood* explain Frances Ann Kemble in 1878. But they do not explain Fanny Kemble in 1829, when she set out to help her family's ailing fortunes. She casts her actions in the mould of filial obedience and family pride, but in her more unguarded confidences to Harriet St Leger reproduced in *Record*, there is personal ambition as well. And it might be the fact of the existence of this ambition – so contrary to the growing ideological hegemony of female modesty – which the older Kemble wants to counterbalance.

After returning from school to live with her family, Kemble could not have been unaware of the increasing difficulties of her father's management. The law suit brought by Thomas Harris, one of Covent Garden's shareholders, hung, Kemble wrote, 'like the sword of Damocles' over the family. In these letters, written through 1827 and 1828, Kemble's awareness of her parents' difficulties forms the background to her determination to do something to help. At the beginning of 1828, she wrote to Harriet St Leger:

They are in sad want of a woman at both the theatres [Covent Garden and Drury Lane]. I've half a mind to give Covent Garden one. Don't be surprised. I have something to say to you on this subject, but have not room for it in this letter. (Vol. 1, 201)

This is also the period when Kemble was writing *Francis the First*, her tragedy performed at Covent Garden in 1832, and in 1827 she wrote to Harriet about it, speculating on the amount she might be paid, and the relative merits of selling the play to Covent Garden, or to a publisher. The contrast between her discussion of this enterprise to Harriet in her letters, and her reflections when writing about it fifty years later provide further texture to Kemble's motivations and actions. The teenage Kemble is 'extremely busy [...] and extremely elated' (Vol. 1, 186) about her play, opining that it has 'some good writing in it; and good situations,' because, as she tells Harriet, with all the confident knowledge of a young woman who has heard her parents, grandparents, uncles, and aunts speak of the theatre all her life, 'a play without striking situations and effects [will not] succeed [...] with an English audience of the present day' (Vol. 1, 187). In August 1829, she wrote to tell Harriet of the crisis in her family's business at Covent Garden.

Do you remember a letter I wrote to you a long time ago about going on the stage? and another, some time before that, about my becoming a governess? The urgent necessity which I think now exists for exertion, in all those who are capable of it amongst us, has again turned my thoughts to these two considerations. [...] These reflections have led me to the resolution of entering upon some occupation or profession which may enable me to turn the advantages my father has so liberally bestowed on me to some account, so as not to be a useless incumbrance to him at present, or a helpless one in future time. (Vol. 1, 291–2)

Kemble represents herself as motivated by family duty and the desire to contribute according to her talents. Her view of the ideal of private, respectable femininity is expressed in terms of its dependency and herself as a potential 'incumbrance' and 'helpless.' She, educated and talented, could contribute to the family enterprise, in what Margaret Oliphant later referred to as 'daughterly work in the artist class.'[38] While Kemble quailed at the enormity of her debut on the stage at Covent Garden, her upbringing in a working theatrical family led her to respond to their difficult situation with characteristic energy and agency. As Jacky Bratton points out, Fanny Kemble was 'living one story, while telling us, and herself, quite another.'[39]

Bratton argues that the theatre as a family business worked to 'pass on inherited skills and talents, and to enable the smooth running of the enterprise, through woman as much or more than through men.'[40] It was in this setting of the family business that Fanny Kemble made her debut. Kemble was literally surrounded by her family on stage: her mother Marie-Thérèse Kemble (*née* De Camp) returned to the stage after an absence of several years to play Lady Capulet, and her father played Mercutio (Fanny explains to Harriet that he will not play Romeo – 'there would be many objections to that' (Vol. 2, 16)), while her Aunt Dall was her chaperone and attendant. The season's attractions also included a revival of Marie-Thérèse Kemble's comedy, *The Day After the Wedding; or, a Wife's First Lesson*, which had premiered at Covent Garden in 1808. So Kemble's appearance was part of saving the family business which had afforded her education as a middle-class lady out of the business. Kemble's 'insider' status as the daughter of a theatrical family and her working knowledge of the theatre gave her prodigious cultural capital, which she converted into other kinds of social and economic capital throughout her career, as a writer and playwright, by her readings from Shakespeare, and as a celebrity.

Kemble used her familial obligations to explain her participation in an enterprise she came to dislike, but more powerfully came to feel she needed to excuse. She could characterize her debut as literally the fulfilment of filial duty, not self-generated ambition, as she commented to her friend Mrs Calcott: 'I feel astonished at what I have dared to do and am thankful that as I did it in obedience to the wills of others, the sin of presumption and its punishment have been alike far from me.'[41] Valerie Sanders comments that in Kemble's account of her debut in *Record of a Girlhood* 'The structure of every sentence accentuates her lack of responsibility for what she was doing:'[42] Sanders sees this as contributing to the instability of Kemble's autobiographical writing, pointing to the problem for subsequent critics and historians in unpicking Kemble's life: 'She says this [her dislike of the stage] so often and in so many different contexts throughout her life, that one must take her at her word [but . . .] Fanny Kemble's uncertainty about her selfhood, at once so separate, yet merged into all the parts she had acted, was compounded by a continued attraction to the stage.'[43] In puzzling over her 'curious' state of mind before her debut, Kemble reflects on her talent and her conflicted feelings about acting:

Though I had found out that I could act, and had acted with a sort of frenzy of passion and entire self-forgetfulness the first time I ever uttered the wonderful conception I had undertaken to represent, my going on the stage was absolutely an act of duty and conformity to the will of my parents, strengthened by my own conviction that I was bound to help them by every means in my power. The theatrical profession was, however, utterly distasteful to me, though *acting* itself, that is to say, dramatic personation, was not; [...] The dramatic element inherent in my organization must have been very powerful, to have enabled me without either study of or love for my profession to do anything worth anything in it. (Vol. 2, 13–14)

Kemble's repugnance to the profession – stage business in every meaning of the phrase – is significant here, and as Sanders argues, Kemble's performance of dispassionate observation of her 'organization' allows her to absolve herself of responsibility and agency. Yet, as Faye Dudden argues, paradoxically Fanny Kemble came to represent a new kind of woman through her talent: 'With this glorious talent she had the power to normalize female public accomplishment, and in doing so to undermine deeply held assumptions about women's nature and capacities.'[44]

It was the first display of this talent, Kemble's fetishized femininity, and promise of maturing power (Kemble was only 20 when she first appeared as Juliet) which rescued her father's business at Covent Garden. Whatever Kemble's misgivings about the disruptions to her preferred quiet life of writing caused by her celebrity, she enjoyed the money and fame of this first season,[45] and she pursued the financial and artistic independence she began to experience in 1829 for the rest of her life.[46] Isabel Hill's contribution, well-meant, could not figure so prominently in the contemporary excitement about nor later memories of this season at Covent Garden. The different careers of Isabel Hill and Fanny Kemble illustrate one of the major distinctions in the late Romantic theatre between those whose work in the theatre was part of a family business, and those who had to find other ways in; a distinction which endured until the 1860s. But Hill and Kemble are not simply opposable as an 'outsider' and an 'insider,' as useful as this opposition might be. Both negotiate a combination of roles and *personae* within a complicated ideological framework – all the more complex because they were working in the theatre during a time of fundamental change in its organization which rendered the theatre at its most unstable for several generations. Despite the differences in the status of their familial connections with the theatre and access to it as a source of income and status, both Kemble and Hill internalized similarly prescriptive notions of middle-class femininity – ladyhood – which caused them distress in the pursuit of equally powerful desires for self-expression and recognition, while performing heroic acts for the theatre's rescue.

Competition

The crisis of Charles Kemble's management at Covent Garden in 1829 was a crisis in its financing, and indicative of the change in London theatre from an oligarchic economic structure to a set of practices based on the principles of free trade and *laissez-faire*.[47] Although Charles Kemble's problems were largely financial, they were reported in the press in terms of a crisis in the National Drama, caused by its decline in standards of writing, performance, and reception. The 'decline of the drama' was, according to Jacky Bratton, 'a concept generated [...] for the particular purposes of a newly ascendant hegemonic fraction,'[48] and public discussion (as opposed to theatre managerial practice) often focussed on the lack of good writing for the theatre. The call for new plays to help rescue Covent Garden in 1829 was one of many moments of crisis in which the supposed paucity of good new play writing disguised the fundamental difficulties of financing the Theatres Royal in widening competition without the forceful protection of the dramatic monopoly.[49] The focus on writing as the cause of the decline of the drama which emerges in this period continued throughout the century, forming a distinct theatrical culture which brought with it discursive formations which served to marginalize the popular, the non-literary, and the work of women. Playwriting competitions were one of the methods adopted in the Victorian (and Edwardian) theatre for generating new plays which conformed to criteria of excellence determined by literary rather than theatrical standards, and conflicts around their establishment, judging, and the afterhistories of performance (or not), attest to the power of ideas about the roles and standards of drama and theatre in this period. The use of competitions to elicit 'good' new plays is of a piece with the new politics and economics of competition pursued by a rising professional and industrial middle-class, and the presence of these practices in the theatre, however contested or ridiculed, is indicative both of the power of the new modes of economic and social thought emerging under the banner of Reform, and of the important position of the (London) theatre in the cultural imaginary of the Victorian period.

What was at stake for women in their participation in playwriting competitions? Susan Carlson and Kerry Powell suggest that the history of women's playwriting 'might be very different' if the theatre were run by 'blind' competitions, implying a greater prominence for women writers.[50] However, any account of women's participation in these competitions is caught between valuing individual women's achievements and noting the difficulties which attend the public prominence of the 'exceptional' woman playwright. Undeniably, women were successful in these competitions. Plays written by women won prominent play-writing competitions in 1843, 1901, and 1913, and their success appeared to position women playwrights at the centre of the revival of the National Drama. Cultural citizenship seemed possible for women, even if political and economic citizenship were largely denied them. The anonymity of such competitions, and the claims to objectivity and high skill in the judgement of them, would also suggest that women received powerful affirmation of their skills and talents. Yet the aftermath of each competi-tion denied such gains, reversed claims about the efficacy of competitions in eliciting 'good' plays, and reflexively condemned the exceptional woman as an oddity and an interloper.

In 1913, *The Era* quoted a report in *Morning Post* that 'Another play competition has been decided in favour of a lady [. . .]. It is singular how frequently such prizes do fall to the ladies.'[51] The *Morning Post* writer then listed three previous competitions won by women playwrights, noting that the winning plays were all comedies, and went on to ponder, yet again, women's shortcomings in the writing of tragedies. The winning play in 1913 was announced as a comedy, *The Minotaur*, by Violet Pearn. This announcement brought a vigorous response from Violet Pearn, who maintained that 'My play "The Minotaur" is a tragedy.' Somewhat tartly, she continues

> The two plays I have written since sending 'The Minotaur' in for the competition 'Mountain Lights' and 'Wild Birds' are also tragedies. [. . .] I find, personally, that it is much more difficult to write comedy than tragedy. [. . .] Possibly women are supposed to excel in the more difficult art because, as all the world knows, the circumstances of their lives keep them remote from tragic events.[52]

It is hard not to read the last sentence as heavily ironic, given female activity in the writing of tragedy and melodrama throughout the century, and the frustration with the limitations of women's lives and experiences increasingly voiced in women's writing from the early Victorian period. Defensive as she may sound, Pearn's rush to correct the record about her writing, and particularly the play which won her the competition, was a wise move, given the other history of women's success in playwriting competitions in the nineteenth century. This other story is one of controversy and outright misogyny.

Two earlier Victorian playwriting competitions, in 1843 and 1901, were both launched as flagship attempts to promote the English drama, opening up its processes to all writers in the hope of eliciting new plays. Benjamin Webster, manager of the Haymarket in 1843, announced his competition for a five-act comedy 'best [...] illustrative of British life and manners of the present day.'[53] His offer of the substantial prize of £500 and a production at his theatre gave many writers something to play for (there were ninety-seven entries), but also provoked public and private criticism from prominent writers of the time such as Charles Dickens, William Thackeray, and Douglas Jerrold.[54] As Ellen Donkin argues, the question of the National Drama became fraught when 'a lady, [...] by no means unknown to literary fame' was known to have won the competition.[55] That 'lady' was prolific playwright and novelist, Catherine Gore, and her winning play was broadly condemned, in an episode which revealed the powerful prejudices against women playwrights which framed the critical reception of their work. Some doubts about the competition were voiced at its announcement, as the *Spectator* advising Webster 'to make the public his jury,'[56] and the *Athenæum* wondered sceptically '[w]hether one will be forthcoming in which there is the true dramatic spirit, remains to be seen.'[57] *Punch* converted the whole competition into a running joke, with spoof entries appearing in the magazine throughout 1843 and 1844, collected by Gilbert A'Beckett in *Scenes from Rejected Comedies*. This was the typical banter of the literary and theatrical *demi-monde* of the time; but it turned into vicious criticism and cliquery when Gore's play was performed. The 'literary gentleman's club'[58] detected a boundary jumper, and closed ranks to repel the 'lady' invader of professional men's territory.

Gore tells some of the story in her 'Preface' to the printed edition of *Quid Pro Quo*, noting the refusal of Charles Mathews and Eliza Vestris to take the lead roles (her complaint has echoes of Benson Hill's annoyance that *The First of May* was chosen 'for the nights that Miss Fanny Kemble did *not* appear'), and the determination of other competition entrants to make their disappointment public. Reviews were uniformly negative, with George Henry Lewes making the most openly defensive statements about the prize-winning play and its production. He excuses his infliction of pain on Gore by reminding her that there are 'ninety-six authors whose self-love has been wounded, whose time has been wasted; ninety-six angry men who need consolation, and who, we cannot but think, deserve it.'[59] The language of his review, its placement in the *Westminster Review* – a periodical which exemplified the 'national discourse of bourgeois progressivism'[60] – all serve to mark off the territory of the drama from the reach of a writer like Catherine Gore – female, populist, and ambitious. But Catherine Gore was not stupid, and realized that what she faced was a masculinist defence of threatened territory – as she comments:

> For the animosity on the part of the pit and the press [...] which succeeded in condemning the very superior plays of Joanna Baillie, Lady Dacre, and Lady Emmeline Wortley, could scarcely fail to crush any attempt of mine.[61]

Netta Syrett expressed similar irritation at prejudiced criticism of her play, *The Finding of Nancy*, winner of the Playgoers' Club competition for new playwrights in 1901. This competition was an attempt to find new plays of quality, and to show that managers were prepared to encourage new talent, rather than using the same well-known names. Some 400 manuscripts were entered, from which Syrett's play about a young middle-class woman living an independent life in London was chosen as the winner. Syrett's prize was to have George Alexander produce her play at the St James's Theatre, and for Alexander and Herbert Beerbohm Tree to take parts in it. *The Finding of Nancy* is a striking dramatisation of a young woman's desperate attempts to change her 'cramped, narrow life'[62] without compromising her optimism, individuality, or respectability. Although the play never names it, the 'life' Nancy seeks, and the self she must find, is bound up with her sexual experience. Syrett's play presents a rather grim view of the respectable middle-class single working woman's prospects, with Nancy's declaring to her art-teacher friend, Isabel:

> I have the misfortune to be fastidious. Theoretically I love humanity. Practically I dislike it babbling on my hearth. Oh yes, there *are* charming people of course. But remember how narrow my groove is. I don't meet them. [...] I think that I am growing older. That life is short: that the days go on one after another: that nothing happens, that nothing ever *will* happen. I think of all the glorious places in the world I shall never see. I think of all the people, the dear charming, interesting people I shall never know. I see life with all its colour and glitter sweeping on without me like some great full river, while I am caught in a little stagnant backwater, held fast by the weeds. [...] I'm

not going to perdition, I shall have no opportunity. [. . .] It's the one thing that women in our position have little chance to do. If I were a shop girl, I could meet the shop-walker round the corner; if I were a duchess that would account for many little eccentricities. But for the modern young woman who works for a living wage, and has the misfortune to be a lady, there is no chance of any kind. Not even of going to the devil. (ff. 7–9)

Eventually, Nancy does 'go to perdition,' and lives with Will Fielding, a married man, for four years. Syrett comments in her autobiography that the play makes it quite clear that Fielding, tied to an alcoholic wife, 'would marry her if he could.'[63] And, indeed, after a series of dramatic misunderstandings, Nancy and Fielding do marry. But this plot was enough to set London theatre gossip alight,[64] and provoked Clement Scott to write a review of the play in the *Daily Telegraph* which Syrett described in her autobiography as 'ludicrous and hypocritical invective.'[65] The review published in the *Daily Telegraph* immediately following the Thursday matinée performance insinuated that Nancy's decision to live with Fielding as his wife was based on Syrett's own experience:

For Miss Netta Syrett [. . .] has many dramatic intuitions: she surveys some problems with acute and penetrating glance: she can suggest character – not the hackneyed characters of the stage, but personalities which are real, vivid, convincing. In the simplest way with the simplest language, she can write out a situation which grips the heart with its painful actuality, and, above all, compose a first act which is so fresh and, at the same time, so absolutely torn out of the bosom of living experience that it takes the house by storm. [. . .] Sometimes, when the unconventional strikes home, because it is real and because 'it has been lived,' they [the audience] respond [. . .] quickly and sympathetically. (10)

Despite an excellent review from such an opinion-maker as Max Beerbohm, who wrote in the *Saturday Review* that 'in my time there has been nothing on the stage so interesting, so impressive, so poignant, as the first act of Miss Syrett's play,'[66] Scott's review had devastating effects, according to Syrett. Rather than the long run Alexander had hinted to Syrett that he planned, the play had only its single promised performance, a special matinée for the Actors' Benevolent Fund, on 8 May 1902. It was never printed, and remains, an overlooked gem, in the Lord Chamberlain's Collection in the Manuscripts Room of the

British Library. And in her autobiography Syrett recounts how she also lost a well-paid teaching job because of the gossip generated by the play – or rather, by Scott's review of the play.[67]

If Syrett received a swingeing review on moral grounds from the powerful critic Clement Scott, other responses, although not so outraged, were just as damaging. Rather than the moralizing of the *Daily Telegraph*, the *Times* ran a campaign of consistent disparagement on the grounds of the triviality of Syrett's play, and other plays and novels like it. Syrett's play was not only written by a lady – it was for ladies:

> That is to say, it assumes as a matter of course that the greatest interest for all of us in life, the thing we want most to hear about, and that we go to the play to see, is the career of woman [...]. Whether Miss is to get married or to die an old maid, [...] are important questions to Miss herself, and indirectly to all the rest of her sex; and the fact that modern fiction is largely written by members of that sex no doubt accounts for the disproportionate fuss which it makes over these things. [...] In *The Finding of Nancy* are to be found all the usual characteristics of feminine fiction. The women unbosom themselves to one another, analyse one another, talk about one another, and generally 'take the stage'; while the man (whose sole business in life is to be in love with women) hang around, unanalysed, but occasionally allowed to say selfish things in order that the women may treat them with half-scornful, half-compassionate irony.[68]

Later that season, in a report on a charity performance of Mrs Ashton Jonson's play, *The Hedonists*, at Wyndham's Theatre, the *Times* critic theorizes satirically that

> A recent competition seems to have given birth to a new dramatic species – the Playgoers' Club play. The distinguishing marks of a Playgoers' Club play, so far as we have been able to collect them from the specimens submitted to the public, are – (1) female authorship, (2) a single afternoon performance before an audience chiefly female, (3) an initial situation wherein a distressed female decides to accept irregular relations with an importunate male, and (4) the discussion of typewriting as female employment. (5 July 1902, p. 10)

These comments are most pointed because they are in response to a high profile public competition, in which a woman outwrote her male peers. But they are part of that critical discourse which has historically connected women's writing with triviality and mediocrity because that writing has often (but not always) been concerned with the issues, life choices, and decisions faced by women. Although the *Times* could hardly be considered in the vanguard of the modernist *avant-garde*, it joins with that movement in its sneering treatment of writing for literary markets which included 'ladies' and children.[69] So at the end of the Victorian period, as at its beginning, the 'exceptionality' of the winning woman precipitated public condemnation of her, and converted her excellence into immorality, triviality, and lack of skill and aesthetic value.

Critical reviews – such as those of the *Telegraph* and *Times* – focussed on the 'women's business' of *The Finding of Nancy*, and its limited interest to theatre audiences. Implicit in this approach is a set of gendered assumptions about aesthetic and commercial theatrical values, which contests the emergent power of the female audience of the last decades of the nineteenth century. These gendered critical assumptions rendered women's experience and female culture invisible, in the same way that, as Viv Gardner argues, the female 'spectatrice' was rendered invisible by the 'social maps' of London and women's access to public spaces.[70] However, Syrett was not the self-absorbed 'Miss' of the *Times*' dismissive review. She was a hard-working writer, earning her living in a range of genres and publications. *The Finding of Nancy* demonstrates Syrett's professional skill at picking up the popular mood of the time and giving it powerful expression in. As 'a middlebrow writer of feminist women's fiction'[71] Syrett worked from within the romance form to attempt to represent the 'truth' of contemporary women's lives. The heightened nature of the play's 'structures of feeling' are part of Syrett's deployment of the conventions of romance fiction. The intensity of Nancy's longing for life in all its variety is a necessary explanation for her decision to take a lover. Syrett represents Nancy's actions as courageous rather than immoral, and through her characterizations of Nancy, Isabel, and the worldly wise Mrs Wingfield, Syrett reveals the hypocrisy of so-called respectable behaviour.

Reading Syrett's play now, it is tempting to draw parallels between Nancy's situation, so powerfully articulated and dramatized, and that of Syrett and many other women writers like her, but not in the prurient way Scott is accused of. However, Syrett's autobiography vigorously resisted such a defeatist story of the sufferings of late Victorian female independence. Syrett remembered that in the 1880s, 'educated girls of any character [. . .] were asserting their right to independence,'[72] and that 'so long as a girl was working at some art, profession, or business, she was perfectly free, and could go about her lawful occasions without censure – even from the censorious.'[73] Syrett's vigorous defence of the freedoms she enjoyed suggests that we resist reading *The Finding of Nancy* as autobiographical, although we might speculate on what Syrett left out or glossed over in her actual autobiography. Ann Ardis argues that Syrett's autobiography was part of a survival strategy based on her experience of expounding an overt oppositional politics in the reception of *The Finding of Nancy*.[74] Syrett's personal experience of over-exposure as an 'exceptional' playwright had the long-term effect of her near withdrawal from the commercial stage, although she was active in establishing, and writing and producing for a children's theatre.[75] Like Hill, Kemble, and Gore, Syrett was undoubtedly a successful working professional, but, as Gardner and others note, even in the late Victorian and Edwardian periods, when women working in the theatre become more numerous and more important than ever before, she faced the paradoxical consequences of her exceptionality. Winning led to loss, because the public exposure of the exceptional playwright who was also a woman was, even at the turn of the twentieth century, still too great a challenge to the gendered ideals of the National Drama.

Syrett's and Gore's successes in playwriting competitions have come to represent for feminist theatre history almost canonical instances of the misogyny of the Victorian theatre industry in its treatment of women playwrights. Historians (myself included) have generally used these incidents to identify and analyze the power of the opposition to women's participation in the profession of the playwright. However, as I have argued elsewhere, Pierre Bourdieu's notion of a field of cultural production gives us the theoretical tools to complicate the tendency to see these episodes as failures. Bourdieu argues that argument that '[T]here is no other criterion of membership of a [literary] field than the objective fact of producing effects within it [. . . and] polemics imply a form of recognition.'[76] By the weight of opposition to their work, Gore and Syrett must be seen as momentarily central in defining the field of the National Drama. The familiar strategies of recuperative feminist scholarship in constructing these women as inevitably and ultimately silenced by patriarchy may not work here: rather, our acknowledgement of their work must accommodate the tensions which arise between playwrighting as a deliberate writerly choice and their often agonising experiences of dramatic authorship and production. The paradox of writerly legitimation through attack theorized by Bourdieu can stop us from replicating the past critical practice of picking out the exceptional woman and focussing on her difficulties, while ignoring the ways in which such exceptionality can throw light on the broader group of writers from which she emerges. So the difficulties faced by the winners of these competitions might lead us to ask about the many writers who were not so exceptional, but for whom playwriting was a 'normal' activity. In other words, rather than base our history and historiography of women's playwriting on the troubled cases of exceptional playwrights, we might consider the field of women writers from which they emerge.

The case of the disappearing playwrights

By tracing the concept of women playwrights as exceptional – as rescuers or winners – this chapter has been concerned with the ways that the high visibility of individual women's theatre work has paradoxically caused other women's work to disappear. In this final section I want to suggest some of the factors contributing to the apparent disappearance of women playwrights at the end of the 1810s, with which Ellen Donkin ends her important survey of eighteenth and early nineteenth-century women's theatre writing.[77] I use the term 'apparent disappearance' because it is my contention that historiographical factors as well as historical changes have served to focus our attention on a few visible cases of writerly difficulty, while overlooking the many women theatre professionals working consistently, if unspectacularly. This is not to dismiss the very real difficulties that many women faced in getting their dramatic writing seen and heard on the public stage, as those visible cases were visible precisely because they collided with the patriarchal foundations of the material and discursive practices of the British theatre industry. However, they do not illuminate the broad range of work women playwrights produced, nor do they identify the important features of such work. On the other hand, I do not wish to claim simply a triumphalist reverse of the disappearing playwright. Rather, my approach is to note the oscillations between recognition and obscurity, visibility, and invisibility, of women playwrights, to attempt to track the dialectical relationship between patriarchal theatre practices and aesthetics, and women's activity within these structures.

In the period after the heyday of women's theatre writing identified by Ellen Donkin, women playwrights *did* disappear. Or rather – a certain type of woman playwright disappeared. The highly visible woman playwright, who was also accepted (more or less) as a professional by her male peers – indeed, mentored by them – and respected in public critical discourse, rarely emerged after the 1810s.[78] Instead, women who aimed for this kind of career (often citing the influence of Joanna

Baillie) found themselves pilloried in the press on the grounds of gender, and blocked and frustrated in their dealings with theatre managers, with the playing out of gender ideology in the everyday negotiations involved in getting new plays staged. Joanna Baillie herself, so Thomas Crochunis argues, was 'writing in an important historical moment between print and theatrical culture,'[79] when the patterns of production and publication of theatre writing were less fixed, leaving Baillie more vulnerable to changes in managerial and audience taste. The reasons for this change from respected female playwright to exceptional – and consequently vulnerable – female playwright are complex, and intricately connected with the general changes in the London theatre industry in the 1820s and 1830s; an industry which, in its turn, was highly sensitive to the profound changes in the reorganization of capital and culture of the early nineteenth century.

While historians such as Marc Baer, Gillian Russell, and Elaine Hadley have tracked the interconnected changes in English political and theatrical organization, in *Illegitimate Theatre in London*, Jane Moody argues for seeing the theatre industry in terms of a more widespread cultural change from a 'legitimate' culture to an 'illegitimate' culture.[80] Building on Moody's model, I would suggest that this change had specific consequences for women theatre workers – actors, playwrights, and managers. London theatre in the first thirty years of the nineteenth century was changed by the rapid growth of the city, producing a new popular audience characterized by geographical and class mobility, working in an expanding city, increasingly organized socially and economically around mechanized labour. Tracy Davis investigates in detail the economic foundations of such changes in the London theatre industry in the first half of the nineteenth century, finding the forces of *laissez-faire* and early industrial capitalism reshaping the theatre's aesthetic and commercial concerns.[81] In tracking a similar changes in the production and consumption of print culture, Jon Klancher writes of the early nineteenth-century reader 'confront[ing] the burgeoning powers of machines, spectacular industrial creation, a reenergized capital,' and a 'mass' readership which needs representation in and by 'inexhaustible images and a ceaseless stream of discourse.'[82] Other historians of this period note the post-Revolutionary pressures on writing in the public sphere working through the oppositional stance of radical politics, and the state's attempts at repression of this writing, creating what Kevin Gilmartin defines as a 'plebeian public sphere.'[83] In the contested communications of this emergent popular culture, as Ian Haywood points out, '[W]omen also had to be excluded from politics, not by force but through an appeal to "decorum" and "modesty." '[84] In whatever way such broad social, economic, and cultural changes are discussed, their impact was to 'unravel' theatrical practices which had, to a certain extent, protected women writers, particularly in the power of the actor-manager to develop and promote playwrights.[85] The theatre manager himself (it was only occasionally herself) had a far less stable economic environment in which to conduct the business of entertainment – the inflation of the Patents, the incursions of the 'minor' theatres, the demands of new audiences for different kinds of diversions – all these factors diminished the opportunities for the kind of protective patronage under which women playwrights apparently flourished in the eighteenth century.

Changes to the economic and social organization of Britain in the early nineteenth century were accompanied by, and productive of, increasingly coercive ideologies of gendered behaviour. Leonore Davidoff and Catherine Hall (among others) argue that the two developments were mutually constitutive, arguing that the 'sexual division of labour within families' was central to the development of the capitalist enterprise.[86] Writing in a literary critical vein, but confronting the same apparent retreat of women into silence after the heady times of the late eighteenth century, Alison Sulloway argues that it was as if there were a 'compensatory equation' affecting the production and reception of women's writing, in which the British movement towards democracy and class mobility – political and economic freedom – influenced by the French Revolution had to be balanced by restrictions on female behaviour and sociability.[87] And these restrictions on the female freedom of speech, produced and policed by gendered ideologies of decorum, occurred within an increasingly repressive atmosphere of state surveillance of radical speech in the late 1820s and early 1820s. Discussing Victorian discursive and social practices, Mary Poovey notes the 'consolidation of bourgeois power' through '[T]he rhetorical separation of spheres and the image of domesticated, feminized morality.' Poovey argues that the Victorian distinction between kinds of labour (she lists 'paid versus unpaid, mandatory versus voluntary, productive versus reproductive') 'created the illusion of an alternative to competition.'[88] In the emerging *laissez-faire* economic culture of the early nineteenth century, its momentum exerting pressure on hierarchies of taste to flatten them out, expand them, or invert them (implied by Moody's tracing of the power of 'illegitimate' culture), commercial pressures moved theatre into areas and genres in which it was problematic for women to venture, given the simultaneous emphasis on models of female behaviour and ideologies of femininity which increasingly required women to disengage from matters commercial or corporeal. If part of what shocked conventional London was the 'grotesque corporeality' of illegitimate theatre,[89] then how much more problematic was participation in this burgeoning illegitimate culture for women, given the equal but opposite movement to enforce female respectability and deny feminine corporeality?

The collision between the economic and cultural changes in the theatre industry and the development of an increasingly gendered notion of bourgeois respectability had further consequences for the career patterns and working practices of women playwrights. As I shall argue in my discussion of Mary Russell Mitford and Felicia Hemans as playwrights, their investment in the 'legitimate' drama was in part dictated by their social identities as respectable women. And in a very practical sense, in a *laissez-faire* market for writing, women were disadvantaged in negotiating, bargaining or demanding payment for their writing; this book is peppered through with examples of the struggles of women to manage their financial affairs. It is noticeable that women playwrights returned to the theatre from the 1860s when patterns of production stabilize again, and although they do not revert to the relative certainty of the Theatres Royal model of the eighteenth century, the pattern for longer runs in established companies, as well as the emergence of not-for-profit theatrical ventures seemed to create a working environment which offered opportunities for women playwrights. The expanding literary marketplace in the early decades of the century had its advantages for women writers – new forms of publication and markets developed into lucrative fields for women writers, and this is not simply a reference to the move women made into novel writing. In the period I am discussing, poetry, short stories, contributing to and editing annuals were all profitable forms of writing for women. Women's work became concentrated in the new media of the period which were typified by their consumption-led characteristics in a feminizing popular culture: the gift book, the annual, the story or poem for the fashion magazine, and of course, the novel, not yet established as a legitimate aesthetic form, and so, according to Gaye Tuchman, available to women.[90]

Looking back on another aspirant woman playwright of the early Victorian period, the published but unproduced Sarah Flower Adams, late-Victorian critic Richard Garnett reflected on her play, *Viva Perpetua*:

> 'Vivia Perpetua' is unsatisfactory as a play, but has deep human interest as an idealised representation of the authoress's mind and heart. [...] The authoress would probably have left a higher reputation [...] if she had given freer scope to her natural instinct for lyrical

poetry, instead of devoting her most strenuous endeavour to the difficult undertaking of reviving the poetical drama.[91]

Because of course the National Drama could not be 'saved' nor the poetical drama 'revived' either by feminine virtue or masculine intellect, however exceptional. The theatre had changed, and with it, women's work as playwrights. But although I can marshal overwhelming material and empirical evidence to show that the 'National Drama' never really existed, and the 'decline of the drama' was no such thing, these concepts as discursive constructions were so powerful as to structure women playwrights' careers to the mid-Victorian period, and our surviving histories of them.

2
Legitimacy

Felicia Hemans and Mary Russell Mitford were two of those 'exceptional' women playwrights whose personal artistic ambitions and desires became entangled in the travails of the National Drama, and the conflict between the ideals of the legitimate drama, and the practices of the commercial London theatre. It was in the 1820s and 1830s, under the influence of Romantic aesthetic ideology, that these two conceptions of the theatre drew apart. As Mary Russell Mitford reflected at the end of her life on her career as a playwright in the 1820s, 'The fact was that, by the terrible uncertainty of the acted drama, and other circumstances, I was driven to a *trade* when I longed to devote myself to an *art*.'[1] My interest here is to track the way that Hemans' and Mitford's playwriting was caught within the conflicts between high cultural notions of the tradition of the English drama, and the commercial and professional realities of the theatre as an industry. To use Thomas Crochunis' concept of 'passionate ambivalence' as he applied it to Joanna Baillie,[2] each woman was positioned ambivalently between page and stage, vitally concerned with both forms of communication, but troubled by difficulties – both aesthetic and material – in their commitment to either. While Crochunis is primarily concerned with the literary implications of this ambivalence, particularly in relation to critical theories of Romanticism, I will be pursuing a close study of the processes of writing and production of women's tragedies: that most 'high' and 'legitimate' of high cultural forms. In the course of this re-mapping of Romantic theatre, and in the later work of women poets and translators whom I discuss in Chapter 4, I find representative women playwrights through whose work a female – indeed proto-feminist – tradition of 'high art' and aesthetic experiment can be traced, in the face of high cultural definitions of drama and playwriting which attempted to exclude women. So this is not entirely a story of women's 'disappearing acts' in the theatrical marketplace (to borrow Catherine Gallagher's telling phrase), although neither is it a victorious recuperation of a lost tradition.

Although they desperately wanted it to do so, those involved in the production and commentary on the theatre throughout the nineteenth century had grave doubts about the capacity for the commercial theatre to produce art. In the late Romantic and early Victorian period, this anxiety was articulated through debates over 'the decline of the Drama' and the 'National Drama.' These debates appeared to be resolved through the Theatres Regulation Act of 1843, but this legislation did little to resolve anxieties about the aesthetic standards of English drama. The Act's emphasis on the legal and financial arrangements of the theatre indicated Parliamentary concerns with government regulation of the theatre as a national cultural institution rather than with the aesthetics of the drama. But within this drawn-out battle for the de-regulation of the London theatre deep class divisions were embedded, as Jane Moody argues, 'Theatrical warfare between minor and patent playhouses, on one level an economic contest about dramatic free trade, dramatised on another an ideological struggle about relationships between social classes and cultural interests.'[3] The Patent theatres consistently used both the law and the rhetoric of the National Drama to maintain control of their theatrical 'property' (the spoken word), but just as consistently faced failure. And the minor theatres, purveying the so-called 'illegitimate' drama without recourse to the letter of the law, also used the verbal and visual discourses of the National Drama to claim membership of this national cultural institution.

The National Drama was an over-determined concept, intricately entangled with hegemonic ideologies of gender, class, and nation, particularly in the establishment of hierarchies of aesthetic value which came to be linked to moral value. Or, more materially, we might see these debates as the defence of particular aesthetic distinctions which are both produced by and operate to maintain class distinctions, as argued by Pierre Bourdieu.[4] Throughout the century, the battle was discursive as well as economic and legislative, so that control of the dissemination of critical opinion, and the very detail of linguistic usages in talking about the theatre and the drama, became sites of the exercise of power. The blurring of aesthetic values with legal regulation and customary practice resulted in that loaded term, the 'legitimate' drama, possessing great currency, even for those who opposed its claims.[5] Notions of legitimacy (and illegitimacy) persisted throughout the century; indeed, the blurred boundary between morals and aesthetics in the notion of legitimacy persists to this day in British practices of funding and spectatorship in the theatre. The term 'not-for-profit' is certainly a more accurate term for what the late Romantic legitimate drama was to become.[6] However, the term does not carry with it the complex connotations of the history of theatre-making in Britain in the nineteenth century in the way that 'legitimate' does. For all the problematic history the term trails after it, the category of legitimacy is one I will be exploring in this chapter, not least because I am interested in what made the idea of the legitimate theatre, and its later concomitant, the literary drama, so attractive for a number of women writers.

The work of the writers I discuss in this chapter and in Chapter 4 confirms the enduring power of the verse tragedy as a literary form carrying with it significant cultural capital, which serious and ambitious women writers were anxious to exploit. But many women writing with the stated ambition of bringing together the apparently separated worlds of the working theatre and high culture expressed disappointment about their own careers, and were increasingly marginalized by their peers. Late in the century, Emily Pfeiffer's rather plaintive remarks in her 'Preface' to her poetic drama of contemporary life, *The Wynnes of Wynhavod* encapsulated the naïve bewilderment of many would-be playwrights throughout the century:

> 'The Wynnes of Wynhavod' [...] was written in the hope that – first attempt as it is at that high prize of a poet's ambition – it might, with the kindly aid of some borrowed technical experience, be found proper for representation on the stage. The first attempt, however, [...] induced an experience of so different a nature, that I was fain to make this earliest example of the treatment to which authors are liable at the hands of managers my last, and to content myself with an appeal to the public on literary ground alone.[7]

Pfeiffer's tentative language here, and the repeated use of 'first attempt' (as a kind of talismanic hope for beginner's luck, perhaps?), is all the more striking coming as it does from an otherwise accomplished poet and translator, who left a substantial sum in her will to endow an acting school for women,[8] and whose poetic work was reviewed widely and positively during her lifetime. Her pinpointing of the problem as her reliance on others – theatre professionals – is typical, and echoes the complaints of women playwrights throughout the century. Their frustrations demonstrate the material effects of the critical and ideological categories these women writers were attempting to manipulate, and the practical consequences of the tenuous connection between models of women's writing – particularly those based on Victorian domestic ideology – and 'art' as represented by the cultural capital of verse drama. However, the effort was thought worth the strife by many women playwrights. This indomitability and perseverance should be celebrated as a significant form of self-definition and a series of political acts by women playwrights throughout the nineteenth century.

Of course, the Romantic conceptualization of legitimacy to which Mitford and Hemans subscribed bore with it the contradictions of practice and ideology embedded in the theatre industry. The suspicion of popular entertainment implicit in the concept of the 'legitimate theatre' was pursued through a century-long aspiration towards the theatre as an art, defined as that which was removed from the grubby businesses of profit and pleasure. But theatre, more than most other forms of cultural production, needs its material base (although this is to minimize the material and industrial basis of other forms of art in the nineteenth century): it needs the flow and energy of financial capital to create cultural capital. The contradictions, then, of a theatre of 'art,' are clear, and here I am concerned with women playwrights who became entangled in the paradoxes of the 'legitimate' theatre, by attempting to manipulate the cultural capital of the 'legitimate drama' in order to claim the citizenship largely denied them through other political and social institutions. Yet the contradictions of the legitimate drama as it was produced through the London theatre industry also served to marginalize women playwrights, and in this chapter I examine both the causes and conditions of this marginalization, and the basis from which women kept fighting, by writing, back.

Mary Russell Mitford and Felicia Hemans and the legitimate drama

With Mary Russell Mitford and Felicia Hemans, I turn to two of the most important and successful writers of the late Romantic period.[9] This sentence does not even need the adjective 'woman' to qualify the noun 'writers.' Mitford's drama and prose fiction and Hemans' poetry made their authors famous and affluent in their lifetimes, achieved critical success, and gave them authority and influence as editors, correspondents, and mentors of their peers. That their reputations dwindled quickly after their deaths into images of quaint, provincial ladies, writing of quaint, provincial topics, is an indication of a literary critical discourse which progressively decoupled 'women' and 'art,' in part by requiring women to write of the suitably 'feminine' topics indicated by an increasingly conservative domestic ideology, while simultaneously defining those areas as trivial and of limited and personal interest, rather than universal import, and therefore not topics from which art could be made. Their invisibility has been compounded by their situation as transitional figures, writing in the late Romantic period, but, as Angela Leighton and Stuart Curran argue for Hemans (Mitford has been little mentioned in these contexts), representing some of 'the characteristic preoccupations of Victorian verse.'[10] This crack in periodization, into which they have disappeared, says more about the exclusionary effects of the professionalizing of literary criticism from this same period, and suggests how a more inclusive history of the theatre might require us to rethink the Romantic/Victorian boundaries which have been for so long dangerously prescriptive, rather than descriptive. If Ann Mellor's work on gender, and Jon Klancher's and Kevin Gilmartin's work on class and readership has been effective in broadening our definitions of Romanticism, it now needs to be complemented by similar work in Romantic and Victorian theatre, particularly in our tendency to see this period as one which entrenches the split between literature and stage, as Jeffrey Cox and Michael Gamer point out, *and* between the Romantic and Victorian periods – the continuities in both these areas are as significant as the breaks.[11] A study of women playwrights who aspired to join literature and the theatre is one starting place for such a revisionist project.

How Mitford and Hemans as fiction writer and poet respectively worked with and around the prescriptions of late Romantic and early Victorian gender ideology is discussed below, as are their personal self-images of themselves as writers; but what is worth stating incontrovertibly here is that as playwrights, both writers were courageously un-'feminine,' taking on proscribed (even censored) topics, interpreting historical events, writing in heroic verse tragedy, and, in spite of misgivings, pushing their work in front of theatre managers to get it performed. I need to make such a statement so boldly because the autobiographical records that both writers have left suggest very different stories: of frustration as playwrights, dispiriting negotiations with managers, wounding critical commentary, and an abiding sense of failure. Both stories are accurate accounts of Mitford's and Hemans' careers as playwrights, seen, of course, from very different points of view. But I do not want, as Anthony Dawson has put it, to write a history where subjectivity becomes subjection.[12] My interest here is to ask what might we understand from the gap between these conflicting accounts of Mitford's and Hemans' careers. What is significant in my re-presentation of their success is obvious by its emphasis on the actuality of women's presence and success in a period from which they have been written out. However, I am conscious of the inadequacy of a merely triumphalist recuperation of these women's writings if my account is at odds with their records of their own experiences. This conflict between narratives is typical of that which runs throughout the whole of this book, and foregrounds the necessity of recognizing the dialectical tensions between women's constructions of their own writing experience, and the evidence of the material traces of their work, as well as the necessity of balancing an account of the very real difficulties women playwrights faced against the equally genuine evidence of their success. In the former is a trail of clues which partially explains subsequent female invisibility, and in the latter is the evidence with which to defy that cultural process of making invisible.

One of the contradictions inherent in the notion of the performed 'legitimate' drama is self-described in Mary Russell Mitford's case. Although I am discussing Mitford's work in the general framework of writing for art's sake, rather than for commercial gain, Mitford declared that she wrote plays for money. In 1821, she wrote to Benjamin Haydon

> I have been very busy [. . .] writing a tragedy. We are poor, you know. When I was in town I saw an indifferent tragedy, of which the indifferent success procured for the author three or four hundred pounds. This raised my emulation.[13]

However, it is important to look at *what* she wrote. She did not write in the 'illegitimate' forms of fast-selling, easily staged farces, pantomimes, or melodramas, nor did she write novels in the conventional three-decker format of the period. Her first public literary productions for money were full-length verse tragedies, and Mitford's self-representation was as a dramatist. In 1825, writing to William Harness, Mitford explains herself in aesthetically driven terms:

> You are the only friend whose advice agrees with my strong internal feeling respecting the drama. Everybody else says, Write novels – write prose! So that my perseverance passes for perverseness and obstinacy, which is very discouraging.[14]

To Thomas Noon Talfourd, one of her principal mentors in theatrical matters, she wrote in the same year:

I deserve disappointment for having against all warning clung to the Drama instead of trying the more laborious but more certain path of the novel writer. The excuse which I have always made to myself has been a persuasion that my talent, such as it is, is essentially dramatic.[15]

Mitford represents herself as driven by strong feelings of emulation, excitement, audaciousness, busyness, perverseness, and stubbornness. Her combination of motives is typical of women (and men) playwrights of the Romantic period: she was attracted by the money and the chance of success, and she was also attracted by the power of the stories she could tell in the five act tragic form. But what happened in the four years between confidently announcing to Haydon that she would try her hand at a tragedy, and her confession to Talfourd that she deserved disappointment?

In what follows, I will use Mitford's account of the writing and staging of her plays *Foscari* and *Rienzi* to trace in detail the experience of a woman playwright engaging with the legitimate theatre. In one of the ironies of this study, Mitford's situation as a provincial 'lady,' isolated by geography and gender from the physical sociability of the London theatre business, and thus at a disadvantage in dealing with managers, actors, and publishers, has actually left us with unique records of her working process and the conduct of her career through the many letters she wrote to her (mostly) male mentors at this time. Her letters also provide one history of the 'theatrical conditions under which the old drama finally toppled.'[16] Mitford seems to have realized quickly that without the support of some powerful men of the theatre, her plays were unlikely to be performed. Her father was often her intermediary in her literary affairs, but as in all business matters in the Mitford family, Dr Mitford proved too often to be a clumsy and untrustworthy agent, although he usually demanded the authority of his role as head of the family. In the writing of *Foscari*, Mitford came to rely particularly on Thomas Noon Talfourd's critical judgement and his professional networks in the theatre and literary circles. When she began to work on *Foscari* in 1821 her letters to Talfourd were full of concerns about the responses of other powerful men of the theatre, as well as questions about the play's dramatic structure and concerns over its theatrical effectiveness. Although she started on *Foscari* in a flush of enthusiasm for the five-act drama in 1821, it was not produced until 1826, by Charles Kemble at Covent Garden. In the course of writing and rewriting *Foscari*, Mitford also dealt with powerful actor William Macready. Mitford quickly realized that if Macready liked the central role, the play had a better chance of being performed. But combined with this shrewd assessment of production conventions in the theatre was an element of hero-worship of the actor. As she wrote to Talfourd 'So Mr. Macready must be Foscari – Write to me, my dear Mr. Talfourd, if you think he would not – write & I stop immediately – one word would be enough – Mr. Macready is my only inspiration' (Letter 1, 21 June 1821). After completing a first draft of *Foscari*, Talfourd asked Macready to read it, and Mitford records her response on receiving Macready's letter to Talfourd about *Foscari*, which Macready had recognized as written by a woman:

> I was not in the least disappointed or disconcerted (except for that terrible 'evidently a lady's') by Mr. Macready's opinion of the play. – Mine has always been much lower – really much lower [. . .] I was therefore not in the least surprised or startled at that – but astonished & delighted beyond measure at the zeal & energy with which he takes up the cause. (Letter 3, n.d.)

Mitford kept working on the play, and produced another draft, sending it to Talfourd, and reassuring him that she would make whatever alterations Macready might suggest 'in case [. . .], he should deem it worth altering' (Letter 5, n.d.). Her uncertainties about the play – or rather, Macready's approbation of it – increased, as did the rather pleading tone in her letters to Talfourd.

> And is there the smallest chance that I may make [. . .*Foscari*] such as Mr. Macready would approve? Pray tell me frankly – you have no notion how much I desire to write such a death as may please him [. . .] Do you think he would like the death by joy for Foscari? It would not be so good as the Doge's – but newer than this certainly – & perhaps in better keeping with the character – shall I try it? (Letter 7, n.d.)

Throughout this correspondence there is a strong sense of Mitford's lack of agency in negotiations, which is in contrast with her determination to succeed as a dramatist, and also in contrast to her abilities and knowledge as a professional writer evident in the tenor of her enquiries to Talfourd. The strings of questions and constant self-deprecation (which must have been quite wearing to receive) belie her actual shrewdness in the writing of plays and the business of the theatre. She was aware of the importance of star actors succeeding in her plays, and this was the main reason she persisted with Macready and Kemble for so long, in spite of their careless handling of her work. She was also aware of the importance of working with a tragic dramaturgy which combined strong parts and strong situations for star actors with suitably spectacular settings and plot incidents. Yet her knowledge is framed by her role as a 'lady playwright' which necessitated a certain element of performed helplessness and *naïveté* in the face of what Henry Crowe calls the 'bickerings, rivalries, jealousies, and debts of the actors and managers'[17] in the course of Mitford's time as a playwright actively seeking the production of her plays.

Mitford's constant search for reassurance may have been in her character, but the contrast in tone between her side of the correspondence and Talfourd's bears out Norma Clarke's general argument that the literary marketplace was for women a place of pain and anxiety, often leading to mental or physical illness.[18] The theatre was generally acknowledged to be a difficult industry for writers, male or female (Douglas Jerrold and George Henry Lewes were both bitter about the trials of the playwright), but for women, these difficulties were compounded by their 'sense of trespass' – in both physical and ideological terms – in moving from the private study to the public stage.[19] The expression of trauma which Catherine Burroughs notes in many women's writings about their dealings with the theatre industry is absent in Talfourd's letters to Mitford; although an aspirant playwright himself (of less immediate success than Mitford), his letters are marked by a knowledgeable and businesslike tone. Talfourd took for granted his access to the places and people central to the London theatre, and his judgement of them. For Mitford such access was problematic. As Ellen Donkin argues, the working areas of the theatre – stage, backstage, and green room – tended to be masculine spaces, into which women entered on sufferance or at real risk to the integrity of their bodies or reputations.[20] As a single woman, Mitford's physical presence in the theatre and manager's offices needed to be chaperoned, and as a poor woman, with a dependent family, the cost and inconvenience of journeys from Reading to London was considerable. The issue of her presence in London was a matter of some controversy in the lengthy negotiations over both *Foscari* and *Rienzi*. In 1822, she received a letter from Kemble about *Foscari*, suggesting that she should meet him to discuss changes needed for its performance; she wrote for advice to Talfourd:

> I suppose Mr. Macready would not object to play the Doge, if Mr. Kemble should wish it – though of course I should not take the liberty to answer for it – Would it be right to leave the choice of performers & all affairs of that nature to the Manager? I suppose so.

I hope you will be in Town for I am – we are – so totally ignorant of theatrical business that to see you only for two minutes would be an inexpressible comfort. (Letter 13, 13 August 1822)

The considerations and arrangements necessary for Mitford to make before travelling to London were outlined in a later letter to Talfourd during negotiations with Macready over Mitford's tragedy *Rienzi*:

Pray forgive the trouble that I am going to give you – Will you have the goodness to ascertain from Mr. Macready whether it is at all necessary that I should see him to hear from himself his suggestions regarding Rienzi & talk them over with him, or whether they are such as may be transmitted through you – If he wishes to see me will you have the goodness to appoint a morning the end of this week, or next week or whenever suits him that I may wait on him at Hampstead for that purpose – & first let me know by one line when to come up. [...] – I had rather not [travel] of course – but still my dear father is now so well recovered [...] that I can leave him without fear – & as I should sleep at the decent Inn where the coach puts up & only stay one day, there would be very little expence or inconvenience in the journey. (Letter 15, 1824)

These journeys, arranged so carefully, proved almost fruitless; indeed, a later visit to see Macready about *Rienzi* became the focus of a public controversy over which Mitford had little control, but which caused a serious rift between her and Macready. Benjamin Harness (another of her mentors) recorded in his diary that:

Received a note from Miss Mitford to tell me that she was staying in town with Mr Talfourd. I called on her and found her in a rather dirty lodging with Mrs Talfourd, some cold ham from the eating house, some seed cake, and a bottle of white wine in the green bottle. She had a long and serious story of complaints to make against Macready.

He had taken a violent fancy to a tragedy of hers, called *Rienzi*, and had written to her to come up to town immediately upon the subject, that she might personally discuss with him some alterations which he was desirous of having adopted.[21]

The changes Macready wanted included 'The second and third act were to be condensed into one. The fifth act was to be rewritten; [...] and it was to be completed without fail in a fortnight.' Mitford did so, and according to Harness, 'returned to town to bring home her work. On giving it to Macready his first, chilling, unfeeling words were "Oh, there was no hurry, we have another piece at the Theatre." '[22] Mitford's frustration had some very public consequences. In 1825, a public letter appeared in *Blackwood's Magazine* under the pseudonym of 'Philo-Dramaticus,' which commented in a veiled way on Mitford's negotiations with Macready.[23] Macready took personal offence with Mitford, who denied all knowledge of the letter, but nevertheless wrote to protest at Macready's treatment of her in terms echoing those of 'Philo-Dramaticus':

> That you did send for me on the perusal of Rienzi; that you suggested many & material alterations; that you assured me, at least that I understood you to assure me, that if altered to your satisfaction you could & would bring out the play; that you subsequently caused Mr. Talfourd to write to me desiring that I would myself bring up the piece to prevent the delay even of a day in case farther changes were requisite; & that when I waited on you at the time appointed you told me there was no hurry for that you had another Tragedy in the Theatre; – all this appears to me true – & without saying such hard words or harbouring such hard thoughts as 'deceiving or betraying,' the disappointment was bitter. (Copied to Talfourd, Letter 22, 12 August 1825)

Macready's diary entries show him still smarting from this public criticism over a decade later, as he takes comfort in Talfourd's falling out with Mitford (probably attributable to Talfourd's professional jealousy of Mitford's success), commenting 'They [Talfourd and John Forster] are much displeased with Miss Mitford, who seems to be showing herself *well up*. She was bad from the beginning. How strange with so much talent!'[24] The endurance of this malice, while it says much about Macready's character, also says much about Mitford's frustration over her dealings with him. In spite of Mitford's fulsome dedication of *Julian* to Macready – 'with warm admiration for those powers which have inspired [...] the tragic dramatists of his age' – he seems to have already judged her 'bad from the beginning,' thus justifying his treatment of her.

Ostensibly, Mitford's career as a playwright was a success. She wrote eight full-length plays, and had five of them performed in the Theatres Royal at Covent Garden and Drury Lane; she earned money, public recognition, and popularity from her writing. She was part of several wide circles of literary men and women, and maintained lively correspondences with other writers in England and the United States, where her prose was also very popular. Yet even the award of a state pension in 1837 only came after her representation of herself as a writer in the most marginal of positions, vulnerable to the vagaries of the theatre industry:

> I took the step of writing at once briefly & plainly to Lord Melbourne – I told him that my poor writings had been the chief almost the sole support of my family – that I had been compelled during the last winter [...] by the state of the theatres to withdraw a tragedy for which I had seemed certain to be paid in ready money – that this disappointment had been followed by a failure of health & spirits which had nearly taken away the power of execution which that very disappointment had rendered doubly necessary, that another such blow or even another such illness would go near to annihilate what little power of comprehension I possessed & deprive me altogether of resource & of hope – that this application had been urged upon me by a friend who knew these circumstances – & that looking at my father's white hairs I had felt emboldened to take a step which no personal conditions could have induced me to take. (Letter 74, postmark 13 May 1837)

Even after her theatrical and fictional successes, Mitford could not take her place in the world of letters – her cultural citizenship – for granted. Her struggle to make a space for herself in the national culture of the legitimate theatre exemplifies the difficult position of women of letters in this period, and her constant illnesses and her almost pathological sensitivity and uncertainty make clear the bodily and mental costs of her cultural investments. Mitford's own comments point to the paradoxical situation into which she wrote herself. In her determination to write drama, she rejected prose fiction and by this rejection she rejected also the opportunity to realize an income in a rapidly expanding market. But her writerly self-image was a matter of deliberate choice: Mitford actually *did* write a lot of prose, most famously *Our Village*, but also in the various annuals and almanacs throughout the 1820s and 1830s. Her primary interest in verse tragedy suggests she had internalized the high cultural valuation of poetic tragedy, and used this form as her way to claim full membership of the theatrical and literary community. The 'high' drama of the legitimate stage, seen at the time as the appropriate form for the nation which inherited the plays of Shakespeare, was a vocation which could be pursued without compromising her status as a lady. However, in quasi-economic terms, she made a cultural investment in a declining market, entering the field of the 'legitimate' drama at the time when its dominance of the theatre industry was waning, when the manager of Covent Garden could delay the production of *Foscari*, on the grounds that sensation and novelty were what audiences demanded. When *Foscari* was performed finally in 1826, it was produced as part of a bill that delivered the 'sensation and novelty' audiences apparently required: it shared the bill with a farce, *Returned 'Killed!,'* and a *'Ballet of Action,' The Deserter of Naples*. And by the end of the 1820s, Mitford's plays were performed outside of the two Theatres Royal, finding more congenial homes in the minor theatres,[25] and contributing to the breaking down of the boundaries of the 'legitimate' and 'illegitimate' which so damaged her career in its earlier stages.

Felicia Hemans' experience as a playwright was similar to Mitford's, except that Hemans represented herself as persuaded by others to offer her play, *The Vespers of Palermo*, to Charles Kemble at Covent Garden. Apparently pushed by her literary mentors (the Reverend) Henry Milman (also a mentor of Mitford's) and (Bishop) Reginald Heber, rather than motivated by the promise of money and fame in the theatre, she tried to balance feminine decorum against the public exposure and comment occasioned by playwriting and production. But her first biographer repeatedly mentions Hemans' 'long cherished hopes' for the play, and reproduces her correspondence with Milman over the period from June 1821 to December 1823 as he advises her and acts as her agent with Kemble. Two and a half years is a long time to work on a piece without wanting it to succeed, publicly and distinctively. However, Hemans' self-deprecation is of a piece with her general approach to her writing career, in which she managed to mask her determination to succeed as a writer behind a carefully constructed persona of the domestic poetess.[26]

Nevertheless, *The Vespers of Palermo* was produced at Covent Garden on 12 December 1823, but had only one performance there, much to the disappointment of Hemans' family and friends. Hemans' sister, Harriett Hughes, recalled the 'uncontrollable state of excitement' of Hemans' sons waiting to hear 'about mamma's play,' the extra newspapers ordered for the reviews, and besieging of the local post office in St Asaph for news of the play's reception.[27] The play's first night failure was put down to the performance of Frances H. Kelly as Constance – she had a speech impediment, or was 'under the influence of some infatuating spell.'[28] That was not the end of the story, however, as Joanna Baillie's advocacy of the play to Walter Scott persuaded Harriet (Mrs Henry)

Siddons to stage the play in Edinburgh, where it met with much greater success. Hemans' network of supportive women writers noted as so significant by Marlon Ross[29] expanded here to include a powerful woman manager from Britain's leading theatrical family, suggesting that whatever the support of Charles Kemble's 'consideration for my interests,'[30] there may be some truth in Hemans' own sense that being a woman was at the root of her bad London reception.

> As a female, I cannot help feeling rather depressed by the extreme severity with which I have been treated in the morning papers; I know not why this should be, for I am sure I should not have attached the slightest value to their praise, but I suppose it is only a proper chastisement for my temerity; for a female who shrinks from such things, has certainly no business to write tragedies.[31]

The Theatres Royal, with their weighty expectations for producing a National Drama, looked awfully suspect as fertile ground for women playwrights in the 1820s.

Perhaps because of this success so hoped for and not achieved in an otherwise extraordinarily successful career, there is a sense of unfinished business with the theatre and performance in Hemans' subsequent writing career. This is, maybe, another manifestation of that oscillation between page and stage which I am arguing is a paradigm for women writers balancing respectability against ambition (however covertly expressed), and, as I shall argue in my discussion of George Eliot, a characteristic of non-commercial women playwrights' working lives that was not confined to the Romantic period. It is not just that Henry Chorley noted Hemans' enduring 'reverence for, or delight in, our own noble old dramatic writers' (78–9), but that Hemans was continually drawn to the expressive possibilities of formal verse drama poetic dialogues. As well as *The Vespers of Palermo*, Hemans wrote and published *The Siege of Valencia* (1823), and *De Chatillon; or, The Crusaders* (published posthumously in 1840), as well as translating other verse tragedies from the Italian (*The Alcestis, Il Conte di Carmagnola*, and *Caius Gracchus*), and casting several of her lyric poems in the form of dramatic monologues or dialogues ('The English Martyrs,' 'Flowers and Music in a Room of Sickness,' 'Wood Walk and Hymn,' 'Burial of an Emigrant's Child in the Forests,' and 'The Painter's Last Work'). Diego Saglia comments that 'Drama was evidently uppermost in Hemans's interests at the time,' and links this focus with Hemans' interests in European oppositional politics, particularly those of Italy.[32] What emerges from reading these plays and dramatic fragments, in relation to Hemans' other writing as domestic poetess, and in terms of the politics of the theatre of her time, is that drama offered her a freedom and strength of expression which was not available in other forms and styles.

Similarly, reading Mary Russell Mitford's plays against the work which is probably her lasting memorial – her pastoral idylls starting with *Our Village* – reveals a tougher and less ideologically 'feminine' intelligence. The differences between her fiction and her drama were recognized during her lifetime, and shaped her reputation then and post-humously, as Sarah Hale's account demonstrates:

> Although her tragedies show great intellectual powers, and a highly cultivated mind, yet it is by her sketches of English life that she has obtained the greatest share of her popularity, and it is on them that her fame will chiefly depend.[33]

In the same work, Hale also comments that Joanna Baillie, while an undisputed genius, might have had 'a more extensive and more popular influence' as an essayist or novelist, and regrets that she did not write an epic poem (574) – suggesting that Hale saw Baillie's genius and moral influence as independent of her chosen medium, and leaving her reader with the strong sense that a talented woman writer should turn to *anything* but the drama. Hale's connection of women writers' influence with particular genres is typical of the period, indicative of the entrenchment of a gendered ideology of genre and medium, and her investment in the connections between gender and genre demonstrate why women's playwriting was so easily overlooked in contemporary criticism, even in a period with a strong tradition of successful women playwrights.

Liberal tragedy

By reading their plays against the grain of their lasting literary reputations – Hemans the domestic poetess, Mitford the ladylike Tory – I want to emphasize the constructive aspects of the dialectical tension between playwriting and femininity this book traces, and articulate the positive outcomes of the risks Mitford and Hemans took. Mitford's and Hemans' plays show how – despite the material difficulties documented above – writing for performance in the legitimate theatre offered broad canvas for aesthetic innovation, intellectual challenge, and politically engaged writing. Indeed, these plays can be read as *proto-feminist* plays which do much to establish a tradition of women's playwriting in the nineteenth century – even a canon, acknowledging Virginia Blain's comment that 'I believe canonicity is a very handy tool, so long as we don't get misled into allowing it to become a hegemony.'[34] Later women writers were drawn to the drama and the theatre for its freedoms of voice, range, and topic, and the work of Baillie, Hemans, and Mitford offered a tradition – a canon of sorts – of writerly practice. Notably, unlike the male and masculinist tradition of the 'theatre of the mind' which Shou-Ren Wang delineates, and which he argues from the mid-nineteenth century 'became obsolete and was ready to retire before the resurgence of stage drama,'[35] women's non-commercial dramatic writing continued, serving specific personal and political purposes throughout the century.

One striking feature of the recent revival of scholarly attention to Felicia Hemans has been her outing as a political poet, albeit masked by the distinct role of 'poetess,' but, as Gary Kelly argues, nevertheless a public poet and a member of the revolutionary class, that fraction which lobbied 'against the restoration of reactionary and repressive monarchic regimes, and in face of emergent working-class political movements,' and was involved in the cultural formation of the modern liberal state.[36] Building on this revisionist version of Hemans, Diego Saglia finds *The Vespers of Palermo* to be an exemplary public discussion of liberal ideas, and the problem of the liberal state, addressing the contemporary geopolitics of Britain and Europe through a tripartite layering of historical reference – to the events of 1282 on which the play was based, the post-Napoleonic settlement of Europe and its political effects in Britain, and the volatile situation of Sicily and southern Europe in the early 1820s.[37] No broad revisionist studies of Mitford exist, and her own avowal of high Tory politics at the time of the banning of her play *Charles the First* (Letter 19, 29 June 1825) suggests that a reading of her plays as resistant to the dominant hegemony might be counter-intuitive. Yet her Italian history plays, *Rienzi* and *Foscari*, draw on a similar view of history and politics as Hemans', as both writers offer a critique of martial and confrontational politics in the nation state. It is not just the interlacing of the affairs of home and state through scenes which make physical the ideological interpenetration of private and public spaces, but the bold approach both 'lady' playwrights take in confronting the conventionally masculine territories of power, conflict, and war, through the *über*-masculine genres of history and tragedy. All three plays view rebellion against tyranny in positive terms, through male protagonists whose rebellion is justified in both national and domestic terms, in what Susan Wolfson and Elizabeth Fay call 'nation-defining, heart-rending warfare.'[38] In Hemans' unproduced play, *The Siege of Valencia*, this connection between home and nation is foregrounded by the situation of the siege, a state of warfare which, according to Simon Bainbridge, 'presents a particular challenge to women, compelling them to cross from the private sphere into the public and from a conventionally feminine role into a conventionally masculine one.'[39] While Bainbridge and others[40] have focussed on the transformation of femininity in Hemans' plays, in my discussion below I will focus on the male protagonists, in order to explore the extent of the challenge Hemans and Mitford make to gendered views of genre and the writing of history. In this case, I am interpreting the way women write about men as a touchstone for their relationship with the proscriptions of the gendered ideology of late Romantic writerly practice, and furthermore, that writing about men in public life and action is an open challenge to those constraints of gender and genre. When Mitford's plays were reviewed with comments such as the *Times* made in a favourable review of *Julian*, it suggests that Mitford and Hemans played for high stakes in venturing to represent the masculine will to power:

> when we reflect that it is the work of a woman, we are only surprised that she has succeeded so well in delineating passions (ambition and revenge) of which she may have read, but the violent workings of which her intercourse with society debars her from perceiving[41]

The Vespers of Palermo, Rienzi, and, to a lesser extent, *Foscari* track the origins and progress of rebellion against tyrannical authority through an heroic male protagonist. *The Vespers of Palermo* makes an argument that links war, freedom, and heroism, but also represents heroism as a quality which is not exclusively masculine. The kingdom of Sicily has been colonized by the 'yoke of France,'[42] but the people still carry the memory of their national leaders: their King Conradin (executed by the French), the Count de Procida, and his son Raimond (who both survived the invasion). Conradin's memory is kept alive by Vittoria, his fiancée, who is now promised by Charles of Anjou to the French viceroy, Eribert, as a human trophy for conquering Sicily. While Procida and his son remain in the shadows to organize a band of rebels, Vittoria becomes the public focus of the rebellion. She agrees to marry Eribert, with full pomp and ceremony, but secretly plans with Procida and Raimond to make the occasion of her wedding the trap for Eribert and the rest of the French occupation. The ringing of the vesper bells, as Vittoria and Eribert and his retinue of Provençal nobles proceed to the church, is the signal for Procida, Raimond, and the Sicilian nationalists to attack the French while they are vulnerable. Vittoria throws off her 'bridal wreath and ornaments' and pronounces the rebellion 'proud freedom!' She challenges Eribert to

> Believe in retribution! What! proud man!
> Prince, ruler, conqueror! didst thou deem Heaven slept?
> [. . .] O blind security! He, in whose dread hand
> The lightnings vibrate, holds them back until
> The trampler of this goodly earth hath reached
> His pyramid-height of power; that so his fall
> May with more fearful oracles make pale
> Man's crowned oppressors! (566)

But just as Vittoria is making the revolutionary's claim to the support of God in the overthrow of tyranny, De Couci and his men come to the rescue of the French, and Raimond is suspected of betraying the Sicilians, because of his love for Constance, Eribert's sister, and his refusal to take unreasonable and brutal revenge on the French. Raimond reveals himself as a hero in the typology of tragic characterization when he challenges his father's plans: 'Must innocence and guilt / Perish alike?' (551) and 'Why should freedom strike / Mantled with darkness?' (558). And in the midst of re-establishing Sicilian self-government, the pursuit of Raimond as a traitor forces even his father Procida to suspect him and pronounce him a traitor, punishable by death. The rest of the tragedy follows the battle between father and son, as well as between the French and the Sicilians. The conflict between father and son takes on national significance because of their positions as leaders of their people, and the cosmic significance of Procida's lack of faith in his son is underlined by the final speech of the play, in which Procida finally realizes the consequences of his loss of faith:

> I have learned
> All his high worth in time to deck his grave.
> Is there not power in the strong spirit's woe
> To force an answer from the viewless world
> Of the departed? Raimond! – speak! – forgive!
> Raimond! my victor, my deliverer! hear!
> Why, what a world is this! Truth ever bursts
> On the dark soul too late: and glory crowns
> The unconscious dead. There comes an hour to break

> The mightiest hearts! – My son! my son! is this
> A day of triumph! Ay, for thee alone!

> > [*He throws himself upon the body of* RAIMOND,
> > *Curtain falls*] (595)

In the closing moments of the play, Procida learns what his son's lover, Constance, always knew: that love must be trusting and sometimes even passive. Procida's tragedy is that he learns this too late, after his son's death (and Hemans' central interest in Procida is suggested by the play's working title, 'Procida' as listed in the Covent Garden accounts ledgers). Earlier in the play, Constance articulates the lesson Procida is yet to learn:

> – Is not the life of woman all bound up
> In her affections? What hath *she* to do
> In this bleak world alone? It may be well
> For man on his triumphal course to move,
> Uncumbered by soft bonds; but *we* were born
> For love and grief. (576)

Constance is the image of the domestic, enduring woman, and thus continues what we might expect of the typical gendering of female dramatic character; but the commanding and powerful Vittoria is also given speeches which acknowledge a different way for a woman to view the world. Throughout the play she is troubled by omens of disaster – Etna's smoke, traitorous looks – and cannot rejoice after the Sicilians' first victory:

> We are free –
> Free and avenged! Yet on my soul there hangs
> A darkness, heavy as the oppressive gloom
> Of midnight fantasies. (573)

Vittoria and Constance's ways of looking at the world are at odds with those of the powerful men around them, and regarded by those men as inadequate and weak. In a scene between Constance and Eribert (II, i), these perspectives clash over Constance's plea for mercy for a young boy. In the face of Eribert's insistence that 'I am not one / Of those weak spirits, that timorously keep watch,' Constance warns him

> Brother! I have seen
> Dark eyes bent on you, e'en midst festal throngs,
> With such deep hatred settled in their glance,
> My heart hath died within me.
> *Eri.* Am I then
> To pause, and doubt, and shrink, because a girl,
> A dreaming girl, hath trembles at a look?
> *Cons.* Oh! looks are no illusions, when the soul,
> Which may not speak in words, can find no way
> But theirs to liberty! (544)

Eribert's insistence on the materiality of power in the face of Constance's emphasis on empathy and feeling is set up on its own terms as a binary opposition between the masculine and the feminine in the play. But it is paralleled by Procida's determination to exert his power by punishing the man he thinks is traitor to his cause – even if that man is his son. He ignores the evidence of his eyes which tells him that Raimond is innocent: 'Thou hast a brow / Clear as the day – and yet I doubt thee, Raimond!' (558), and in doing so, also ignores what the play establishes as the closest of bonds – that between parent and child. Montalba becomes the most vengeful of the Sicilian nationalists, driven by the grief of the loss of his children; the occasion of Eribert and Constance's argument cited above is her plea on behalf of a Sicilian mother for leniency towards her son. Here Hemans cuts across oppositions which might otherwise neatly align masculinity with oppression and femininity with freedom-fighting to give us alternative versions of masculinity, such as Raimond's, which rejects unthinking violence. Procida must learn through bitter experience that his desire for justice has been corrupted by his over-whelming pride. Although the French are defeated, the cost of Procida's public victory and private lesson is the death of his son. It is Hemans' final twist on the gendered plot mechanics of tragedy, which as Catherine Clément has shown, usually require the woman to die.[43] In *Vespers*, the son Raimond must die in order for Procida to learn his lesson about the truth and power of feeling, rather than force.

A similar rupture of the bonds between father and son is charted in *Foscari*, Mary Mitford's version of the story of the Doge of Venice and his son Francesco Foscari. While Hemans' play was not considered a London success, Mitford's play was received with some pleasure, albeit qualified by statements which we must regard as typical of the treatment of women's playwriting in the period. Critical responses focussed on Mitford's deployment of the emotional force of tragedy, her investment in history, and the parallels between her play and that of Byron's *The Two Foscari*. These boundary-riding reviews of *Foscari*, *Julian* (her first play to be performed, although written later than *Foscari* or *Rienzi*), and *Rienzi* made sure that Mitford did not stray too far into that realm marked out by that most publicly celebrated of Romantic poets. Mitford herself acknowledges her potential trespass, making sure to announce in her author's preface that

> her piece was not only completed, but actually presented to Covent Garden Theatre, before the publication of Lord Byron's well-known drama: a fact which happily exculpates her from any charge of a vain imitation of the great Poet, or of still vainer rivalry.[44]

Indeed, as her letters to Talfourd, Harness, and others reveal, Mitford began writing *Foscari* in 1821, started negotiations with Charles Kemble for the production of *Foscari* in January 1822 (although wondering 'by the way people say that Mrs. C. K. is the critic – is it so?' (Letter 11)), and received Kemble's undertaking to produce the play in October of that year in a letter to Talfourd in August 1822 (Letter 13). Her composition of *Foscari* thus ran parallel with Byron's but reviewers were not to know that Mitford had been 'tossed about between him [Kemble] and Macready like a cricket-ball – affronting both parties and suspected by both, because I will not come to a deadly rupture with either'[45] for several years, and that *Foscari* was actually her first attempt at writing stageable tragedy. Public opinion sought to compare Mitford's version with Byron's and with the historical record, perhaps perversely pleased they could point out that

> our readers will perceive that Miss Mitford has by no means closely adhered to the historical facts, and that her drama bears no resemblance whatever either as to time or action to the tragedy of the *Foscari* by Byron; but that she has taken a detached portion of the history, and filled up the details from her own imagination.[46]

In this, and other comments, Mitford's imagination is represented as that part of her artistry which must make up for the deficiencies of her (gendered) knowledge. Thus her inaccuracies and departures from or embroideries of the known record should be gallantly excused. As Mitford's novelist friend, Mrs Hofland, told Samuel Carter Hall after the first night of *Rienzi*: 'Macready told me it was a wonderful tragedy – an extraordinary tragedy *"for a woman to have written."* The men always make that reservation, my dear; they cramp us, my dear, and then reproach us with our lameness.'[47] The critic of the *New Monthly Magazine* is explicit about Mitford's scope and literary 'manners' in respect of her gender in its review of *Foscari*:

> of all writers, a female is most entitled to be treated with respect and consideration. The habits of female life are not friendly to the exercise of the more vigorous ability; and women, successful in authorship, have not seldom stained their laurels by a too obvious use of strong picturing, and forbidden modes of sentiment and language. But the present writer has honourably kept her pen immaculate; and we should be glad to see her popularity increase, even if it were only for the sake of her example.[48]

The paucity of tragedies from women playwrights was also cause for treating the play differently, as *The Literary Gazette* argues:

> That the tragedy [...] will be eminently successful, we do not expect. The authoress has not always made the most of her situations [...]. As a whole, however, it reflects no little credit upon her talents; and when we take into consideration the remarkable fact, that, with the single exception of the *Percy* of Hannah More, there is no such thing upon our stage as a successful tragedy from a female pen, we ought still more warmly to express our satisfaction at the result.[49]

In these reviews, couched in terms of chivalrous concern, the central critical criteria by which women's work was to be judged are articulated. The rare – and even more rarely successful – 'female pen' (More's *Percy* was first performed in 1777, almost half a century earlier) wrote from the 'habits of female life' which were dissociated from the affairs of the world, necessarily unstained and 'immaculate' but deserving of 'indulgence' – that is, protection from the rigours of standard judgement. This exceptionality, as Angela Leighton argues, was 'one of the woman poet's most disabling inheritances.'[50] That these are typical comments about one of the most successful playwrights of the Romantic period is a stark reminder of the force of gender differentiation as a critical principle in the period.

In spite of public and private pressures on Mitford (which she had also internalized as evidenced by her letters to male mentors) to observe the gendered decorums of writing by producing a piece (like Goldilocks' porridge) not too powerful, but not too sentimental, *Foscari* imagines and creates on stage a world of violent emotion which is closely – indeed, causally – connected with men's performance in public life. The aging Doge (the elder Foscari of the play's title) is challenged by the rather thinly characterized antagonist, Erizzo, whose personal ambition drives the plot to overthrow the Doge by proposing Donato as the new Doge. Donato is the Doge's oldest friend, and his daughter Camilla is betrothed to the Doge's son, Francesco Foscari, with whom his son, Cosmo, was brought up. When Erizzo fails in his attempt to oust the Doge, he resorts to criminal means, framing the Doge's soldier-son, Francesco, as the murderer of Donato. Circumstantial evidence works against Francesco, as he was clandestinely visiting Camilla, and was seen leaving from her window at the same time that Donato is heard calling 'Murder!' (III, i, 122). In the Ducal palace, Cosmo accuses Francesco of murder (III, ii) and demands justice; Francesco is tried and pronounced guilty, although such is his belief in his honour that he refuses to speak in his defence at his trial: 'Why should I speak / When I have nothing but my knightly word / To prove me innocent?' (IV, i, 141). Camilla is brought in to testify against Francesco, at which point she loses her reason, like Ophelia, overwrought by grief at her father's death apparently at the hand of her lover. Instead of death, Francesco is sentenced, by his father, to exile, and Camilla decides to go with him, in spite of her brother's taunts that she is a parricide, a 'murderer's bride' (V, i, 150). In the final scene, on the seas shore, the Doge parts from his son, but the action is halted by Cosmo and Erizzo entering to stop Camilla from leaving Venice. Francesco is fatally stabbed by Cosmo, but not before the news that the real murderer of Donato has been found (a mercenary paid by Erizzo) and Erizzo confesses to his overwhelming urge to power. Francesco dies pardoned by his father, who *'Flinging off the Ducal bonnet'* proclaims that: 'Now I am free! / Now I may grieve and pity like a man!' (V, ii, 160).

This is the incendiary mix of high politics and familial connections into which Mitford launches her spectator. The play is saved from outright advocacy of revolutionary principles by the characterization of the chief rebel, Count Erizzo, as a bitter and devious man – an anti-hero against Foscari's obvious honour and heroism – thereby undercutting Erizzo's public professions of democracy by revealing his personal amorality. So Erizzo's attempt at overthrowing the power of the Doge is represented as a plot of private ambition, rather than public idealism, and his critique of the Doge as an absolute ruler is shown to be prompted by jealousy rather than principle 'He rules us as a king – this Foscari, / An absolute king, haughty and imbecile / As any Eastern sovereign!' (II, i, 101).

Mitford's representation of Venetian politics combines these public and combative scenes of government with intimate domestic scenes in the family home of Donato. In setting up the plot to supplant the Doge Foscari, Mitford emphasizes the ties of friendship and family feeling which connect Donato and the Foscari: Donato refuses to plot against the Doge as his oldest friend (II, i), and the Doge hopes for Cosmo and Francesco to become brothers through Camilla (I, ii). The staging of the play also makes material the interconnectedness of family palazzi and the Senate house, by blurring the distinctions between public and private space, so that life in these *élite* families is imagined as always on show, and even private action accountable in the public record. Characters move from public meeting places, like St Mark's or the Senate house, to apartments within their homes, which are also spaces where public policy and governance are shown to be conducted.

Reviewers read this dramaturgical technique largely in terms of its opportunities for large-scale staging within the limits of legitimacy, commenting that

> Considerable pains [...] bestowed upon the appointing and getting up of the piece. The scenery is splendid, and there is a fancifully arranged dance introduced into the banqueting scene in the third act. [...] Miss Mitford is entitled to this high commendation – that she has produced a tragedy of the legitimate drama – not a pantomime of moonlight, and procession, and tinsel.[51]

Interestingly, however, the play does not contain the spectacular scenes of conflict of Hemans' *Vespers*. The action in *Foscari* is more solidly political and psychological, and Mitford's point about the dangers of power and ambition is made through her combination of familial and state politics. While Erizzo is the obvious villain, corrupted by his ambition, the character of the Doge presents an even more compelling – because the character is not a pattern villain – example of the hazards of power. He is required to judge his own son and pronounce sentence, bound implacably by his public position, even in the face of Camilla's pleas:

> I am not
> A King, who wears fair mercy on the cross
> Of his bright diadem; I have no power
> Save as the whetted axe to strike and slay,
> A will-less instrument of the iron law
> Of Venice. (IV, i, 137)

In this statement he refutes Erizzo's charge that he exercises power tyrannically. But his liberation as a father only comes at the expense of the death of his son, when the Doge casts aside his bonnet – the symbol of his public role – to feel 'like a man.' Again, the woman survives, while it is the death of a young man which forces other characters to realize their sins and weaknesses.

While *Foscari* ultimately upholds a political system ordered by influence achieved through honour (particularly in battle) and grounded in deference, respect, and family hierarchy, in *Rienzi*, produced at Drury Lane in 1828, with Macready in the title role, Mitford connects rebellion with democracy represented as a liberal cause.[52] Indeed, the play endorses democracy as a populist movement, and a mode of government which brings out the best in all ranks of society. The son of working parents, Cola di Rienzi leads a rebellion in Rome against the aristocratic and tyrannical Ursini, whose arrogant misrule of Rome he opposes. But when his rebellion is successful, and Rienzi himself is ruler of Rome – although he rejects the popular call for him to become emperor, wishing to be simply 'the Tribune of the People' (II, i, 28) – he too falls prey to the inconsistencies of power, and becomes rigid and tyrannical himself. Rienzi is overthrown and killed by the same mob of citizens whom he stirred into rebellion at the start of the play. However, at play's climax – but too late to save his life – Rienzi realizes the delusions both of his own ambitions, and the general weakness of his fellow citizens. In defiance of the citizens who call for vengeance, blood, and liberty from Rienzi, whom they now call 'perjured tyrant' he answers:

> For liberty! Go seek
> Earth's loftiest heights, and ocean's deepest caves;
> Go where the sea-snake and the eagle dwell,
> 'Midst mighty elements, – where nature is,
> And man is not, and ye may see afar,
> Impalpable as a rainbow on the clouds,
> The glorious vision! Liberty! I dream'd
> Of such a goddess once; dream'd that yon slaves
> Were Romans, such as ruled the world, and I
> Their Tribune; – vain and idle dream! Take back
> The symbol and the power. What seek ye more? (V, ii, 78)

George Daniel calls this 'majestic image [...] equal – we had nearly said *superior* – to anything in modern poetry. It is perfectly noble, and almost sublime.'[53] In Mitford's work, it maintains a certain ideological ambivalence: offering the ideal of liberty, while closing off the possibilities of human attainment of such a dream. Although Mitford herself does not claim kin with any literary school, the ideological ambivalence of the denouement of *Rienzi*, with its valorization of liberty, but its rejection of the possibility of achieving it, is perhaps typical of Romantic writing in the 1820s, after the disillusionment of the grand projects of liberty of the French Revolution and the clashes between individuals and the repressive state in Britain in the eighteen-teens. Mitford's plays – and I am thinking particularly of *Rienzi* and *Charles the First* here – demonstrate both an attraction to and rejection of grand projects of national freedom, chiefly in her understanding of the dialectical tensions between the heroic ideals of revolutionaries and the private and emotional consequences of political action. And it is this conviction that the apparently impersonal forces of history and politics have their basis in the agency of the feeling individual which gives Mitford her liberal edge, but one which speaks critically of masculine power from a woman's point of view. One could argue here for Mitford in the terms which Gary Kelly employs in representing Felicia Hemans as a member of the 'revolutionary class' of Britain which was active 'against the restoration of reactionary and repressive monarchic regimes, and in face of emergent working-class political movements.' This class was, according to Kelly, a 'predominantly middle-class reading public [...] who had just become or were demanding to become the political nation.'[54] Mitford's plays engage with the dreams, fantasies, *and* practicalities of revolution; her revolutionaries have families, love, and suffer emotional pain.

Mitford's representation of national politics is always grounded in what George Daniel calls her 'happiest style' – that of the domestic scene (8). As she announces in a note to the published edition, '[F]or the female characters I am wholly responsible' (3). It is through her creations of Rienzi's daughter, Claudia, and Lady Colonna, the wife of Rienzi's antagonist, Stephen Colonna, that Mitford focusses her critique of the unfeeling will to power. The play represents women's intuitions about character and emotion as an alternative mode of knowing, often in conflict with male characters' certainties about policy, status, and power. The women are ultimately correct in their judgements of others, although their convictions run counter to those of their male relatives. Lady Colonna warns her husband Stephen Colonna about Rienzi's capacity for opposition early in the play, in the face of Colonna's dismissal of him as a malcontent,

> He hath turned
> A bitter knave of late, and lost his mirth,
> And mutters riddling warnings and wild tales
> Of the great days of heathen Rome; (II, i, 19)

In Claudia Rienzi's case, her premonitions of the danger of her father Rienzi's actions, and her commitment to stay with her father, whatever happens, lead to her death on her father's breast at the close of the play. Rienzi's courage, like that of Procida's in *Vespers*, is shown by his lack of fear in facing the people.

But Mitford reminds us that women can also show courage: when her husband flees Rome, Lady Colonna stays to fight Rienzi for her son, and Claudia will not be parted from her father and dies with him. Mitford's appropriation of masculine territory was noted by critics of *Foscari* and *Rienzi*, from George Daniels' relieved discovery that she could also write like a woman, in his comment that 'If, in the character of Rienzi, Miss Mitford has shown that she can write with masculine energy, let Claudia bear witness that her wonted dominion over the heart is still in full force;' (8) to the *New Monthly Magazine*'s prediction that 'we are mistaken if, in her future productions, she does not leave us with any pretence for tracing the weaknesses of the poetess or the woman.'[55] Again, statements like this one bring us up short, by reminding us of the critical atmosphere into which Hemans and Mitford ventured. Statements like these remind us of the reasons beyond those of 'bad writing' for the adverse response to Hemans' *Vespers of Palermo*. This kind of critical opinion also identifies the courage these women mustered in putting their work into the public realm, and makes us realize how much more courageous are women writers who hold strongly to patterns of feminine virtue in the face of representations of masculine power. While such a moral and sexual economy might now be thought of as essentializing and conservative, in the face of the masculinist guardians of high culture and legitimacy, looking for the inevitable revelations of female 'weakness,' such dramaturgy has the feel of a feminist protest.

3
Money

For men in the nineteenth century, work for money was usually a given; for women, work for money needed to be disguised as something else. Yet – perhaps because of this – women's writing was often concerned with money, to the extent that Ellen Moers traces a tradition of 'feminine realism' in women novelists' concern with the material facts of money, attributing their fascination with 'the Real' to their denial of access to it.[1] Although I argue that women routinely worked as playwrights, this was always done in an often painful dialectic with social and cultural proscriptions on their participation. In previous chapters, I have explored the consequences of casting women playwrights as exceptional, encouraging women playwrights only at moments of crisis in the theatre, but barring them from its permanent ranks, and requiring that they display a level of precocity and excellence to excuse their public prominence. In this chapter, I want to move from these rescuing angels to discuss the work of women who worked within the commercial theatre as it was constituted in various forms across the nineteenth century – that is, women playwrights who routinely worked for money, in theatres where the house takings were as important as aesthetic achievement or legitimacy.

These were the women playwrights who wrote mostly for the 'minor' theatres before de-regulation of the theatres in 1843, created the fashion for sensation in the 1860s, and were prolific in the commercial West End theatres at the end of the century.[2] In looking at the range of this work, I trace the defining contribution made by women playwrights to popular culture. Women have long been recognized as influential consumers of popular culture, but in this chapter I identify the ways in which women writers were also significant producers of that culture, making contributions to the public sphere through their participation as professional playwrights. Furthermore, this contribution came from women across the social classes, from the working or lower-middle class writer-managers such as Mrs Denvil (at the Pavilion in the 1830s), to Caroline Boaden and Eliza Planché as members of theatrical families in the legitimate theatres, to the 'de-classed' position of actress turned writer Mary Braddon, and the middle-class, fashionable, and suffragette connections of Madeleine Ryley and Clo Graves.

It may have seemed that women playwrights disappeared after the fame and influence of Joanna Baillie dispersed, and the novelty and promise of women such as Mary Russell Mitford was forgotten. In the late eighteenth century a 'normal' season included plays by Susannah Centlivre, Hannah Cowley, Elizabeth Inchbald, and Sophia Lee, at the turn of the century Baillie's publication of *Plays on the Passions* (1798–1812) took the literary world by storm,[3] and in the 1810s writers such as Lady Dacre (Barbarina Brand) and Mary Berry gained attention and notoriety as playwrights. But notwithstanding the validity of the sense of crisis for women playwrights constant in women's own accounts of their careers at the time, it is important to recognize that women *did* remain active as playwrights in the mainstream theatre throughout the nineteenth century. Numerically, the figures may not look impressive: my tabulations of the numbers of titles produced by women show they produced (roughly) 12 per cent of the plays across the century,[4] and John Russell Stephens argues that women's involvement as playwrights in the first half of the nineteenth century 'about matches their proportional involvement in the literary profession as a whole.'[5] This is a modest figure compared with women's presence in other literary markets, but given the obstacles to their active participation women's theatrical writing was not negligible, particularly if we consider the way women combined playwriting with writing in other genres and media. Furthermore, they were active in one of the principal mass media of the nineteenth century, participating in the public sphere of a democratizing and modernizing culture.[6]

In the 1820s and 1830s the expansion of the London theatre industry, with enlarged audiences, and new theatres built to cater for them, offered new markets and opportunities for playwrights. Discovering how women writers responded to these opportunities, and under what conditions, is part of my interest in this chapter. While stories of male playwrights' experiences of adjusting to changing conditions in the industry have figured prominently in theatre histories of this period, particularly their focus on underpayment and exploitation of their labour by theatre managers,[7] complaints from women playwrights (when they are extant) focus on other aspects of treatment than payment. Women's playwriting was positioned differently because of the growing ideological pressure not to regard women's work as labour to be paid for, and for the ideology of domestic respectability to place women only within the frame of home and family, even when, as we shall see, there is considerable evidence to the contrary. This has had lasting effects on British theatre historiography. Women who wrote for the commercial theatre were made invisible by the masking of playwriting within narratives of family and home, as well as the writing out of popular and commercial theatre from British theatre history. Conversely, women who focussed their playwriting energies and ambitions on creating work of aesthetic or lasting value found that their work was displaced in the material practices of the theatre by the popular and the commercial: to literalize Pierre Bourdieu's metaphor of cultural capital, they staked their capital on a declining market. And as Bourdieu demonstrated of the French middle-class in the post-Second World War period, the relationship between cultural and economic capital is generally an inverse one,[8] although as Morag Shiach comments, 'the possession of these [privileged] forms or access to these practices becomes both the expression, and the guarantee of social dominance.'[9] Women writing for the 'legitimate' theatre could manipulate the cultural capital of legitimacy in order to claim the rights of participation largely denied them through other political and social institutions, whereas women playwrights working for the popular stage mobilized their social capital of theatrical connections through family or literary networks. This became more marked after the 1843 Theatres Regulation Act, with the 'retreat' of women writers into the dramatic closet or the middle-class drawing-room regarded as a history of failure. It has taken feminist Romanticist theories of the closet drama to rescue this work, and recognize closet drama as a body of theatre theory and praxis (principally through the work of Catherine Burroughs). So through the triangulation of 'legitimacy,' 'money,' and 'art' I encapsulate the main body of my argument about the development of women's writing for the theatre across the nineteenth century in terms of the difficulties for women playwrights thrown up by the conflicts between theatre as an art and theatre as an industry. In this chapter, building on Jane Moody's conception of an alternative 'illegitimate' theatrical culture which challenged and ultimately dominated its 'legitimate' other, I will examine the way that women manipulated different kinds of cultural and social capital to participate in the London theatre. In the next, I look at the apparent retreat from the competitive and commercial arena of the theatre industry to write for an idealized concept of performance as a driver of social, political, or ethical change.

My discussion of the playwriting of the many women who wrote for the popular theatre in London throughout the nineteenth century is divided into three phases, corresponding to my reading of the patterns of the theatre of the period. Unlike the genres of poetry and fiction, commercial theatre writing and theatrical practice generally (acting, production, staging, publicity, reviewing, and so on), cannot easily be mapped onto the conventional divisions of the long nineteenth century into Romantic, Victorian, and Modernist periods, in those literary conceptualizations which have come to stand for much more than chronological periods. Rather, in this chapter, I trace the broad continuities of practice from the 1820s until the late 1850s, with a noticeable break in the early 1860s. This rupture was represented aesthetically and ideologically by the phenomenon of the sensation drama, and in material practice by the embedding of long running season of a single play; a practice which was in part produced by the success of a number of sensation dramas. After the 1860s, while many of the aesthetic, ideological, generic, and thematic qualities of the popular theatre remain continuous with those of the earlier part of the century, there were significant changes in theatre production and management practices related to theatre managements' desires to maintain and increase the middle-class audience attracted by the sensation phenomenon, and the increasing mobility of audiences in terms of class, gender, and geography. The growth of a female audience in the last two decades of the nineteenth century, in line with the emergence of the female consumer, had a significant impact on both the commercial and the avant-garde theatre.

Women playwrights in the popular theatre, 1820–1860

Unlike the high visibility of women playwrights working in the 'legitimate' theatre women writing for the minor theatres and in popular genres were rarely hailed as saviours of the stage, but nor did they carry the complicated burdens of expectation and behaviour which aspirations to legitimacy entailed. Sometimes their work received particular press attention – particularly if they had plays produced at the Theatres Royal or the Haymarket – but mostly it did not, and was considered as part of the standard fare of the London theatre business during a period of transition from the stability of the late eighteenth-century organization of the profession into the model of free trade and flow of capital the theatre was to become after 1843. Playwrights such as Caroline Boaden, Adelaide (Mrs Charles) Calvert, Elizabeth (Mrs George) Conquest, Eliza (Mrs T. P.) Cooke, Catherine Crowe, Mrs Denvil, Mary (Mrs Joseph) Ebsworth, Sarah Lane, Maria Lovell (née Lacy), Mrs Herman Merivale, Elizabeth (Mrs Alfred) Phillips, Eliza Planché, Elizabeth Polack, Melinda (Mrs Henry) Young, and Margaret (Mrs C. Baron) Wilson all worked in the theatre, often in partnerships with their husbands, and all had several plays produced. These are the women who come nearest to the masculine model of the hack playwright, such as William Thomas Moncrieff, Edward Fitzball, or Douglas Jerrold, yet their work is rarely as prominent or prolific.

There were women whose work patterns are partly congruent with those of men – Mrs Denvil is an obvious example whom I discuss below, and from an earlier period, the prolific and commercially astute Jane Scott is a prime instance – but for the most part women playwrights in the commercial theatre had to organize their working lives quite differently. As Stephens notes, the playwriting profession in this period was predicated on masculine patterns of sociability and employment.[10] In a society dominated by ideologies of gender which attempted to control the physical and discursive arenas in which men and women could operate, the visible, working woman was felt to be an anomaly – even an affront. This is not to say that women did not actively engage in the public sphere, through work (working-class women were increasingly urged into factory work as compliant factory workers[11]), writing, performance, entrepreneurship, and governance. There is a growing body of historical evidence and argument which indicates that the notion of the division of men and women in to the 'separate spheres' of the (masculine) public and (feminine) private was an ideal, and blinkers us to contemporary reality and its material practices in the first half of the nineteenth century.[12] However, it is not possible simply to jettison the concept. The circulation of the theory of separate spheres and its associated precepts for and constraints on female behaviour, particularly the modelling of the 'proper lady,' had material consequences for the conduct of women's lives, and the records of their activities and achievements they left. This seems to have been the case even for women in theatrical families who, although ambiguously placed in respect to class hierarchies and the hegemonic middle-class values of domesticity and privacy, nevertheless desired respectability, as it was understood within the profession. And the early career of Fanny Kemble demonstrates how success in the theatre profession was no bar to upward social mobility, although her case is an unusual one. Overall, how women negotiated their working identities through family and profession, in the face of (or under the cover of) discursive constructions of Victorian ideals of femininity, then becomes of central interest to a study of women playwrights, particularly when considered in parallel to the ways that women negotiated the increasingly differentiated and opposed discourses of legitimacy ('high culture') and popular culture in the theatre.

What is striking about the mainstream or commercial theatre is its possibilities for activity and agency of women playwrights, exemplified by the work of a number of women who wrote comedy, farce, and melodrama for theatres in central London. Theatres such as the Haymarket, the Strand, and the Olympic were located in what is now known as the West End, but which in this period was in formation as a distinct social terrain. As Davis and Emeljanow argue, the West End came to be defined primarily by its 'cultural and commercial status' in part established by the presence of the Patent theatres, Drury Lane and Covent Garden at the north-eastern-most edge of the area, and the Haymarket theatre (given a summer license in 1766, and so a 'legitimate' Theatre Royal together with Drury Lane and Covent Garden), at the border of the fashionable district of St James's.[13] In response to the dramatic expansion of London and the commercial possibilities this offered entrepreneurs, other theatres, such as the Olympic, the Adelphi (formerly the Sans Pareil, built by John Scott for his daughter, Jane), the Strand, the St James's, and the English Opera House (or the Lyceum),[14] were built or expanded in this area of central London prior to 1843. The activity of these and other theatres in the growing London suburbs led to an almost constant agitation on the part of the Patent theatres to maintain their rights to the spoken drama, and challenges from the 'minor' theatres to exploit the lucrative possibilities of new and more mobile London theatre audiences.[15] In this period of the formation of the West End as a cultural and commercial centre for Londoners and tourists alike (identified by Davis and Emeljanow as 1840–1880),[16] theatres were beginning to attract a mixed but theatrically knowledgeable audience, and one not averse to controversy – either theatrical or political.[17] The Olympic, the Strand, and the Haymarket, all theatres in which the plays of Caroline Boaden, Elizabeth Phillips, Elizabeth Planché, Anna Maria Hall, Margaret Wilson, and Catherine Gore were performed, were part of this growing West End tourist and commercial market, in which female participation and consumption, although problematic in the 1830s and 1840s, was to become increasingly important. Although discussions of the problems of theatre-going in the 1830s often focussed on the presence of undesirable femininity – in the bodies of prostitutes – particularly at Covent Garden and Drury Lane, 'respectable' women were much prized as audience members in the West End.[18] And women's plays on stage suggest that theatre managements were not unaware of the ways in which this work could be used to attract specific audiences. Again, this is not to posit an anachronistic third-wave feminist consciousness of the late twentieth century on the part of managers, playwrights, or audiences. Rather I want to suggest that in an increasingly commercial industry, within an economy in which consumption, as opposed to production, was becoming a dynamic force, a fit between the product displayed, its creators, and its consumers was one way of developing and maintaining an audience. And in the work of the women who wrote plays for the minor theatres in the West End, there are some suggestive symmetries between the comic or farcical plots of middle- and lower-middle class life, and the lived experiences of parts of the audience.

Family networks

For women playwrights working within the London commercial theatre professional life was typically bound up with family structure and family business, as most of these women entered the profession through familial connections.[19] As Jacky Bratton points out, the theatre was one family business in which women were visibly active, whatever the anxiety about publicly acknowledging such activity.[20] However, playwriting was an activity which could be cloaked and pushed back into the private, domestic part of family life and the family business. In the women I discuss below, familial connections are predominantly those of wife and daughter, and these positions offered both opportunities and constraints, the family concern often enabling women's activity and rendering it invisible simultaneously. However, on balance, we might speculate that these women's experiences were not so wearing or shocking as those of the rather less protected women playwrights who lacked such workaday family introductions to the theatre, such as Isabel Hill, Felicia Hemans, or Mary Russell Mitford. This is necessarily speculative, however, as one abiding feature of the careers of the women I discuss here is that they left very little in the way of accounts of themselves, their working lives, their imaginative lives, or their family lives. And it is a feature of the market-led nature of their plays that the scripts render up very little of specific biographical information, however much the scripts of these women tell us about the general structure of feeling (to use Raymond Williams' term) of middle-, lower-middle and working-class life.

I would rather be able to discuss these playwrights independent of familial connections, but to do so would be to ignore a central reality of women's lives. I am particularly interested in the category of daughter-hood because in the paucity of biographical data about most of the women I look at, the role of daughter to a father (rarely mother) involved in a high status job in the theatre often resulted in recognition and a record – however cursory – of the daughter. Caroline Boaden provides an example of the frustrating mix of information and oblivion we have in such a case of high profile father and daughter involved in the same family business. Boaden was an actress and playwright who had at least six plays performed between 1825 and 1838, and then, in a familiar pattern, her name disappears from the public records of the theatre. As an actress, she did not achieve great critical acclaim, but her family name gave her the face-saving judgement of 'respectable failure' in her performance as Lady Teazle at the Haymarket in 1827.[21] As a writer, Boaden was much more successful, but there is still a tendency for her personality to slip into the background of her father's career. Her plays were performed mostly at the Haymarket, cementing a familial relation-ship with that theatre. She was an honorary member of the Dramatic Authors' Society (women could not be full members, but were invited to take honorary status), and five of her plays were published by Cumberland soon after their production, further indices of her success. But in the *New Dictionary of National Biography* Caroline Boaden is included in the entry for her father, James Boaden, who was a playwright as well as prolific journalist, critic and biographer.[22] James Boaden's son, John, then merits a separate entry but Caroline does not. Apparently, John's work, 'although pleasing, did not rise above mediocrity'[23] a critique which could apply just as well to Caroline's plays; however, as an exhibitor at the Royal Academy and the Society of British Artists, John Boaden had both the institutions of high culture and his gender speaking for him.

So daughterhood here envelops Caroline Boaden in the family talent and name. But how might daughterhood allow for the possibility of rebellion against the expectations of that role? While Elizabeth Kowaleski-Wallace pursues her 'daddies' girls,' Maria Edgeworth and Hannah More, as *'case studies in complicity,'*[24] I am cautious in assuming complicity in the case of Caroline Boaden. Her plays – even her dramas – are so resolutely light and iconoclastic, and her farces fully exploit the oppor-tunities of that genre for representing disrespectful children and stupid father-figures particularly in the slapstick elements of physical theatre and the parody of domesticity which were such prominent aspects of English farce.[25] *William Thompson*, for example, is described briefly by one critic as furnishing 'the less squeamish class of play-goers with abundant laughter,'[26] while the *Examiner* comments on its 'monstrous incongruities,' although referring to the author throughout as 'he' until the final sentences: 'The piece, we should think, cannot fail to please the lovers if broad humour. Since writing the above, we have heard that Miss Boaden is the authoress' leaving a telling silence at the end of the review.[27] Her critique of paternal interference was not simply a function of the generic expectations of farce – her well-received serious drama, *Fatality*, was noted for its critique of the marriage of convenience arranged for an adopted daughter by 'a worthy man and *kind father*, but bigotted [*sic*],' and is generally praised for its dramatic spirit, and revelation of the folly of marriage without love.[28] Is it possible, then, that Boaden's work was an attempt at independence from the overwhelming family name? Particularly one so connected with an investment in chronicling the star actors of a previous generation who established the stage as a place of intellectual and cultural capital.

Of Caroline Boaden's plays, three – *The First of April*, *William Thompson*, and *Quite Correct* – were comedies or farces which relied on physical humour and stage machinery. Her other published plays, *Don Pedro the Cruel and Manuel the Cobbler*, *Fatality*, and *A Duel in Richelieu's Time*, were dramas or melodramas. The reception of Boaden's plays in these two genres is often different, and suggests that while critics were delighted to be entertained with the physical humour at which Boaden excelled in arranging, they were less certain about her melodramas. The mildest of comments was made by the *Athenæum* about *A Duel in Richelieu's Time*, commented on the unsuitability of the Haymarket for tragedy, but the *New Monthly Magazine* calls the play 'as clever and effective as it is offensive to good taste and injurious to good morals.' The *New Monthly Magazine* critic continues in this censorious vein, connecting the play's skill in entertaining its audience with its lack of moral fibre:

> the object and effect of [the play's narrative] is to excite the feelings to a painful degree; that excitement being in itself the *end* sought for, not the *means* to any thing else; and, what is still worse, the excitement is made to grow out of a spurious and mischievous sympathy with feelings and actions that are at variance with the principles of society at least, whatever they may be with human nature.

The judgement of the script closes with that oft-repeated killer line:

> the materials of this clever but worthless production [. . .] we are the less inclined to tolerate [. . .] that it is *the work of a lady*, –[29]

In contrast, both the conservative *Times* and the Radical periodical, the *Examiner*, find much to commend in Boaden's earlier translation of a French drama, performed and published as *Fatality* in 1829. It too deals with the tricky issues of marriages of convenience, potential infidelity, and suspected adultery, but, as D.——G. (George Daniels) remarks, 'Miss Boaden has told the story with simplicity and effect,'[30] while the *Examiner* approves of the sentiments of the play, finding the French worldliness which was to so offend the *New Monthly Magazine* in *A Duel in Richelieu's Time* to be a welcome antidote to the hypocrisy of 'our moral, bible-distributing and gin-promoting nation.'

> The sentiment so common in the mouths of our moralists, of holding up to infamy and execration a fallen, and *therefore* unfortunate woman, we never can subscribe to so long as justice is not meted out to the other and avowedly the stronger party.[31]

Clearly Boaden's treatment of infidelity was in accord with the writer's own views, and in a radical paper such as the *Examiner* this iconoclastic statement in response to a play might be expected. However, the near-contempt with which Boaden's later play is regarded by the *New Monthly Magazine* suggests her choice of topic (and its foreign source) touched a deeper nerve, and that the expectations of the 'proper lady' and the dutiful daughter were upset by her unambiguous representation of the adulterous Duchess de Chevreuse, Marie de Lagnes, combined with the outright criticism her characters express of the King and his court (and Emma Robinson's play *Richelieu in Love* was banned for this same reason in 1844[32]).

There is obviously much to explore in the clash between Boaden and the public opinion makers over her drama, *A Duel in Richelieu's Time*, and such clashes between women playwrights and critics over their treatment of serious topics of morality persist throughout the nineteenth century. Yet I find the general approval of Boaden's comic writing, and particularly her knowledge of and control over stage business to be a fascinating aspect of her writing, given that within the same expectations of respectable femininity, Boaden's choreography of actors' bodies into ridiculous positions and situations could have been potentially troubling for audiences and critics alike. Yet, by following the rules of engagement for farce, Boaden could play with otherwise forbidden thoughts and situations to the delight of her audiences, and some critical acclaim. Critics were on much surer ground with Boaden's comedies and farces. D.——G. comments in his 'Remarks' on the farce,

The First of April: 'Miss Boaden is a decided patroness of the practical joke, and a perfect mistress of its merry machinery.'[33] And D.——G. was not the only critic to appreciate Boaden's ability to create laughter. The *Times* asserted that her farce, *William Thompson, or Which is He?* is 'so extremely comical and whimsical, as would set at defiance the gravity [...] of the most rigid follower of Jeremy Collyer's [*sic*] anti-theatrical principles.'[34] *Quite Correct*, first performed in 1825 at the Haymarket, appeared regularly on the same bill with John Poole's comedy, *Paul Pry*, in which comedian John Liston had a huge hit as 'Paul Pry.' With this double bill, and Liston playing the lead in Boaden's play as well as in *Paul Pry*, Boaden's success was ensured.[35] Boaden's use of farce, in contrast to her adaptation of French plays, allows the playful deconstruction of conventions of gender and class, revealing them to be performative and coercive. Her comedies exploit the possibilities 'for the expression of dissenting points of view that do not entail radicalism *and* that can be undone within the text as part of the comic operation of plot' which Misty Anderson finds so compelling in women's comedy.[36]

Boaden gives no quarter in the broad comedy of her farces. *William Thompson* takes the theme of mistaken identity to cruel lengths in the accidental incarceration of the *wrong* William Thompson in a genteel nursing home, which is really a prison-like mental asylum. *The First of April*, that play so fully enjoyed by George Daniels, demonstrates strikingly the possibilities of daughterly disobedience in its ridicule of the father-figure, Sir Bumpkin Pedigree, while invoking a strongly nationalist – but metropolitan – sense of proper behaviour. Much of the humour is predicated on a laughing acquiescence to both the ridicule of English provincials (in this case, Yorkshiremen) and foreigners – specifically, the French – set against the popular memory (in 1829) of the invasion panics at the beginning of the century. *The First of April* replays elements of the plot of Oliver Goldsmith's *She Stoops to Conquer*, in the trick played on the pompous Sir Bumpkin Pedigree (played by William Farren, a celebrated comedian of the period) by his rebellious nephew, Colonel Airy (played by Vining, another star comic actor). Airy and his lover Clara send Sir Bumpkin to the Castle while telling him it is an inn, and over the course of the evening discompose Sir Bumpkin so much that his wanderings about the Castle (an army garrison) cause him to be arrested as a French spy by the Governor of the Castle.

As is usual in classic English comedy and farce, more is at stake than the physical humour of ridiculing a pompous man; Sir Bumpkin is forced to concede to his nephew's demand for his inheritance, and consent for his marriage. Boaden does not pull back from grotesque representation in the character of Sir Bumpkin, while Airy's revenge seems suddenly serious when Sir Bumpkin is held at gunpoint and threatened with summary execution. This is the classic stuff of comedy, masking social critique of pretension and pomposity in verbal and physical humour, but firmly making its point about the damage done by the patriarchal power of an older generation in blocking youthful love and ambition (in his aunt's bequest that Sir Bumpkin arbitrarily withholds from Airy). Intriguingly, the 'female pen' here in Boaden's hands creates a play which is at least as cynical about human behaviour, and certainly more disrespectful of moral authority, than her much criticized melodrama.

Caroline Boaden was a daughter of a well-known man of the theatre, and my speculative argument about her positioning in the theatre industry suggests that her comedies can be read not only as existing both within the family business of the theatre, and thus drawing on the social capital of her thorough knowledge of stage business, but also playfully impertinent about men of her father's generation in her creation of the ridiculous buffoons such as the two William Thompsons and Sir Bumpkin Pedigree. Boaden's knowledge of theatre history, as it was embodied through her family pursuits (her father as biographer and playwright, herself as an actress performing the comic repertoire of the English National drama) gives her the clear vantage point of an insider. The advantages of this position are exemplified by the fact that the role of William Thompson the Second (who is mistaken for the mad William Thompson) was written for leading comedian John Liston, although in the end, John Reeve played the role. Liston did, however, play Grojan in her farce *Quite Correct*.[37] The casts of Boaden's other plays were similarly starry. Her unmarried status (while performing and writing at least) also had some advantages, as she maintained a singular identity and was not transformed on marriage into the *femme couvert* of British legal theory and practice. This is in contrast to D.——G.'s need to unpack the theatrical heritage of playwright Maria Lovell, who had a hit in 1851 with *Ingomar the Barbarian*, a melodrama with aspirations to legitimacy which stayed in the repertoire until late in the century – the best-known production in 1883 featuring Mary Anderson as Parthenia, making her debut on the English stage, although reviewers of that revival judged the play 'old-fashioned,' 'wearisome,' and 'artless.'[38] Lovell's heritage was obscured by her married name, as George Daniels explains in his 'Remarks' to her second and rather less successful domestic drama, *The Beginning and the End*; she 'is a lady not unknown to literary and histrionic fame,' married to the playwright George Lovell, and as Miss Lacy, an actress with Charles Kemble and Macready.

But, adds Daniels, Lovell 'may also boast of hereditary dramatic honours' as the grand-daughter of Michael Lacy, Garrick's partner and colleague of Sheridan.[39] Although she has left few records other than her plays, we can speculate that Lovell's career was enhanced by the social capital (knowledge, contacts) of her theatrical heritage, at the same time as her position as a wife obscured that genealogy – which is why Daniels takes such pains to tell us about it.

The effects of simultaneously masked public identity combined with insider status reverberate in a number of accounts of women playwrights working within the theatrical mainstream. James Robinson Planché's account of Elizabeth (known as Eliza) Planché's playwriting exemplifies the ease with which women's activities were dissolved into the domestic paradigm, even though the reality must have been different if evidence of other writers' careers is a guide. In recounting his wife's work as a playwright, James Planché presents her successful career as a brief excursion out of domesticity, but always framed by that domesticity. He makes no mention of any difficulties or checks she experienced, nor of the personal effort and real physical and mental labour involved in writing. In his 'Professional Autobiography,' *Recollections and Reflections*, James Planché mentions in a footnote that 'Mrs. Planché had amused herself by translating and adapting several French dramas. [They ...] had considerable success, and still keep the stage.'[40] Planché's achievements appear in her husband's autobiography, framed by his prefatory 'Advertisement' in which he explains that his memoir is 'limited as strictly as possible to [...] public and professional matters [...] avoiding reference to my own family and private affairs' (vii). His wife's work, apparently, is a private family matter, notwithstanding the very public productions and reviews of her plays which exist. Writing in the 1870s, his brief recognition that his wife's plays are still performed thirty years after she wrote them is an indication of success indeed, in a profession that treated most scripts as ephemeral. And, in a pattern typical of a number of women playwrights from the first half of the century, Elizabeth Planché does not leave her own memoirs – all we have is her husband's account written thirty years later.

If we compare James Planché's account with the material facts, a very different picture emerges: that of a wife who made a substantial contribution to the family business. Planché wrote nine plays, all of which were performed at either the Olympic Theatre under Madame Vestris' management (with which her husband was associated), or at the Haymarket. They received good reviews, good runs in their first seasons, and numerous revivals through the next two or three decades.[41]

The first casts were of high quality, featuring comic actors of the standing of William Farren, Charles Mathews, Madame Vestris, and Ellen Tree, to whom Planché's play *The Ransom* was dedicated. Her professional standing can also be gauged by her honorary membership of the Dramatic Authors' Society. Interestingly, her comedies offer a version of middle- and lower-middle class domestic life which might be designed to cause alarm in an attentive husband, as plays such as *The Welsh Girl*, *Folly and Friendship*, and *A Handsome Husband* feature assertive young female characters (written for Madame Vestris or Ellen Tree) who are all too conscious of their power over the men who love them. In *Folly and Friendship*, the heroine, Helen Melrose, forces a declaration from her admirer, Augustus Tavistock, simply by playing her demure, ladylike role to the hilt: 'Miss Melrose, in spite of what you call my inattention, I didn't mean it. I loved you fondly. I do love you to distraction.'[42] In the midst of her plot to bring Tavistock to the point, Helen sings to the audience of what they have already seen:

> Oh women for contrivance
> By far outwit the Men
> They twist and turn just like a worm
> And Turn and twist again (f. 328)

In *The Welsh Girl*, Madame Vestris plays Julia, married to Alfred against his uncle Sir Owen Griffiths' wishes. Alfred and Julia concoct a plot to trick Sir Owen into approving of the marriage and clearing Alfred's debts. Winning Sir Owen's favour is Julia's task, and she does so by pretending to be a young Welsh girl, Taffline, come to the great house to get on in the world. Julia's charming of Sir Owen, in the role of an innocent Welsh country girl, often veers to the edge of propriety as in the double meaning of 'falling' in her explanation of why she is afraid to move forward to greet Sir Owen:

> when I left my native village they told me that a young girl like me should be very careful, particularly if I went into great houses, and saw great people; for if I made one false step, and had a fall, I should never rise again, look you.[43]

Julia is adept at role-playing, and plays the innocent so well that crusty Sir Owen falls in love with her and proposes to marry her. He is quite besotted by her, and made to appear ridiculous. While Planché remains within the conventions of comedy, the comic plot plays on deep anxieties about cross-generational sexuality and class inequality; as Julia tells Sir Owen, still in role as Taffline,

> Ah! I think I understand what you mean. Your nephew, look you, does wrong to marry a lady of his own rank, and about his own age, and one he has loved for some time [...] – but *you* do quite right when you propose to marry a poor, unknown, untaught, little Welsh girl, young enough to be your grand-child. (27)

As well as finally getting his consent to their marriage, Julia is able to use her power of attractiveness over Sir Owen to force him to agree to clearing Alfred's debts, and so the play ends happily, although Sir Owen still suffers the humiliation of being tricked.

Although it is based on a patently ludicrous premise, the core of the plot of *A Handsome Husband* cuts close to home, as it deals with the hidden reasons for marriage, and the accommodations couples must make for each other. It is set in the present (1836) in a '*drawing-room elegantly furnished*,'[44] in the home of Mr and Mrs Wyndham (Charles Mathews and Madame Vestris). Mr Wyndham married Laura when she was blind, but after 'two months of bliss' (4) he was forced to leave the country to attend to a lawsuit. Two years later, he has returned and is to be reunited with his wife. But in the meantime, she has regained her sight. Wyndham is distraught as although his looks 'would not alarm a sensible hackney-coach horse' (4) he is certain that he is not handsome enough to keep his wife happy now she can see; for him, her blindness was her great attraction. What follows is a typically convoluted and ridiculous plot in which Laura mistakes Henry Fitzherbert, the suitor of her friend, the newly widowed Mrs Melford, for her husband (whom she has never actually seen), and Fitzherbert opportunistically humours her mistake when she throws herself into his arms. When Wyndham returns with a plan to introduce himself to his wife as Mrs Melford's husband, the comedy proceeds through a tangle of spouse-swapping, which if treated seriously would certainly threaten early Victorian proprieties, particularly in the representation of women in intimate and physical contact with men who are not their husbands (with the comedy of the first Olympic production intensified by the extra-theatrical knowledge amongst most of the audience of Mathews' and Vestris' off-stage relationship). Gradually, the plot is untangled, and the 'piece went with a bounce, and bang to its conclusion, amidst the laughter and applause of the audience.'[45] Reviewers find little to criticize in any of Planché's pieces, remarking generally on her 'smart, lively' writing, and the 'unaffected and unpretending' dialogue of *The Welsh Girl*, with the hope that this play's success will 'lead her to new efforts.'[46] The *Times* calls *Folly and Friendship* 'happily conceived, and pleasantly dramatized,' and notes the good reception for *The Sledge Driver*.[47]

So to refer to this work of his wife's (who died in 1846) as if it were simply a light amusement to fill in her spare time, seems to us today not only belittling, but indicative of James Planché's need to underplay both his wife's work and her success to preserve a semblance of bourgeois respectability in his own upwardly mobile career and life story. In James Planché's memoirs, the respectability conferred by work for royal connections, bourgeois familial gendered divisions of life and work, and increased leisure time and wealth all serve to balance out the threat to his social position constituted by his family's work in the theatre. In this narrative form, James Planché's wife's ability to 'amuse herself' by adapting plays from the French not only indicates her superior education and talents, but also implies that she undertook these activities for pleasure rather than profit, both signs of her husband's increasing status and wealth.

The careers of Elizabeth Conquest and Mary Ebsworth offer similar examples of public erasure which masked a high degree of involvement and professional competence. Conquest married into a far less socially aspirant family than the Planchés, but one with a substantial theatrical tradition in the minor theatres. Her work was central to the family business, but almost completely disappears in records of the family's work. Allardyce Nicoll's 'Handlist' of play titles from 1850 to 1900 includes three pieces attributed to her authorship, none of which exist in the Lord Chamberlain's Collection of Plays. This is probably because they are ballets, without accompanying scripts to fix the otherwise ephemeral creation of choreography. In addition to performing with her husband George, Elizabeth Conquest took over the running of her mother-in-law's ballet school attached to the male Conquests' (father and son Benjamin and George) Grecian Saloon. The school provided the dancers for the Grecian's pantomimes, and was responsible for the stage training of many performers, including Kate Vaughn. Conquest family biographer Frances Fleetwood recounts that 'everyone agrees that it provided an excellent training' with Elizabeth Conquest and her brother William Ozmond in charge, and Elizabeth also supervising and choreographing the ballet in the famous Grecian pantomimes, and 'at intervals [. . .] producing a flourishing quiverful of Conquests.'[48] Elizabeth Conquest's contribution to the family enterprise as a prolific producer – of the next generation of workers in the family business, of star performers, and of lucrative entertainments – is typical of the central role played by wives and mothers in theatrical families in the training of sons and daughters for the profession. Noting this combination of production and reproduction, and building on the work of Leonore Davidoff and Catherine Hall in *Family Fortunes*, Jacky Bratton argues that the importance of women in theatrical families as 'not simply [...] consumers, progressively separated from production, but equal sharers in the work and sometimes as the major creators and transmitters of cultural capital.'[49]

Mary Ebsworth was another performer and playwright located in a complex web of theatrical familial associations. Her father was Robert Fairbrother, popular actor, friend of Sheridan's, and teacher of fencing; one of Mary's brothers, Samuel Glover Fairbrother set up a theatrical publishing business, and Mary married the playwright and musician, Joseph Ebsworth in 1817. Their eldest daughter, Emilie, also married in the theatre, to Samuel Cowell, a comedian. In a genealogical *tour de force*, Jacky Bratton shows how Emilie's marriage to Cowell links the Siddons family, through connections with the Fairbrothers and the Ebsworths, to the early twentieth-century writers and actors, the Batemans and the Comptons.[50] In such webs Mary Ebsworth's plays have been caught and forgotten, although she wrote four plays, all successfully performed at minor theatres between 1822 and 1834, two of which were published. Her melodrama, *The Two Brothers of Pisa*, and her comedy, *Payable at Sight; or, The Chaste Salute*, were published by her husband, Joseph's and brother's (Samuel Fairbrother) short-lived publishing venture, Joseph Ebsworth's 'English and Foreign Dramatic Library, and Caricature Repository,' based in Edinburgh, at the time that he and Mary were performers at the Theatre Royal there. In common with the melodramas of Elizabeth Polack, Madame Laurend, and Mrs Denvil, Ebsworth's melodramatic writing is full-blooded, offering grand roles for the local Coburg (Victoria) company in the first production there in 1822, the cast including favourite Thomas Potter Cooke as Count D'Oristan, the heroic, but stern and remorseless Chief Magistrate, and Mary's husband Joseph as the Calabrian prisoner who attempts to escape from a charge of murder by implicating Lorenzo, one of the two brothers of the title. Both Lorenzo and his brother Pietro were played by young women, Miss Taylor and Miss Watson, while other local stars, such as Mrs Weston, were also given strong roles. Although the play was written for a 'minor' theatre, it contains grand rhetoric and high-flown statements, such as this statement by the Count after saving someone from execution:

For ages the law has outraged humanity by spectacles of death; but is mankind the better for it? For one guilty wretch that dies upon the scaffold, ten are rendered callous and hurried into crime. Horrible alternative of a world, that only purifies itself from past evils, to witness greater![51]

Here Ebsworth plays to the strengths of her actors and the desires of her audience to enjoy powerful language and uplifting ideas. If her melodrama actually reads like hundreds of others produced at the Coburg in these years, then I take that to be an indication of her professional knowledge and facility, exercised in the face of public opinion about both the degraded nature of the drama in the minor theatres, and the inability of women to write serious plays.

Women playwrights and bourgeois comedy

The freedom offered by farce and domestic comedy for women playwrights to satirize the very conditions and ideologies of domesticity which conditioned their own lives is taken up with great glee by a number of women playwrights, particularly in the 1840s and 1850s. An early example of the kind of farcical sketch which becomes a staple of women playwriting right through to the end of the century is exemplified in Catherine Gore's farce, *A Good Night's Rest*. The plot is minimal, but involves a husband, given only the name 'Stranger' in the script, observing a woman whom he mistakes for his wife entertaining another man. The Stranger sees this from his neighbour Snobbington's room, catching sight of his wife's silhouette through a window like a voyeur. In the course of its half hour of playing the farce touches on marital infidelity, the old rivalry of the two men over a woman, and the madness of sexual jealousy as the Stranger systematically destroys Snobbington's room in his agitation over his wife. Yet the play's humour works off its characters' neurotic insistence on the proprieties of bourgeois domesticity, even when the lower-middle class communal life of boarding houses, genteel poverty, and the presence of over-close neighbours work against maintaining such respectability. Indeed, it is the demonstration of the very necessity of preserving respectability in the face of threatened chaos through the breakdown of class and gender boundaries which drives such farces and comedies. In performance, the piece employed broad physical humour in a 'brisk succession' of practical jokes, so that 'the audience were kept in a continued roar, and the sternest despiser of the illegitimate drama could scarcely have refrained.'[52]

Gore's play is a miniature but typical example of comedies and farces by playwrights such as Mrs Hallett, Anna Maria (Mrs S. C.) Hall, Mrs Valentine Bartholomew, Margaret (Mrs Cornwell) Baron Wilson, and Elizabeth (Mrs Alfred) Phillips. Of these playwrights, I will focus on Elizabeth Phillips, a prolific playwright and actress who wrote for her own skills as a broad comedian, but was also adept at picking up touchy issues.

The striking thing about Elizabeth Phillips' playwriting is her clear-eyed estimation of her own skills as an actress, her writerly generosity towards other performers, and her ability to write for her strengths, even if this means she played characters who were the butts of jokes, rather than romantic heroines. The cast lists of her plays show that although she often played the lead role, this was also exchanged for a comic or character female role, in which she was not afraid to send herself up as a performer. In *Caught in His Own Trap*,[53] playing Madame Vonderbushell, Phillips plays the part of a mature matron, trying to trick Vraiment, a determinedly bachelor lawyer who calls a wife 'A snake' and children 'Damned hungry little ogres!' (6), into marriage, and at the same time arrange for the marriage of her daughter to François, Vraiment's nephew. In his misogyny, Vraiment even goes so far as to tell his nephew that if he, Vraiment, ever marries he will forfeit 20,000 francs, and so it becomes a battle of wills and wits between Madame Vonderbushell and Vraiment each to wear the other down for the money. And here one can see Phillips' canny writing as a performer, as she develops her role through a series of swift and witty exchanges with Vraiment, played by leading comedian William Farren, in the quickfire mode popularized a century later by the Hollywood screwball comedy. When the two characters first meet, Vraiment remembers Madame Vonderbushell as

the pretty Englishwoman he [Vonderbushell] married some 15 years ago. [...] Bless me, how you are altered. (*She stares at him.*) Do not misunderstand me, madame – I mean, how you are improved.

MAD. Yes, fifteen years ago I was a green young girl.
VR. Ah, there's nothing green about you now, Madame.
MAD. I trust not. – green things are generally sour.
VR. True, madame, and our most delicious fruits are not gathered 'till the autumn. (10–11)

But while Phillips might give herself the best comic lines in this play, as we can see above, they come at a cost. In this play, the cost is playing 'up' in age and having it made a point of comedy in the dialogue. In *An Organic Affection*, in which Phillips played actress Mademoiselle Joliejambe, she again writes for herself great comic lines and situations, but these are delivered with a ridiculous French accent, and her character is a figure of fun throughout the play.[54] In *Katty from Connaught*,[55] Phillips plays the heroine, Katty, who sets out to win back the love of Sir George Ellis, from whom she had parted unhappily five years earlier. To do this 'Katty' (actually Miss Mable [*sic*], sister of Lady Stanfield) 'assumes the manners and dialect of a raw Irish servant girl,' which Mrs Phillips apparently did with 'great spirit,'[56] and included in her repertoire a country ballad as well, which according to the *Theatrical Mirror*, she sang 'with much sweetness.' According to the rather more staid *Athenæum*, 'the whole piece depended upon' Mrs Phillips' performance,

> and she supported it with admirable *naïveté* and humour. We have now for some time looked upon this actress as possessing much talent, – and the more we become acquainted with her the more we admire its extent and force. [...] She accomplished all [...] with a power and ease which set her in the first rank of low-comedy performers.[57]

In these, and other, approving reviews, read in conjunction with her plays, what is notable is the extent of Mrs Phillips' professional acumen, and the reliability of her performances in the dual roles of actress-playwright – the one prepared to do whatever it took for a laugh, the other happy to turn out serviceable vehicles for her own and other actors' stage business.

Women melodramatists in the minor theatres

Caroline Boaden and Elizabeth Planché, although now forgotten minor playwrights of the early Victorian period, had some visibility and recognition which has survived in various documents. Their plays were performed in theatres which are now part of the West End (although it was not labelled as such at the time) of highly visible, commercial theatrical production, attracting mixed audiences from beyond the local area. Their plays were (mostly) published in cheap, widely available editions, which have survived today. They were reviewed, not always favourably, but noted as part of the sphere of public entertainment. My next subject is an example of the women playwrights who worked beyond these West End theatres, and as a consequence of their gender and class position, in that process which Davis and Emeljanow describe in terms of the Orientalizing of working-class theatre,[58] their work has left very little trace. Heidi J. Holder suggests that the ideal of the 'lady playwright' was not so oppressive in the East End as in the West, and she and Jim Davis document the successful careers of two East End playwrights, Sarah Lane and Melinda (Mrs Henry) Young, working in the 1860s and 1870s.[59] But earlier in the century, women playwrights such as Mrs Denvil (and I have no other name for her), Madame Laurend, Margaret Wilson, Mrs Yarnold, Mrs Hallett, Elizabeth Polack, Charlotte Barnes, Mrs T. P. Cooke, and Mary Ebsworth emerged briefly and brightly as promising and active playwrights for the south bank and East End theatres, the Britannia, the Pavilion, and the Victoria (now the Old Vic). And then they disappeared, leaving few of the traces of writing careers, except published plays and manuscripts in the Lord Chamberlain's Collection.

I want to focus on Mrs Denvil who is perhaps one of the most 'invisible' of women playwrights in this book. Her career can only be traced in outline around a series of absences – starting with her first name. She can be identified as the wife of actor-manager W. G. Denvil, who first came to public notice in the 1830s as an actor. He received early attention for his role in the actress-writer Mrs Edwin Yarnold's play, *Marie Antoinette; or, the Lover of the Queen*, played at the Royal Kent (or Kensington) theatre in September 1834,[60] and soon after made his debut as Shylock in the Drury Lane production of *The Merchant of Venice*. Obviously, there had been some gossip about Mr Denvil – James Planché comments on theatre manager Alfred Bunn's promotion of him as 'a second Edmund Kean,' and Denvil, 'starving as he was' writes Planché, had no choice but to take the work offered him at the Theatres Royal.[61] Although the *Athenaeum* gives him a rave review, duly comparing him with Kean,[62] the *Times* critic opines that he is not entirely 'that creature of perfection which his ill-judging friends would fain describe him to be.'[63]

Not a creature of perfection indeed, as by 1847, after going into the management of the Royal Pavilion and the Effingham theatres, he was declared insolvent under his original family name of Gaskell.[64] The Denvil family name next occurs in the public record in a report of the trial of the milliner Jane West who was accused of robbing children on the streets of Shoreditch. Eleven-year old Isabella Denvil, 'daughter of the actor of that name' was one of those accosted on the Kingsland Road.[65] Tracing the Denvils through the pages of the *Times* turns up further mention of two other young Denvil girls, Clara and Alice, Clara as a child performer in *Midsummer Night's Dream* at the Princess Theatre in 1859, and Alice in George Conquest and Paul Merritt's adaptation of

D'Ennery and Cormon's *Les Deux Orphelines*, as *The Blind Sister*, at the Grecian in 1874. If we can assume that all these Denvils are related then the picture that emerges from the public record is of a family business in the theatre, certainly not as successful as the Planchés or the Conquests, who remained living and working in the area of London local to the theatres Denvil had managed.

Mrs Denvil's thirteen plays were part of this enterprise. But the information is patchy, and it is in a case like Mrs Denvil's where the impact of the low cultural status of theatres such as the Pavilion and the Effingham is felt. Very few records of minor theatres have survived, and they rarely deal with the minutiae of management in the way that British national archival collections preserve the daybooks and ledgers of Covent Garden, or the playbills of Drury Lane. The plays by Mrs Denvil which are published are to be found most accessibly in the Frank Pettingell Collection (now held in the Templeman Library University of Kent at Canterbury),[66] her authorship and their production histories indicated by hand-written annotations to the scripts. Copies in the Pettingell Collection are catalogued under Mrs Denvil's name, unlike the records of the British Library, where Mrs Denvil is invisible as an author. After 1843, several manuscripts under Mrs Denvil's name can be found in the Lord Chamberlain's Collection of Plays, indicating that for the Royal Pavilion and the Effingham the extension of the Lord Chamberlain's licensing powers made at least an administrative change to their production practices. The survival of her printed plays and some manuscripts, in the Pettingell Collection, originally built up by popular comedian Arthur Williams (1844–1915), points to the endurance of these cut-down adaptations of popular novelties and sensational melodramas in small theatres throughout England. The scripts were published by the Purkess's Pictorial Penny Press in very cheap editions of fragile paper (even more so than the Dicks or Lacy's editions of this time), rarely amounting to more than eight or nine pages. Although quite graphically and lavishly illustrated on the front cover, the text is crowded into two columns, and there are few production details such as first performances, authors, or cast lists. Everything about the texts as material objects suggests that they were published as cheap souvenirs of popular performances, or for local amateur and itinerant performers. Although they are the only documents we have of Mrs Denvil's work, they are probably also unreliable guides to the actual performances of her scripts – again, the production of her plays appears to have been rapid to the point of improvisation. The note attached by W. G. Denvil to the cover of his wife's manuscript of *The Poisoner and His Victim; or,*

Revenge Crime and Retribution indicates the pressures of speed under which a theatre like the Pavilion worked; Denvil requests that 'This piece being required for *Monday* Night, an early reading of the drama will be esteemed – as the interest of the Establishment depends on Novelty.'[67] Even a carefully prepared (and uncharacteristically lengthy) adaptation of Harriet Beecher Stowe's novel, *Dred*, written for the Britannia Theatre and played in 1856, has extensive evidence of production changes and cuts in the surviving manuscript.

It is probably just as well that the Denvils were able to manipulate the loopholes in the pre-1843 legislation and practice governing the London theatre industry so that Mrs Denvil's plays were not submitted to the Lord Chamberlain's office, as her plays are almost entirely adaptations and reworkings of popular plays and novels from other theatres in London. In providing plays for her husband's theatres, Mrs Denvil follows the common practice of producing novelties very quickly, cashing in on the money-spinning fashions at theatres further west in adaptation or perhaps plagiarisms of current attractions in central London. And for an actor-manager to have a writing wife able to exploit the market quickly, especially in the marginal financial situation in which the Denvils seemed to exist, must have been a valuable asset. Mrs Denvil was a hard-working theatre professional, and she knew her market; while there is no record of her as a performer, she produced numerous rapidly moving melodramas, designed to draw in a local working-class audience for sensational entertainment. Importantly, East End theatres sought to provide their audiences with the same kinds of entertainments as the theatres in the West End, without the inconvenience of having to make the journey west for working people who laboured long hours. In a play like *Susan Hopley; or, the Servant Girl's Dream*, Mrs Denvil combines the occult elements of Gothic melodrama with a focus on the vulnerable working-class heroine of contemporary domestic melodrama to create an exciting entertainment which also provides a semi-literate audience with a staged version of one of its favourite novels. Denvil's melodrama was an adaptation of Catherine Crowe's novel, versions of which, according to Arthur William's annotation on the cover of the copy in the Pettingell Collection, played at the Queen's Theatre, the Royal Albert Saloon, and the Victoria. Although it was not Mrs Denvil's version that ran for over a hundred nights at the Victoria, but George Dibdin Pitt's, Mrs Denvil's version at the Royal Pavilion took its place in the general fashion for adaptations of the extremely popular novel. Like the melodramas of Mary Ebsworth, Eliza Planché, or Mrs T. P. Cooke, the play stages highly fraught events – murder, dream visions, revenge – using high-flown dramatic speech for the vulnerable heroine (albeit in diction highly unrealistic for a servant girl) whose actions and heroism are contrasted with the low comedy of the butler and other servants. That is to say, Mrs Denvil's version of *Susan Hopley* fits the template of the domestic drama with its class and gender conflicts, which Douglas Jerrold claimed as his invention.[68] Away from the scrutiny of the press and the opinions of the 'literati,'[69] Mrs Denvil could write like any other playwright – that is, write like a man – without being called to account for holding the pen of a lady.

1863 and the sensations of the season

In the late winter of 1863, stage adaptations of Mary Elizabeth Braddon's sensation novels, *Lady Audley's Secret* and *Aurora Floyd*, dominated the London stage. *Lady Audley's Secret* was first published in book form in October 1862, and by March 1863 the story of the blonde bigamist had appeared on five stages in London, filling both West End and East End theatres, in a cross-class theatrical phenomenon. William E. Suter's version opened at the Queen's Theatre, in Tottenham Court Road on 21 February 1863. It was followed a week later by George Roberts' (pseudonym of Robert Walters) adaptation at the St James's Theatre opening on 28 February, and Colin Henry Hazlewood's version for the Victoria Theatre on 25 May. The play's notoriety and popularity was confirmed by the appearance of a burlesque version by Henry Byron, 'Comical Conglomerative Absurdity,' *Eighteen Hundred and Sixty Three; or, The Sensations of the Past Season, with a Shameful Revelation of 'Lady Someone's Secret,'* which opened on Boxing Day, 1863 (always the opening day for the new Christmas pantomime).[70] Together with *East Lynne*, *Lady Audley's Secret* would go on to become a staple of theatre managements internationally, as both plays made the transition to broadcast media, lasting well into the twentieth century in commercial theatres' repertoires.[71]

Adaptations of *Aurora Floyd* followed closely on the heels of *Lady Audley's Secret*, mirroring the appearance of two novels, which were published in the same year, and to which Braddon herself referred as 'my pair of Bigamy novels.'[72] Benjamin Webster's and Charles Smith Cheltnam's adaptations opened on 11 March 1863 at the Adelphi and at the Princess's Theatres respectively. These were followed by William E. Suter's adaptation at the Queen's Theatre, 30 March, and continued to move outward from the West End through London with Colin Henry

Hazlewood's *Aurora Floyd; or, The First and Second Marriage* (with the variant sub-title: *The Dark Duel in the Wood*) on 20 April at the Victoria in the East End, and John Beer Johnstone's version at the Marylebone Theatre in West London in May. In July of that year, *Aurora Floyd* was dramatized for the Théâtre du Châtelet, Paris, meeting with a sensational success there.[73] Hazlewood's adaptations of *Lady Audley's Secret* and *Aurora Floyd* were staples of the Britannia's repertoire, and from there Hazlewood's scripts travelled the world. In March 1868, stage manager Frederick Wilton notes a letter from Thomas G. Drummond (an actor formerly with the Britannia, and now in Texas, USA) asking for manuscripts of Hazlewood's including his adaptations of Braddon.[74]

Some critics who desired to maintain certain standards in theatre-going did not welcome this domination by sensation drama. Henry Morley noted in his diary:

> *April* 13. – The list of performances at London theatres this week would, with but one or two exceptions, be an insult to the taste of the town if it did not indicate a lamentable change in the class to which the drama looks for patronage.[75]

Henry Morley's general comment on the dominance of sensation drama comes after his specific reference to the Adelphi Theatre's *Aurora Floyd* as 'garbage' fitted only for the 'literary taste in the uneducated' (243). His comments reflect the endurance of the debate over the decline of the drama into the mid-Victorian period, and foreground the fact that middle-class literary critics were as concerned with the dangers of class fluidity implied in sensation fiction and drama as they were with its challenges to bourgeois respectability and conventional morality.[76]

In spite of this extreme reaction from one critic, and the moral panic over sensation fiction whipped up by what Patrick Brantlinger identifies as the 'hysterical extreme' of public commentators,[77] newspaper reviewers were far less contemptuous of Braddon's novels on stage than might be expected. However, it should be noted that as I have only been able to locate daily press reviews of the version of *Lady Audley's Secret* playing at the decidedly middle-class St James's Theatre, the unspoken class-based bar on reviewing East End and transpontine theatres was apparently still in operation in 1863, despite the popularity of the play. However, responses to this production might confound our assumptions about Braddon's reception generally, as theatre critics were more open to the play's narrative and its representation of 'interesting' characters, appreciating the entertainment offered through strong feeling, and the opportunities for witnessing powerful acting. It was the stage version that Braddon herself recommended to Bulwer-Lytton on the strength of Miss Herbert's performance.[78] These were the themes of all the reviews of the St James's production. The usually staid *Athenæum* was uniformly complimentary about the production, noting first of all the 'numerous as well as fashionable audience' which received the piece with enthusiasm.[79] Describing her as a 'bold, fascinating woman, with a fatal secret,' the *Athenæum* predicts that Miss Herbert's professional reputation 'will be increased by her fortunate assumption of the character' (338). The *ILN* also comments on Miss Herbert's ability to draw on 'the opposite forces of dramatic art,' explaining this critique with an analysis of the character of Lady Audley as 'prompted to crime by hereditary insanity and untoward circumstances, and therefore impelled by both external and internal motives.'[80] The *Times* noted the difference between the role of Lady Audley, 'the bold, bad, fascinating woman,' and the 'meek sufferer[s]' which Miss Herbert had previously played, commenting on the physical force and intellectual power necessary to impersonate the 'hardened, indomitable, handsome wickedness.'[81] The *Daily Telegraph* went so far as to attribute the success of the production to its acting: 'beyond all, the success of the night was owing to the acting of Miss Herbert, whose assumption of Lady Audley was one of the most remarkable achievements which we have witnessed for some time.'[82]

When *Aurora Floyd* appeared on stage, there were inevitable comparisons of the two heroines: in reviewing Charles Cheltnam's adaptation at the Princess's Theatre, the *Times* judged that

> Aurora Floyd is not so striking a personage on stage as Lady Audley. She has her temper, and can be resolute but, altogether, she is more sinned against than sinning, and a halo of amiability is cast upon her by her affection for her husband.[83]

The *Athenæum* echoes this judgement, arguing that the fact that Aurora is 'neither thoroughly good, nor thoroughly bad' is 'an essential weakness [. . .] as a dramatic representation.'[84] The *Daily Telegraph* was rather more enthusiastic, seeing the ambiguity of Aurora's character in a positive light:

> Here we have a heroine who is not less attractive because she is loveable and human, and a story which is not less exciting because it happens to be possible. How delightful is its heroine, the wild, bright impulsive

girl, who errs from no love of evil, but mere excess of life and ardour, and whose punishment abates her spirit only to render it more engaging.[85]

Although all reviewers are complimentary about Amy Sedgwick's performance at the Princess's, the *Times* had more praise for Avonia Jones' rendition of Aurora in Benjamin Webster Jnr's version at the Adelphi Theatre. Jones' Aurora was 'not merely a young girl in difficulties, but the spoilt, quick-tempered, ill-regulated girl of the novel.'[86] As with Miss Herbert's performance of Lady Audley, reviewers' comments exhibit the tendency to identify the actor with her role, attributing the power of each actor's representation to her personal qualities; such a slippage was a professional hazard for actresses, particularly in such morally and ideologically sensitive roles as Lady Audley and Aurora Floyd. The confusion of creator with creation is mirrored in the earlier reaction to Braddon herself: besides the general execration of her character as one which was able to imagine such stories of female degeneracy as those of *Lady Audley's Secret* and *Aurora Floyd*, her 'bigamy novels' were written at a time when Braddon was subject to scrutiny over her own marital arrangements. Although she left the stage as a performer, her fiction writing never really left a theatricalized public realm which tended to fuse the identities of female author and female protagonists.

These difficulties over clear characterization and dramatization in *Aurora Floyd* were overcome with the representation of Stephen Hargreaves, or 'Softy,' who is made into the melodramatic villain of the piece. Actor George Belmore, usually a low comedian, played the role in the Princess's production and 'scene by scene grew into importance, until, in the last two acts, he thoroughly fascinated the audience into attention.'[87] In creating Softy as the outright villain, one of the central requirements of melodrama was met by a clear alignment of good characters against evil. All adaptations of *Aurora Floyd* are structured so that the final scene is a confrontation between Softy and those he persecutes. This gives Softy a very strong scene, as the *Times* notes: 'when the wretched criminal was dragged off the stage frantic with despair, and shrieking out supplications [...] the audience acknowledged their satisfaction by a burst of surprised applause.'[88] However, in both John Beer Johnstone's and Benjamin Webster Jnr's adaptations, it is Aurora herself who confronts Softy, thus giving the actress an opportunity to create a powerful image of breaking the bounds of conventional feminine behaviour. The *Daily Telegraph* comments that this scene was played by

Avonia Jones 'with unusual spirit, and [...] infused it with an amount of vigour which was cordially applauded.'[89]

My principal interest in this survey of responses to stage adaptations of Braddon's novels is not with the quality or detail of the adaptations, but with the cultural work that they do, particularly as they are representative of the widespread adaptation of women's texts for the stage. I am particularly interested in the popularity of Braddon's bigamous heroines on stage which was a marker of Victorian popular culture's shift into modernity through the representation of 'women's stories' on the popular stage. This shift was intimately bound up with challenges to the Victorian conception of 'the proper lady' in her fictional and material versions, and was distinguished by an emphasis on the power of women's emotions and their simultaneous commodification. Critical attention to the 'power of affect,' to use Ann Cvetkovich's term,[90] in the staging of Braddon's sensation novels was divided between appreciation of the wide audience appeal of these adaptations, and a muted condemnation of their sensational material and mode. Inevitably, sensation dramas adapted from sensation novels were caught up in the public 'moral panic' precipitated by the novels. And, as is common with moral panics then and now, public anxieties about sexuality were focussed on women and their behaviour within the economy of a gender ideology which attempted to identify women solely with their domestic and reproductive roles. Class also played its part here, as sensation drama and sensation fiction reconfigured class-based anxieties about the externalized threat of the deracinated, dispossessed working-class male of the industrial and social stage melodramas of the 1830s and 1840s (and their concomitant fictional forms in the 'Condition of England' novels) into the feminized, domesticated, fair-haired 'angel of the house' of the bourgeois and upper-class British life of country houses, hunting, and dinner parties.

Literary historians have recognized that the sensation novel was not a unique genre, but a mode with its antecedents in stage melodrama, the Gothic novel, and popular newspaper fiction such as Reynolds' *Mysteries of London*.[91] Lyn Pykett argues that the sensation novel was a 'site in which the contradictions, anxieties and opposing ideologies of Victorian culture converge and are put into play.'[92] That the sensation novel – and by extension, the sensation drama – focussed on the strong feelings and independent actions of apparently respectable middle- and upper-class women was central to critics' ambivalence about these texts, to the extent that Kate Flint argues that contemporary critics found Aurora Floyd's 'capacity for spontaneous action' such as horsewhipping a groom more problematic than the architecture of the plot of bigamy and deceit.[93] But sensation in adaptations of Braddon's novels was not just a matter of creating effects (and affect) by stage machinery, which Dion Boucicault established as the dominant mode in his spectacular melodramas of the late 1850s.[94] In these women's stories, sensation was created by what Lyn Pykett has described as the 'irruption into the narration of that feeling [...] which is repressed in the narrative,'[95] by the character-function of the heroine. This emphasis on the feeling woman constituted an historical moment in which extreme pressure was placed on one of the most fragile fault lines of Victorian ideology and social practice: the attempt to control female bodies and desires. Sensation fiction of the 1860s and its associated dramas, as Ann Cvetkovich succinctly puts it, 'marks the moment at which sensations became sensational.'[96]

While recent studies of Braddon have questioned earlier feminist enthusiasm for her novels as subversive,[97] it is worth considering the potentially transgressive nature of stage adaptations of Braddon's novels, particularly in their return to an originating genre and mode for the sensation novel – that of melodrama. Pykett reads women's sensation fiction in part through a Bakhtinian model of dialogism between the 'popular form' of melodrama and the 'official form' of middle-class domestic fiction. She argues that the popular form of melodrama destabilizes and exposes the contradictions of the 'proper feminine' even as these novels (particularly through their conservative endings) seek to reinforce conventional femininity.[98] So the return of these texts to the stage brings with it this politics of representation, and I would argue, the most significant element of this return is the embodied representation of the feeling (sensational) woman (body). As Lady Audley and Aurora Floyd take centre stage, both literally and metaphorically, a space is claimed for the female voice and body, for Pykett's 'improper feminine.' It is the act of articulation, as much as what is articulated, that is important here. For the female character – no matter how much she is finally restricted by the plot of melodrama – the very taking of the stage as a physical, vocal, passionate, active, and self-activating human being is significant. The presence of a powerfully feeling woman on stage is reinforced by a stage performance practice which emphasized the grandeur and scope of the articulation of female experience. This acting style in turn developed to accommodate the heightened language of melodrama and the experience it points to. Taken together, performance style and language work to create an iconic sign of woman in which performance energy is concentrated and focussed to a high degree.

It is here that we can best locate Mary Braddon and her adapters' uses of the affective power of melodrama, and here that the politics of feeling have most significance in her novels and their stage adaptations. A powerful energy pervades Mary Braddon's early sensation novels, which proved enduring staples of popular entertainment from the sensational melodramas of the 1860s to the emergent British film industry before and during the First World War, when there were four film versions of *Lady Audley's Secret* and three of *Aurora Floyd* between 1906 and 1915.[99] These novels have become templates for 'women's stories' in popular entertainment to this day, and if their precise plot lines of bigamy and murder have not been repeated exactly, their patterns of masochistic female suffering and victimization are constantly replicated. This reading of the cultural work of adaptation departs from Kerry Powell's rather defeatist argument that the frequent adaptation of women's fictions for the stage was 'a massive assault against women writers that is both textual and sexual in nature' in which women's fictions were 'refitted for a masculinist theatre.'[100] Whether or not Braddon's ideological import is ultimately subversive is for me less important than the cultural work of putting female bodies and experience at the centre of theatre going. The trend for woman-centred sensation drama (as opposed to the male-centred melodrama of the previous sensation period of the 1830s and 1840s) was to have a profound impact on the commercial theatre industry in the last third of the nineteenth century.

Commercial theatre in the *fin de siècle*

My focus on the fashion for sensation dramas in 1863 is not intended to invoke a precise moment of change in theatrical practices precipitated by the popularity and power of women's writings for performance – such a view would be historiographically naïve. Yet the domination of the London stage by adaptations of two novels, similar in plot elements, by the same author, points to a paradigm shift in the sensibility of the popular stage, similar to the shift into domestic melodrama represented by, for example, the multiple versions of Douglas Jerrold's *Black-Ey'd Susan* thirty-four years earlier (even though productions of *Black-Ey'd Susan* did not saturate the London theatres as adaptations of Braddon's novels did). However, in focussing on *Lady Audley's Secret* and *Aurora Floyd* on the London stage, I want to draw attention to their role in characterizing 'a modern, high-speed, industrialised culture.'[101] An increasingly important element of that culture was the body and agency of the women, albeit as fetishized objects, but increasingly as writing subjects of modernity. The cultural debates of the 1860s which focussed on the feminization of popular culture in a moral panic over sensation fiction bore resemblances to similar concerns in the 1890s over 'New Woman' fiction.[102] Such frenzied reactions reinforced in literary judgements which, as Nicola Thompson argues, judged that '[T]he more popular a novel, the more appealing to a mass audience, the more suspect the quality of the work.'[103] In what follows, I want to investigate the role of women playwrights in the shift to a feminized culture as a constructive movement. In the process, I hope to stage a rescue of women's writing for the commercial theatre, an aspect of women's writing which has been left stranded between the exclusive definitions of high modernism on one hand, and anti-populist proselytisers for the literary drama on the other.

Our understanding of the cultural landscape of last decades of the nineteenth century and the early twentieth century has, until very recently, been dominated by the aesthetic values of contemporary modernist artists, and later twentieth-century critics who, as Ann Ardis argues, have tended to read modernism from within its own values.[104] Avant-garde artists and critics of the period mounted a vigorous campaign to reject the past wholesale, in a 'reaction formation,'[105] which Lynne Hapgood describes as the 'modernist sense of rupture [which] was, of course deliberately constructed.'[106] Historiographically, we have tended to lose sight of the continuities from early to late Victorian playwriting and on into the Edwardian period. While there *are* differences between the plays women wrote in the 1890s and those they wrote in the 1830s, they are not such as to require us to discard the earlier work as superseded in a modernist revolution. As well as doing vital recovery work for the recognition of women's writing by viewing the late nineteenth-century theatre through the frame of women's playwriting, I am suggesting that other histories might be told about the theatre at the turn of the twentieth century. In this way, women's playwriting for the popular stage in this period is both significant in itself, and as an example of what is overlooked in the standard historiography of late nineteenth-century British theatre.

As well as the attempt by some artists and critics then and now to establish modernism as the defining aesthetic practice of this period, and cast other forms of cultural production into invisibility, women's playwriting of this period was also caught up in the boundary-riding involved in the campaign for the literary drama. While the two movements were not identical, they did share a number of precepts and assumptions, as both rejected the sentimental and domestic tendencies of popular culture, tendencies which were inevitably cast as feminine.[107] Although some advocates for the improvement of British drama expressed an almost traumatized protest at the theatre work of the modernist avant-garde, in for example, critical responses to *A Doll's House* or *Alan's Wife*,[108] they were also disturbed by contemporary mass culture, particularly in its populist and feminized forms. The late nineteenth-century version of the 'decline of the drama' lament argued through the binary oppositions of art versus commerce, drama versus theatre, literature versus entertainment, intellect versus feeling, and, by implication, masculine versus feminine. These oppositions have remained with us, shaping theatre history, enforcing the hierarchy of art over commerce, and until recently, casting other approaches into the wilderness.

To sample a range of middle-class and middle-brow periodical articles on the state of the English theatre in the 1860s to the turn of the century is to trace the formation of this version of theatre history. This comment in 1863 from the *Cornhill* is typical: 'That our drama is extinct as literature, and our stage is in a deplorable condition of decline, no one will venture to dispute.'[109] In 1869, *Macmillan's Magazine* opines that 'It is in England only that the glory of the drama has gone down, and it is a fact much to be deplored, for it coincides with an undeniable degeneracy of taste, and it suppresses the noblest form of expression affected by the national tongue.'[110] In the *Temple Bar*'s discussion of 'The Present State of the English Stage' in 1871, the degradation of the drama is attributed to just five causes: the influence of the lessees, the influence of the playwrights, the influence of actors, the influence of professional critics, and the influence of the audience.[111] Just what is left as a benign influence on the theatre is unclear, but in the course of this discussion the *Temple Bar* makes an interesting argument which pinpoints very neatly one of the central binary oppositions in hegemonic attitudes of the period.

> A lessee is entitled to look to a safe and decent livelihood [...]; but the more ardently he professes to honour and be enamoured of his art, the smaller, comparatively, should be the return that contents him. (460–1)

The opposition between art and commerce is a familiar one in the nineteenth century, but by the latter part of the century it led to a further critical articulation of the oppositions between art and entertainment, and drama and theatre. G. H. Lewes, for example, writes that: 'The

drama has an immediate and an ulterior aim. Its immediate aim is to
delight an audience; its ulterior aim is the ennobling and enlarging of
the mind through the sympathies –'[112] Unfortunately, Lewes does not
mention how these two aims might both be achieved, and how theatre
professionals might make a living by both delighting and ennobling.

These oppositions are marked in the commentaries of Henry Arthur
Jones. Jones consistently attempts to decouple theatre from entertainment, rewriting the history of English theatre as one solely of aesthetic
striving for moral and educational improvement. In his introduction to
his first collection of polemical pieces *The Renascence of the English
Drama*, Jones states that he has been fighting for 'a recognition of the
distinction between the art of the drama on the one hand and popular
amusement on the other, and of the greater pleasure to be derived from
the art of the drama.'[113] The problem with contemporary English drama
is that 'It is a hybrid, an unwieldy Siamese Twin, with two bodies, two
heads, two minds, two dispositions, all of them, for the present, vitally
connected. And one of these two bodies, dramatic art, is lean and
pinched and starving, and has to drag about with it, wherever it goes,
its fat, puffy, unwholesome, dropsical brother, popular amusement'
(11). Indeed, in a later lecture at Harvard he argues that one of the
'Corner Stones of Modern Drama' is 'The severance of the drama from
popular entertainment: the recognition of it as a fine art which, though
its lower ranges must always compound with mere popular entertainment, and be confused with it, is yet essentially something different
from popular entertainment, transcends it, and in its higher ranges is in
marked and eternal antagonism to popular entertainment.'[114] But it was
in his early essay 'The Theatre and the Mob' that Jones showed himself
to be fundamentally at odds with his age: in echoing Matthew Arnold's
anxieties about a culture dominated by philistinism, Jones writes 'And
as the Elizabethan drama reeks of the spirit of Raleigh and Sidney and is
relative to the age of the Spanish Armada, so the Victorian drama reeks
of the spirit of successful tradesmen and is relative to the age of
Clapham Junction.'[115] Drawing on Arnold, Jones laments that an
authentic English drama cannot emerge because of the lack of unity of
England as a nation: his despair at this is a rejection of the diversity and
multiplicity of cultural products and communities which marks late
nineteenth-century British capitalism, modernity, and the theatre.[116]

By the end of the century polemic had solidified into orthodoxy
which valued drama over theatre, art over entertainment, and Englishness
over foreignness. Theatre history in the making also reflected the Victorian
model of inevitable progress, revealing an unremarked appropriation of

evolutionary ideas.[117] In 1899, Clement Scott wrote in *The Drama of Yesterday and Today*, that: 'We have arrived, step by step, steadily and by slow degrees, at the year 1865, which is a landmark in the history of the English stage during the Victorian Era.'[118] The 'landmark' was Marie Wilton's 'discovery' of playwright Tom Robertson (484–7). Similarly, William Archer identified three stages in the 'rehabilitation of the British drama, each associated with the name of a remarkable man.'[119] First is the 'Robertson stage,' then the 'Pinero stage,' and finally, the 'Shaw stage.' His discussion of this last stage is most significant for the dichotomies between the popular and the aesthetic, the performed and the reading drama that Archer sets up as central to the improvement of the English theatre:

> The first two movements came from within the theatre itself. [...] But the third movement proceeded from without. [...] Economically, it was at first, and has continued to be in some measure, an endowed movement. [...] if the Shaw drama had been forced to pay its way, as were the Robertson drama and the Pinero drama, it would long ago have died of starvation. (338)

Elsewhere, Archer distinguishes between the literary and the non-literary drama, echoing Jones' argument that until the English drama is read as well as performed, 'our drama will remain unliterary, frivolous, non-moral, unworthy of its past and of our present stage of advancement in other branches of literature and art.'[120] Bernard Shaw himself followed the practice of most innovators in his critique of what had gone before: his opinion of Robertson's plays and the 'school' of drawing-room drama he influenced was that they were nothing but 'a tailor's advertisement making sentimental remarks to a milliner's advertisement in the middle of an upholsterer's and decorator's advertisement.'[121] Shaw's emphasis here on the commodification and commercialisation of the theatre makes manifest that he saw Robertsonian realism as a 'deceptive substitute for a genuine critical realism.'[122] Archer, Jones, Scott, and Shaw replicate and renew old Romantic debates about the superiority of the literary drama over the popular theatre, even though the evidence of audiences, managements, and performers throughout the nineteenth century suggests that the popular theatre, no matter how frivolous or non-educational, was the great survivor. This model leaves out more than it can include – necessarily so, as the model is predicated on the kind of unity that Jones and Arnold seek, but cannot actually find, in their studies of contemporary English culture.

So this was the cultural landscape within which women playwrights at the end of the nineteenth century worked, encountering, on the one hand, a modernist aesthetic which rejected the domestic, the sentimental, the conventional in favour of an oppositional critique of bourgeois culture, and on the other, a campaign for a literary drama, which excluded the domestic, the sentimental, the entertaining. And, as Andreas Huyssen has noted, cultural debates in the second half of the nineteenth century intensified anxieties about a feminized mass culture into the 'identification of woman with the masses as political threat.'[123] To suggest what lay between these views contending for dominance of the theatre profession *and* its history, I want to look at the reception of the work of two prominent women playwrights of the period, Clotilde (Clo) Graves, and Madeleine Lucette Ryley. Their work, taken together with my accounts of the work of Florence Bell, Lucy Clifford, and Florence Marryat in Chapter 7, demonstrate some of the significant features of the feminizing of popular culture, and will, I hope, provide a starting point for further discussion. While I am conscious of a certain selectivity in my focus on just two writers here, by no means do I wish to suggest that these writers be considered canonical. Indeed, I see Graves and Ryley as representative of any number of women writing for the mainstream theatre of the period, and my discussion should be read in conjunction with the surveys of late nineteenth-century women playwrights' work provided by Susan Carlson and Kerry Powell.[124] Like the women playwrights I discuss from the early Victorian period, Ryley and Graves were not exceptional: their work emerged from the professional networks and material practices of the London theatre industry.

In quick summary, let me outline the grounds for presenting Ryley and Graves as representative. First, they were prolific writers, Ryley producing sixteen full-length plays between 1895 and 1907, and Graves writing seventeen plays between 1886 and 1909. It should also be noted that although both were extraordinarily successful playwrights during their lifetimes they have since dropped almost completely out of view: only four of Ryley's plays were published – *An American Citizen, Jedbury Junior, Mice and Men,* and *Mrs Grundy* – while the others remain in manuscript in the Lord Chamberlain's Collection of Plays, or fortunately preserved in beautifully bound typescript volumes at the John Rylands Library, Manchester.[125] Similarly, Clo Graves' work has languished; of her seventeen plays, the only ones to be published were *A Mother of Three* and *The General's Past.* Another feature of their careers which was increasingly typical of late Victorian women playwrights was the international dimension of their careers. Graves was Anglo-Irish, and travelled much in Britain and abroad as an actress, before settling in Berkshire in the 1900s; under the pseudonym 'Richard Dehan,' she published fiction set in diverse locations. Her novel, *The Dop Doctor*, for example, whose best-seller status in 1910 has dwindled to near invisibility a century later,[126] was set against the background of the Boer War in South Africa. Ryley, although born in London, made her stage debut in New York and was identified as an American throughout her career.[127] She might seem out of place in this study of *British* women playwrights, but her integration into the London theatre scene in the last decade of the nineteenth century and the first decade of the twentieth illustrates the internationalism of the popular theatre. Ryley's career follows the pattern of earlier actress-playwright, Anna Cora Mowatt, who moved easily between London and New York in her career as a performer, whose play *Fashion; or, Life in New York* was a runaway success on both sides of the Atlantic in the 1850s, and whom Adrienne Scullion nominates as one of the most influential women in the American theatre in the nineteenth century.[128] Besides, Ryley is even more invisible (if that is possible) in the standard reference works on American literature than she is in those with a British remit.[129] Both Graves and Ryley moved from being actresses to playwrights – Clo Graves reportedly took up acting because she wanted to become a playwright;[130] and Madeleine Ryley moved into playwriting at the end of her musical comedy career. Although Ryley married, and Graves remained unmarried, both women's careers illustrate the opportunities for independence and public profile without censure for professional women at the end of the nineteenth century: Graves trained at the Royal School of Art in Bloomsbury, illustrated her own writing, apparently was known for wearing man's dress, and lived by her pen; Ryley's plays became ubiquitous on the stage and she was the fêted 'authoress' of the society pages of recreational magazines. Both women were involved in the suffrage movement, Madeleine Ryley famously saying when asked if she would ever write a suffrage play:

> No. I have thought of doing so several times, but the difficulty is not to miss the broad issues in dwelling on one of the irritations. [. . .] Remedying small disabilities is the insidious method of delaying the great result, and it is the great uplifting, that the responsibilities of full and perfect citizenship will give us, that we are waiting for.[131]

Both women were well-connected in the networks of artistic London, as suffragists, but also in the mainstream theatre. Ryley worked with

Johnston Forbes-Robertson and his company on several of her productions, while Graves collaborated with actress, playwright, and later theatre manager Gertrude Kingston, and Lady Colin Campbell. While David Mayer comments that collaborative writing in the popular theatre at the end of the century 'resembled an assembly-line' for writing hits,[132] I would argue that Graves' collaborations are indicative of the development of female-centred networks of professional women, helping each other in the face of a still male-dominated theatrical industry, as outlined by Julie Holledge in her account of the growth of feminist theatre in the late nineteenth and early twentieth centuries.[133] Finally, both women wrote plays for the mainstream commercial theatre of London, in popular genres: mainly comedies of contemporary life, broadly realist in style, but not Naturalist in their aesthetic or ideological approaches or content. It is this last characteristic which has proved to be critical in the systematic forgetting of their work, and has outweighed what are interesting and productive careers. While it is understandable that their work may have faded in comparison to the blast[134] of protest that Eleanor Marx, Elizabeth Robins, Janet Achurch, Marion Lea, and their colleagues found in Ibsen and his like, what is less reasonable is our continuing acceptance of this model, and the transformation of this mix of generational and aesthetic politics into a model of historiography and an hierarchy of aesthetic value.

Like the adaptations of Mary Braddon's novels in spring 1863, in the summer of 1902 Madeleine Ryley's plays seemed to dominate the London West End. Throughout May and June a revival of *Jedbury Junior* (first seen in London in 1896) played at the Shaftesbury, and Forbes-Robertson's production of Ryley's new play, *Mice and Men* transferred from Manchester to the Lyric,[135] running for the next year; meanwhile a short and relatively unsuccessful season of *The Grass Widow* was interspersed with the *Jedbury Junior* revival at the Shaftesbury. *Jedbury Junior* and *Mice and Men* display all those characteristics which the campaigners for the New Drama sought to expunge from the stage. *Mice and Men* was described on its premiere as 'sentimental and idyllic,' 'slight to fragility,'[136] in contrast with its robust predecessors by William Wycherley, and David Garrick. But several reviews commented approvingly precisely on the play's value as entertainment, the *Times* called it a 'very wholesome entertainment' which was received with manifest enthusiasm on its first night,[137] while the *Era* commended Ryley for the fact that 'there is not an unpleasant word in it, not an offensive or disagreeable line.'[138] This was not the first time Ryley had disarmed her critics through pleasantness and good humour: her first play which was an immediate hit, *Jedbury Junior*, opened in 1896 to some decidedly mixed opinions by reviewers. At stake was the play's genre and theatrical provenance: the *Times* critic, in disgruntled mood, compares the play to a 'domestic drama or comedy of the Henry J. Byron type, though written without that author's distinguishing humour and geniality.' The reviewer goes on to complain that the 'lady has not expended much invention in the building up of her plot, the materials of which have served before,' and continues to point out what the reviewer feels are the hackneyed elements of the marriage plot of the play, before conceding that the performances are 'interesting enough' and the piece 'achieved a fair amount of success.'[139] The *Era* too identifies Henry J. Byron as the governing influence of the play, noting Ryley's adoption of Byron's 'easy superficialities, cheerful "go-as-you-please" methods, indifference to artistic canons, and general brisk, careless cheerfulness.'[140] The *Athenæum* takes an odd line over these genre confusions, which seem 'to challenge condemnation at all points,' regarding them as part of the play's success. 'Thanks, however, to its very defects of construction – extraordinary as such a statement may seem – it not only escapes censure, but wins approval.' This is a play which the *Athenæum* would like to condemn for its 'hovering' uncertainly between domestic comedy and farce, 'violating probability alike in character and incident, ill made and worse equipped,' but cannot because of the way Ryley confounds generic expectations, and moves from farce to 'scenes of domestic tenderness' which cause the audience to 'vainly [. . .] suppress a tear' just when they expected to 'snigger.' This reviewer's difficulty in placing Ryley's play continues throughout the review, his perplexity with the play resulting in a series of aporia which amount to a critical shrugging of the shoulders at Ryley's playwriting skills and the taste of the popular audience.

> Why the interest is tender, we know not, but tender it is. The piece is manifestly trivial and inept. Its opening action shows the hero abandoning for a garret the fashionable apartments he has occupied, hoping thereby to soften the heart of a dictatorial sire. Nothing whatever comes of this device, except that the hero drinks brandy-and-soda out of a teapot. [. . .] Obviously, then, it may be urged, the play is incapable of being defended. [. . .] It is equally true, however, that it needs no defence. [. . .] in spite of its defects the play proves sympathetic and human.[141]

While equally frank about the play's apparent shortcomings, the *Theatre* attributes the success of the play to the sex of its author: Ryley's play, while at many points 'amateur' is so fresh, so fragrant, and so charming, as to insure for it a cordial welcome. With the courage of her sex, the authoress does not hesitate to set probability at defiance, and to demand from her audience a measure of make-believe not always to be relied on in these prosaic days. Luckily, however, the appeal is not in vain, and, despite its obvious shortcomings, *Jedbury Junior* conquers by virtue of its delightful qualities.[142]

My interest here is not to evaluate these critical opinions in the light of a close analysis of Ryley's plays (although such a study of Ryley's work is warranted), but to identify both the pleasure and the unease in critical reactions to her two most successful comedies as representative of reaction to the increasingly visible presence of women playwrights in mainstream theatre. From these reviews we can start to articulate the conditions of women's professionalism as playwrights at the end of the Victorian period. I would point to the way that the language of respectability and the 'proper lady' no longer dominates reviews of Ryley's playwriting, in spite of the fact that the plots of *Jedbury Junior* and *Mice and Men* revolve around the possibility of bigamy, and intergenerational and cross-class marriage respectively. Although there is a ghost of the expectations of 'the work of a lady' we are familiar with from the early Victorian period, critics also discuss Ryley's dramaturgical skills, her borrowings from earlier writers, the appeal of her plays to the West End audiences, and her ability to write pieces to suit her actors. While their comments are not always complimentary, these are all topics appropriate to the discussion of a professional writer's achievement, and where Ryley's gender is invoked, as in the *Theatre*'s infatuated review of *Jedbury Junior*, it is to remark on Ryley's courage to invite her readers into the full enjoyment of the theatricality of theatre as much as to question her claims to respectability. While Susan Carlson reads Ryley's plays as 'cautious yet playful' and politically conventional or even conservative in their commitment to 'marriage *de rigueur*' in contrast with Ryley's avowed suffragette position,[143] my reading of Ryley's reception suggests there is a further interpretation to be made, which acknowledges the ideological work of women playwrights making women visible on the stage even in the most conventional of forms. Rather than seeing Ryley's triviality and fun as damaging to the National Drama or evidence of the woman writer's immoral propensities in daring to write for the theatre, they are held up as examples of successful and welcome popular entertainment. And the acknowledgement that a woman's play can be 'sympathetic and human' in spite of its faults can be seen as the partial admission of a woman playwright to that form of cultural citizenship which had been contested territory for women playwrights for most of the nineteenth century.

However, notwithstanding Ryley's charm offensive on the London stage, this territory *was* still embattled. Kerry Powell identifies theatre reviewers' surprise at the plethora of women playwrights plays on the stage at the same time in the 1890s,[144] although as I have shown, such saturation was not so exceptional, and reviewers' surprise is part of an ideologically inflected practice of forgetting. Plays which attracted this specific critical notice included Clo Graves' smash-hit, *A Mother of Three*, first produced in April 1896, while a month later another play by Graves and her collaborator Gertrude Kingston (who also performed the title role), *A Matchmaker*, opened at the Shaftesbury Theatre.[145] *A Mother of Three* harks back to the long English tradition of farce, while its opening scene retains (for me, at least) parodic echoes of the opening chapters of *Little Women*, in which the four March sisters, in a household with an absent father, must use their ingenuity to survive as respectable middle-class ladies. Graves' playful picture of lively sisterhood in poverty frames the play in domestic and intimate terms, and remains engaging, for all the farce of mistaken identity and sexual impropriety that ensues. It was the changes rung by farce on propriety on which reviewers focussed attention – together with acknowledgement of the play's great success with its audiences. The *Era* closes in on Mrs Murgatroyd's (the mother of three) cross-dressing (as her husband) in her decamping lodger's clothes, commenting that in

> the comical consequences of Mrs Murgatroyd's rash assumption of masculine attire, some of the lines [are] broad enough to prove that the modern female dramatist is, to say the least, not squeamishly prudish.[146]

The *Theatre* calls the play 'at once bright, clever, and inspiriting,' commenting that

> Nor is it likely that an irresponsible public will regard the fact as detrimental to their enjoyment that some of the allusions contained in the piece are decidedly of the risky order.[147]

Graves' risky dialogue and incidents are part of a theatre scene which now includes the 'irresponsible' public, in a relationship with the playwright in which each is seen as egging the other on into further iconoclasm. But this is not condemned outright – indeed, these comments are made in the context of discussing what Graves has done with the traditions of farce. The *Era* playfully announces that Graves has been the 'discoverer of a new motive;' while identical twins have traditionally been used in farce, triplets (the three Murgatroyd daughters) have not. Bernard Shaw muses on Graves' Irishness – '[T]he Irish have a natural delicacy which gives them a very keen sense of indelicacy' – and wonders whether Graves, in an attempt to outdo the success of *Charley's Aunt* or *The Strange Adventures of Miss Brown* (a collaboration between Harriet Jay and Robert Buchanan) decided to reverse the usual cross-dressing of a man into a woman, to give us a woman dressed as a man.[148] Of course, what these reviewers choose to forget is the long burletta and pantomime tradition of cross-dressed women; however, I find it significant that in spite of adverse criticisms of *A Mother of Three* for its loose plotting, its absurdities and improbabilities, it *is* being discussed within the frame of English farce. Whatever rank she might be given in the hierarchy, Graves is being accorded a place in the English popular tradition, although we might wonder at critics' forgetting of a female tradition including Caroline Boaden writing for Liston, and Mrs Phillips writing for Farren (not to mention Susannah Centlivre and Elizabeth Inchbald).

The 'riskiness' of Graves' work emerges in reviews of her other play to open in 1896, *A Matchmaker*. Again, reviews of *A Matchmaker* try to be disapproving, on the grounds of the play's 'frivolous chatter' and 'invertebrate' nature, 'possessing little coherence and no cohesion' although the same review in the *Theatre* does not deny that the play has 'some ingenuity and not a little cleverness.'[149] The *Era* is perhaps the most enlightening about the grounds for adverse critical reaction: the play lacks 'unity of design,' 'centrality of motive,' and 'backbone,' but it does have

> plenty of wit and humour [...], abounds in smart sayings, and contains some clever, if rather cynical, character-drawing, and some shrewd hits at modern worldliness. Nor is it without that spice of mild impropriety without which no play written by a lady would be complete; and the scene in which, after the fact of their being man and wife has been exposed, the Hon. Charles Soper and Mrs S. go off to bed together with only one candle is one of the most piquant and effective in the piece.[150]

Bernard Shaw's review also foregrounds the women playwrights' 'naughty' humour, opining that they have 'some bright dramatic talent between them' even if the play seemed thrown together.[151] After decades of reviews in which 'pen of a lady' is held to higher standards than her male peers, 'the mild spice of impropriety' and female 'naughtiness' fairly leap out at me. But they also gives me pause. Both reviews clearly indicate a loosening of the double standard of the 'proper lady,' yet suggests the substitution of that set of gendered codes of behaviour with another, in which the woman playwright's role is to titillate. So any triumphalist claims I might be tempted to make about the progress of women playwrights as professionals must be tempered by an acknowledgement that women's playwriting was still judged by gendered criteria focussed on gender difference, which now included a more overt acknowledgement of the sexualized nature of the critical assessment of theatrical pleasure. Yet, as Carlson and Powell suggest, Graves' work should be regarded as part of the 'tussle' over what constitutes British theatre.[152] Responses to the plays of Ryley and Graves suggest that while critics can still carp about women's inability to structure plays as they 'should' be put together, there is less of a sense that women should not be playwrights at all. Indeed, women's plays are now *expected* to provide uproarious laughter, spice and risk, charm, enjoyment, and entertainment. This is not to say that men's plays were not also regarded in this way, but my analysis serves to identify the ways in which women's playwriting at the end of the nineteenth century was visible and normalized in a way that had previously been contested. And although the terms of critical approval – Ryley's charm and freshness, Graves' spice and humour – were loaded with gendered assumptions, they also indicate the extent to which conventionally feminine attributes had become absorbed into the popular aesthetic, and how commercially viable such an aesthetic was. Of course, this popular aesthetic is one that has, until recently, been overlooked, in part because of this feminization. Yet my preliminary explorations of this territory suggest that there is more to find in a feminist theatre history of the popular theatre than we suspected.

Through these plays, and the hundreds like them, by women playwrights such as Florence Bell, Aimée Béringer, Lucy Clifford, Pearl Craigie ('John Oliver Hobbes'), Florence and Gertrude Warden, Gertrude Kingston, Harriet Jay ('Charles Marlowe'), Kate Sinclair, Rosina Filipi, Ina Cassilis, Kate and Eva Bright, and Mabel Freund-Lloyd, a female version of the world is made increasingly prominent on stage. Even if women playwrights themselves desired to be treated no differently from men, this rarely happened, and, as I argue in this book and elsewhere, the conditions under which women wrote for the theatre were so substantially different from men as to make it difficult for us to read them in the same ways.[153] Kathy Mezei is only one of many feminist critics to claim that the 'essence' of feminist narratology is 'the *context* of how stories are told, by whom, and for whom.'[154] One context which came increasingly to bear on women working in the public sphere of writing – as journalists, novelists, playwrights – in the last decades of the nineteenth century, was the hostility to their growing presence. Marysa Demoor's study of the professionalization of women writers as reviewers and contributors to the *Athenæum* argues that this overt hostility focussed on what was seen as the threat of 'the so-called feminisation of culture,' and masculinist defences included obstruction of women's participation in the sociability of literary and artistic London as men barricaded themselves into clubs such as the Garrick – the 'weapon used by savages to keep the white woman at a distance.'[155] However, as Lynda Nead argues persuasively, the debate over women in public in this period suggests that their growing presence was an entrenched fact, and increasingly significant in economic as well as cultural terms, although Judith Walkowitz identifies the existence of 'male pests' as late as the 1890s.[156] Nevertheless, women's increasing visible presence and economic power were significant in the last decades of the nineteenth century, as studies of late Victorian commodity culture also locate women at its centre as consumers (as well as objects),[157] and in the theatre female spectators made the new trend for matinée performances viable.[158]

Such debates over women's physical presence in London remind us that all the women who wrote in the nineteenth century, for money, for the commercial stage, were participating in the public sphere. And the theatre was no simple adornment of public life; it was part of a network of communications and mass media which played a significant part in conceptions of Englishness throughout the century. However much it was disparaged or belittled, now and then, women had a presence in the theatre, one of the few fields in Victorian Britain where women could participate with anything near to the advantages men took for granted in most aspects of their lives.[159] The realization that on the stage, women had some (but only some) of the advantages of men in terms of work, salary, and opportunity was one of the influences in the founding of the Actresses' Franchise League in 1908.[160] With this recognition of comparability came women's accompanying understanding of the extent of male privilege and advantage. Such knowledge is, however, encoded in much women's playwriting throughout the period before the suffragettes. But the precariousness of masculine

advantage is also embedded in these domestic comedies and farces
I have surveyed, and crucial in the melodramas. It is as if, in the deliberate creation of chaos which was central to comic genres, the 'uneven
developments' of Victorian gender and class ideology, as they were
gathered together in the representation of domesticity, were performed.
The fissures and ambiguities which Mary Poovey finds in Victorian
middle-class ideology were put on display, played with, and played out,
in ways which constantly challenge Victorian conventions of both
femininity and respectability.[161] Women's plays help us to identify the
intersections of gender and class ideology, showing how the one was
dependent on the other. And in their 'ordinariness,' their focus on
sentiment and feeling, their popularity and entertainment value, they
also tell a story about the feminization and democratization of the
public sphere.[162] What is significant here is the staging of the domestic
in public – in the family business of the theatre, in the fictional representations of parlours and drawing rooms on stage. In a later chapter,
I will use women's playwriting to look further at the intertwining of the
domestic and the public spheres. In the next chapter, I will look at what
was at stake when money was not, and how writing for performance
(even imagined ones) was significant in the development of a broader
Victorian feminist writing tradition.

4
Art

The binary opposition between money and art in the Victorian theatre is a troubling one, and in using it I am conscious of the danger of simply perpetuating the Victorian valorization of writing for art over writing for money. However, it was an aesthetic and discursive opposition which, although mutating over the century, remained fundamental to the structuring of the London theatre industry, and one which women had to negotiate. To see the ways in which women writers did this is to acknowledge – again – the work of class and gender in the Victorian theatre, and also to observe the ways that discursive constructions could have material effects. Furthermore, understanding these divisions in the nineteenth century are important as they form the foundation of a set of concepts which still dominate British thinking about theatre, art, and, money – concepts which do not match the basic facts of the theatre industry – but indicate much more interestingly the 'cultural capital' attached to specific playwriting and production practices. In this chapter, I will look in detail at two areas of women's playwriting where money – success in the commercial or mainstream theatre – was not the principal motivation for embarking on dramatic writing. In the examples of the dramatic writing of George Eliot and Augusta Webster, we can see the enduring power of poetic drama, its lure for serious and ambitious women writers, and a tradition of women's performance writing which, like the work of Hemans and Mitford, was grounded in sympathetic presentation of rebellion. And in the work of women translators of Ibsen, I am interested in the ways that women were instrumental in campaigns to introduce a new school of drama to the stage in the late nineteenth century, driven by feminist principles.

Late Victorian poetic drama: George Eliot and Augusta Webster

It may seem as if a reading of women's verse drama of the late nineteenth century is a step aside from the complexities of understanding the way women writers attempted to accommodate the demands of the theatre industry within their self-fashioning, or interrogating the conditions of invisibility of women working successfully in the commercial theatre with which I have been concerned so far. In George Eliot and Augusta Webster, we find women writing poetic drama with limited aspirations towards performance, and, by the 1870s, a recognizable tradition of women's poetry to provide them with literary 'mothers.' When George Eliot and Augusta Webster actively pursued verse drama, together with other poet-playwrights including Emily Pfeiffer, Katherine Bradley and Edith Cooper (writing as 'Michael Field'), Harriet Childe-Pemberton, and Katherine Hinkson Tynan, earlier women writers such as Joanna Baillie, Mary Mitford, Felicia Hemans, Laetitia Landon, Sarah Flower Adams, and Elizabeth Barrett Browning provided them with models for a cultural form which 'presents women as speakers, as actors, as agents, in a way that lyric or third-person narrative poetry cannot,'[1] and in more general terms, Angela Leighton argues that women poets wrote within 'a self-consciously female tradition.'[2] In addition, the impact of Robert Browning's dramatic monologues was to bring together the power of performance – with its directness and action of character-based speech – with the cultural capital of poetry, their combined effect heightened in Browning's work by a dash of that moral and aesthetic shock which characterized Victorian sensation.

And yet, to assume that the writing of verse drama was an uncomplicated retreat from the cultural marketplace is to participate in precisely the kind of divisive cultural tactics which contributed to the stunted sense of professional self that Mary Russell Mitford expressed so eloquently. The historical record suggests that Eliot and Webster and their peers *did* look towards the theatre, albeit not in the 'passionately ambivalent' way that characterized Joanna Baillie. Actual performance possibilities aside, Catherine Burroughs reminds us that closet drama is 'private' and non-performative only in certain ways and from specific points of view; Burroughs demonstrates how closet drama can be read to identify its intense engagement with politics, and professional issues of dramaturgy and theatre theory. Marjean Purinton states even more boldly that 'Closet drama is not escapist literature.'[3] Following Burroughs' and Purinton's lead, my discussion of the playwriting of

Augusta Webster and George Eliot is driven by the assumption that women writers continued to use the dramatic genre in order to thrash out issues of both political and aesthetic significance throughout the century.

By the 1870s, divisions between high and popular culture embedded in public discourses about the theatre had hardened into accepted wisdom and history. Women writers in the 1870s and early 1880s wishing to work in either drama (as genre) or theatre (as medium), or both, who were mindful of the proscriptions against the commercial theatre or lacked connections in the theatre industry, were hard-pressed to find an appropriate means of expression. The translation of continental European Naturalist and Realist playwriting was not to make an impact until the mid-1880s, and the political engagement in the popular sphere encouraged by the suffrage movement was a turn of the century phenomenon. Eliot and Webster found different ways to present ideas and themes in their poetic dramas, but, interestingly, their writerly judgements found that the dramatic form was an appropriate and attractive one. Of further interest to me is the comparison between the kinds of writers that Eliot and Webster became, through their lifetimes and posthumous reputations. Eliot's self-fashioning as sibyl, released from quotidian concerns of child-rearing and household management (much to Margaret Oliphant's disdain) to create her art, and her positioning at the centre of the canonical 'great tradition' of English literature, contrasts strongly with Webster's involvement in public political life, her homely and practical writerly character during her life-time, and her languishing reputation since. Both women were happily partnered to supportive husbands,[4] although Eliot was famously not married and conscious of her anomalous social position and its implications for her professional life. Webster, on the other hand, was open (in private correspondence at least) about the impact of house, wifely and motherly duties on her writing, as she tells Edmund Gosse that

> I don't think you are quite as much as half right about women not giving their whole souls to their art. They don't, but it is only because they are prevented. [...] I don't suppose I am the only woman living a happy life (so far as all else a woman can want for her best happiness goes) who knows what it is to feel a longing for a prison or a convent that she might at least now and then have the certainty of a half hour's unbroken time to think her own thoughts in.[5]

Given George Henry Lewes' involvement with the theatre as critic and playwright, it has always puzzled me that George Eliot's engagement with the theatre and drama was so ambivalent.[6] Of course, partners in life do not have to be partners (or even fellow-travellers) in art and work, and Eliot herself simply may have felt the reverse of Mary Russell Mitford's 'strong internal feeling respecting the drama.' It may also have come down to money – by the late 1860s she could not have earned enough from dramatic writing, and she would have known of Lewes' frustrating career as writing comedies and farces, fictionalized in the exasperated account of an aspirant playwright's travails in *Ranthorpe*. There was also the thorny issue of reputation and the problematic status of the theatre, and those writing for it, an acute concern for Eliot in many ways. However, other aspects of Eliot's life and work suggest opportunities for and a serious interest in the theatre. Eliot's use of performers, artists, and theatrical settings, and her use of highly visual set-pieces and theatrical *tableaux* in her novels,[7] as well as the more quotidian consideration that through Lewes, Eliot had 'insider' access to the London theatre industry, cause me to speculate on an imaginary body of work produced by George Eliot for the London stage. There are traces of this possibility in Eliot's biography, and ghosts of Eliot's dramatic impulse in her verse dramas, *The Spanish Gypsy* and *Armgart*.[8] However, the reputation Eliot sought was in contradistinction to the problem of the 'literary' on the English stage at this time, and her own anxieties about the 'production and circulation of bad literature' and her attempts to 'disengage herself from the literary marketplace she had conquered'[9] obviously mitigated against Eliot's entry to the commercial marketplace that was the London theatre. Poetry was one literary pursuit which (apparently) eschewed the requirements of the marketplace, and brought with it high cultural capital; it was also an activity in which serious women writers (such as Felicia Hemans) had excelled before – whatever might be Eliot's opinions of those writers. However, in what follows, I explore Eliot's attempts at dramatic poetry in *The Spanish Gypsy* and particularly *Armgart* as *drama*, and even as theatre, for an example of the way that even the most canonical of Victorian women writers found performance both irresistible and resistible.

The journey of *The Spanish Gypsy* from prose drama, written with an eye to the possibilities of its performance,[10] to dramatic poem was painful and difficult for George Eliot. Her anxiety about the piece, her research for it, and her struggle to find an appropriate form for this historical drama set in Spain in the late fifteenth century continued over several years, from her start on it as a drama in 1864 to its publication as a long poem in 1868. Eliot's biographers note her commitment to the project over several years,[11] and attribute its metamorphosis from drama to poem to Lewes' influence on Eliot's work, particularly his views as a critic 'of the incompatibility of art and amusement in the theatre,' and his opinion that Eliot 'lacked dramatic ability.'[12] Although *The Spanish Gypsy* became a long poem in what Isobel Armstrong labels the 'apparently "masculine" form' of 'dramatic-epic'[13] – a mixture of blank verse, verse dialogue, and even prose – the traces of its making in the biographical record suggest a sense of unfinished business with the dramatic form, to which Eliot returned in *Armgart*. With the publication of *Armgart*, Eliot seems to have solved some of her writerly concerns about dramatic form. This dramatic poem had no genesis in plans for an actual stage production, as had *The Spanish Gypsy*. In using the dramatic form, but clearly signalling its reading rather than performing status by publishing *Armgart* in the book *The Legend of Jubal and Other Poems* (1874), Eliot absolved herself from the kinds of compromises for stagecraft and stardom which Mitford had constantly made, the oscillations between page and stage which epitomized Baillie's work, or the sneering critiques which greeted Hemans' staged verse dramas. Gail Marshall comments that as a mature writer Eliot rejected the stage of her time as a medium, because of her fear of 'the body's potential for detracting from, even denying, the art of the playwright given prevailing performance conditions,' preferring to 'appeal to a discrimination which would embed the performance within an aesthetic and literary tradition, rather than remaining fixed in a moment of spectacle.'[14] Perhaps because of Eliot's own rejection of the stage, the sparse critical attention given to *Armgart* rarely considers the verse drama in the context of women's playwriting. Biographers read the piece as a poem, which, like *The Spanish Gypsy*, is seen as part of Eliot's 'creatively scrappy' middle years,[15] touching on Eliot's own experiences, but not as their 'direct expression.'[16] *Armgart* is seen to prefigure Eliot's concern with women, art, and performance in *Daniel Deronda* as exemplified in the character of the Alchirisi, or as a kind of prelude to writing *Middlemarch*.[17] However, perhaps *because* of the aesthetic and material considerations mitigating against the stage for Eliot, it is even more significant that she chose the dramatic form for a piece of writing which intersected the period of genesis and composition of the early parts of *Middlemarch*.

What happens when we consider *Armgart* as drama? The few literary critics who do so speculate on the freedom the dramatic form allows Eliot.[18] With *Armgart*, rather than weigh her down, as happened in the composition of *The Spanish Gypsy*, the genre seems to have liberated

Eliot to imagine a different kind of heroine in a narrative in which, as Rebecca A. Pope puts it, 'the diva doesn't die.' And Pope goes on to make an interesting case for the re-evaluation of Eliot's heroines in her major fiction based on the continuing artistry and agency she allows Armgart at the conclusion of the drama.[19] Kathleen Blake argues that the poem offers 'a double critique of the conflict of art and love for a woman,' in that it presents no easy solution to the profession/marriage dilemma in which Armgart finds herself, but that the conflict is not solved by 'the woman artist's contempt for her own sex.' Ultimately, according to Kathleen Hickok, Armgart is punished 'for her lovelessness and conceit,' not her ambition.[20] While acknowledging the importance of these feminist readings of *Armgart*, both for the drama itself, and for the light it sheds on Eliot's mature fiction, my analysis of the piece as a play below focusses Eliot's use of the possibilities inherent in dramatic dialogue and physical setting. My final point is to extend my discussion of the significance of Eliot's focus on the vexed questions of the place and fate of the female artist, through a brief exploration of the metatheatricality of Eliot's verse drama – that is, its use of performance within performance to draw attention to the constructedness of gender roles. In the light of Catherine Burroughs' detailed argument about Baillie's use of the closet drama as a form of theatre theory, and Burroughs' argument for seeing Baillie's plays as active interventions into the stage practices of her time, whether or not her plays were performed, we can see Eliot within a tradition of women's playwriting which uses the dramatic form itself to offer a critique of the aesthetic and sociological conditions of women's artistic practice.

The singer Armgart is starring in the formerly male castrato role in Gluck's *Orpheus* when the play opens.[21] She is looked after by her cousin Walpurga, and courted by the Graf Dornberg, who characterizes her as having 'Caesar's ambition in her delicate breast' (77). Armgart refuses the Graf's offer of marriage, declaring that 'The man who marries me must wed my Art –/Honour and cherish it, not tolerate' (111) and predicting that as a woman *she* would be the one who would have to give up 'that something else for which each lives/Besides the other' (107). A year later, Armgart has recovered from a serious illness, but the cure ruins her voice. Armgart accuses the Doctor of murder and protests at the lack of choice she was given:

> You never told me, never gave me choice
> To die a singer, lightning-struck, unmaimed,
> Or live what you would make me with your cures – (119)

But Armgart still refuses to think about marriage to the Graf. In a powerful scene of unusual frankness between two women, Walpurga taxes Armgart with her selfishness, and her attitude of scorn for ordinary women who wear the 'placid mask / Of woman's misery' (135). Walpurga's viewing of Armgart's loss of voice as 'a new birth – birth from that monstrous Self' (140) reconciles Armgart to a life of teaching other singers. She maintains her devotion to the principle of work, and tells her teacher Leo that she aims to pursue her work not for her glory but for other's delight: 'I would take humble work and do it well –' (146).

The dialogism of drama is central here to Eliot's exploration of possibilities for her female characters, as Eliot does not give us a play in which it is easy to empathize or identify comfortably with one character or another. Armgart's self-regard and scorn for more ordinary people are met by Walpurga's harsh truth-telling; if Walpurga has a point about Armgart's arrogance, Armgart is right in her protection of her great gift. Similarly, while Armgart's apprehension of being crushed 'within a mould / Of theory called Nature' (104) is all too accurate, the Graf's love for her is strong and persistent, and represented to us as of some value in his willingness to learn 'A more submissive speech' (105). Released from the formal necessity of a unifying narrative voice, Eliot is able to explore contrasting voices and points of view, without having to reconcile them, and although the play reaches resolution, it does so through a dialectical process of contending voices, without an active narrator, rather than Eliot's more familiar narrative webs of interconnection.

Armgart is short – just five scenes, in one setting, over the period of a year, and a cast of only five characters. Although published as a poem, and read – if at all – as a closet drama, it is firmly located in an imagined three-dimensional performance space, even if that space is not envisioned as a theatre's stage. The fictional setting is a domestic space, a private drawing-room, removed from the working spaces of the rehearsal room and the stage on which Armgart performs. Yet women's drama is often distinguished by its conception of domestic space in close relationship with working (or public) space, continually blurring the apparently sharp separations along gendered lines demanded by Victorian domestic ideology. The dialogue and action create an important relationship between Armgart's domestic space and her working space. The realities of Armgart's profession, and the effects of her talent, are present in her private salon and shape her personal and emotional life. Throughout the five short scenes there is an energetic sense of characters coming and going -- entering from and exiting to a wide and compelling world beyond the drawing-room, exemplified by the Graf's first entrance in travelling dress hurrying from the 'panting roaring steam' (76) of his train. The imaginative creation of spaces (theatre, rehearsal studios, trains across Europe) beyond Armgart's salon gives extra force to Armgart's sarcastic reaction to the Graf's suggestion that in marriage she would be 'Concentering your power in home delights / Which penetrate and purify the world' which Armgart translates as 'warbling in a drawing-room' (103). When Armgart loses her singing voice, and cannot contemplate even this limited arena of performance, the enclosure of the domestic and the poverty-stricken is played out through Armgart's sense of entrapment within the play's setting, and it is significant that the play concludes with Armgart deciding to travel. She will return with Walpurga to her home, but there is also a sense that she needs to escape the enclosing walls of the salon in which she celebrated her success. Her new resolve in life requires movement beyond her self-created world, and immersion in, as Rosemarie Bodenheimer suggests, 'the life of the uprooted, the marginal, the displaced.'[22]

To this strong sense of the physical space established by the play's dialogue and action, Eliot adds a powerful visual gestural language, creating a series of *tableaux* which encapsulate the action. On Armgart's first entrance she is muffled in a fur cloak, but then '*throws off her hood and mantle, and shows a star of brilliants in her hair*' (80) in a pose which echoes visually the triumph of her just-finished performance, and her place as 'the queen of song!' (80). Armgart's entrance in Scene IV after the rehearsal in which she realizes her voice has disappeared is a visual set-piece, which emphasizes how deliberately Eliot deploys the visual and gestural possibilities of the stage in *Armgart*.

> WALPURGA *starts up, looking towards the door.* ARMGART *enters, followed by* LEO. *She throws herself on a chair which stands with its back towards the door, speechless, not seeming to see anything.* WALPURGA *casts a questioning terrified look at* LEO. *He shrugs his shoulders, and lifts up his hands behind* ARMGART, *who sits like a helpless image while* WALPURGA *takes off her hat and mantle.* (116)

In this *tableau*, Eliot economically shows us the extent of the disaster, and the rest of the dialogue in the scene serves mostly to elaborate on this. The visual, plastic, and spatial possibilities of theatrical form allow Eliot to express extreme emotion instantly. Although, as Marshall argues, Eliot may have been wary of the contemporary stage because of the dominance of stage effect over language, and visceral sensation over thought, in the play she writes here, protected from considerations of *actual* performance, Eliot in fact stages a series of telling pictures which underline a powerful affective structure in *Armgart*.[23]

In choosing to write a play about a female performing artist, Eliot employs the framing device of metatheatre – that is, theatre about theatre. Robert J. Nelson argues that metatheatre in the nineteenth century turns the play into a confessional, by its melding of 'the man and the artist, the player and the role.'[24] That is, the representational frames usually separating the theatre and the extra-theatrical worlds are removed, and the continuity between the life of the performer on-stage and off is stressed. And it is in the plays about actresses where the confessional aspect of metatheatrical melodrama is strongest and also dramatizes most interestingly the Victorian ambivalence about the performance and theatricality of the self. In dramatizing a crucial episode in the life of a performer, which results in the singer's retreat from the public stage, Eliot plays out both her own ambivalence about self-display,[25] but also those concerns of her culture about female performance. By the simple moral economy of Victorian anti-theatricality, Armgart is punished for her presumption and ambition as a public performer by the loss of her voice. Yet Eliot's dialogism persists: although Armgart can no longer perform at the end of the play, she does not retreat into domesticity. Instead, she plans to pass on her knowledge to others in a continuing commitment to her art. Leo (her teacher) uses a maternal metaphor in consoling and encouraging Armgart in her new plan – 'Mothers do so, bereaved; then learn to love / Another's living child' (148), but Armgart speaks of her new vocation with the same indomitable ambition for excellence as she had for her singing. She plans to 'take humble work and do it well' (146). Armgart's skill and knowledge, potentially 'unfeminine,' are justified by her possession of a talent which is considered as a higher gift throughout the play. In this way, performance, and performing talent such as Armgart's, becomes an epistemological position, as Armgart knows the world through her music in a way that is beyond gendered conventions or expectations. As a confessional, *Armgart* is dynamically dialogic through Eliot's use of the figure of the female performer to interrogate the basis of gendered identity, and to suggest that the social codes of gender are themselves performances which can be challenged. The dramatic form gives Eliot the freedom to play both sides, without the 'explaining, moralizing narrative voice' of her fiction,[26] and her metatheatrical frame and focus on stage performance foregrounds the notion of self as a social performance. While Eliot's misgivings about the capacity of the theatre of her time to produce serious art may have kept her from dramatic writing for the theatre, in *Armgart* she appropriates key features of the stage to explore female identity in ways she could not through her narrative fiction.

Augusta Webster's writing career presents some striking contrasts to George Eliot's, not least that of the remarkable difference in their subsequent reputations. Eliot's position at the centre of the canon of English literature and Webster's invisibility exemplify the processes of hierarchization and exclusion that operated during their lifetimes and which have been slowly dismantled since the 1960s. Like Mitford several decades earlier, Webster's dramatic writing seems to have become invisible through a combination of bad timing in literary and cultural fashion, as well as meeting the usual obstacles to the recognition of any woman writer's work. Angela Leighton argues that in contrast with the model of sensibility she traces from Felicia Hemans, Webster was 'a determined literalist of the imagination [...] prosaic and dramatic.'[27] Dorothy Mermin describes Webster's poetry as 'forceful and erudite,' arguing that through her dramatic monologues, Webster 'vastly enlarges the range of voices through which women poets can speak.'[28] However, in spite of recent renewed interest in Webster's dramatic monologues,[29] there has been little study of Webster's drama, although of all the late Victorian literary dramatists, Webster was briefly judged to be most likely to be successful on the public stage.[30] Her dramatic writing was not part of the populist or commercial theatre I discussed in the previous chapter, and, in an irony central to the late nineteenth-century clamour about the literary drama, her plays were largely overlooked as possible renovators of the drama in the debates over Ibsen and Naturalism. The neglect of Webster – almost immediately after her early death – is another instance of the way Victorian aesthetic and cultural judgements still frame theatre historiography and literary criticism, as judgements of literary value or historical significance are made from within an already determined position, without a clear laying out of the biases inherent in it. My intention here is not simply to reverse this practice by exploring Webster's verse drama to reveal its hidden 'value' but to take seriously Webster's use of the dramatic form. To do this, I will look closely at her ambitious drama, *In a Day*, which as it happened *was* produced in a matinée performance, but received bad reviews in its one outing as a stage drama, although the critic does not give us any evidence or reason for his dismissal of the piece:

> The production at Terry's Theatre, at an afternoon presentation, of Mrs Augusta Webster's previously written drama of 'In a Day' only served to show that it is unfitted for stage presentation. Miss Davies Webster as the heroine showed histrionic possibilities.[31]

In focussing on an apparently 'unsuccessful' play, I am challenging a tendency in theatre historiography which relies on the 'unproblematic acceptance of theatrical production as the organizing principle of dramaturgical history,'[32] and literary criticism which accepts past judgements uncritically. Why should bad reviews *then* govern our critical and historical analyses *now*, over a hundred years after Webster's death, especially as we have come to see very clearly the gender-inflected nature of theatre production and reviewing?

In a Day (published in 1882, performed 1890) is set in ancient Greece under Roman rule, and continues Webster's pursuit of 'strong' poetry in the ideas and situations it presents. As Leighton points out, Webster's contemporary reputation for 'strength' tended to be a coded reference to her predilection for 'socio-political content,'[33] and *In a Day* is nothing if not politically engaged. But unlike her dramatic monologues, which approached difficult topics directly 'without subterfuge or apology,'[34] Webster uses the distancing techniques of historical drama as they developed in the nineteenth century: an exotic setting, emphasis on historical codes of honour, and a certain sensuous exoticism in its dramatic incidents. Although the play does not conform to the conventions of the 'toga play' as defined by David Mayer – principally, it is not concerned with the conflict between pagan Roman and early Christian culture[35] – Webster's use of the classical setting performs a version of what Bertolt Brecht was later to call the *Verfremdungseffekt*. By distancing his or her audience in time or space from the narrative, it is argued, the playwright requires the audience to withhold empathy (central to the Aristotelian dramaturgy of affect) and think about the issues presented via the plot, particularly through a series of dialectically opposed choices to be made. While neither Webster's political intentions nor her dramaturgy were so programmatic as Brecht's, her move from the direct contemporaneity of her lyric poetry to historical settings in several of her dramas does significant cultural and ideological work, particularly in her critique of ideas about freedom, honour, and knowledge, deriving from her own culture's gendered divisions and exclusions. Webster adroitly manages a balancing act between politics and poetics as she works within the conventional field of literary production to enable her visibility and acceptance (at least during her lifetime). Her use of verse drama and the dramatic monologue throughout her writing career are consistent with the general trends of unacted verse drama in the nineteenth century as defined by Shou-Ren Wang, 'by presenting both the external world of objectivity and the inner world of subjectivity.'[36] Yet, according to Susan Brown, Webster's dramas are constructed on the assumption that subjectivity is constructed through 'the processes of social determination,' and her dramas move between this understanding and the 'linguistic mediation of subjectivity.'[37]

As well as providing a forum for the dramatization of ideas about gender, love, and slavery, Webster's choice to set *In a Day* in ancient Greece under Roman occupation fulfils an immediate contemporary political purpose. Sixty years after *In a Day*, Virginia Woolf wrote that 'not knowing Greek' is not to know 'the literature of masterpieces.'[38] For Woolf, 'knowing' Greek was more than knowledge of the mechanics of vocabulary and grammar. It was a route to knowledge of the beginning of literature – in Greek 'there are no schools; no forerunners; no heirs' (12) – and its enduring resource. In Greek drama, she writes, we meet characters 'before their emotions have been worn into uniformity' (5). But as Woolf well knew, knowing Greek was an exclusive knowledge, reserved for young men. Even past Woolf's generation, Greek was the basis of the education of a 'gentleman,' but not that of a 'lady.' Not knowing Greek shut Victorian women out of the 'masculine' realms of poetry, acting as 'both a sign and a cause of [their] exclusion.'[39] Unusually for a woman educated in the mid-nineteenth century, Webster *did* know Greek. Yet this was not a result of her precocity nor her parents' advanced ideas; rather, it was justified in truly Victorian ideological terms of woman as helpmeet, as Webster learnt Greek to help her brother learn the language. She put her sisterly knowledge to good use, however, by publishing two well-reviewed translations from the Greek – Aeschylus' *Prometheus Bound* in 1866, and the *Medea* of Euripides in 1868, although the former was published with an 'Editor's Preface,' which provided, publicly at least, a male academic stamp of approval for her work:

> The reason why the title-page of this book bears the name of an Editor as well as that of a Translator is, that my wife wished for some better guarantee of accuracy than a lady's name could give, and so, rightly or wrongly, looked to me for what she wanted.[40]

I speculate that this was a strategic move, to silence contemporary critics who might doubt (Mrs) Webster's abilities in the masculine study of the classics, and indicates little about Webster's real confidence in her translations. Given that Webster persuaded her husband to leave his comfortable post as Fellow of Trinity College, Cambridge, and begin a new career as a solicitor in London, so that she could become immersed in London literary life, it is hard to imagine Webster needing her husband's imprimatur for her translation. However, the inclusion of her husband's 'Editor's Preface' does suggest that she was shrewd about the conditions of women's entry to the literary marketplace.

Given the Victorian cultural understanding of Greek as a 'masculine' language, Webster's choice of a Greek setting for *In a Day* already stakes out the territory of gendered knowledge and experience. The plot and characters she creates emphasize these themes. The play concerns a rich Greek of Achaia, Myron, who is also an enlightened man and master. He is shown to be on terms of equality with his slave, Olymnios, and Olymnios' daughter, Klydone (the part played by Webster's daughter Margaret in the play's one performance). The play opens at dawn of the day Myron plans to wed Klydone, his slave. The opening conversation between them immediately sets off the play's dialogue about freedom and slavery, placing these topics within the relationships between men and women underscored by socially constructed gender identities. Myron finds it easy to declare his love for Klydone, and does so throughout the play in often extravagant and exotic terms. On meeting Klydone at dawn going about her work on his terrace Myron protests at her 'fretful task.' Klydone protests, countering that

> That's a man's share.
> We women, even they that are not slaves,
> Have never leave of life to take but best:
> The best sweet flowers, and costing never a care,
> Are for the butterflies and choiceful bees
> And men like thee.[41]

Klydone's freedom of thought and opinion is clear here, as is the equality of minds between them in this encounter, in contradistinction to her social position as a slave. She emphasizes her freedom within slavery when she rejects Myron's love and offer of marriage; she taxes him with her position as his slave, while at the same time claiming her own type of freedom:

> I am thy slave. But never think to move me.
> Some rights the law accords me, this I'll hold.
> No truth, no love, no service, but a slave's. (5)

Klydone's apparent defiance of her master has something of Cordelia's resistance to King Lear, loving within her bond, but in Webster's tragedy (for the play *is* a tragedy by conventional definitions), neither Myron nor Klydone is represented as self-divided. Indeed, the tragedy of the play comes from external and social sources of oppression, linked to the Roman imperial domination of Greece, and unenlightened Roman views on the relationship between master and slave.

During their banter in the garden, Klydone agrees to marry Myron after he has promised to free her, and her father, Olymnios, before the wedding, to be held the next day. Olymnios remains sceptical, partly because of Myron's self-confessed desire to 'take life soft and loverlike, / So woo the sweetness of it' (8). Klydone, in a remarkable declaration of emotional freedom and power, after hearing Myron's praise of her, declares

> Thou hast heard him, father. I, had'st thou prevailed,
> Would call thy prudence best and bid him use it,
> And never would have wept. He should be judge:
> Does he need love, or all that thou hast said?
> Does he need one of those high dames, or me?
> Me, me, and love. His heart was in his voice. (10–11)

This opening scene sets the tone for the rest of the play: Myron's relaxed sensuality, Klydone's irrepressible confidence, and Olymnios' sternness and pessimism will all be tested by the political events of the play. In the following scenes, Myron is denounced as a conspirator against Rome; and in the strength of his innocence, he decides to answer the charge, rather than running into exile. His accuser, Lavinius, requires proof of Myron's innocence, and calls for the evidence of Myron's slaves. The evidence of slaves must be tested by torture, and knowing of their close relationship, Lavinius calls for Klydone and Olymnios to give evidence. Again, rather than flee Achaia, Klydone gives evidence, but cannot withstand the torture and betrays Myron. As the Roman guards surround Myron's house and garden on the evening before his marriage to Klydone, he and Klydone take poisoned wine, while Olymnios dies of grief, his strength dissolving suddenly, as Myron comments 'When sorrow swells these iron-pent hearts they break' (92).

These events are heralded in the first scene by the entrance of Myron's friend and provocateur, Euphranor, who attempts to involve Myron in an uprising against the Roman rulers of Achaia. Euphranor introduces another conception of freedom to those embodied by Klydone and Olymnios. To Myron's protest that 'Name me a ten, a half ten in our town, / Thou'dst trust to rule one street,' (19), Euphranor argues that

> We know them not;
> Nor they themselves – since how should they be proved?
> These marble stones we tread bind down the earth;
> Is the earth therefore barren in itself? (19–20)

Euphranor's conviction of the potential for all to be capable of self-rule is akin to Klydone's confidence in the freedom and equality between individuals granted by love, or her father's sterner doctrine of self-control:

> What is a slave, Euphranor?
> I, since my manhood, never was but free:
> More free than Myron; maybe more than thou.
> I am the master of my will; I rule:
> He but obeys himself and all desires.
> [. . .]
> I tell thee none can make me slave or free,
> None save myself. Freedom is of the soul:
> Bind my mere body, torture me, compel,
> Yet I am free, and 'tis but God can reach me. (16–17)

These complementary views of freedom are expounded by Webster's characters in relation to their commitments to love, and tested against the political events of the play. In Klydone, for example, Webster gives us an account of a character, enslaved legally, but – like her father – not mentally or emotionally. Indeed, so strong is her love, that she declares to Euphranor that 'I would liefer still be Myron's slave / Than empress of the world and not his love' (28). But her love is not all-conquering, nor is it passive in a stereotypically 'feminine' characterization. When the false accusation of conspiracy against Myron is known, it is Klydone who actively makes plans for Myron's release, and against his wishes goes to give evidence in his support. However, she fails in the test of torture, her father railing against her as a 'wincing mindless babe, / A crouching thing distraught by pain, and faithless,' but blaming himself for believing her eagerness and putting her 'unproved, unpractised, to the touch' (74). There is no uncontested position of sympathy allowed the spectator in this play – each character is presented making decisions which have consequences which contribute to the sequence of events. If Klydone's eagerness leads to Myron's betrayal, Myron's relaxed sensuality leads to passive complacency. Olymnios' stern creed of self-sufficiency cannot compass Klydone's pleasure in the world, nor recognize that her eagerness outpaces her strength. Euphranor's talk of uprising against Roman rule, while principled, is careless and dangerous. Thus, Webster uses the dialogic nature of drama to require her audience to think as well as to feel.

Webster's focus on issues of freedom, strength, and love pose questions about codes of honour and individual behaviour which the play encourages us to understand more broadly. The challenge to the concept of slavery, embodied in the relationships between Myron, Klydone, and Olymnios, and its parallels with the position of women, both in the fictional setting of her play and in its application to the world of her audience is clear. This is developed alongside Webster's discourse on honour, and honour, together with strength and freedom, is located in the characters of women and slaves. This feminist reversal of convention is exemplified in the contrast between Klydone's bravery and sense of honour and Myron's complacency and naïveté. Webster's reversal of the usual gendered binary of tragedy – that is, a plot structure based on the fundamental assumption of female passivity and foolishness and male action and honour – poses questions about other possibilities for the social organization of human life. Like Euphranor's argument with Myron over the potential of Greeks to rule themselves if Roman domination were overthrown, Webster's representation of female honour and action suggests the capacity of women to judge for themselves, take action, and behave honourably if given the opportunity. We are shown that if Klydone failed, it was not because of any constitutional female weakness, but as an immediate result of the cruel torture inflicted on her, and, more broadly, her socialization into a femininity which failed to equip her with the necessary mental or physical strength for her ordeal.

My point is an equivocal one. Eliot and Webster use the dialogic, defamiliarizing, and metatheatrical possibilities of dramatic writing to engage in what Isobel Armstrong calls 'a "masked" critique'[42] of the gendered ideologies of femininity and domesticity. Like the tragedies of Hemans and Mitford, Eliot and Webster's poetic dramas offer hitherto overlooked evidence for a feminist tradition in Victorian theatre writing. Yet the aesthetic 'burial' of their dramatic writing blunts the edge of their critique somewhat, by making their work invisible, notwithstanding critical discussions seeking to retrieve the power of closet drama. In the next decade, however, explicitly feminist engagement with the theatre, through a different mask – that of translation – offers a model of feminist activism through the theatre, although again at the cost of making other kinds of women's playwriting, particularly that of the mainstream theatre, once more invisible.

Translation, realism, and the New Drama

The 'New Drama' and the 'New Woman' coincided significantly in the London theatre industry in the 1880s and 1890s, particularly in the translation and production of plays by Henrik Ibsen. The promotion and production of Ibsen's plays in England intersected with the broader political projects of several women writers, actresses, and producers, for whom campaigns for socialist and feminist political change included aesthetic reforms in the theatre. The New Woman drama of the late Victorian period has been one of the few areas of women's playwriting to have received detailed attention from theatre historians and literary critics, perhaps because of the way it seems to prepare for the specific political engagements of suffrage drama, and for the ways in which the New Woman so neatly prefigures concerns of third-wave feminism from the late 1960s. I will not rehearse the broader themes and issues of New Woman drama here as they have been well covered by previous literary and theatre historians;[43] rather, I will focus on the involvement of Catherine Ray, Henrietta Frances Lord, and Eleanor Marx (known as Marx-Aveling until her death[44]) and her circle in the cultural importation and translation of Ibsen's drama to the English stage. The work of these women as translators, critics, and promoters of Ibsen's drama offers a brief study of the ways in which the largely masculinist movement for the New Drama – a literary drama of ideas – could also serve feminist and socialist political goals. In this version of the New Drama there is a partial resolution of those divisions, often so problematic for women playwrights, between the popular theatre and the literary drama.

Although much critical energy has been spent on tracing Ibsen's extraordinary influence on late Victorian English drama and theatre, it is rare for historians to comment that it was largely the work of three women which introduced Ibsen to English audiences. With the exception of Edmund Gosse's critical essays on Ibsen's poetry and *Peer Gynt* in the early 1870s[45] (which did not include translations of Ibsen), it was women writers and activists who first translated, performed, promoted, and produced Ibsen's plays in Britain. Of course, as Thomas Postlewait documents, William Archer became the central mover in the 'Ibsen campaign,' but it was the otherwise obscure writers Catherine Ray, and Henrietta Frances Lord (signing herself as Frances Lord) who provided the first translations, and Eleanor Marx who organized the first performance of an Ibsen play in Britain, as well as providing early translations of several Ibsen plays. Catherine Ray published her translation of *Emperor and Galilean* for Samuel Tinsley in 1876, and Frances Lord (who had spent 1878–1879 in Stockholm) published *Nora* (her translation of *A Doll's House*) in 1882. Of Catherine Ray there is almost no record (she appears in neither the *New DNB*, 2004, nor the *NCBEL*, 1999), other than her children's novels of German and Scandinavian life published after her Ibsen translation. This neglect was briefly acknowledged by an anonymous critic of the Charrington-Achurch production of *A Doll's House* in 1889 who noted that 'I have not noticed that any of the critics have mentioned the fact that Miss Ray was the first to introduce Ibsen to the English public. I am afraid she found that her efforts were not appreciated.'[46] Frances Lord's translation of *A Doll's House* survived for longer and more prominently, providing the text for Eleanor Marx's first staged reading of the play in 1885, but like Marx's own translations, was absorbed into William Archer's Ibsen project.[47] Lord also translated *Ghosts*, and was involved with the Christian Scientist and spiritual healing movements of the late nineteenth century – a combination of interests not unusual in this period of experimentation with alternatives to Victorian bourgeois lifestyles in which many of the 'Ibsenites' were involved.[48]

Catherine Ray's introduction to her translation, along with Gosse's essays, constitutes the earliest English-language analysis of Ibsen's theatre. Although Ray offers only *Emperor and Galilean* in translation, her introduction draws on her knowledge and reading of all Ibsen's work to the mid 1870s. She points to the two very different styles of Ibsen's work – his historical dramas and his romantic plays – noting that the 'difference between the two groups is great enough to warrant the supposition that they could scarcely be written by the same person.'[49] Ray responds to his work as poetic drama, finding in Ibsen's representations of male selfhood his explorations of the moral drives of character and action. *Brand*, she argues, is the story of 'a man who believes the voice within him is the only thing he has a right to listen to,' (52) and *Peer Gynt* 'is a sketch of a purely egotistical man' (53). However, writing before the publication and first performances of *A Doll's House* and *Pillars of Society*, Ray's critical analysis does not specifically focus on the sexual and social politics which later British commentators find so compelling in Ibsen, and Ray's interest in Ibsen's dissection of character stops short at relating his plays to the kinds of progressive social movements which caused such controversy a decade later.

Frances Lord's translation of *Et Dukkehjem* (*A Doll's House*), as *Nora*, first appeared in the *avant-garde* journal *To-Day* in 1882, and was then published independently with a long preface which included her analysis of *A Doll's House*. Lord views the play as principally setting out to tell the truth about marriage, which is, according to Lord, 'still an unsettled problem.'[50] As soon as 'a great and popular poet' writes about marriage, she writes, 'we see how little woman's own voice has been heard in other poetry' (4–5). Lord's approach is a feminist one, which values the play chiefly for its arguments about the inadequacies of late nineteenth-century bourgeois marriage, although her time spent living in Scandinavia gave her a clear sense of the controversy caused by the play on its first production. Lord's approach is theoretical as well as theatrical, and she develops in this preface one of the first of the *Doll's House* sequels, imagining that if Nora had not taken the initiative to leave the doll's house, twenty-five years later Helmer would stay a 'gentleman' but never learn to be 'a real man,' and that eventually 'His principles would dry up into mere maxims, his duty, honor, taste, and judgement into routine, till he ended in being one of those faultless persons whom no one would dream of exchanging ideas with on any subject, great or small' (17). Nora would become selfish 'with the self-ishness that is more or less in every natural woman's heart which, unchecked and suppressed, destroys either her whole woman's person-ality or the happiness and honour of all around her' (22). The bourgeois conditioning of men and women into gentlemen and ladies is, Lord argues, 'social murder whose results are most disastrous for human destiny' (20), and will remain so while society thinks it is desirable for a woman to have no soul (8). The trajectory of Lord's argument, and her imagining of a future for Ibsen's characters, indicates the way in which *A Doll's House* became a focal point for radical thought, and 'acquired an anti-establishment cachet.'[51] Lord's analysis typifies the response of British radicals of the late nineteenth century, who had as much interest in the extra-theatrical relationships between British progressive activism and what seemed to be Ibsen's radical feminism, as in Ibsen as a theatre artist.

Lord's translation was the subject of some decidedly territorial sparring between Archer and Lord; in a review of Lord's translation in the *Academy* (1883), Archer accuses 'the lady who has attempted an English version of *Et Dukkehjem*' of having neither good enough Norwegian nor English to 'reproduce the crispness and spontaneity of the dialogue,'[52] going on to 'suspect' that the translation was made from a Swedish translation of the original Norwegian (62). But his broader objection is to Lord's critical approach to Ibsen: having first damned her with the faint praise that 'the defects of her work proceed from lack of knowledge, not from want of care or enthusiasm' (62), Archer casts doubt on the 'so-called' (62) 'Life of Henrik Ibsen' with which Lord prefaces her translation. Archer retitles it 'Ibsen and the Marriage Question' and suggests that it 'may' help the reader 'though it be "through a glass darkly"' to appreciate the power of Ibsen's work (62). Lord replied briefly the next week, insisting that she had worked from the Norwegian original, and her dramaturgical practices were undertaken 'for the practical convenience of actors.'[53]

My aim here is not to weigh the merits of the various translations of Ibsen for their accuracy or dramatic quality, but rather to identify the cultural work done by the feminist-sponsored appearance of Ibsen's plays in London in the mid-1880s. Archer may well have been right about the quality of Lord's translation, but what I find more interesting is the difference in each writer's assumptions about the end and purpose of their translations. Lord's emphasis is on the play as a script for performance, and on performance as an intervention in the current state of relations between middle-class men and women. Archer is more concerned with introducing Ibsen as a 'prophet of the New Drama' (to use Thomas Postlewait's phrase), and protecting a literary approach to Ibsen founded on the principles of textual and aesthetic fidelity. His protectionism is of a piece with other campaigns for the advancement of the English drama, to which I have already referred, and which, in the 1880s, Simon Shepherd and Peter Womack argue, constituted a push to professionalize play writing in order to exclude certain types of writers and plays.[54] Archer's enthusiasm for Ibsen is put to work as a prescriptive model for an improved English (literary) drama and (realist) staging practice, as opposed to Marx and Lord's broader interest in Ibsen's plays as vehicles for social change. Additionally, Archer may have been exercised by a sub-conscious awareness of the gendering of translation as a reproductive rather than productive activity, thus attempting to counterbalance his pursuit of the 'feminine' reproductive activity of translation by an increased insistence on the 'fidelity' and 'chastity' of others' translations. If, as Lori Chamberlain argues, the cultural anxiety over translation from the late eighteenth century was because 'Translations can, in short, masquerade as originals, thereby short-circuiting the system' then Archer is employing a typically masculinist strategy to establish his own mastery in the apparently feminine arena of reproduction, by insisting on translations which do not 'threaten to erase the difference between production and reproduction.'[55] Archer's concern with correctness and authenticity smacks also of Victorian gendered discourse in matters of aesthetics, all the more ironic in this case because of Ibsen's interrogation of the moral basis of such patriarchal behaviour in *A Doll's House*. His masculinist boundary-riding simultaneously to exclude pretenders and to establish his own authority in professional terms, extended to his commentary on an amateur performance of Lord's *Nora* by the Scribblers' Dramatic Society in 1885, in a fund-raising evening for the Society for the Prevention of Cruelty to Children. Archer is roundly dismissive of audience, actors, and script, comparing the performance of Lord's translation of Ibsen to a performance of the 'bad' quarto of Shakespeare's *Hamlet*.

> Imagine the conception of Shakespeare which a spectator who had never heard of him would have received from this performance of Hamlet. As far, or further, from the truth is the conception of Henrik Ibsen conveyed by the Scribbler's travesty to the minds of those who witnessed it.

Archer concludes by again dismissing Lord's translation as clumsy, and stating that 'though I believe it has attracted attention in one or two narrow circles [...] it has been little noticed by the press, and has certainly not reached the general public.'[56] However, in an editorial act that seems designed to establish his mastery, Archer used Lord's translation, revised by him, in a volume of three of Ibsen's plays published in the Camelot Classics series in 1888, edited and introduced by Havelock Ellis.

One of the 'narrow circles' attracted to Lord's version of *A Doll's House* was that of Eleanor Marx and her common-law husband, Edward Aveling. Eleanor Marx is the third and most active of the women pioneers of Ibsen's work, and arguably, her 'version' of Ibsen is the most powerful in its influence on subsequent interpretations of Ibsen in

Britain, although it is William Archer who is remembered as Ibsen's champion. Rather than inhabiting one of the 'narrow' circles dismissed by Archer, Marx's life and work as an activist, writer, and feminist-socialist extended the concept of what it was possible for a woman to do in the late nineteenth century, and her work across a range of media and genres was a model of activism which was an influential precursor for the suffragette performances I discuss in the next chapter. And, like the other women I discuss in this chapter, Marx's engagement with the theatre of her time came from a passionate belief that the theatre was a significant art form which could play an important role in feminist and socialist movements for reform. Although Yvonne Kapp contends that Marx's various theatrical ventures were 'of no great importance to Eleanor,'[57] I would in fact argue the reverse: in a position where she had some choice of activities and commitments, Marx *chose* the theatre in several important ways. Gail Marshall's view that Marx's connections with Shakespeare 'straddle, or rather actively unite, both her personal and public political lives'[58] could apply more broadly to Eleanor Marx's involvement in the theatre and her work with several of Ibsen's plays. Like that other daughter of socialist radicals, Helen Taylor,[59] Eleanor Marx seriously investigated acting as a career by seeking training with veteran actress, Mrs Vezin in 1881. The usual disadvantages to middle-class women of going on the stage – loss of caste, hard physical work, vulnerability to sexual harassment – seemed either to have been negligible or outweighed in Marx's judgement by the independence, income, and intellectual exercise of the stage. Although Marx did not progress onto the professional stage (as Helen Taylor did briefly) her training was not wasted. Marx acknowledged the confidence and technique to move an audience she gained through her actor-training, and put it to good use in her later career as a political organizer.[60] Marx and Aveling and their circle (including George Bernard Shaw) were also involved in a series of amateur dramatic performances staged as fund-raisers for various socialist causes and groups.[61] However, it was Marx's commitment to Ibsen which was instrumental in bringing together her personal and political activities.

Eleanor Marx's letter to Havelock Ellis in 1886 inviting him to a reading of Lord's translation of *A Doll's House* as *Nora* is often cited as one of the defining moments of Ibsen's cultural translation into the English theatre. Inviting Ellis to a reading of the play in her Bloomsbury home, Marx wrote that 'I feel I *must* do something to make people understand our Ibsen a little more than they do, and I know by experience that a play read to them often affects people more than when read by themselves.'[62] Marx staged the play literally in her drawing room, with a cast of socialist luminaries, highlighting the personal connections upon which political networks in London were founded. Marx played Nora to her husband's Torvald, May Morris (William Morris' daughter) played Kristine Linde, and Bernard Shaw was cast as Krogstad. Recently, a number of critics have commented on the irony of Marx and Aveling playing opposite one another, 'convinced that Ibsen's "miracle of miracles" had already happened in their domestic Eden.'[63] Certainly, that same year Marx and Aveling had drawn on *A Doll's House* to illustrate their essay, *The Woman Question*, and the version of Ibsen's play they created in that essay contributed to their utopian vision of future marriages under socialism. Like Frances Lord, they imagine the marriage of a future Nora and Torvald, but unlike Lord, they describe a marriage of equals, in which husband and wife will be able to 'look clear through one another's eyes into one another's hearts.'[64] Their amateur production of Ibsen 'carried a frame of reference very much of their own making,'[65] typical of the way the 'Ibsenites' appropriated his work in London in the mid-1880s.

If this drawing-room production of a play about the necessity of leaving such claustrophobic spaces had an impact on a small circle of bohemian intellectuals, then several later events in which Marx was the driving force put the plays of Ibsen in front of a much wider audience. The first, in 1888, was the inclusion of her translation of *An Enemy of Society* (now generally known as *An Enemy of the People*) in Havelock Ellis' edition of three plays by Ibsen. Marx studied Norwegian specifically to translate Ibsen, and went on to publish her translation of *The Lady from the Sea* as a separate volume in 1890, followed by hers and Aveling's production of that play in a matinee at Terry's Theatre in 1891. Havelock Ellis' 1888 edition of Ibsen plays was seen by Ibsenites then, and historians now, as marking the arrival of Ibsen's work in the English literary consciousness. The lasting impression of Ibsen's work in performance in Britain was created by the first public season of one of his plays in London: Charles Charrington and Janet Achurch's production of *A Doll's House* in 1889. Again, Eleanor Marx was instrumental in getting this play in front of an audience – she and Janet Achurch approached Henry Irving for a subsidy of £100 for Achurch and Charrington to stage a comedy, *Clever Alice*. Instead, Marx and Achurch staged the first professional production of *A Doll's House*, at the Novelty Theatre. Irving saw the production, and according to his grandson, commented that 'If that's the sort of thing she wants to play she'd better play it somewhere else.'[66] With the help of Irving's hundred pounds, the production was a critical success, attracting what Sally Ledger calls 'a dazzling array of bohemians and intellectuals [...] an "alternative" and highly politicized audience' and a 'roll-call of New Women,'[67] and its short season lost 'only' £70. The production would have run longer if Achurch and Charrington did not have a commitment to tour Australasia, where they continued performing *A Doll's House*. Achurch continued to work with European avant-garde dramatists, producing her own translation (with C. E. Wheeler) of German Realist playwright, Gerhart Hauptmann's *The Coming of the Peace* in 1900. The Ibsen controversies continued, particularly after the first seasons of *Hedda Gabler* and *Ghosts* in London, but after her influential work in introducing Ibsen to her circle of intellectual and socialist friends, Eleanor Marx moved into a phase of intense activity as an organizer of the labour movement. However, her work as a translator of Ibsen, together with her earlier translations of *Madame Bovary*, her father's work, and that of Russian political writers places her as one of the most influential cultural mediators of the nineteenth century, drawing together the internationalist movements of socialism and feminism in Britain.[68]

Eleanor Marx, Catherine Ray, and Frances Lord's translations were quickly superseded, revised, or adapted in the movement to reform the British stage at the end of the nineteenth century. In the (often self-publicizing) hands of the reformers of the drama and advocates of Ibsen such as Archer and Shaw, the work of their female peers was set aside, and subsequent histories have continued this invisibility. This has had significant consequences for the orthodox historiography of British drama and theatre. The effect of Archer's promotion of Ibsen, in particular, was to establish a version of Ibsen in Britain mediated through Archer's preference for the well-made play, and, as Errol Durbach argues, Archer's attraction to Ibsen mainly as 'the champion of a fundamentally well-made form of Realism.'[69] Ibsen's poetic and epic dramas, such as *Peer Gynt* or *John Gabriel Borkmann*, have always figured less significantly in British Ibsenism, in contrast with Catherine Ray's discussion of the two aspects of Ibsen's work. But Marx, Ray, and Lord served Ibsen well. Their persistence introduced his work to an influential group of London intellectuals who began to see the potential of the theatre for circulating ideas for social change.[70]

How did Ibsen serve them? As is the constant refrain of this study, the answer to this question is a dialectical one, framed by 'yes, but...' Women's work as translators and disseminators of the New Drama was a double-edged sword. Well done, translation can be an invisible art, and one that was well-adapted to Victorian ideologies of respectable femininity.[71] Women as translators, especially from French and German – the feminine languages – were at the service of a master text, exercising their knowledge as facilitators, nurturers, and midwives of others' ideas, without intruding their own ideas or identities. But translation could also be a disguise, a mask, or a cover for the translator's own interests. Translating Ibsen (and likewise Mary Morrison's translations of German Naturalist playwright Gerhart Hauptmann, or Henrietta Corder's translations of Richard Wagner's libretti) enabled women to become innovators in the theatre, albeit under cover. The resurgence of interest in the last decade in Eleanor Marx's life and work has read her championing of Ibsen biographically, with various critics commenting on the ironic parallels between Marx's life choices (particularly her partnership with Edward Aveling) and the roles she played in the Ibsen campaign.[72] However, my intention here is to identify Marx's place (and to a certain extent her peers, Ray and Lord, although there is much less evidence of their intentions apart from their actual translations) in British theatre history as an innovator. At the end of the Victorian period, women theatre workers were central to a reformation of the English theatre, and, although it was in some ideological conflict with the popular tradition of women's theatre writing (a division the suffrage activists of the early twentieth century tried to repair), it is significant that it was in the service of late Victorian feminism that one of the major influences on British playwriting in the late nineteenth and early twentieth centuries was introduced to the London stage.

5
Home and Nation

In 1868, Eliza Lynn Linton wrote that:

> There is a great demand made now for more work for woman, and wider fields for her labour. We confess we should feel a deeper interest in the question if we saw more energy and conscience put into the work lying to her hand at home.[1]

In this chapter I want to explore the connections between women's work in the home, and their participation in that widest of fields, the nation, through the practices of the theatre. Although Linton fashions their relationship into a moral hierarchy, clearly valuing the claims of home over those of 'wider fields,' I want to explore the more complex interpenetrations of representations of home and nation in women's playwriting, and the interdependence of the material practices of home theatricals and the national stage. In doing this I will chart a double movement, as home theatricals brought the commerce and concept of performance into the home, and domestic ideology gave women the theoretical scope to participate in aspects of nation-making. Home and nation may at first appear to be diametrically opposed as concepts and places but they are linked through women's negotiations with and challenges to domestic ideology in the act of taking up the playwright's pen.

In feminist literary studies since the late 1960s, the truism that from the time of the French Revolution British social life was increasingly organized into the separate spheres of masculine public life, and feminine private life, has been immensely productive of important recuperative literary and historical work about women's lives and art. However, the tensions between the ideology of the separate spheres of life for men and women, and the reality of social practices of the late eighteenth and nineteenth century have also been regularly noted. Linda Colley argues in her overview of the role of women in the formation of the British nation state in the late eighteenth century that '[A]t one and the same time, separate sexual spheres were being increasingly prescribed in theory, yet increasingly broken through in practice.'[2] Anne K. Mellor pushes this view much further in her argument that histories of women's writing in the Romantic period founded on either an acceptance of the separate spheres of men and women, or later Habermasian notions of a public sphere limited to 'men of property,' are simply not supported by the historical evidence.[3] Mellor's argument, drawn principally from a study of the writing of Hannah More, and emphasizing the importance of women's writing on the stage as part of the public sphere, is supported by the archival work of Amanda Vickery, who is most vocal of all in her criticism of the acceptance of the separate spheres ideology as a description of the lived experience of women in the late eighteenth and early nineteenth centuries.[4] Mary Poovey has discussed in detail the effects of the 'uneven developments' of Victorian gender ideology, and found within it fissures and ambiguities: 'the middle-class ideology we most often associate with the Victorian period was both contested and always under construction; because it was always in the making, it was always open to revision, dispute, and the emergence of oppositional formulations.'[5] And in a study of mid-Victorian domestic ideology as it was constructed and contested through popular periodicals, Hilary Fraser, Stephanie Green, and Judith Johnston conclude that 'Our aim, then, has not been to demonstrate a seamless story of progress [...] but to read that narrative as comprising multiple and competing discourses.'[6]

And yet I keep returning to the power of these contested formulations of domestic ideology over women's conceptions of themselves as artists, and as the dominant criterion for evaluations of women's theatre writing. In looking at women who sought legitimacy and respectability as playwrights, it is clear that they went to some lengths to conform to hegemonic ideas of 'the female pen' wielded from 'the woman's place.' Michel Foucault has famously speculated that fictional discourse can 'induce effects of truth.'[7] Mary Poovey identifies the connections between ideology and subjectivity when she argues that '[B]ecause gender roles are part of familial, political, social, and economic relationships, the terms in which femininity is publicly formulated, dictates, in large measure, the way femaleness is subjectively experienced.'[8] Writing about women writers in the 1830s and 1840s, Norma Clarke similarly identifies the power of ideology to structure individual experience of subject status and public institutions,[9] and Catherine Waters notes the same influence of the powerful discourse of domesticity on lived practices in the mid-Victorian period in her discussion of the fictions of that most insistent of enthusiasts of domesticity, Charles Dickens.[10]

The domestic ideology which attempted to proscribe women's participation in the national, public, and political debates was also open to manipulation from within, and it is through these manipulations that I want to examine women's playwriting as it engaged with both issues of theatre within the home, and the connections with the public world of commerce that these brought, and with issues of the nation. Barbara Caine's analysis of the strategies of Victorian feminists as they worked from within domestic ideology frames my readings of the work of women playwrights in these areas. Through a reading of Sarah Stickney Ellis' *Women, Wives, Mothers*, and *Daughters of England* series, Caine argues that the power of the moral and educative mission enfolded within domestic ideology meant that 'the idea of "Woman's Mission" served at one and the same time to discipline women and contain their demands – and to offer them a vastly new and extended scope for action.'[11] The apparent moral and gender conservatism of domestic ideology was used by feminist agitators throughout the century, argues Caine:

> By emphasizing the connection between the female body and women's moral qualities, [...] feminists took up the construction of femininity evident in domestic ideology, but moulded it to their own purposes [and] established a basis for demanding political representation and female inclusion within the political world.[12]

In her popular series, Ellis' argument proceeds from the central importance of women's work as educators (as mothers, wives, or governesses) within the home, arguing in *The Mothers of England* that

> all the statesmen of the rising generation, all the ministers of religion, all private and public gentlemen, as well as all men of business, mechanics, and labourers of every description, will have received, as regards intellectual and moral character, their first bias, and often their strongest and their last, from the training and influence of a mother.[13]

This is a prime case of the continuance into the early Victorian period of that domination of the public sphere by 'the values of the private sphere associated primarily with women – moral virtue and an ethic of care' which Anne Mellor finds during the Romantic period.[14] And this, argues Caine, formed the basis of later feminist demands for good education, the preparation and opportunities for productive employment and independence from men.[15]

At the same time that Ellis was arguing for women's domestic duties as the foundation of righteous national governance, there is evidence that home performance (in its widest sense, including recitations and charades) developed as an important alternative to public entertainments. As Victorian middle-class anxieties about the maintenance of class difference through distinction and privacy were manifested in a discursive anti-theatricalism, home performance offered a solution to the perceived difficulties of public performance. The aesthetic value of theatre as 'art' could be appreciated in privacy with control over content and behaviour, and the desirable educational benefits of performing and spectating could be imparted safely to children. But home theatricals also involved activity and energy, and a study of women's domestic theatrical activities must recognize these 'hobbies' of women at home as work which connected the apparently domestic and private middle-class home with the commercial business of the theatre. While recent discussions of the popularity of home performance rest convincingly on charting the retreat into the home by the middle classes,[16] a study of the *actual* activities involved in home performance suggests that retreat was actually something of a mirage. In fact, home theatricals are revelatory of important work by women in creating the sociability of domestic and communal life which was essential for maintaining middle-class culture. Paradoxically, in their role in the creation and maintenance of the ideal of 'home,' home performances actually blurred categories of social space. Furthermore, I will argue that home theatricals, rather than helping us to track the Victorian retreat into domesticity, add substantially to other evidence of the extent to which the (private) home was imbricated in the (public) commercial world.

Plays for the parlour

The realities of performance within the middle-class home are discernible principally by the material traces left by these commercial interests. From the evidence of over forty published scripts by women writers specifically flagged as catering for home theatricals, the domestic market was actually targeted as a number of 'niches'. There are volumes of charade dialogues and scenarios, such as *Charade Dramas for the Drawing Room*, *Charade Plays for the Parlour*, and *Plays for the Parlour; A Collection of Acting Charades*. There are many volumes specifically designed for children, such as *Fairy Plays for Performance*, *The Doll Dramas*, *Dramas for Boys*, and *Little Plays for Little People*. There are a number of collections of scripts designed for women only, such as *Home Plays for Ladies*, and *Dramas for the Drawing Room*, and for male performers in series such as *Dramas for College, Camp or Cabin*. And there is a huge array of reciters, collections of poems, extracts, and addresses for home and amateur recitation.

There are few traces of the work of women playwrights in these niche markets, except for the scripts themselves, and the one exception of Florence Bell, whose combination of proper lady and professional writer I discuss in the following chapter. Of the other writers, Eliza Keating emerges as a typical playwright in this market, and demonstrates the versatility and productivity to cater for most of the specific groups of performers identified in Lacy's and French's series. Under series titles such as *Fairy Plays for Home Performance* and *Home Plays for Ladies* published by Thomas Hailes Lacy, she was a prolific writer for the home theatricals market, producing some eighteen collections of plays, mostly scaled down pantomime versions of fairy stories and charade dialogues, but including scripts in the *Dramas for Boys* and the *Home Plays for Ladies* series. Her work was probably first published in the 1860s, after some of her pantomimes were licenced for public performance in Brighton and Birmingham between 1858 and 1860;[17] but there is no official record of the production of her plays written for home performance. While it is obviously difficult to generalize about this range and number of plays, some trends emerge in Keating's style which are representative of material written for home performance generally. Most of her plays are comic and parodic, in the style that J. S. Bratton identifies as typical of the comic ballad for the Victorian drawing-room incorporating parody and punning in 'a distinctively Victorian comic mode.'[18] This humour is also the dominant mode of pantomime, and many of Keating's plays for children are, indeed, scaled down pantomimes. They omit the harlequinade, which was in decline after 1843 anyway,[19] and present a fully plotted fairy story – the 'opening' of the traditional pantomime. Obviously these plays do not contain the spectacular transformation scenes of early nineteenth-century pantomime, although some are quite elaborate in setting, in spite of authorial disclaimers of the simplicity of setting the plays in the parlour or drawing room. *Aladdin; or, The Very Wonderful Lamp! A Fairy Extravaganza in Two*

Acts, for example, contains the following stage directions which come near to the scenic effects of a mainstage transformation scene:

> *The Magic Gardens in perspective; a small lamp with a brass chain, on a pedestal in [the] centre. This scene may be managed by means of a painted background, representing rows of very formal trees with flat circles of gold, silver, red, green, and blue foil paper, to represent precious stones, stuck on here and there.*[20]

Although this scenery might seem fairly elaborate for improvised home performance, its intricacy and the embedded instructions for making it are typical of scripts for home performance. Other adaptations of fairy stories for children's performance include instructions for creating special costumes from materials available in the home: in Louisa Greene's *Nettlecoats; or, The Silent Princess*, there are illustrated directions for making Stork costumes from calico and newspaper cut and painted to resemble feathers, and for making the storks' heads from light basket work or papier mache.[21] Florence Bell also gives directions for making an ogre's or beast's head, in her book, *Fairy Tale Plays and How to Act Them*, which also includes a fifty-five page introduction covering acting techniques – both physical and vocal – costuming, make-up, and detailed directions for the dances to accompany the plays.[22] Elsie Fogerty's adaptation of Tennyson's *The Princess* 'Adapted and Arranged for Amateur Performance in Girls' Schools' is another script with substantial introductory instructions about casting, elocution, movement, singing, and music.[23] These informative introductions competed with a growing range of instruction books written specifically for amateur performance, which were advertised alongside lists of scripts suitable for or especially adapted for amateur and home performance.[24]

Notwithstanding these instructional addenda to playscripts, and the numerous guides to amateur theatricals later in the century, most drawing room plays assume that readers, home performers, and potential audiences are familiar with the conventions of mainstage melodrama, farce, comedy, extravaganza, and pantomime. The standard of performance assumed by the level of linguistic expression and theatrical business is high, and all plays call upon a range of virtuoso skills from their performers and arrangers. Most noticeable is the heavy emphasis on music and singing, and their integration in the performance. Eliza Keating's 'Fairy Extravaganza' *The Yellow Dwarf* contains fourteen cues to specific songs or tunes over its playing time of about forty minutes. The music ranges from a burlesque version of the folk song, to pieces from the *Beggar's*

Opera, to Mendelssohn's wedding march, to the vocally demanding and showy song 'I'll Be No Submissive Wife.' Similarly, *Aladdin* includes music from Haydn, Mozart, and parlour favourites such as 'Home, Sweet Home,' itself originally a theatre song. This would seem to be strong evidence for the interdependence of home theatricals and their place in domestic life with the public theatrical culture of the mid-century.

Domestic transgressions

But 'getting up' a play, while presented in the scripts and 'how-to' guides as wholesome and educative, could offer possibilities of transgressing the conventions of feminine and masculine sociability. As late as 1880, Mary Collier (Lady Monkswell) recorded in her diary that:

> We are now working hard getting up our play 'General Engagements' [...] We have had several most amusing rehearsing dinners & teas. Last night I declare it was a perfect orgy, the more Walter [Pollock, playwright and co-author of the play] embraced Marian [Collier, *née* Huxley] in the last scene the more angry Jack [Huxley, Marian's husband] became. I roared with laughter. I have a very small part, in which I make violent love to Jack so I don't mind.[25]

These sorts of dangers could operate to constrain women's involvement as actors or spectators, but were also opportunities for adventure which could be taken up with delight, as Mary Collier demonstrates (although of course, Jane Austen regarded the situation differently in *Mansfield Park* seventy years earlier). Augustus Mayhew gives a comic account of the improvisation and license allowed in presenting charades at Christmas time in the *Illustrated London News*.

> There is no difficulty about the acting. A little ingenuity and tact are required in rapidly dressing up the different characters [...]. At my uncle's, we always turned the front drawing-room into 'the house,' and made a stage of the back one. The folding-doors serve capitally for a drop scene. You have to ring a bell before you open the doors. It gives quite a theatrical allusion to the performance.[26]

What emerges from these accounts is that the preparation for performance was at least as exciting as the performance itself. Indeed, C. Lang Neil writes that 'the excitement and bustle of fitting up a play is an attraction in itself' and that the *esprit de corps* which develops is a tangible social good.[27] In their book of advice to amateur performers, the Pollocks also emphasize the enjoyment of participating in or observing amateur theatricals, in spite of the fact that it is a lot 'less trouble' to see 'the real thing' done by professional actors in a public theatre.[28] In these views of home performance, a licensed element of play is attached to the educative and decorative functions of drawing-room theatricals.

However, David and Susan Garland Mann argue that it was the possibility of educating through drama which attracted many women writers to experiment with dramatic writing from the last decade of the eighteenth century.[29] Discussions of the moral and social education provided by home theatricals also provide a record of upward social mobility. As class and social positioning gradually became less dependent on birth and inheritance, other ways to police and distinguish class hierarchies and differences became important. Speaking and moving well were among the markers of class and education to become significant in the nineteenth century, and the home was still the most important place for such education. In 1858, the *Illustrated London News*, that representative journal of middlebrow and middle-class life, carried a report of a lecture by a Mr D. Puseley, demonstrating 'how an entertaining evening might be secured by the domestic hearth' by recitation. 'The pieces recited were mostly his own, and were such as almost any gentleman of ordinary education could produce, and, therefore, such as might be readily extemporised at any respectable fireside.'[30] Anne Bowman introduced her charades as 'pleasant and harmless fireside recreations,'[31] and J. V. Prichard introduced his scenarios with the claim that 'foremost among the beneficial effects which the culture of Art has exerted upon society stands the successful production of a series of Tableaux Vivants, or Living Pictures.'[32] Florence Bell uses her introduction to *Fairy Plays* as an opportunity to deliver general strictures on the behaviour of children: 'Feet also appear to be extremely inconvenient parts of the person, especially those of boys.' Performing is seen as a way of teaching children deportment, 'an art' she writes, 'which they seldom master in private life.'[33] Thus, an apparently anti-theatrical class used a controlled form of performance practice to teach the signs of respectability and gentility, suggesting how performative and mobile these signs were in Victorian Britain. Furthermore, the transmission of these signs (both bodily and moral) was based on the employment of feminine accomplishments in music, speech, deportment, and handicrafts, which were transformed from apparently superfluous frivolities into the negotiable currency of respectability.

Home theatre and commercial practice

The educative work of women in the home, so encouraged by Sarah Stickney Ellis in general terms, was framed by a whole industry catering to amateur performance, either in the private home or later in the more public venues of amateur dramatic clubs. In most of the printed scripts designated for home or amateur performance, there are four to six pages of advertisements catering to amateur performers, ranging from advertisements for scenery in wallpaper-like rolls, to advertisements for scripts and joke books. These accoutrements to home entertainment point to the gradual transformation of Victorian society into a culture focussed on consumption and commodities. This is the contradiction at the very centre of the idea of the home as a place of refuge, a self-sufficient and self-sustaining environment, and emphasizes the theatricalization of Victorian social life – both public and private – in spite of anti-theatrical protestations throughout the century. The ideals of domesticity and the gendered separations of private and public life *do* underpin home plays and their accessories, but these are also part of a network of industry and commerce which services the home, and indeed, must necessarily do so in order to maintain the appearance of the home a special and separate place. The very act of publication challenges claims about the private nature of such work, and the evidence of an increasingly lucrative market for home and amateur theatricals further stresses the commercial reality of this activity. The plays also point to a whole area of previously unrecognised women's work, which has been labelled as 'hobby' or 'accomplishment,' but in the economy of the household and its improvement and entertainment, needs to be seen for what it is – work which keeps the private home connected to the public world.

Plays for the nation

Like the Victorian home, the nation was both a material place and a symbolic space. Benedict Anderson has pointed out the conceptualization of the nation through discursive practices as much as the materialities of geography and landscape, positing the nation as an 'imagined political community.'[34] But what theoretical and material space is made for women's playwriting in the history of British theatre in their encounters with 'the nation' as an imagined concept? Without the general acceptance of women's right to speak publicly on matters of national policy, any woman who did so was suspected of unwomanly behaviour and feelings, and so what she did say was discounted. But this is not to say that women did not find ways to participate in debates over national policy and national character. In what follows, I will explore a series of case studies of women playwrights' participation in the public sphere, through their playwriting on Reform politics, patriotism, and, that ultimate symbol of national participation, the vote.

Party politics: Comedy and reform

Maybe the domestic ideology theorized by Sarah Stickney Ellis was used by later Victorian feminists to argue for their economic and moral independence from men, but in the 1830s and 1840s in independence from men could be understood in many ways, not all of them publicly admissible, when Catherine Gore was active as a novelist and playwright. Like Felicia Hemans and L.E.L., 'Mrs Gore' was a prolific professional writer whose work supported her family, although she did not make a virtue or vocation of domesticity as did Hemans. Indeed, her reputation as a writer was quite the reverse of the domestic feminine 'corner of the table' or 'two inches of ivory,' an aspect of her career which caused her some difficulty, but also offered her some freedoms. Like Hemans and L.E.L., however, Gore can be identified as a Romantic cosmopolitan (to invoke Stuart Curran's description of L.E.L.),[35] who took Europe as her canvas (she wrote in and about Paris, Poland, and Hungary, as well as England and Ireland), and exploited the commercial opportunities of the new literary marketplace of the late Romantic period. Gore produced over seventy novels, sixteen plays, many pieces of journalism, as well as numerous contributions to the fashionable albums and annuals of the 1830s and 1840s, and also produced ten children. This combination of production and reproduction seems to have been the consequence of the contradictions implicit in early nineteenth-century constructions of femininity. Although her contemporary biographers do not state it outright, Gore wrote for money to support her family. Like many middle-class women whose playwriting was part of a broader writing career but were not members of theatrical families, Gore turned to playwriting because of a feckless husband. Having fulfilled her role as a 'proper lady' by making an appropriately respectable and prudent marriage to a Lieutenant Charles Gore of the 72 Regiment of Foot in 1823, Gore found her husband to be inadequate in the support of his family, and their move to Europe for much of the 1830s was in part to live more cheaply and enable him to pursue various business ventures, before he became an invalid and died abroad in 1846.

Gore turned the experience to good effect with her travel writing, tales of Poland and Hungary, and her pictures of high life in Paris, Berlin, and various European watering places. Her professionalism had to be carefully cloaked in the public performance of a lady, although as I have discussed elsewhere this character was also held against her.[36] Certainly, when she inherited a substantial property in 1850, she was less active as a writer. She is now best known as the author of a number of 'silver fork novels,' but she also wrote sixteen plays, including the 'Prize Comedy,' *Quid Pro Quo*. The discussion of Gore in Richard Horne's *New Spirit of the Age* is damning with faint praise of her 'teeming eloquence' and 'clever' and 'impudent' writing.[37] However, her plays were performed at the Haymarket, the Adelphi, and the St James's theatres, with managements and casts which made claims to legitimacy and high quality in the 1830s and 1840s. Such a position in the theatre industry suggests the success of her work in commercial, if not aesthetic terms, and of course, the debates over legitimacy, high culture, and the National Drama during the period of Gore's playwriting activity meant that her work was judged in this highly politicised and partisan atmosphere; as both Ellen Donkin and I argue elsewhere, in this respect her gender further told against her in contemporary critical estimations of her work.

Gore's pre-eminent status in recent studies of early nineteenth-century women's playwriting has largely come about because she won Benjamin Webster's prize of £500 for the best modern five-act comedy in 1843. The storm of protest which followed the revelation of her authorship of the play and the concerted critical damning of it in performance in 1844 have been offered in some detail as examples of the barriers to women's participation in the early Victorian commercial theatre.[38] More significantly, Gore's trials over *Quid Pro Quo* have led Ellen Donkin to question the very definition of playwright in this period. These are pertinent questions, but in the focus on Gore's difficulties over *Quid Pro Quo*, the success of her other plays, and their characteristic representation of contemporary issues has been overlooked. Very little comment has been made by theatre historians on Gore's novel writing, and the limited commentary on Gore's fiction almost completely ignores her work as a playwright. In what follows, I want to read Gore's writing in these two genres together in order to present her as a political writer, engaged with matters of the day. She wrote about parliamentary and party politics from the standpoint of a domestic ideology: in her comic writing about party politics and aristocratic society, Gore manages an ingenious negotiation between the maintenance of respectable femininity and political engagement. In Gary Kelly's words, she participated in 'refashioning the feminine for the revolutionary middle classes in distinction from models of transgressive courtly woman of the *ancien régime* and from transgressive plebeian woman of the widely publicized Revolutionary events of 1789 to 1792.'[39] While Barbara Leigh Harman argues that the woman's political novel dramatizes the 'points of entry' of women new to public life – often literally physical moments of entry or presence[40] – I want to investigate the ways in which Gore observed and commented on topical political issues from the more ambiguous position of a well-connected society woman. It is clear from Gore's private correspondence, especially her letters to the Duke of Devonshire, that she had access to the kind of aristocratic circles about which she wrote, as she passed on gossip to the Duke, asked his advice, sought his patronage for her son, and arranged visits.[41] But her novels and plays display a scepticism about this world, all the more cutting for her demonstration of insider knowledge.

As a political writer, Catherine Gore, as Winifred Hughes argues, 'touched a popular nerve [in her] open preoccupation with shifting class boundaries and insecurities' during the Reform period of the late 1820s and 1830s.[42] Hughes argues cogently for the 'radical instability of tone' of the silver fork school emerging at the 'crucial juncture of political and cultural emergence' of the middle class of the Reform era, citing Edward Lytton Bulwer's observation of the general political import of what he calls 'fashionable novels' which 'unconsciously exposed the falsehood, the hypocrisy, the arrogant and vulgar insolence of patrician life.'[43] This understanding of the context of Gore's work is important for what follows; so too is Gore's imbrication – knowingly or otherwise – in debates over reform of the national constitution. Her early plays and novels provide a commentary on those debates from a culturally feminine and domestic point of view, offering yet another version of 'National Drama' as an alternative to the masculinist, high cultural ideal promoted by the Whig 'constitutionalists' in the National Drama debates.[44]

Julie Carlson and Betsy Bolton place the analogy between theatre and the nation at the centre of their respective studies of Romantic drama.[45] For both of them, women – actual, represented, figurative – are the crucial connection between the theatre as a social space for the performance of fictions which reflect and reconstruct the extra-theatrical world, and the nation, as it is both imagined and constituted through legislative and institutional practices. Bolton explains what she calls 'spectacular nationalism' through a sketch of the history of the *theatrum mundi* concept in English political thought, arguing that after 1688, the English saw the 'playhouse as a microcosm of the state,' where '[S]pectacle made power visible,' (12) and that in the Romantic period, there was an 'ubiquitous [...] analogy between theatre and nation' (5). In their accounts of national theatres, Carlson and Bolton argue that the instability and liminality of the stage allowed significant gaps for the expression of female subjectivity, however contested. I want to read Gore in this context, although my study of her work will move from these rather abstract frameworks to an examination of the material practices of a working professional in an industry reorganizing itself in through the *laissez-faire* and entrepreneurial model of capitalism of the early Victorian period. What is significant is the central point of connection between theatre and the nation state, arising from a recognition of the import-ance of the theatre in the discursive construction of the nation; and the opportunities this situation offered for a writer like Catherine Gore to comment on both the state of the theatre and the state of the nation. In reading Catherine Gore within this context, I am further complicating concepts of Romantic theatrical nationalism, by arguing for a *popular* and *feminine* imagining of national community, which develops a comic vision of the nation-state, in conversation with, but not equivalent to, the high cultural discussions of the period.[46] In the nationalist vision of Gore's work, the female presence can be disruptive and contributes towards instability, but this is represented within the generic conven-tions of classic comedy, in which chaos is created so as to produce an improved order. Chronology and historical specificity are significant here too: by the early 1830s, the revolutionary impulses of the first generation of Romantic writers (or the reaction against them, *pace* Burke) are history themselves, and British radical thinking has moved from the enthusiasms of revolution and counter-revolution, to the discourses of self-improvement and constitutional reform.[47] Thus Gore, viewed as a late Romantic writer, offers an example of Romantic ideals as they are translated into a popular and populist vision.

The three themes whose connections I have outlined above: Reform, the theatre, and the nation are brought together in Catherine Gore's first (produced) plays in 1831, *The School for Coquettes*, and *Lords and Commons*.[48] Against Gore's reputation as a frivolous and inconsequential writer, I want to propose Catherine Gore as first and foremost a political writer, and one of the most successful of her age. These plays, and her novels of the 1830s, when read together, offer a unique insight into the Reform era, and particularly, aristocratic and non-titled genteel women's political roles in it. Gore's position was an interesting one – neither entirely an insider's nor an outsider's view. Her first performed play,

The School for Coquettes, was produced at the Haymarket in the summer of 1831, and ran in repertory through to October of that year with a revival in the next year – a success in anyone's terms.[49] The production rode the Reform excitement of the times, as the *Spectator* review mentioned that 'The epilogue, by Mr. BULWER, contained some clever illusions to the Reform Bill, which were much applauded.'[50] The *Spectator*'s comment, to be expected from a pro-Reform journal, contradicts evidence given the following year to the Select Committee, asserting that playwrights and managers tended to avoid direct mention of politics, and particularly Reform, because political agitation 'is one of the most destructive things that can be' for attracting theatre audiences.[51] Bulwer-Lytton's epilogue, spoken by Honoria, the heroine of the play, is underscored by George Colman's (the then Examiner of Plays) pencil in several places in the manuscript lodged with the Lord Chamberlain's office; although it is not the 'blue pencil' spoken of by playwrights as the censor's cut, it serves to mark the political points about which Colman was nervous as clap-traps for the actress.

> *Shall I reform, but gently – bit by bit –*
> And grow a very moderate coquette*?*
> *A change too sweeping should I not repent*?
> And after all, what husband is content?
> If once to please the wretch, I stoop to mend
> Say can you tell me where the thing will end?
> May not the creature next contrive to see
> *My weekly routes require a Schedule B!*
> May he not lop exclusive seats away –
> *And place the Opera under schedule A?*
> No yet content to curb my faults alone
> Ask universal suffrage for his own!
> Extend the Electoral franchise of his frown
> And bring my wardrobe to an annual gown?
> Well I must hope – and come what will –
> I'll stand – if you permit me – on the Bill* [Examiner of
> Play's asterisk here] (ff. 198–9)

The political interest of the play was not just articulated by the theatrical MP's epilogue: Gore's plot and dialogue brim with multiply-layered references to reform, and Bulwer-Lytton's epilogue just makes sure the audience has not missed them, as well as serving to provide a final moment of complicity between the audience and the actors.[52] *The School for Coquettes* centres around the young Lady Honoria, daughter of Lord Marston, a 'pounce and parchment gentleman' (f. 97) and member of the Cabinet, and 'tied to the drudgery of office, all the jealousies of ministerial distinctions, all the pestiferous slavery of Downing Street' (f. 100). While Lord Marston, Honoria's father, is lugubriously moralistic, Lady Marston is in exile on the Continent, deemed by her husband 'a heartless coquette!' (f. 102), fleeing his reproofs and her 'evil conscience.' While Lord Marston tried to bring up Honoria without her mother's apparent faults, he was too busy and worn-down by public political office to check 'those fashionable follies which betrayed her Mother' (f. 103), and although Honoria is married to the upright and moral Howard, she is still undomesticated in her habits, attending parties, flirting with other men, and generally refusing to settle down as a sober wife to Howard. While he is made abjectly miserable by this, and powerless to exert himself in the face of Honoria's apparently superior (sexual) power, Honoria confides to her cousin Frederick that she has been trying to make Howard jealous, but that, in spite of all her efforts, he maintains 'the most philosophical equanimity' even in the face of her flirting and dancing (ff. 127–8). She intends to continue the plot, by starting 'a most ostentatious flirtation' with Frederick to try to 'provoke him [Howard] to call you out!' (f. 128). Frederick has his own intrigue, having secretly married Amelia, 'the orphan daughter of an Englishwoman of rank named Ravensworth who bequeathed her on her death bed to the Ursuline Convent at Ravenna' (f. 129). Frederick must somehow find a way to gain his uncle, Lord Marston's approval of the marriage, in the face of his relatives' plots to marry him to heiress Caroline Hampton, whom Frederick describes in protest as 'a little missified, milk and water nonentity in a muslin frock!' (f. 122). As is the way in this kind of plot, Caroline is in love with Colonel Donnelly, an old friend of Frederick's, and for most of the play, we follow the quick-witted and insouciant Honoria's attempts to bring Amelia into the family circle, and advance the match between Caroline and Donnelly. The play's more serious moral theme is carried by the eventual revelation of Amelia's true identity as the daughter of Lord and Lady Marston, and Honoria's sister. The theme of reform is woven through the play as the reform of character and manners. In its more serious form, Lord Marston's reform is in his realization at the end of the play of the wrong he had done his wife in suspecting her behaviour; and in its comic form, the radical edge of reform is implicit in the ridicule of the 'exquisites' and 'exclusives' such as the pompous Lord Polter.

So 'Reform' is the basis of a good deal of punning and satire in this play, and Gore keeps returning to the idea that any national Reform must also involve the reform of manners and of the heart. She uses the character of Frederick, returning to England after a long sojourn in Italy, as a lens through which to view the upper echelons of aristocratic power as, for example, when he and Donnelly discuss Lord Polter:

I thought all that sort of exquisition and exclusiveness had become obsolete in good society? – that the great world had experienced a radical reform?

Donnelly. And so it has! – but the standing evils, you know, retain a vote for life. We have a few relics of the tape and buckram school – a Lord Polter or two – still extant, and it is proposed at the clubs that on their decease they shall be converted into mummies, and deposited at the British Museum as Zoological specimens of the extinct class of exclusives.

Frederick. It seems then, they will at length be of some use in the world? (f. 148)

Similarly, even the emotional and moral pointing of the final scene of family reunification is undercut by Honoria's light-hearted final speech:

Yes! my dearest sister your welcome home has chanced in a turbulent and anxious moment but it has at least enabled you to witness Honoria's reformation – and given you a useful lesson in the School for Coquettes. (f. 283)

That the radical Reforms contemplated by her characters are the reform of manners, of fashion, of love, and of polite society, but not explicitly Parliamentary, is part of Gore's allusive comic technique. In this play, and her next, *Lords and Commons* (first performed at Drury Lane in December, 1831) Gore sets up the reform battle as one which engages characters not only in the legislative debates of the off-stage world, but also in the inter-generational battles traditional to classic stage comedy. The topical nature of her comedies is recognized by reviewers who, although their opinions differ as to the quality of her plays, all agree that Gore's writing is spirited and lively, and almost lives up to her reputation as a novelist. Yet there is some caution about Gore's entrance into the scene as a playwright: as the *New Monthly Magazine* observes,

Mrs. Gore is the only female writer of the day who has indicated the capacity to produce a sterling comedy, representing the actual manners of the day, and the state of society out of which those manners spring. But Mrs. Gore has 'indicated' that capacity merely, not evinced it; and [...] not in the two comedies which she has produced. [...] Mrs. Gore may be assured, that to write a comedy is no slight task.[53]

The *New Monthly Magazine* goes on to fire a warning shot about women writing comedy, arguing that comic playwriting is as specialized as writing tragedy, with the implication that it is also, like tragedy, a male genre. Given this mixed reception of her early plays, which combined praise for her evident skills with an admonitory, pedagogical tone – telling Gore what she *should* do to write 'a sterling and original comedy' (*New Monthly Magazine*, 23) – then perhaps the general outcry when Gore won Benjamin Webster's prize for a modern comedy in 1843 should come as no surprise.

Although most press reviews judged *Lords and Commons* as less successful than *School for Coquettes* – which had, after all, an extraordinary success for a first comedy running over 30 nights in its first season – the topicality of its humour was never questioned. Indeed, *Figaro in London* points this out in its knowing puff for the play:

our friends the Lords and Commons, who are thus brought by Mrs. Gore, in a spirit of ultra-reform, into *one house*, as if more than one house of legislature was decidedly a superfluity. We hope we shall find that there will be a pretty *fair representation*, though we must not be too sanguine.[54]

In *Lords and Commons*, Gore explores the reforms of decadent aristocratic behaviour required by new forms of economic growth driven by the merchant and professional classes. She contrasts the prudent and hard-working banking families of Quotient and Melville, with a portrayal of the threadbare aristocrats, Lord Sauntington and Lord Martingale, whose aimless lives seduce the young Frank Melville and almost cause the ruin of his bank (run by his less flamboyant partner, Quotient) and his family. Frank is the protégé and adopted heir of Sir Caleb Cabob, a retired Indian nabob (played, according to the *Literary Guardian* by William Farren in capital 'spluttering' style)[55] who disapproves of Frank's dissipated habits and aristocratic hangers on. When Sir Caleb threatens to disinherit Frank, Frank's so-called friends desert him, but not before pressing him for payment of his debts (ff. 550–1). Of course, Sir Caleb's threat of disinheritance was part of a plan to teach Frank a lesson about the value of hard work, and in the final scene, Frank is revealed as the nephew of the snobbish Countess of Newford, who agrees to the marriage of her daughter Juliana with Frank, particularly on hearing that Frank is Sir Caleb's heir after all. Frank promises to change his life style and manners so that 'happiness and reformation are the order of the day! [. . .] my future assiduity and application to business shall merit all your indulgence!' (f. 566).

While Gore's political writing was wrapped in the conventions of social comedy for the stage, as a novelist she was free to approach politics directly. However, Gore's approach in her fiction remained superficially light, her situations and observations composed from the domestic point of view. Yet domesticity is never far removed from national politics and party interests. These connections are made explicit in *The Hamiltons, or The New Æra*,[56] in which the 'new era' is Britain in its post-Reform Bill state. The 'new era' is also a summary of the fate of Susan Hamilton, who starts the novel newly married wife to the son of a Tory peer, Lord Laxington, who sacrificed his entire family to his international political intrigues, so that, as Gore's omniscient narrator comments: 'thus, most unconsciously, the gentle Susan was made a scape-goat to the intrigues of a cabal of politicians' (Vol. II, 5). Writing from within the world of political power, Gore's narrator draws constant parallels between the intrigues of the Season and those of the Government, Parliament, and the battles between the Tory administration and the Whig ascendancy. More tellingly, the fate of Susan Hamilton and George IV are juxtaposed through the structure of the narrative, emphasizing – with quite pathetic effect – the heartlessness of political life, and its exploitation of the feeling individual. As the king lay dying, writes Gore, 'The Whigs were gathering in twos and threes; and the people hailed their appearance as that of the sea-birds which harbinger a storm' (Vol. II, 280).

> Meanwhile, in a remote room of that stately castle, whence expresses were now hourly despatched, with tidings of the decline of the king, and where every breath and every murmur was supposed to prognosticate a change, sat Susan Hamilton, watching over the cradle of a little helpless, dying child, – the extreme point of that awful chain of being which commenced in the chamber of Majesty. (Vol. II, 280–1)

Susan ends the novel as Lady Claneustace, married to the Marquess Claneustace, a reformed aristocrat, whose estate is a utopian model of benign government enabled by the post-1832 political settlement:

The admirable administration of the Claneustace farms, mines, canals, and rail-roads, is cited in parliament, and studied as a model by travellers of all nations; and the Marchioness has not only her own happiness to attribute to the love and protection of her husband, but indulges in the heartfelt joy of knowing the welfare of thousands to be secured by his interposition. (Vol. III, 318)

Throughout the novel the narrator's rhetorical and direct address to the reader (and so present and active is the narrator that it is hard to resist identifying the narrative voice as that of Gore) is constantly satirizing the decadence of the Tory aristocracy, and looking forward to the Whig ascendancy. Gore is by no means a Radical democrat, as her sympathies are firmly in the aristocratic Whig camp, and from this stand point she indulges in some stringent satirical criticism of 'Old Corruption' in both its legislative and social emanations. The connections between the affairs of high politics and the domestic lives of those same politicians are pursued in others of Gore's novels written in the age of Reform, although none of them links parliamentary Reform, social reform, and personal morality so systematically as *The Hamiltons* or her early stage comedies. But casual domestic discussions of cabinets and prime ministerships pervade her novels of this period, such as *Women as They Are*,[57] *Diary of a Desennuyée* (1836), and its sequel, *Woman of the World* (1838).[58] In *Women as They Are; or, The Manners of the Day*, Parliamentary politics is the essential background to the lives of the women of the title. Lord Willersdale's political troubles ('Catholics or Corn') form an important emotional pivot for the heroine, Helen, his wife, as Willersdale's secrecy about his political activities leads her to doubt his affection and trust. In *Woman of the World*, Gore makes specific reference to the political changes after 1832 in her Preface. After two years of 'strict seclusion' the *Désennuyée*, Mrs Delavel, re-enters London society, and the narrator – Gore's pseudonym 'H. Hartson' – takes the opportunity to comment on English society:

The coteries of the day differ in fact more extensively than they are aware of from the coteries of yesterday [. . .]. The splendid year 1838, with its crowns and sceptres, stars and garters, heralds and helter-skelter hopes and promises, is an era of deeper interest than its sallow, pensive, desponding elder sister; and as the human mind is roused to a more active exercise of its powers by the conflict of stirring events, the London of this passing month is not to be trifled with! [. . .] England is wide awake. [. . .] we have attained '*le commencement d'un commencement*,' an epoch of brightness, joy, and consummation. (vii–viii)

Here is Gore's own view of the transitional from late Romanticism to the early Victorian period: a post-Reform society inspired by its new young queen, eager for a more rational and well-ordered future.

In these plays and novels, including her prize-winning comedy *Quid Pro Quo* (1843), Gore shows the interconnections of domestic life, romance, high finance, and electoral politics. In her romance plots, Gore harks back to the sentimental comedies by Goldsmith and Centlivre of the eighteenth century; in her revelling in the absurdities of snobbery and ambition her model is Jane Austen – albeit much broadened. But her combination of these models and conventions of comedy with the sharp political commentary on Reform in *School for Coquettes* and *Lords and Commons*, or the election plot in *Quid Pro Quo*, is Gore's own, and rare to find in early nineteenth-century drama or fiction by men *or* women. Gore is particularly interested in the women who are connected with powerful men; women who, because of fierce social and legal constraints, were powerless to deal directly with the consequences of corruption but had to live with the results. And as a woman and a writer – an outsider to the direct exercise of power – but moving in circles with those who did wield legislative and economic power, Gore has a sharp satirical eye for the effects of power and money on their owners, and those caught in their turbulence. Read in this light, Gore's work provides a unique insight into the social and political landscape of the early Victorian period. It is an insider's view as her fiction, drama, and letters demonstrate an easy familiarity with the politics of making and breaking national administrations. In this respect, Gore's dramatic and prose fictions align themselves with the non-fictional role of aristocratic women described by K. D. Reynolds who argues that 'It is at [the] interface between the social and the political that the aristocratic woman found a role which, while having limited impact on the content of political discourse, was of immense importance in defining its context.'[59] And if her plays and novels sometimes read like stream-of-consciousness gossip, the 'great deal of smart dialogue,'[60] it is the insiders' gossip of the wives, daughters, mothers, and sisters of men in power.

Performance and suffrage

In turning to women's writing for performance in the suffrage cause, I move from a mostly discursive construction of an imagined community and an allusive, tangential approach to national politics to a set of direct, embodied, and material practices which sought to effect revolutionary change. Of all of women's work in theatre and performance in the long nineteenth century the work of the suffragettes (and their immediate predecessors, the New Women dramatists) is the best known, perhaps because their work most closely reflects the concerns of third-wave feminism since the 1970s.[61] And it was through the activism of feminists in the campaign for women's suffrage that theatre was brought squarely into the political realm, not least because, as Lisa Tickner points out, suffragists were interested in women artists' potential (and actual) 'autonomy, creativity and professional competence.'[62] In its exploitation of the theatre to question the conventions of Victorian femininity, suffragette theatre was the first 'agitprop' (agitational propaganda) theatre, although it has been overlooked in this context. Suffragette theatre moved performance from conventional theatre stages (although the AFL staged regular matinées in West End theatres), into meetings and lecture halls, pageants, street meetings, and semi-private meetings in homes and clubs, reiterating the early Victorian connection of the home and the nation, but this time with radical intent. The direct actions of the suffragettes – stone throwing, window breaking, newspaper selling, public speaking – created performances of protest, designed for both effect and affect in public spaces. Theatricality here was more than just the feigned 'show' which made many Victorians so uneasy – it was an attempt to provoke and express strong feelings (of outrage, disgust at men's hypocrisy and social injustice) when measured argument and change by constitutional means was deemed to have failed; this was the commitment to activism at the heart of the suffragette movement.

The show of suffragette performances was also important: suffragette spectacle emphasized beauty and decorativeness, because, as the Pankhursts argued, they did not have to become like men to have a vote like men.[63] Wendy Parkins has argued that dressing up and dressing well became crucial political tactics in the suffragist and suffragette campaigns, as 'suffragettes seized tactical opportunities for political protest from the everyday practices of modern life.'[64] Barbara Green finds in the public activities of the suffragettes 'a theatricalized and sensationalized femininity, catering to and challenging a public gaze.'[65] So the visible signs of class distinction and respectable femininity, usually marking the boundaries of proper female behaviour, were transformed into the tools of the political fight for the recognition of women as political subjects and citizens. Famously, women put their lives and their bodies at risk, from starvation campaigns and gruesome force feeding, to the heroic and martyred action of Emily Davison in 1913. Theatrical shock tactics in public, as well as more conventional forms of theatrical performance, gained an urgency and power from the juxtaposition of apparently decorous ladies, well-dressed and polite, with stone throwing, shouting, fighting women's bodies.[66] Ironically, what shocked Edwardian observers has sometimes blinded later historians of radical politics; the prevalence of signifiers of respectable femininity and middle-classness in suffragette demonstrations and public events (such as pageants) has subsequently worked against the recognition of these events as revolutionary political events in the post-1968 understanding of oppositional political spectacle and radical theatre.[67]

However much the suffragette movement in its public activism consciously rejected the previous forty years of constitutionalists' battles for the female suffrage, the 'spectacular activism'[68] of suffragette protest was not wholly cut off from the past struggles of the Victorian woman writer or artist. Suffragette activism, and the range of performances it encompassed, dramatized in striking terms women's negotiations with the constraints of the gendered domestic ideology of the nineteenth century. The emphasis on dress as part of the politicization of everyday practices was part of this recognition of women's past, and so too was the move to think back through their mothers, in suffragette analyses of the historical position of women. The suffrage fight gave women the theoretical tools to do this in a way that was not available to their feminist mothers and grandmothers. Elizabeth Robins focusses on this point in her speech 'The Suffrage Camp Revisited' in 1908, when she wonders aloud why '[t]hese excellent people [Sarah Stickney Ellis and Anna Jameson] failed to further the Cause they advocated.'[69] Her answer is that Victorian women themselves were flattered into believing the myth of the 'Exceptional Woman,' a concept used by male public opinion to cordon off 'those women whose capacity could not be denied' but which allowed all other women to be regarded as unfit to be involved in public affairs (65). Robins' answer to the divisiveness of the Exceptional Woman is 'Combination.' Robins, thinking and writing after her encounters with Ibsen and the Ibsenite socialists and feminists,[70] and in the midst of one of the most powerful British collective political movements of the twentieth century, had a theoretical framework within which to analyze the phenomenon of exceptionality which so bewildered writers such as Isabel Hill, Felicia Hemans, Catherine Gore, and Mary Russell Mitford. But her analysis does not reject the achievements of these women. Indeed, Robins was, like many other activists, concerned to continue the Victorian women's strategy of claiming power through the very domestic ideology which sought to control women's speaking positions. In her introduction of politics to the stage as a place 'from which they could begin to speak out of silence,'[71] Elizabeth Robins employed the tactic of staging the '"womanly woman" to score feminist points,'[72] giving a self-consciously oppositional edge to previously oppressive definitions of woman as object. 'How do they know what is womanly? It's for women to decide that,' states suffragette Ernestine Blunt in *Votes for Women!*[73] In their protests the suffragettes continued to claim the leadership in moral and spiritual matters claimed for women by Sarah Stickney Ellis in the 1830s and 1840s, transforming this into the basis of their demands for formal political, legal, and economic rights,[74] in a future 'reformed nation' in which women would take their place as full citizens.[75]

This is the context within which I want to discuss two short suffragette plays by Evelyn Glover, *A Chat with Mrs. Chicky* (1913) and *Miss Appleyard's Awakening* (1913) which, although republished recently, have not attracted the kind of critical attention I think they merit.[76] They are typical of the kind of short, consciousness-raising sketch which was often performed as part of a larger suffragette meeting. With the establishment of the Actresses' Franchise League in 1908 came the high profile offered by public performances involving well-known actresses such as Violet Vanbrugh, Nina Boucicault, Lena Ashwell, Eva Moore, Lily Langtry, and Kitty Marion, labelled the '*franchisseuses*, those fascinating women of the stage who made everything bright.'[77] Regular benefit *matinées* were a good way of raising funds and public attention to the suffrage cause, as we can see from the *Times* review of an event at the Scala Theatre in 1909 which judged the matinée to be an afternoon of 'real and sustained purpose,' or the *Era* review of the 'gratifying success' of the matinée at the Aldwych in 1910.[78] Inez Bensusan, in particular, saw the potential for playwriting in the suffragette movement, and set up the AFL's Play Department, recruiting established and aspirant writers to produce short sketches for performance in these matinées and for touring Britain as part of the job of enlisting women into the Cause.[79] Evelyn Glover was one of the writers Bensusan encouraged (Beatrice Harraden, Gertrude Jennings, Madeleine Ryley and Cicely Hamilton were others) to produce theatrical sketches and plays which could be performed in all sorts of circumstances.[80] In this milieu, Glover's pair of parlour sketches sit interestingly within two traditions of theatre writing: the parlour dramas of home theatricals, and agitprop. They were not pieces which attracted attention at high profile matinées. They are characteristic of the suffragette art which Katharine Cockin argues challenged masculine aesthetic standards and artistic practices by promoting 'collaboration rather than competition; removing the barriers between professional and amateur; and interrogating, if not rejecting, the aesthetic distinction between art and propaganda.'[81] Glover's plays have a similar feel to Brecht's *Lehrstücke* (teaching pieces) which he wrote to train his actors in the late 1920s: she writes short and pointed dramatizations of arguments and ideas, without complicated plots, sets, or performance styles, and the pieces served much the same purposes of training suffrage activists in public performance, and providing plays which brought together suffrage groups in a recognition of their shared purpose.[82] Glover's sketches use comedy to show how politics is inextricably intertwined with domestic life, and they mobilize conservative views of women to subject them to comic reversal and ridicule of the illogical ideas on which the anti-suffrage case was based. They use the methods of defamiliarization and dialectic which we now attribute to Bertolt Brecht, in the reversals of so-called 'common sense' and demonstration of the sound logic of the arguments for women's rights. Moreover, Glover emphasizes the suffragists' concerns with class, refuting the common criticism – both then and now – that the suffragists were privileged middle- and upper-class women interested only in their rights, and not the legal rights and economic conditions of working women. Working women take centre-stage in Glover's pieces, demonstrating greater wit, understanding, and logical thinking than their 'anti-' (women's suffrage) social superiors.

Both plays are set in drawing-rooms, represented as exclusively female domains of work and leisure. In *A Chat with Mrs. Chicky*, the physical work involved in maintaining the respectability of the middle-class parlour is made obvious, as Mrs Chicky *'with sleeves rolled up, skirts pinned high, etc., is discovered scattering tea-leaves from a jar on the carpet'* (105). She continues to sweep and dust – to comic effect – throughout the dialogue with Mrs Holbrook, the 'anti' whose brother employs Mrs Chicky. Mrs Holbrook speaks to Mrs Chicky with the automatic assumption of superiority, telling Mrs Chicky she wants to find out her views on Women's Suffrage, but actually wanting to tell Mrs Chicky what she ought to believe. But this is a character who cannot even get Mrs Chicky's name right, and reveals her utter ignorance of the political and social principles of the Cause almost every time she opens her mouth:

> The fact is that a few women who haven't got anything else to do have some ridiculous idea that they ought to have votes, and do men's work instead of their own and interfere with the government of the country, and if you and I and millions of other women who know better don't stop them at once we shall simply have England going to rack and ruin! (106)

Mrs Chicky's simple and affecting example of the poor woman whose baby died of pneumonia because she was not allowed by law to take her baby into her own warm bed – 'because Parlyament 'ad made a lor about it' (107) – confounds Mrs Holbrook, as does Mrs Chicky's knowledge that 'Votes wouldn't give women a bit of a voice in drorin' up the lors about their own affairs, then?' (108) or her heavily ironic observation that "Twouldn't never do for those as know most about 'omes to 'ave anythin' to do with fixin' rules for 'em' (108). Mrs Holbrook is bested in each of her pronouncements about the evils of women's suffrage by Mrs Chicky's pose of unassuming common sense, and her more varied life experience, from her marriage to a French man which makes her French (much to the surprise of Mrs Holbrook) to the experience of her soldier brothers who cannot have the vote, by which Mrs Chicky establishes that 'then the vote 'asn't got nothin' to do with fightin' for your country' (110). Mrs Holbrook's testy counter-argument that it is about men's superior physical strength is contradicted by the physical action of Mrs Chicky pushing Mrs Holbrook in her armchair bodily across the floor '*with perfect ease*' (110), and Mrs Holbrook's final parting statement that nothing will make her alter her mind is capped by Mrs Chicky's down-to-earth response:

> (*picking up hearthbox and dust-sheets*): Oh yes 'M., I've 'eard of that before. (*Pauses at door.*) You see 'M. my husband lived in France till just before we was married, an' *'e kep' MULES!* (113)

Mrs Holbrook is left open-mouthed at this piece of working-class impudence, but it is a terrific laugh line on which the actress playing Mrs Chicky (Inez Bensusan in the first production) exits, and allows the audience a final moment of complicity in their beliefs, expressed in a collective laugh at the bested Mrs Holbrook.

Miss Appleyard's Awakening goes further in showing the stages of conversion of a uncommitted woman into a suffragette through an encounter with the stupidity of the anti-movement. Mrs Crabtree calls on Miss Appleyard with the aim of getting her to sign a petition in support of preventing members of the Anti-Suffrage Society (surely the acronym is a joke in itself) from political canvassing. In the course of their conversation, Miss Appleyard comes to realize the illogical and contradictory elements of the anti-position. After Mrs Crabtree leaves, indignantly, Miss Appleyard calls for her servant, Morton, and asks for the Suffrage Society papers she had thrown away that morning as she has decided she now wants to read them.

Morton: I'll bring them, m'm. (*Hesitating.*) If you'll excuse my saying so, m'm, Cook and me think there's a deal of sound common sense in this Suffrage business.

Miss Appleyard (*slowly*): D'you know, Morton, I'm beginning to think it's quite possible you may be right!

Curtain.

As Carole Hayman comments, it is the classic scenario of the mistress being taught by the maid (116), and again typical of the suffragette interest in the representation of working-class characters in their own terms. It is clear in the interchanges between Miss Appleyard and Morton, and Morton and Mrs Crabtree, that Morton has a degree of autonomy that is unusual for a maidservant; this alerts the audience to Miss Appleyard's predisposition to conversion to the Cause. That she is revealed at the end of the sketch as the character most educated in suffrage matters reinforces the strong ethic in the suffrage movement of a commitment to the realities of working women's lives. From Annie Kenney's inspirational activism with factory workers, to the Pankhursts' intellectual and activist roots in Manchester Radical political traditions, to the outspoken and independent servants in Glover's sketches, suffrage activism sought to make visible the invisible labour of women on which all men and women relied. It is at this level of analysis that I take issue with Katharine Cockin's assertion that in these plays the 'narrative dynamic conforms to the promise that property-owning women would represent working-class women.'[83] In *A Chat with Mrs. Chicky* in particular, Mrs Chicky has all the good lines, where she can milk the audience's laughing response. And at a more serious level, the drama-turgical use of what Brecht would label the *Gestus* – the inscription on the actor's body or in her gestures of the socio-economic circumstances in which the character is placed – of the servant in *A Chat with Mrs. Chicky* makes visible the physical labour on which Mrs Holbrook's ordered world of bourgeois propriety is founded. It is a feature of the play's comic style, but also an important political *gestic* element of the play, that Mrs Chicky does not stop working throughout her dialogue with Mrs Holbrook. She sweeps, she dusts, she blacks the grate, she moves Mrs Holbrook bodily out of her way, she undertakes all manner of dirty and 'unladylike' labour, all the while appearing to defer to Mrs Holbrook's greater knowledge of the proper sphere of a woman, and her place in the world.

It is quite possible to read much of the future development of twentieth-century radical activist theatre nascent in these sketches. I have already demonstrated how one might read Glover's plays (anachronistically, as she was writing a decade earlier than Brecht) in terms of Brecht's principles of *Gestus* and dialectic to identify how Glover is making a space for the usually invisible woman to speak. We might also consider these plays in terms of Augusto Boal's liberatory dramaturgy of Forum Theatre and Invisible Theatre, where the contradictions of an oppressive social situation are revealed through improvised debates, games, and the staging of 'real' situations.[84] Forum Theatre requires the ability to imagine and then embody a different outcome – the maid instructing the mistress – of a social problem in fictional terms, so that the possibility of pursuing this scenario in the world beyond the performance is opened up, and the 'spectactors' (participant observers) have experimented with changing their behaviours and responses. Boal's Forum Theatre also requires his 'spectactors' to play their oppressors, and much of the humour of Glover's pieces comes from the relish we can take in the sheer awfulness of the antis, Mrs Holbrook and Mrs Crabtree. That relish must also be communicated by the actresses playing the roles in the comic spirit of revelation of ridiculousness, and a kind of Bakhtinian carnivalesque of female misogyny. In claiming a place for these plays (and in their name the many others Bensusan commissioned for the AFL Play Department) as constitutive of the radical performance traditions of the twentieth century, I am conscious of bringing a heavy weight to bear on a couple of short sketches. Yet I do not think that this is an overblown claim; these plays were part of a larger project of suffragette performative activism which moved astutely between a radical feminist vision of a future and an articulate understanding of the historical forces which produced the position of women as it was at the turn of the twentieth century. Thus the *Pageant of Great Women*, organized by the Women Writers' Suffrage League and the Actresses' Franchise League, in featuring iconic women of the past – some of whom, such as Hedda Gabler, might not seem such obvious feminist heroines[85] – celebrated the historical roots of a women's culture in traditional terms. By showing women what they had already achieved, it laid the groundwork for a later radical feminist self-determination in the light of a female tradition of self-representation.

Patriotism

The First World War presented a different kind of political crisis for women writers than that of Reform and the new Victorian era, or the campaign for the vote, as the momentum of the campaign for women's suffrage was halted, and women's work in the theatre, as elsewhere, was directed towards the defeat of the nation's common enemy. Specifically women-centred (or even feminist) concerns moved aside for national concerns. The public struggles of the suffrage campaign, which made women visible as active citizens and speaking subjects, were increasingly absorbed into the war effort, but not always with feminist arguments foremost, as Katherine Kelly documents in her analysis of the change in Inez Bensusan's Women's Theatre programmes in 1915 from overtly political pieces such as *Votes for Women!* to 'a more varied and light entertainment bill – the fare that would most often appear [...] before the troops.'[86] After 1917 the Women's Theatre seems to have left no record (Kelly, 131) and Claire Hirshfield argues that even by 1916 stalwarts of the AFL Play Department 'had begun to glimpse a future from which the cause which had preoccupied them [...] had vanished.'[87] Hirshfield notes that after the war, the drive of the suffrage movement to claim the stage for women as playwrights, actors, and producers, on grounds of equality with men, dissolved into a campaign for a National Theatre, and the impetus for 'drama as an appropriate vehicle for female liberation' diminished (135). However, women theatre professionals participated fully in war work, and whatever regrets may have been felt then by activists for the loss of the ideals of feminist collectivist theatre work and its material practices as forged by the Women's Theatre, the war had a central role in liberating women into public life. In this concluding section, I am going to look at one example of a forgotten woman playwright, whose war propaganda melodramas demonstrate how strongly the connection between women, the home, and the nation persisted, even under the unprecedented exigencies of the First World War.

Mrs F. G. Kimberley (and I have no other name for her) was a prolific playwright and managed the Theatre Royal, Wolverhampton (and later the Grand Theatre, Brighton) with her husband throughout the war. The company was very much a family concern, as Mrs Kimberley told the *Era* in 1913, involving herself as 'actress, authoress, manageress,' her husband, and their daughter, who at fourteen in 1913, was being 'carefully trained' as a singer.[88] The *Era* reporter rehearses Mrs Kimberley's achievements as a playwright for whose fifteen plays managers clamour, and as a busy manager of the Wolverhampton theatre and the various touring companies she and her husband have on the road. She admits to starting to write plays out of 'ambition [...] and perhaps a little petty conceit' in the course of her career as a singer and then dramatic actress. Here is the verbatim account of the career of actress- or wife-turned-playwright that I can only surmise for Eliza Planché, Mrs Cooke, Mrs Denvil, and Mrs Arthur Phillips, but whatever Mrs Kimberley's confidence in 1913, her career had a less than satisfactory ending in the 1930s, when she was rather desperately canvassing for work. Her letter to novelist and playwright Compton Mackenzie, of the Bateman-Compton theatrical family, sets out the sad story of decline after the War which must have been typical of theatre professionals engaged in the kind of populist melodrama which Mrs Kimberley wrote and produced.

> I am an old PRO and you may have heard my name as I have possessed many Theatres in my time and toured many Cos [companies]. I wrote my own plays for years and some ran years. With the advent of TALKIES came ruin. Bus[iness] went to zero and Banks got scared and called in overdraft. [...] I must earn a living and I cant live on dreams. I WANT YOU TO READ THE MS and tell me if you think it any use or hopeless to go on. I know my name is known to the popular public. as [sic] a girl I used to do bus with your Father and his partner Milton Bode to whom I am well known. [...] After so many years of management &c and affluence I feel my position deeply.[89]

But during the war, Mrs Kimberley's patriotic melodramas did good business. Plays with such stirring and sensational titles as *The Pride of the Regiment* and *A Spy in the Ranks* and *The Soldier's Divorce*[90] played successfully in the late years of the war, the Kimberleys making known their commercial success with an advertisement in the *Era* announcing the takings for three weeks of *A Soldier's Divorce* at £1575, and offering the production as a substantial attraction for other theatres to take on.[91] Although the Reader of Plays in the Lord Chamberlain's Office (in this instance Ernest A. Bendall) commented tersely that in 'this little melodrama [...] most of the characters are in the army or in love with men who are,' but that it was '[H]armlessly effective in its crude conventional way,' this rather snobbish summary does not do justice to Mrs Kimberley's ability to capture the democratic mood at the end of the war. The *Era* judges the message of the play to be 'right well' preached: 'nothing extravagant, simply plain, straightforward truth, but it is in the telling that the authoress excels, and she can certainly add this to her many previous successes.'[92]

What is striking about these three war plays is their ability to tap into a proletarian sympathy with the ordinary soldier, celebrating both the qualities of the 'Tommy' and his faithful wife or sweetheart, and introducing quite pointed attacks on the moral character of men and women of the upper classes. The Lord Chamberlain's Office notes this aspect of *The Pride of the Regiment*, calling it a 'simple-minded dramatic melodrama,' about 'a brave young soldier who gets his head turned by the adoration of a silly "society" girl for his khaki.' The reader concludes that '[T]here is no verisimilitude in the sketches either of military or of civil life; but there is no offence in the well-meant attempt to point one of the morals of the War.' However, *The Pride of the Regiment* raises the issues of personal and sexual freedom, bravery, and class in a remarkably open way, and Wolverhampton and London audiences were apparently more than receptive to the play's message.[93] Bobbie Hamilton, the 'Pride of the Regiment' who wins the Victoria Cross, is lured from his childhood sweetheart Betty by the aristocratic Hilda St Clair. Bobbie's father, a farmer, is wary of such class mixing: 'Let Society women stick to their Society men. Our class to our class I say. In my opinion they can't be mixed, breeds breed and what's cooked in the meat comes out in the dripping' (f. 11). The viciousness of the upper classes is revealed however, when Bobbie returns from his final battle permanently injured, and Ralph, Hilda's former lover, persuades her to reject Bobbie:

> the novelty has worn off. The Khaki lads are coming home shattered, limbless, in fact in all sorts of conditions. They are being discharged and in their civilian clothes they cannot hide their wounds and they sicken you. [...] you only see his scarred face, his injured arm and his coarse manners. (ff. 27–8)

To add insult to Bobbie's injury, Hilda tells him that 'You were a fool in your last battle to try and save that private Tommy and get yourself injured – marked for life' (f. 34). The play is remarkably frank about its characters' motivations, and this is particularly striking in its representation of the upper-class women in the play, who see the brave Tommies as their sexual playthings, attractive for their khaki uniforms and the virility they represent. Mrs Kimberley evidently knew her audience in industrial Wolverhampton and at the working-class Elephant and Castle theatre in South London. The play finishes with the desperate Hilda dishonouring herself to procure a divorce from Bobbie, who until this point has honoured his marriage promises to her. A letter is brought to Bobbie telling him that Hilda is staying at the Chadley Hotel that night as Ralph's wife. Bobbie reads the letter: 'I have tried in every way conceivable to make you break our marriage tie. I have failed. You working class are evidently stronger to honour than we are,' and in the final picture of the play, Bobbie is reunited with Betty, his childhood sweetheart who has waited patiently for him and is not repulsed by his war-damaged body (f. 57).

Official concerns were raised, however, by Mrs Kimberley's last war play, *A Spy in the Ranks*, where her standard class-conflict plot of a senior, upper-class officer betraying his working-class colleague, Ronald Lee, is in this case complicated by the fact that the upper-class officer, Captain John Culling (the name was later changed to Oppenheim in response to the Lord Chamberlain's concerns),[94] is actually an enemy spy, trained by his German parents

> to serve my Kaiser as they serve their country; I have lived here all my life, but I serve my German land, here I am disguised as an Englishman, here I can find out so much & send it across to my friends and serve my country, that is why I hate this Ronald Lee, I hate him as I hate all British. (f. 11)

Culling's betrayal is both in battle and sexual, as he seduces Lee's wife, Miri, a woman he rejected before the war, heartlessly telling Miri's friend, Barbara that 'My people belong to the great social world – entirely different. She was a good girl, she's a good wife, and – there you are' (f. 3). On the evidence of another working-class soldier, Griggs, Culling is denounced as a rapist and a coward, as Griggs recounts how he found Culling:

> with a pure straight young girl in his billet, she was crying, crying for help and I gave it, I saw her safely away, and she thanked me. He cursed me – he swore vengeance on me, and By Heaven he had it. (f. 20)

In this melodrama, the resolution is not found through divorce and the restoration of pre-war affections, but the death of Culling, stabbed by Griggs who avenges the false accusations made by Culling against the innocent Ronald Lee.

The settings rarely move to the front (although *A Spy in the Ranks* offers an exception to this general trend, with its sensational scenes in No Man's Land), concentrating instead on the domestic contexts of the soldiers' lives. Indeed, Mrs Kimberley's plays dramatize the situations of the women left behind during the war, focussing on their moral and emotional struggles with the consequences of war. As I have noted already, there is a remarkable sexual frankness in these plays, as men and women declare their desires openly, and there is a matter-of-factness about the incidence of divorce. Whereas the highly emotional melodramas of Lucy Clifford or the society comedies and dramas of Lucette Ryley or Pearl Craigie hint discreetly at departures from the norm of monogamy, in Mrs Kimberley's plays successive rearrangements of the central couples in each play – and her plays are structured around at least two sets of couples – are a standard part of each plot. However, for all the sexual freedom represented in these plays, Mrs Kimberley's female and male characters rarely step out of stereotypical feminine and masculine roles; the women are either good and faithful working-class girls or upper-class temptresses, while the men are steady working-class soldiers, or upper-class men who generally avoid doing their duty for their country. So the conventional connections between class and morality in melodrama, as noted by Michael Booth and Peter Brooks,[95] are not disturbed in these plays, although the emphasis is significantly shifted. The working-class characters are no longer 'helpless and unfriended' victims of aristocratic tyranny;[96] rather, the plays show these characters, including the women, exercising choice and control over their lives. Furthermore, for all the emphasis on duty and patriotism as a motivation for action in Mrs Kimberley's plays, there is little of the jingoistic sentiment about Britain and Empire that Michael Booth finds in the 'Drury Lane imperialism' of the 1890s.[97] None of Mrs Kimberley's plays reinforce the pre-war order; indeed, they dramatize a world in which the class and moral certainties of the Victorian period are swept away, and a new era of self-determination by young working-class men and women is presented on stage. This is stated overtly in *The Pride of the Regiment*, when the Squire's son asks that his father's employee, now his equal as an enlisted man, stop calling him 'sir.' The Army, it seems, levelled social difference in a way that peace time political campaigns never did: 'Surely all the time we have been in training you have had time to forget I was ever sir to you. [. . .] I know you far more now Bill as a man than I ever knew you as one of our employees' (f. 6). Read as political plays, Mrs Kimberley's melodramas offer a grass-roots approach to democracy and a model for post-war Britain as a meritocracy, where individuals will rise or fall according to their moral characters.

Two central issues emerge throughout the variety of forms and approaches women use in writing about and around specific political questions. One is the issue of genre: across the century, women habitually used varieties of comedy and melodrama to approach topics of national importance directly. In earlier chapters, I have shown how the cultural capital of five-act verse tragedy and poetic drama allowed women to interrogate fundamental questions of national importance, such as national principles of freedom and democracy, but for the discussion of immediately topical issues women playwrights resort to the popular genres of comedy and melodrama. The equation of cultural capital with authority and legitimacy, expounded in different ways by Pierre Bourdieu and Loren Kruger, seems in this case to be balanced against the opportunity for insouciant and direct topical commentary, its impact deliberately disguised by the use of less authoritative forms and genres. Evelyn Glover can 'hide' her critique of women's misogyny behind the ridiculousness of her play's situations and their farcical physical comedy, and Catherine Gore can disguise her critique of 'Old Corruption' with the trivialities of fashionable drawing-room comedy. My second theme is that of the dialectical relationship between domesticity and the nation, as it plays out in the treatment of political topics, and this is very closely related with my first point about populist genres. The theatre is an hitherto overlooked area for what Hilary Fraser and Judith Johnston identify as the intersections and contradictions of 'the political public domain of national government' and the 'political private domain of domestic government.'[98] In the comedies and melodramas I have discussed, the domestic is invariably constructed in the face of the national, and women's experience of being caught between the two realms is dramatized either in comic subversion or melodramatic over-statement. As Isobel Armstrong points out in her study of Victorian poetry, 'the politics of women's poetry in this century cannot necessarily be associated with the uncovering of particular political positions but rather with a set of strategies or negotiations with conventions and constraints.'[99] This is also the enduring story of women's playwriting throughout the nineteenth century, and reading its political trajectory is in part a matter of tracking the ways in which women playwrights negotiated and subverted the constraints of respectability, 'ladyhood,' and professionalism. The use of domestic settings from which to approach debates about the nation – as in Gore's synecdochic use of the reform of individual manners to stand for the reform of structures of governance – and the dramatization of the domestic behaviour of women and men as having national significance – such as Mrs Kimberley's explorations of patriotic principles through the actions of ordinary individuals – point to women playwrights' use of populist genres to represent the authentic, lived experience of their audiences. This is the point Sheila Stowell makes in her rehabilitation of realism for feminist political ends, identifying in the feminist theatre of the suffragette period a powerful use of realism for political purposes, in contradistinction to feminist scholarship which suggests that realist modes occlude oppositional critique.[100] What these trends add up to, I propose, is an awareness in women's playwriting about national political issues of the democratic principle of paying attention to the lives of ordinary people and specifically attending to the voices of women, in theatrical languages and forms that also emerge from the popular and the ordinary.

Conclusion: The Playwright as Woman of Letters

In 1908, Elizabeth Robins used the language of collective political action to declare war on the 'Exceptional Woman' for the sake of all women's progress, rather as Virginia Woolf later wrote about the need to murder the Angel of the House to enable women writers to work freely. In this concluding chapter, I want to look at the careers of some women who worked outside the framework of the 'Exceptional Woman' or 'exceptionality' as it was constructed earlier in the century: writers of the second or third rank (if we're counting this way) who included playwriting as a normal part of their 'portfolio careers' as professional writers, or as Susan Croft titled her bibliography *She Also Wrote Plays*.[1] Florence Bell, Florence Marryat, and Lucy Clifford were all successful playwrights, whose reputations rested largely on other work, and in this way are representative of many other women in the literary marketplace at the end of the century. Apart from Florence Bell, wife of industrialist Hugh Bell, these women made their livings of necessity by their writing. They were all well-connected, educated, middle- and upper-middle class – indeed Marryat was at various times quite a wealthy woman through her work – and all were vitally interested in the theatre, both as another avenue for income and professional recognition, but also for its own sake. A love of theatre for its own sake is a complex cultural and psychological mix of impulses and desires not to be overlooked, and in spite of the obstacles in their way, women playwrights sought the desire for immediate and palpable fame that could come from writing a successful play, the promise of a quick and lucrative financial return if the play were a success, the sense of community and even surrogate family that could develop in the process of getting that play staged, and the importance of the catholic and more democratic audience which the commercial theatre served. At a more quotidian level, acknowledging the extent of women's theatre work is particularly important in the latter part of the Victorian period, as it was a growth area for women's writing. Plays written in the 1890s account for almost half of women's output as playwrights over the century, and this trend is in line with the increase in the numbers of women working in other 'non-traditional' fields in the theatre as documented by Tracy Davis.[2] In the last decades of the nineteenth century, women engaged in the public life and work of the theatre with increasing confidence, and a growing sense of the political significance of their increasing visibility in the public sphere.

Florence Bell

When Florence Bell (variously known as Mrs Hugh Bell or later, Lady Bell) adapted Elin Ameen's story as the play *Alan's Wife* with Elizabeth Robins for performance in 1893, she was already in the middle of a successful career as playwright and essayist. Robins wrote of her in *Theatre and Friendship*:

> Lady Bell was moving quick and vivid among us so recently – writing and godmothering her great Yorkshire pageant; editing the letters of her step-daughter Gertrude Bell; occupying her place in the front row on London First Nights – that I feel it a blow to the continuity of life itself to be told she is already little known to the general public and not known at all (as Henry James and I knew her longest) under the name of Mrs. Hugh Bell. [...] I have never lived so close to a woman of so many gifts and interests.[3]

As Robins notes, Bell was an energetic and busy woman, doing the unpaid work of running a large household which included several relatives of her husband, the industrialist Hugh Bell, upholding the public position of 'Lady' required by her husband's business and social position, as well as maintaining a steady output of writing across a wide variety of genres. The range of Bell's work reveals her to be a truly professional writer – a woman of letters – able to move from translations and adaptations of French plays, to children's literature, to sociological essays for the French journal *La science sociale*, and English journals on a variety of topics, from personal memoirs to informed and detailed studies of working-class reading habits. As well as *Alan's Wife*, Bell's claim to 'serious' literary attention is derived from her pioneering observational work of sociology, *At the Works* (first published in 1907), subtitled *A Study of a Manufacturing Town* – Middlesbrough, where her husband's iron works were based. The close observation of what Bell calls 'a piece of prosperity'[4] (in post-industrial Britain it is salutary to remember this late Victorian view of Middlesbrough) in Bell's account of working-class life in *At the Works* is also evident in her earlier essay (1905) 'What People Read' on working-class reading practices,[5] and her play *The Way the Money Goes* published in 1910, and produced by the Stage Society in 1911.[6] But we should not overlook her other writing, including over fifty plays – one-act comedies, chamber comedies, dramatic sketches, plays for children, and translations. Bell thought theatrically first and foremost, evidenced by her output and by the constant stream of ideas, comments, and plans on her own and Robins' theatrical writing projects in her private papers.

The striking thing about uncovering Bell's career as a writer and particularly as a playwright is how hidden it has been for someone so prolific, capable, and broad-ranging. There is one obvious reason for this, which does not reflect well on literary scholarship, and that is the lingering assumptions about the likely achievements of and interest in the work of a woman of her class and background, perhaps supported by Bell's own commitment to the conventional roles of her gender and class. She was a member of an extended upper-middle class family, and married into one whose wealth derived from heavy industry. Her principal public image was of the wealthy society matron, and photographs of her suggest she had a formidable presence (supported by Angela John's account of her in the *New DNB*).[7] But after reading her plays in the light of that portion of her private papers preserved for us, I want to suggest that this was a disguise. As well as running her large family home and fulfilling the social obligations of the wife of the principal employer in the area, Florence Bell was also involved in some of the most interesting intellectual projects of the late nineteenth and early twentieth centuries. After all, as well as her own sociological investigations, Bell was the editor of the letters and papers of her step-daughter Gertrude Bell, the explorer, and collaborated with Elizabeth Robins on the translation and adaptation of that ground-breaking feminist play, *Alan's Wife*.

Alan's Wife was first produced at the Independent Theatre, on 28 April 1893. The Independent was a theatre set up in protest against the continuing censorship of the Lord Chamberlain. As a private subscription theatre, the Independent was exempt from the stringent blue pencil of the Lord Chamberlain, which so dogged other playwrights of the New Drama at the end of the nineteenth century (Bernard Shaw's

problems with *Mrs Warren's Profession*, for example). *Alan's Wife* tele-
scopes three major events in the life of Jean Creyke – the wife of the
title, played by Elizabeth Robins – into three scenes, so the effects of her
actions and emotions are amplified by this contraction of fictional
time. In the first scene Jean is happily awaiting the birth of her first
child, but the scene ends with the news of Alan's death in an accident
at the works; in the second scene Jean has given birth, not to the fine
sturdy boy in the image of his father about which she had fantasised in
the first scene, but to a deformed child, whom she bravely decides to
kill, so that he will not have to be as she says 'hideous and maimed, [. . .]
stumbl[ing] through this terrible world.'[8] In the third scene, Jean is
facing her death by hanging, unrepentant, but certain of the rightness
of her action. As she says in her penultimate speech:

> I've had courage just once in my life – just once in my life I've been
> strong and kind – and it was the night I killed my child![9]

As Catherine Wiley comments, representations of the New Woman
tended to end in either the marriage or death of the woman at the end
of the play, her disruptive presence necessarily erased by the law of the
father.[10] A twenty-first-century feminist reading has no difficulty in
seeing how Bell and Robins subverted this tradition by representing
Jean Creyke's actions as comprehensible and not the result of
madness,[11] and her death as noble and demonstrative of her integrity.
Furthermore, as Elin Diamond argues, the play destabilizes 'the conventions of realist texts, [and . . .] insist[s] on the untranslatability of a
woman's (body) language before the law – the law represented by the
dramatic fiction and the representational law of realism.'[12] Both Wiley
and Diamond focus on the extreme effect Robins' performance and the
play as a whole had on William Archer's friend and Ibsen-influenced
critic, A. B. Walkley, who argued in *The Speaker* that the play 'ought
never to have been written.'[13] Walkley was apparently so shocked as
to insist that he saw the bloodied corpses of both Alan and Jean's
strangled baby, when both Robins (in private) and William Archer (in
print) denied that such a staging was done. As Diamond and Wiley
argue, such a response creates a male hysteric of the critic, no longer
able to rest in the patriarchal assumptions of the stage's legibility and
legitimacy.[14]

Other critical responses were not so extreme – perhaps, ironically,
because other critics were not so invested as was Walkley in an Ibsenite
call for stage realism and reform, and so could revert to critical judgements

based on moral and aesthetic criteria familiar throughout the century. *The Theatre* called *Alan's Wife* 'a remarkable play' and an 'appalling tragedy' but goes on to maintain that

> although it satisfies these requirements of art, it must be set outside the boundaries of art, as too pitiless, too painful a reflection of the facts of life. [...] Hopeless, harrowing, horrible, the tragedy proved distressing in the last degree, and called forth some passionate protests against the exhibition on the stage of the crude horrors of existence.[15]

It is unclear here whether the reviewer is referring to voiced protests in the auditorium during the performance – no other review mentions this – or registering his own response in his review. The review is full of praise for Elizabeth Robins, however: 'While she was on the stage, it was impossible to call in question the reasonableness of her actions, and the impression created by the piece, a very extraordinary and ineffaceable impression, was almost solely due to her inspired performance' (p. 335).

The *Athenæum* carped that they had expected different sorts of plays from the Independent – plays which might evade decorum to 'tickle the ears' of subscribing matrons and maids – and, one might add, titillate prurient *Athenæum* reviewers with hints of forbidden flesh and intimations of libidinous passions they could only dream of. But instead, 'we may have too much gloom. Even on the West Coast of Ireland it does not always rain.'[16] The discontented reviewer judges the play too 'shudderingly nude' and 'revolting' in its truth of detail to 'pretend to be a play' (p. 582). Elizabeth Robins is praised for her 'great feeling and force,' but the *Athenæum*'s review maintains a general air of peevish disappointment at being shocked in the wrong kind of way. The *Times*, too, finds in the play 'a tolerably large admixture of that element of the gruesome without which the studies of the "new school" are seldom complete. It is a sketch of artisan life done in the darkest colours.'[17] The *Era*, in an otherwise anodyne review, is also full of praise for Elizabeth Robins, judging her to rise 'to a fine height of tragic expression' in the child murder scene but is critical of the play, on both moral and aesthetic grounds. The piece is called 'eccentric' in its structure and 'amateurish' in its form, and opines that 'the process of artistic selection has not been employed in the proportioning of the three acts.' The *Era*'s final judgement of Jean Creyke is not the outrage of Walkley, but rather, the taciturn statement that Jean is 'simply an ignorant, cruel, and presumptuous person.'[18]

While Robins' writing and performance in *Alan's Wife* mark her as a feminist forerunner, as does, indeed, the whole pattern of Robins' life – her suffragette work (over which she and Bell disagreed), her economic and sexual independence, her writing of *Alan's Wife*, *Votes for Women*, and *The Convert* – the work of her collaborator, Florence Bell, requires further attention. We can recognize in Robins a set of concerns which fits the pattern of third-wave liberal feminism. Bell's professional career requires a different framing, and one which can accommodate her domestic concerns, her sense of the social obligations arising from her position and wealth, and her production of the ephemera of theatrical and literary life: children's books, one-act farces, her community pageants, her children's plays and fairy plays, her essays on how to entertain at parties, and conversational gambits for every occasion. Catherine Wiley's otherwise intriguing argument about the transference of hysteria from the female performer's body to the male critic's body in the case of Walkley's response to *Alan's Wife*, almost completely erases Florence Bell's intellectual (if not bodily) presence in the play, and indicates further difficulties about Bell's class position, which supposes Wiley, 'must have prevented real communication between her and her subjects' in Bell's work on women's lives in Middlesbrough.[19] Such a judgement seems based on a superficial assessment of Bell's life and work, particularly in the light of her pioneering work as a sociologist, about which Deborah Epstein Nord comments that Bell arrived at 'an understanding of the project of social investigation rare in investigators, male or female.'[20] According to Nord, the trajectory of Bell's investigation in *At the Works* leads her to shift her enquiry onto the role of the middle classes in national family and reproductive life, '[T]he gulf between classes and the investigator's distorting objectification of the working class have become apparent to her through the affiliation of gender' (230). In what follows, I want to read Bell's work in the context of her domestic and social class position, looking at how she was able to combine her two worlds – one concerned with the new literature and ideas of the *fin de siècle*, the other with charity bazaars and Red Cross garden parties. A central feature of Bell's life as a woman of letters was her close friendship with Elizabeth Robins, and the mutual support evident in their relationship from Bell's first invitation to Robins to appear as a reciter in a charity bazaar in 1891; 'enthralled' by Robins' performance of Hedda, Bell writes that she 'shd like to go constantly!'[21] The focus on Robins as a radical New Woman and feminist in the pattern of a late twentieth-century feminism is entirely understandable – she was one of those women whose heroism enables us to speak and write and vote as we wish now – but to focus on Robins at the expense of Bell is to ignore the evidence of a long collaboration and intellectual partnership between Robins and Bell, as well as an important friendship which sustained them both.

> Tomorrow we are all going off for an expedition into the Oezthal till Monday. Molly and I are coming back that day, the others are going on. I rather doubted, in fact, if we shd start with them at all as itd be a load off my mind if I cd finish the French book this week – Its nearly done. But when I foolishly told Hugh the cause of my hesitating, he said 'Dont make the mistake of making a burden of a pleasure' (meaning the writing) After all youve come away for a holiday. Yes I thought but the holiday is from the housekeeping and the works and arll sarts!! Still I see that I mustnt present this occupation of mine too seriously – Tho it has its comic side that tonight for instance when I have C-Carrs [Comyns Carrs] letter, yours saying of Heinemanns possibility, and one fr Arnold, that I must still keep up the fiction that it *must* be done in a trifling ladylike manner at odd moments or it will be taking it too seriously![22]

> Oh Lisa [Bell's name for Robins], I cant help thinking how blessed it must be from his point of view of writing to come and go at one's own will! because it is sure to come back to you all the zest in it, and everything else, when you get into the atmosphere in which you have written before. – Im at this moment feeling desperate at the way that life ties me round – oh if I could go away some where and hear nothing and have to do with nothing! but that is not how life is arranged.[23]

Like Augusta Webster, Florence Bell was often in despair over the incompatibility of her multiple lives. It is in her letters to Robins, informal and unfettered, that she can unburden herself about the strains of pretending that her writing is 'trifling' rather than the central concern of her inner life. Bell's friendship with Robins, like many between women with children and those without, gives her a safe space in which to admit to the busy mother's heretical fantasy that perhaps she would rather not have children and a husband. Yet we can read the results of her immersion in the 'ladylike' part of her life in her series of popular and well-reviewed one-act comedies, such as *A Joint Household*, *Time is Money*, *In a Telegraph Office*, and *An Underground Journey*, seeing them as a documentation of the female culture of late nineteenth-century

London, and imbricated in the developing networks of collaboration between women theatre workers in this period.

Bell's play *A Joint Household* lays out the difficulties of house-keeping for comic effect, at the same time reminding us of the importance of female friendships; the play itself is situated in a network of professional and personal relationships. It was first performed at Steinway Hall, London, on 13 March 1891, with Henrietta Cowen (who also wrote plays) as the overbearing Mrs Smithers, and Elizabeth Robins playing her hapless friend, Mrs Tallett. The play is a frivolous comedietta which makes a joke of a bossy and hypocritical woman, Mrs Smithers, who ruins her husband's plans for a joint household by the seaside for the summer, with his friends, the Talletts, by her overbearing and suspicious behaviour. There is a delight, however, in the awfulness of Mrs Smithers, and the sweet and ladylike revenge that Mrs Tallett wreaks, by – accidentally on purpose? – handing Mrs Smithers a letter to Mrs Tallett from Mr Smithers, asking Mrs Tallett not to mention to Mrs Smithers that he, Mr Smithers, had once proposed to Mrs Tallett – before she became Mrs Tallett, that is. It is the sort of farcical situation just this side of *risqué* that English drawing-room comedy is founded on. What is such fun in this piece is that, like so many other plays of this sort by women playwrights, the domestic trivia of life are placed at the centre of staged representations of women's lives, and largely for women spectators. It might be a power exercised through domestic tyranny, and it might not be a subject position that we are at all comfortable with now, but in Bell's domestic world we see women without men taking the stage. And in an account of women's playwriting over the century, these domestic female bodies need to be translated just as much as the subversive body of Jean Creyke in *Alan's Wife*.

Like many other of Bell's one-act comedies, such as *Time is Money*, *In a Telegraph Office*, *Between the Posts*, and *An Underground Journey*, *A Joint Household* was repeated, including a performance with two other of Bell's one-act plays, *In a Telegraph Office*, and *Between the Posts* at the Sloane Square Parish Hall, on 11 May 1893, less than a month after the (anonymous) premiere of *Alan's Wife*. Of these plays, and the difficulty of doing them justice, the *Era* writes that they are 'like most of Mrs Hugh Bell's pieces, [...] slight, sketchy, and amusing. Indeed, a mere outline description gives but a poor idea of one of these smart *saynètes*.'[24] One of the other plays in this bill, *Between the Posts*, was first produced as *L'Indècis*, and was well-known as the play in which the fashionable French actor Coquelin played. The *Theatre* called it 'an exquisite piece of comedy' at its first performance in 1887.[25] *Dramatic Notes* commented that, 'It was no small compliment to our countrywoman that her little play was so brightly written, and contained such lively sallies of wit, that M. Coquelin accepted it to play the title *rôle;*' the review going on to note 'the call for the author at its close.'[26] Bell's lady-like cosmopolitanism in her command of French, usually regarded as a decorative female accomplishment of upper-middle-classness (Angela John records that on first meeting her son's fiancée, Bell spoke to her in French to assess her accent)[27] here enables quite a professional *coup*. The neatness and entertainment value of Bell's one-act comedies is acknowledged in a review of *An Underground Journey*, also first produced in February 1893, a month before *Alan's Wife*:

> Mrs Hugh Bell has no need to rush all over the earth, after the fashion of most writers for the stage, before she can find a subject to treat. Her dramas lie practically ready-made in drawing-rooms, offices, where men and women congregate, and observation finds material to work upon. [...] The trifle has all the light wit and naturalness which Mrs Bell's commediettas generally possess[28]

How far from *Alan's Wife* are these plays can be judged from the almost complete critical silence on them after their first performances. While Bell was actively writing and involved in the theatre from the 1880s through to the 1910s, her plays were widely reviewed and well-received, but a century later, they have disappeared from the critical story we tell about the 1890s. Bell's fate as a playwright is repeated so many times, for both men and women, that perhaps it is not worth remarking on. But if we are to do justice to the achievement of a play like *Alan's Wife*, as part of the New Drama produced by and about the New Woman as a proto-feminist literary movement, we also need to be able to account for the popular and the frivolous that flourished alongside it. Through the working collaboration and personal friendship of Bell and Robins, we can start to make visible the connections between these two apparently separate worlds, and, in terms of the material practices of the contemporary theatre, there is a continuum – of actors, writers, critics, and audience – from the popular to the *avant-garde*.

Part of the problem we face in discussing women's collaborations and professional networks is that we still do not have much of a language or a history for doing so. There are some models of women's organisation and working together, but these tend to focus on particular types of exclusive relationships. Tess Cosslett's study of women's friendships deals with fictional friendships in the New Woman novel, interrogating the marriage plot, but commenting that indeed, much New Woman fiction struggles with the lack of formal structures and plot patterns which allow novelists to explore female friendships and ways of life which do not culminate in marriage. Cosslett's comments on the fictional construct could also serve as a critique of historical and biographical accounts of women such as Robins:

> In the attempt to create 'New Woman' as a fictional type, she was often constructed as a heroic *individual*: the odds she had to battle against increased the impression of the injustices done to women, and her isolation increased the impression of female heroism.[29]

Martha Vicinus provides an extended – and still unmatched – study of independent women and female communities, but Vicinus' study is concerned with those separate – or indeed separatist – communities of women such as women's colleges, schools, and charity organisations. The commercial theatre posed very different problems of professional engagement for women. As numerous feminist theatre historians have pointed out, the difficulty for women in the theatre was that if they wanted their work developed, produced, and performed, they had to inhabit the public social space of the theatre on an equal footing with men, something that remained exceedingly problematic throughout the century. Accounts of the *fin de siècle* drama abound with personal and professional attempts to change the principles of casting women for looks and beauty, or trying to circumvent the power of male theatre managers – Robins herself embarked on theatre management in this political vein,[30] and even the milder Lena Ashwell (milder in that her management was not stated to be overtly feminist) maintained that one of her aims as a manager was to provide decent working conditions for women actors, and here she included artistic considerations such as the tenor of women's roles.[31]

Bell and Robins' collaborative relationship, of which *Alan's Wife* was only the most recognizable product, was actually a long and complex negotiation, not only each with the other, but with the intersecting but different social worlds they inhabited. But it was in the commercial theatre that these spheres overlapped, because as much as she was identified with the *avant-garde* of the New Drama, Robins started her career in the popular theatre, and this is where the majority of Bell's plays were performed. It is in this arena that the work of usually invisible women playwrights – invisible in that they fit neither into a high cultural model of literary drama, nor a feminist model of transgressive woman writer – can make a substantial contribution to challenging patriarchal theatre history. Bell's occupation of the position of 'lady' and her collaboration with Robins in proto-feminist work may not be contradictory. Instead, what I note here is the way that Bell's work brings together the women's cultures of domesticity and collaboration she inhabits in her work with Robins, and the patriarchal culture which gives her a privileged position from which to speak, to insert the female culture into the mainstream theatre. The effect of this as – if not a feminist act – then certainly a female-centred act, can be gauged by the level of annoyance George Bernard Shaw registers in his rant about the presence of women's hats in a matinée at the Comedy Theatre in 1896.

> it was by the merest accident that I saw any of these entertainments. The stalls were filled for the most part by quite the most disagreeable collection of women I have ever see. They all wore towering hats, piled up, for the more effectual obstruction of the view, [...] is the privilege of not only obstructing the view, but making all your commonly humane neighbours feel sick everytime they look at you, confined strictly to women? [...] I mention these matters [...] simply to warn people who go to matinées what they likely to get in return for the price of their stall;[32]

Shaw's warning to 'people' obviously does not include the women already going to matinées, although as Susan Barstow and Viv Gardner record, the matinée audience was largely female.[33] In the midst of his fantasies of setting up a guillotine in Trafalgar Square to do away with the offending hats, Shaw saw a 'couple of Mrs Hugh Bell's drawing-room pieces, trivial but amusing enough on their scale' (73). His description of the audience suggests that there was a continuity between the worlds represented on stage and those inhabited by the audience. Certainly, as Susan Barstow argues, the largely female matinée audiences of the 1890s developed a particular empathy with on-stage heroines;[34] Barstow focusses attention specifically on the early seasons of Ibsen, but those principles of empathic identification can surely be extended to other writers and heroines. So Bell's apparently frivolous plays about drawing-rooms, or children's plays about fairies, offer an opportunity for the stage and off-stage display of women's culture, which Shaw found rather challenging. I would even go so far as to claim that Bell's introduction of that culture into the public culture of the late nineteenth-century theatre constitutes a politicized feminist act.

Florence Bell is the final 'lady' of this study. I have focussed on her as my first example of the significance of paying attention to the place of playwriting within a woman's writing career because her case has been

so overlooked, and seems at first to offer so little for recuperative feminist theatre and literary history. While Bell is not another Hannah More –
a 'bad fairy' of feminism – her anti-suffrage views, for example, or
her tendency to play Lady Bountiful in her role as Lady Bell in
Middlesbrough may have proven off-putting to previous scholars, as
Catherine Wiley's comment indicates. So too was her immersion in the
popular mainstream theatre, with apparently little potential for subversive
readings offered by the experimental theatre of the 1890s or the varieties
of sensation theatre popular since the 1860s. My next examples are
women of letters who represent other aspects of women's writing
identities, and other effects of incorporating playwriting in their
careers: Florence Marryat, the woman writer as entrepreneur, and Lucy
Clifford, the novelist and playwright as intellectual.

Florence Marryat

Florence Marryat (1838–1899) typifies the woman writer as entrepreneur, and her stage career as playwright and performer was part of a
range of innovative literary activities, which included the wonderfully
inventive group-authored novels, *The Fate of Fenella* and *Seven Christmas
Eves*.[35] The lists of authors of these two 'round-robin' fictions suggests
the extent of writers' networks in late Victorian London, as they include
literary and theatre critics, novelists, playwrights, and essayists. The
inclusion of Anglo-Australians Rosa Praed and Justin McCarthy indicates also the international dimension of the London literary world.
Florence Marryat was part of the British literary world by birth and hard
work. She was a daughter of novelist Captain Marryat, and from a long
line of well-connected Marryats, characterized by one of her father's
biographers as a family of several generations of 'very distinctly middle-
class [. . .] active people with a marked tendency to use their pens.'[36]
This activity and energy is clear in Florence Marryat's life, and she, like
her father, seems to have made and then run through several fortunes.
In Florence's case, however, as Helen Black quoted her in 1893, 'Others
have spent it for me [. . .] and I do not grudge it to them.'[37] Though
Marryat was principally active as a novelist (she wrote over ninety
novels), her novels were frequently dramatised, and at one time nine
adaptations of her novels were running simultaneously in provincial
theatres,[38] – including *The Gamekeeper, Her Own Enemy, Only a Woman,
Her World Against a Lie, Woman Against Woman, Miss Chester*, and
Charmyon. Most of these adaptations were written by Marryat, alone or
in collaboration, and Marryat herself often performed in them; she

played the 'strong-minded, masculine' role of Hephzibah Horton in *Her World Against a Lie* in 1881, an independent literary woman and advocate of women's rights who suggests to the heroine, Delia, that she could obtain a protection order to stop her husband living off her earnings. Marryat was due to perform in *The Gamekeeper* in 1898 (just a year before her death in 1899) but was stopped by a sprained ankle. Helen Black wrote in obvious awe of Marryat's energy:

> Miss Marryat's talents are versatile. After a long illness when her physicians recommended rest from literature, believing an entire change of occupation would be the best tonic for her, she went upon the stage [...] and possessing a fine voice, and great musical gifts, with considerable dramatic power, she has been successful, both as an actress and an entertainer. [...] She has toured with D'Oyley Carte's *Patience* companies, with George Grossmith in *Entre Nous*, and finally with her own company in *The Golden Goblet* (written by her son Frank). Altogether Miss Marryat has pursued her dramatic life for fifteen years, and has given hundreds of recitations and musical entertainments which she has written for herself. One of these last, called 'Love Letters,' she has taken through the provinces three times, and once through America. It lasts two hours; she accompanies herself on the piano, and the music was written by George Grossmith. Another is a comic lecture entitled, 'Women of the future (1991); or, what shall we do with our men?' She has also made many tours throughout the United Kingdom, giving recitals and readings from her father's works, and other pieces by Albery and Grossmith.[39]

Marryat's own notes towards an autobiographical account in a letter to an unknown recipient reiterate her activity and productivity:

> Seven children – I joined Mr D'Oyley Carte's 'Patience' Company in the Provinces to play the part of Lady Jane – Author of 'Love's Conflict', 'Veronique,' 'The Life and Letters of Captain Marryatt [*sic*]' etc. – My sister, Eva, who was on the stage, was at that time fulfilling a stock engagement in Glasgow, playing in 'The Colleen Bawn' and 'Anna Chute.' – In 1875 I was much engaged in giving dramatic readings in different parts of the country – [...] I was editor of the magazine, 'London Society', at that time[40]

The sense of a female agency in Marryat's career is strong, notwithstanding what Talia Schaffer has called her 'furious autobiographical testimony' about the inequalities women suffer in marriage and divorce in *The Nobler Sex*,[41] and counters Kerry Powell's argument of textual and sexual assault by the theatre on women writers. Although Marryat's work lacks the explicit political dimension of her near contemporary New Woman writers, her dramatization of the feeling woman as a passionate and powerful speaking subject in her plays is ideologically challenging, and all the more interesting for its location in the popular theatre, rather than the emerging 'fringe' of private theatres, clubs, and experimental venues in the late nineteenth century.

Her melodrama, *Miss Chester*, was written in collaboration with Sir Charles Young, which reopened the Holborn Theatre in October 1872.[42] The title character, Miss Chester, is the companion of the juvenile heroine, Isabel Montressor, niece and ward of Lady Montressor; Miss Chester appears to be hardened against the claims of love and sympathy, advising Isabel:

> if you wish to fight successfully the battle of the world, you must ignore the very existence of a heart. It can never lead you on to any happiness. It may plunge you into irremediable error – might even persuade you to place your faith in such a lie as love! (7)

Of course, the audience is quickly shown that her bitterness is a façade to cover Miss Chester's extreme despair over the lost loves of her life – her husband and her son. These characters appear early in the play in disguise: Miss Chester's husband, Sir Arthur Ashton, first appears as the Bohemian drinker and gambler Michael Fortescue, and their son Rupert lives as Lady Montressor's younger son. Isabel is in love with Rupert, although destined to marry his elder brother, Lord Montressor. On the day Rupert is 21, the family solicitor visits to reveal that Rupert is not Lady Montressor's son – her real son died at birth while she was delirious with fever – but he is actually the illegitimate son of the Earl of Montressor's sister, Lady Gertrude, who had eloped with a man who had a first wife already living. Rupert leaves the Montressors, intent on living the Bohemian life of drinking and gambling. But he is involved in a duel with his drinking and gambling companion, Michael Fortescue, over Fortescue's plan to ruin the eldest son of Montressor, and when Rupert is apparently mortally wounded, Miss Chester's speech brings down the act curtain:

> As surely as we three shall stand before the judgement seat of God, the boy your guilty hand has now struck down, *is your own son!* (29)

The final act of the play unravels the complicated relationships of the Montressors, revealing Miss Chester to be Lady Gertrude, Rupert her son, and Michael Fortescue to be the errant Sir Arthur Ashton and husband of Lady Gertrude, who has recently inherited his father's title and estate, which lies next to that of the Montressors. Sir Arthur is contrite and a reformed man since the shock of fighting his son, and the apparent irregularity of his marriage to Lady Gertrude is duly explained, its legitimacy publicly reinstated, after Ashton apologizes publicly to Miss Chester, while Rupert is free to marry Isabel Montressor.

The interest of the play focusses unusually on the older lovers, Miss Chester and Michael Fortescue, as they negotiating the reuniting of their family. The emotional force of the play relies particularly on the part of Miss Chester, giving Mrs Herman Vezin, who played the part, a powerful role (the same Mrs Vezin who gave Eleanor Marx acting lessons). While reviews of the play were mixed, all critics commented on the power of Vezin's performance, and the way that this created the success of the play with the audience.[43] The temptation to read the play autobiographically must be resisted, but the *Era*'s comments about the power of the character of Miss Chester – '[T]he quiet touches [...] of the woman suffering in silence' – suggest a dramatization of female experience beyond the clumsy melodrama which the *Athenæum* criticizes. The heightened melodramatic mode of the play is characteristic of Marryat's other plays and novels as Andrew Maunder discusses them,[44] sensational to the point of near impropriety, but always giving powerfully rendered accounts of female experience, particularly of the marginal or outcast woman (*Facing the Footlights, Her World Against a Lie*) from a sympathetic insider's point of view. As Maunder comments, Marryat's use of this material 'is an example of the way in which nineteenth-century women writers entered public discourse and, through narrative enactment and projection of fictional characters, published their opinions on the most absorbing topics of the day.' And Marryat's constant seeking out of the next new thing through which to communicate with her reading or spectating public ensured that her work had an energetic public presence. One of the features of popular entertainment throughout the century, but of particular importance in the late decades, was the variety and busyness of cross-genre adaptation and borrowing in popular culture. This aspect of the commercial theatre stood women writers like Marryat in good stead. They adapted their novels and short fictions for the stage, converted plays to films (after 1895), used their research for non-fiction writing to inform their dramatic fictions, produced translations and adaptations of European plays and prose fiction, wrote roles for themselves, designed commercial entertainments, or staged readings of their works. Theatre, as one of the mass media of the age, was an important part of Marryat's career, enabling her to develop her self-representation through direct contact with her audience.

Lucy Clifford

Like Florence Marryat, Lucy Clifford was determinedly professional in her pursuit of a literary career which included writing for the stage. Given the enduring prejudices against the theatre even at the end of the nineteenth century, what is notable about Clifford's writing career is the way that she combined the *élite* intellectual networks developed through her marriage to William Kingdon Clifford, Professor of Applied Mathematics at University College, London, with long working and social relationships within the London professional theatre industry. Even a brief look at Clifford's correspondences, and the records of her friendships and professional and social networks show how inaccurate it is to maintain a divide between the worlds of 'high' and popular culture, in terms of writerly *habitus*, at the end of the nineteenth century. The advanced thinkers with whom Clifford was connected through her intellectual circle, such as T. H. Huxley, Leslie Stephen, Grant Allen, and Eliza Lyn Linton,[45] also included those vitally interested in and working in the theatre, such as Thomas Hardy, Elizabeth Robins, Mary Braddon, and latterly Henry James. Clifford knew George Eliot and G. H. Lewes well enough that on William Kingdon's death, Eliot sent her a heartfelt note, alluding to her own widowhood – 'I understand it all . . . There is but one refuge – the having much to do.'[46] She was also a close confidante of Henry James, sharing as they did theatrical ambitions – despite James's great disappointments for his own playwriting, his letters to her are full of commentaries and critiques of her plays both before and after their production, and he relied upon her for all sorts of advice about the practical arrangements of his life, in a relationship Marysa Demoor and Monty Chisholm describe as one of 'complete trust and reciprocal encouragement.'[47] Conversely, Clifford's theatrical work gained her intimacy with the Compton-Bateman theatrical dynasty, and with theatrical manager Clement Shorter, as well as Henry Irving's manager and novelist, Bram Stoker, and eminent actor-manager husband and wife team, the Kendals.[48]

Yet for all her connections into the *élite* circles of British intellectual life, Clifford's own literary work was resolutely popular. And the extent to which this still seems a disjunction which needs explaining indicates the extent to which a modernist rejection of popular culture is embedded in the historiography of the *fin de siècle*. Clifford first came to public attention with her novel *Mrs Keith's Crime: A Record* (1885), a study in extreme maternal devotion.[49] The whole novels builds up to – or even seems to exist for – the dramatic ending when Mrs Keith kills her daughter, Molly, before she herself dies so that she is there when her daughter dies. The impact of this topic was such that when *Alan's Wife* was produced anonymously almost a decade later, it was rumoured that Clifford was the author. Clifford's later story 'The End of Her Journey' was another quite notorious success: it was first published as a short story in *Temple Bar* in 1887, was adapted by Clifford herself as a play, *The Likeness of the Night*, and ran for 63 performances at St James's Theatre in 1900,[50] and was then adapted into film by producer Percy Nash. Both the stage and film versions were a reworking of the classic love triangle, where Bernard Archerson, a barrister, has married Mildred for her money, forsaking his true love, Mary. After a few years of marriage, Bernard and Mary meet again, and Bernard maintains Mary and their son as his alternative family in a villa in Hampstead. Mildred suspects something amiss, and discovers the second Mrs Archerson. Mildred goes on a cruise with friends, and disappears in a storm. The sub-text for the audience is, of course, that Mildred has committed suicide, and when Mary finds out about her predecessor's sacrifice she ends the relationship with Bernard. The curtain falls on a typical melo-dramatic tableau, made all the more powerful by Mary's use of the water imagery which had been connected with Mildred throughout the rest of the play:

Mary. (*Putting out her hands again with a gesture of despair.*) Keep back! Keep back! Between us flows the sea –
(*He* [Bernard] *half staggers; they stand looking at each other aghast.*) (146)

While this brief plot summary sounds like a masochistic fantasy, the representation of the self-centred man, content to ruin two lives because of his desire for material and worldly comforts, is scathing. We are left in no doubt about Clifford's view of the evils of the system of selling women into marriage, and their powerlessness to resist such usage through their investment in a romantic ideal, at odds with the pragmatic views of love and marriage apparently held by those who become their husbands.

Clifford's plays continued to be demanding and challenging while remaining within the generic conventions of melodrama and comedy. Her drama *The Latch*, produced by Lena Ashwell at the Kingsway in a matinee programme of one-act plays in 1908, was seen as 'a harrowing theme of a tragic domestic complication, powerful in a grim way.'[51] *A Woman Alone*, first performed in 1914, about a mis-matched husband and wife who decide to part, shows how frustrating such a marriage is for a woman with 'brains, energy, interests,' but how 'unsatisfactory in the long run so-called freedom is for a woman.'[52] Her study of the entrapment of women in marriages with dominating, even brutal men is the theme of *The Searchlight*, another sensation melodrama set in the milieu of the comfortable middle and upper classes.[53] Even Clifford's comedies, such as *The Hamilton's Second Marriage* and *A Honeymoon Tragedy* have an edge of social commentary.[54] Like her melodramas, Clifford's comedies are firmly located within the drawing rooms and holiday resorts of the affluent and powerful, and use that vantage point to make sharp observations of the consequences of unequal power relations between the sexes. Although Clifford espoused relatively conservative political views – like Florence Bell, whom she knew, she was not a supporter of the suffragette movement, for example – her work was ideologically challenging in its female-centredness, and its use of popular forms to dramatize the vulnerability of middle-class women who subscribe to the gendered ideology of home and hearth. As an admiring reviewer of the London West End production of *The Likeness of the Night* (it had a London suburban and a Liverpool try-out run) wrote:

> Mrs W. K. Clifford [...] has dealt with a very possible – we might almost say a very common – situation in a quite commonplace way. The women are very human and we feel for both.[55]

The response to Clifford's plays, and their challenging material, might be compared with the critical responses to Lucette Ryley and Clo Graves' comedies, I discussed in Chapter 3: in spite of a framing discourse which still saw women playwrights as exceptional, and complained about 'ladies' plays,' it is possible to identify a shift in the theatre industry's attitudes to women playwrights at the end of the Victorian period.

My earlier discussion of Lucette Ryley and Clo Graves as writers of popular theatre placed them in that critical and historical no-(wo)man's-land between the modernist avant-garde and the New Drama or literary drama. Peter Bailey makes a convincing argument for regarding the mass entertainment industry of the turn of the twentieth century as 'popular modernism,'[56] I would locate the work of Ryley and Graves, together with Marryat, Bell, and Clifford within this category. However, I do not wish to expand the conventional definition of modernism to incorporate the work of popular women playwrights of the turn of the twentieth century, but rather to turn attention to those texts which stood alongside the canonical texts of modernism.[57] Rather as Ann Mellor asks us to consider the shape of Romanticism if we were to focus our attention on the women who wrote between 1780 and 1830,[58] I am interested in Rita Felski's question 'what if feminine phenomena, often seen as having a secondary or marginal status, were given a central importance in the analysis of the culture of modernity?'[59] As Felski points out,

> a feminist reading often reveals striking lines of continuity between dominant discourse and aesthetic counterdiscourse in terms of a shared valorization of Oedipal models of competitive masculinity and an overt disdain for the 'womanly' sphere of emotion, sentiment, and feeling. (27)

This approach helps us to make distinctions between modernism and modernity, rather than collapsing the one into the other, and overlooking other cultural phenomena.

The result in the theatre is that women playwright's 'popular modernism' uses the situatedness of women within Victorian domestic ideology to provide a sustained account of middle-class life from within the 'doll's house' (as Ibsen would have it). But this is not always a compliant writerly practice, as modernist theories might have us believe. In dramatizing femininity from within, women's plays do not always concur with Ibsen's metaphor of the doll's house as place from which to flee. They are ingenious in demonstrating female characters' coping strategies and potentially subversive avoidance of restrictive codes of feminine behaviour. This is what Bailey argues in more general terms in his discussion of the theatres of mass entertainment at the end of the nineteenth century, in which performers and playwrights 'engage[d] with the world of popular experience, acknowledging anxieties and aspirations which they may often have shared,' in order to offer knowledge for negotiating the increasingly complex modern world.[60] For women playwrights, this meant producing theatre work within the conditions of contemporary femininity, with its *fin de siècle* emphasis on consumption and display. However, rather than considering this from either the point of view of Arnold's 'aesthetics of evaluation' adopted by the proponents of the literary drama, or as complicitous with a degraded mass culture as modernist critique framed the period, Bailey's argument offers the possibility of seeing such cultural production as offering 'some immediate [...] advantage in the transactions of everyday life and the tactics of self-staging' (18). In a cultural atmosphere increasingly nervous about feminization as a version of decline and degeneration, female self-staging had important ideological implications.

To be a playwright and a woman in the nineteenth century has long been thought of as a contradiction in terms. Recent scholarship in this field has emphasized the ways in which, throughout the nineteenth century, definitions of 'the playwright' were almost exclusively masculine, the institutions of British (and specifically English) national culture raised obstacles to women's participation in the theatre, and the conditions of the London theatre industry – its definitions of professional, its modes of organisation, its arrangements of capital and financial speculation – militated against women's careers as playwrights. There is indeed incontrovertible evidence of this, and this is what recent feminist scholarship in the field (including my own) has concentrated upon. However, if we regard Florence Bell, Florence Marryat, and Lucy Clifford as my final representative examples of women playwrights, and in many ways typical of most working women playwrights across the century, I would argue for an amended view of Victorian women playwrights as, if not a normative model for Victorian women writers generally, at least not aberrant. We should begin to consider playwriting for women as an activity which formed part of the portfolio career of the professional woman writer. Furthermore, I want to remember that women playwrights in the nineteenth century were numerous, and visible if we look in the right way for them, rather than continue the masculinist historiographical tendency of the nineteenth century to consider them as exceptions, like 'a dog's walking on his hind legs,' as Samuel Johnson quipped about women preachers. For these women to succeed in the theatre was not without its difficulties, but the obstacles they faced made their work all the more powerful and urgent. The industrial practices of the theatre, its sociability, public exposure, physical engagement – all things seen as theoretically problematic for 'respectable' middle-class women – required women writers to engage all the more actively as professionals, even when vociferously maintaining that they shrank from such mercenary business.

Of course, it *is* still necessary to recognize a tension between the disabilities of what Mary Poovey calls writing as a 'proper lady' in a profession shaped by what John Russell Stephens describes as the bohemian, clubbable atmosphere of the London theatre, and women's active participation in the profession of the playwright. Indeed, throughout the nineteenth century this dialectic is never really resolved, except by writing women out of theatre history and literary record. But after immersing myself in women playwrights' letters, plays, fictions, and journalism, I would argue that it is important to recognize women's success in this alien territory, and suggest that these active, busy women of the second and third rank of writers provide us with an important alternative model for the professional woman writer in the Victorian period. The theatre offered them agency, and through that, public opportunities for self-definition. The writing of Bell, Marryat, and Clifford and the hundreds of others like them represent a female theatrical tradition which is diverse and many faceted – just like the male tradition – but connected if by nothing else than by an appreciation of the particular conditions of being female in the nineteenth century. Whether this is overtly charged by conflict between women's desires and Victorian gender ideology, as in Clifford's plays, subversively sensational as in Marryat's, or observantly witty as in Bell's, these plays tell us about the construction of modern femininity from within that process. The apparently trivial parts of life – marriage, children, money, and frocks – are given weight in these plays as central experiences of women's lives, so that the objectified and fetishized female body under the male gaze on the nineteenth-century stage is given the opportunity to assert her subjectivity and speaking power. When the work of women playwrights is factored into our landscape of Victorian theatre, a pattern emerges which can help us to disentangle playwriting from masculinity, and which does not regard plays about the minutiae of ordinary domestic life and familial relationships as trivial. In short, the study of women playwrights offers us a theatre history which allows for the marginal, the feminine, the popular, and the non-literary to be included in a history of an important national cultural institution.

Appendix
Nineteenth-Century British Women Playwrights: A Checklist

This Checklist is drawn from Allardyce Nicoll, 'Handlist of Plays,' *A History of English Drama, 1660–1900*, Vol. IV, *Early Nineteenth Century Drama, 1800–1850*, and Vol. V, *Late Nineteenth Century Drama, 1850–1900* (Cambridge: Cambridge University Press, 1970), James Ellis and Joseph Donohue, *English Drama of the Nineteenth Century, An Index and Finding Guide* (New Canaan: Readex Books, 1985), *Index to the Pettingell Collection* (Harvester Microform), and the catalogues of the British Library (on-line OPAC and Manuscripts catalogues, and the Lord Chamberlain's Collection of Plays card index). As my interest is in the productions of plays, I have given the date and place of first performance where available. Place of performance is London, unless stated otherwise. If there are no details of first performance, I have given details of publication. Sometimes not even this information is given in bibliographic sources.

Achurch, Janet
Frou-Frou, Comedy, Manchester, 9 December 1886.
Coming of Peace, The [with C. E. Wheeler; trans. Hauptmann], 1900.

Acton, Jeanie Hering [Mrs Adams, Mrs Jeanie Hering Adams-Acton]
Darkest Hour, The, St John's Wood, 6 April 1895.
Dulvery Dotty, Terry's, June 1894.
Triple Bill, The, St John's Wood, 2 March 1894.
Who's Married?, Bijou, 22 June 1893.
Woman in Black, The, St John's Wood, 21 December 1895.
Woman's Wit, Sunnyside, Langford-place, Abbey-road, 20 July 1893.

Adams, Catherine
Feminine Strategy, Drill Hall, Basingstoke, 11 November 1893.

Adams, Florence Davenport
Home Fairy, A, in *Children's Plays*, No. 1–12 (London and New York: Samuel French, [1900]).
King in Disguise, A, in *Children's Plays*, No. 1–12 (London and New York: Samuel French, [1900]).
Lady Cecil, The, in *Children's Plays*, No. 1–12 (London and New York: Samuel French, [1900]).
Little Folks' Work, The, in *Children's Plays*, No. 1–12 (London and New York: Samuel French, [1900]).
Magician and the Ring, The, in *Children's Plays*, No. 1–12 (London and New York: Samuel French, [1900]).

Midsummer Frolic, in *Children's Plays*, No. 1–12 (London and New York: Samuel French, [1900]).
Prince or Peasant, in *Children's Plays*, No. 1–12 (London and New York: Samuel French, [1900]).
Princess Marguerite's Choice, in *Children's Plays*, No. 1–12 (London and New York: Samuel French, [1900]).
Sleepers Awakened, The, in *Children's Plays*, No. 1–12 (London and New York: Samuel French, [1900]).
Snowwhite, in *Children's Plays*, No. 1–12 (London and New York: Samuel French, [1900]).
Three Fairy Gifts, Assembly Rooms, Worthing, 7 April 1896.

Adams, Mrs Edward
Don Pedro, Prince's Hall, New Cross, 18 October 1892.

Adams, Sarah Fuller Flower [Mrs William Bridges Adams]
Vivia Perpetua: A Dramatic Poem in Four Acts. With a Memoir of the Author, and Her Hymns (Privately printed, 1893).

Allen, A. M.
Madcap Prince, The, Pleasure Gardens, Folkestone, 13 April 1894.

Alleyn, Annie
Woman's Love, Prince of Wales, Manchester, 22 August 1881.

Alma-Tadema, Laura [Miss Laurence]
Childe Vyet, or the Brothers, in *Four Plays* (London: The Green Sheaf, 1905).
Merciful Soul, The, in *Four Plays* (London: The Green Sheaf, 1905).
New Wrecks upon Old Shoals, in *Four Plays* (London: The Green Sheaf, 1905).
Unseen Helmsman, The, in *Four Plays* (London: The Green Sheaf, 1905).

Anderson, Mary [Mrs Antonio de Navarro]
As You Like It [arr. of Shakespeare].
Romeo and Juliet [arr. of Shakespeare].
Winter's Tale, The [arr. of Shakespeare].

Anstruther, Eva
Secret of State, A, St Cuthbert's Hall, Earl's Court, 23 June 1898.

Antonini, Mademoiselle
Incognito, The, Her Majesty's Richmond, 11 June 1881.

Archer, Frances Elizabeth [Mrs William Archer]
Lady From the Sea, The [with William Archer, trans. Ibsen].
Wild Duck, The [with William Archer, trans. Henrik Ibsen].

Archer, Miss
My Life, Gaiety, December 1882.

Aria, Eliza
Runaways, The, Criterion, May 1898.

Armitage, Ethel
Archibald Danvers, M. D. [with G. Southam], Pavilion, Southport, 20 October 1893.

Ascher, Mrs Gordon
Horn of Plenty, The, Central Hall, Acton, 15 December 1897.

Ashley, Evelyn Unsworth [Mrs J. B. Unsworth]
For Queen and Country, Bijou, Neath, 26 December 1890.

Attenborough, Florence Gertrude
Alfred the Great, a Drama, The Ballad of Dundee, and Other Poems (London: W. Reeves, 1902).
Atalanta in Arcady, a Pastoral Play (London: Musical News, [1903]).
Won by Wit [music by A. Robey], Myddleton Hall, Islington, 16 October 1895.

Aveling, Eleanor Marx, *see* Marx, Eleanor

Aylmer, Mrs John
Charlatan, The, Torre Parish Rooms, Torquay, 5 February 1889.

Bache, Constance
Hansel and Gretel, Daly's, 26 December 1894.

Baillie, Joanna
A Series of Plays: In Which it is Attempted to Delineate the Stronger Passions of the Mind-each Passion Being the Subject of a Tragedy and a Comedy (London: T. Cadell & W. Davies, 1798–1812), 3 volumes.
Alienated Manor, The in *The Dramatic and Poetical Works* (London: Longman, Brown, Green, and Longmans, 1851).
Beacon, The, Edinburgh, 2 February 1815.
Bride, The, in *The Dramatic and Poetical Works* (London: Longman, Brown, Green, and Longmans, 1851).
Constantine Paleologus; or, The Last of the Caesars, Liverpool, 10 October 1808.
Country Inn, The, in *Miscellaneous Plays* (London: Longman, 1804).
De Montfort, Drury Lane, 29 April 1800.
Election, The, English Opera House, 7 June 1817.
Enthusiasm, in *Dramas* (London: Longman, Rees, Orme, Brown, Green, and Longman, 1836).
Family Legend, The, Edinburgh, 29 January 1810.
Henriquez, Drury Lane, 19 March 1836.
Homicide, The, in *The Dramatic and Poetical Works* (London: Longman, Brown, Green, and Longmans, 1851).
Martyr, The, in *The Dramatic and Poetical Works* (London: Longman, Brown, Green, and Longmans, 1851).
Match, The, in *The Dramatic and Poetical Works* (London: Longman, Brown, Green, and Longmans, 1851).
Phantom, The, in *The Dramatic and Poetical Works* (London: Longman, Brown, Green, and Longmans, 1851).
Rayner: A Tragedy, in *Miscellaneous Plays* (London: Longman, 1804).
Romiero, in *The Dramatic and Poetical Works* (London: Longman, Brown, Green, and Longmans, 1851).
Separation, The, Covent Garden, 24 February 1836.
Stripling, The, in *The Dramatic and Poetical Works* (London: Longman, Brown, Green, and Longmans, 1851).

Tryal, The, in *The Dramatic and Poetical Works* (London: Longman, Brown, Green, and Longmans, 1851).

Witchcraft, in *Dramas* (London: Longman, Rees, Orme, Brown, Green, and Longman, 1836).

Balfour, Mary Devens
Kathleen O'Neil, Belfast, 9 February 1814.

Bancroft, Marie Wilton
Accidents Decide Our Lives, Royalty, 1895.
My Daughter, Garrick, 2 January 1892.
Riverside Story, A, Haymarket, 22 May 1890.
Tables, The, Criterion, June 1901.

Baring, Stephanie
Snatched from Death [with Walter Beaumont], Novelty, October 1896.

Barker, Miss
Lady Barbara's Birthday, Brighton, 12 February 1872.

Barmby, Beatrice Helen
Gísli Súrsson, 1900.

Barnes, Charlotte M. [Mrs Conner Barnes]
Octavia Bragaldi; or, The Confession, Surrey, 9 May 1844.
Forest Princess, The; or, Two Centuries Ago, Liverpool, 16 February 1848.

Barnett, Miss
La Femme Sentinelle, Drury Lane, 7 February 1829.

Barry, Helen
Night's Frolic, A [with Augustus Thomas adapted from G. von Moser], Strand, 1 June 1891.

Barrymore, Mrs W.
Evening Revels, 10 November 1823.

Bartholomew, Anne Charlotte Fayerman [Mrs Valentine Bartholomew, formerly Mrs Walter Turnbull]
It's Only My Aunt!, Marylebone, 14 May 1849.
Ring, The; or, The Farmer's Daughter, Queen's, 29 January 1833.

Bateman, H. L.
Fanchette; or, The Will-O'-the-Wisp, Edinburgh, 6 May 1871.
Geraldine; or, The Master Passion, Adelphi, 12 June 1865.

Bateman, Isabel
Courtship of Morrice Buckler, The [with A. E. W. Mason from his novel], Grand, 6 December 1897.

Beauchamp, Emily
Anti-Matrimonial Agency, The, Gaiety, Dublin, 9 March 1876.
Matrimonial Agency, The, Strand, 8 December 1897.
Yes or No, Dublin, 2 May 1877.

Beckett, Mrs Harry
Jack, Royalty, 14 June 1886.

Beerbohm, Constance
April Shower, An, in *Little Book of Plays, for Professional and Amateur Actors. Adapted from the French* (London: George Newnes, 1897).
Charity Begins At Home, in *Little Book of Plays, for Professional and Amateur Actors. Adapted from the French* (London: George Newnes, 1897).
Chatterbox, The, in *Little Book of Plays, for Professional and Amateur Actors. Adapted from the French* (London: George Newnes, 1897).
He and She, in *Little Book of Plays, for Professional and Amateur Actors. Adapted from the French* (London: George Newnes, 1897).
Little Surprise, The, in *Little Book of Plays, for Professional and Amateur Actors. Adapted from the French* (London: George Newnes, 1897).
Secret, A, St George's Hall, 26 June 1888.

Bell, Florence Eveleen Eleanore [Mrs Hugh Bell, Lady Bell]
Alan's Wife [with Elizabeth Robins], Independent Theatre Society at Terry's, 26 April 1893.
Angela (London: Ernest Benn, 1926).
Beauty and the Beast, in *Chamber Comedies: A Collection of Plays and Monologues for the Drawing Room* (London: Longmans, Green, 1904).
Best Children in the World, The, in *Nursery Comedies: Twelve Tiny Plays for Children* (London: Longmans, Green, 1893).
Between the Posts [*L'Indécis*], Newcastle, 9 September 1887.
Bicycle, The, Comedy, 12 March 1896.
Blue or Green? Comedy, 12 March 1896.
Cat and Dog, in *Nursery Comedies: Twelve Tiny Plays for Children* (London: Longmans, Green, 1893).
Chance Interview, A, St George's Hall, 12 June 1889.
Cinderella, in *Nursery Comedies: Twelve Tiny Plays for Children* (London: Longmans, Green, 1893).
Cross Questions and Crooked Answers [written with Frances Bell] (London and New York: Samuel French, [1899]).
Crossing Sweeper, The, in *Chamber Comedies: A Collection of Plays and Monologues for the Drawing Room* (London: Longmans, Green, 1904).
Foolish Jack, in *Nursery Comedies: Twelve Tiny Plays for Children* (London: Longmans, Green, 1893).
Giving Him Away, in Crawfurd, Oswald, *Dialogues of the Day* (London: Chapman & Hall, 1895).
Golden Goose, The, in *Nursery Comedies: Twelve Tiny Plays for Children* (London: Longmans, Green, 1893).
Great Illusion, The, West, Albert Hall, 28 July 1895.
Hard Day's Work, A, in *Chamber Comedies: A Collection of Plays and Monologues for the Drawing Room* (London: Longmans, Green, 1904).
In a First-Class Waiting Room, in *Chamber Comedies: A Collection of Plays and Monologues for the Drawing Room* (London: Longmans, Green, 1904).
In a Telegraph Office, Parish Hall, Sloane Square, 11 May 1893.
Jack and the Beanstalk, in *Chamber Comedies: A Collection of Plays and Monologues for the Drawing Room* (London: Longmans, Green, 1904).
Jerry-Builder Solness, St George's Hall, 19 July 1893.
Joint Household, A, Steinway Hall, 13 March 1891.

Karin, Vaudeville, 10 May 1892.

Last Words, in *Chamber Comedies: A Collection of Plays and Monologues for the Drawing Room* (London: Longmans, Green, 1904).

Little Petsy, in *Nursery Comedies: Twelve Tiny Plays for Children* (London: Longmans, Green, 1893).

Lost Thread, A, Prince's Hall, 20 May 1890.

Masterpiece, The, Royalty, 15 April 1893.

Miss Dobson, in *Nursery Comedies: Twelve Tiny Plays for Children* (London: Longmans, Green, 1893).

Miss Flipper's Holiday [with Harriet Bell] (London and New York: Samuel French, [1900]), French's Acting Edition.

Modern Locusta, A, in *Chamber Comedies: A Collection of Plays and Monologues for the Drawing Room* (London: Longmans, Green, 1904).

Monster in the Garden, The, in *Nursery Comedies: Twelve Tiny Plays for Children* (London: Longmans, Green, 1893).

Nicholson's Niece, Terry's, 30 May 1892.

Not to Be Forwarded, in *Chamber Comedies: A Collection of Plays and Monologues for the Drawing Room* (London: Longmans, Green, 1904).

Oh, No! in *Chamber Comedies: A Collection of Plays and Monologues for the Drawing Room* (London: Longmans, Green, 1904).

Public Prosecutor, The, in *Chamber Comedies: A Collection of Plays and Monologues for the Drawing Room* (London: Longmans, Green, 1904).

Quite By Ourselves, in *Nursery Comedies: Twelve Tiny Plays for Children* (London: Longmans, Green, 1893).

Rather a Prig, in *Nursery Comedies: Twelve Tiny Plays for Children* (London: Longmans, Green, 1893).

Reliquary, The, in *Chamber Comedies: A Collection of Plays and Monologues for the Drawing Room* (London: Longmans, Green, 1904).

Sixpenny Telegram, A (London and New York: Samuel French, [1887]), French's Acting Edition.

Superfluous Lady, A, Lyric Club, 2 June 1891.

Surprise, The, in *Chamber Comedies: A Collection of Plays and Monologues for the Drawing Room* (London: Longmans, Green, 1904).

Swiss Times, The, in *Chamber Comedies: A Collection of Plays and Monologues for the Drawing Room* (London: Longmans, Green, 1904).

Time is Money [with Arthur Cecil Blunt, pseud. 'Arthur Cecil'], Newcastle, 5 September 1890.

Underground Journey, An [with C. H. E. Brookfield], Comedy, 9 February 1893.

Unpublished Ms, An, in *Chamber Comedies: A Collection of Plays and Monologues for the Drawing Room* (London: Longmans, Green, 1904).

Viceroy's Wedding, The, in *Chamber Comedies: A Collection of Plays and Monologues for the Drawing Room* (London: Longmans, Green, 1904).

Waterproof, The, in *Chamber Comedies: A Collection of Plays and Monologues for the Drawing Room* (London: Longmans, Green, 1904).

Way the Money Goes, The (London: Sidgwick & Jackson, 1910), 1911.

What Happened to Henny Penny? in *Nursery Comedies: Twelve Tiny Plays for Children* (London: Longmans, Green, 1893).

Wigwam, The; or, The Little Girl from Town, in *Nursery Comedies: Twelve Tiny Plays for Children* (London: Longmans, Green, 1893).

Woman of Courage, A, in *Chamber Comedies: A Collection of Plays and Monologues for the Drawing Room* (London: Longmans, Green, 1904).

Woman of Culture, A, in *Chamber Comedies: A Collection of Plays and Monologues for the Drawing Room* (London: Longmans, Green, 1904).

Wrong Poet, The, in *Chamber Comedies: A Collection of Plays and Monologues for the Drawing Room* (London: Longmans, Green, 1904).

Bell, Frances [with Florence Bell]
Cross Questions and Crooked Answers [see above].

Bell, Harriet [with Florence Bell]
Miss Flipper's Holliday [see above].

Bell, Minnie
Gavotte, The, Steinway Hall, 1 April 1890.
Is Madame at Home? Prince's Hall, 23 May 1887.
Lady Browne's Diary, Strand, 28 June 1889.

Bennett, Emelie
Among the Amalekites, Portsmouth, 22 June 1889.

Beresford, Isabel
Until the Day Break, Bijou, 17 May 1898.

Beringer, Aimée Danielle [Mrs Oscar Beringer]
Agitator, The, Hicks, 9 December 1907.
Bess, Novelty, 17 November 1891.
Bit of Old Chelsea, A, Court Theatre, 8 February 1897.
Holly Tree Inn, Terry's, 15 January 1891.
Jim Belmont, Metropole, 1 October 1900.
My Lady's Orchard [with G. P. Hawtrey], Glasgow, 23 August 1897.
Plot of His Story, The, St James's, May 1899.
Prince and the Pauper, The, Gaiety, 12 April 1890.
Salve, Opera Comique, 15 March 1895.
Tares, Prince of Wales, 31 January 1888.
That Girl [with Henry Hamilton], Haymarket, 30 July 1890.

Bernhardt-Fisher, Mrs
Claire, Prince's Hall, New Cross, 7 May 1887.

Berry, Mary
Fashionable Friends, The, Drury Lane, May 1803.

Bessle, Elizabeth
Tinted Venus, The, Bramblebury, Wandsworth Common, 12 October 1889.
Electric Spark, The, Olympic, 8 May 1889.
Gringoire [with S. H. Basing], Park Town Hall, Battersea, 4 February 1890.
Love's Labours Lost, Park Town Hall, Battersea, 15 April 1891.
Understudy, The, Opera Comique, 30 July 1892.

Bloomfield, Helen
Euston Hotel, The, Royal Pavilion, 8 May 1845.

Boaden, Caroline
Don Pedro the Cruel and Don Manuel the Cobbler!; or, The Corregidor of Seville! Surrey, August 1838.

Duel in Richelieu's Time, A, Theatre Royal, Haymarket, August 1832.
Fatality, Theatre Royal, Haymarket, 2 September 1829.
First of April, The, Theatre Royal, Haymarket, 31 August 1830.
Quite Correct, Theatre Royal, Haymarket, 1825.
William Thompson; or, Which is He? Theatre Royal, Haymarket Theatre, 11 September 1829.

Booth, Mrs Otto von
Corinne [from the novel], Standard, May 1885.

Braddon, Mary Elizabeth [later Mrs John Maxwell]
Dross; or, The Root of Evil, 1882 (Hastings: Sensation Press, 1999).
For Better, for Worse, Westcliff Saloon, Whitby, 6 September 1890.
Genevieve, Alexandra, Liverpool, 6 April 1873.
Griselda, or the Patient Wife, Princess's, 13 November 1873.
Loves of Arcadia, The, Strand, 12 March 1860.
Marjorie Daw (London: J. & R. Maxwell, [1882]).
Married Beneath Him, 1882.
Missing Witness, The, 1882.
Model Husband, The, Surrey, 28 September 1868.

Adaptations of Mary Braddon's novels

Lady Audley's Secret
Hazlewood, Colin Henry, *Lady Audley's Secret*, Victoria, 25 May 1863.
Roberts, George [pseud. of Robert Walters], *Lady Audley's Secret*, St James's Theatre, 28 February 1863.
Suter, William E., *Lady Audley's Secret*, Queen's, February 1863.

Aurora Floyd
Cheltnam, Charles Smith, *Aurora Floyd; or, The Deed in the Wood*, Princess's, 11 March 1863.
Hazlewood, Colin Henry, *Aurora Floyd; or, The First and Second Marriage* [variant sub-title: *The Dark Duel in the Wood*], Britannia, 20 April 1863.
Johnstone, John Beer, *Aurora Floyd*, Marylebone, May 1863.
Suter, William E., *Aurora Floyd*, Queens, 30 March 1863.
Webster, Jr, Benjamin, *Aurora Floyd*, Adelphi, 14 March 1863.

Henry Dunbar
Hazlewood, Colin Henry, *The Outcasts* [*Henry Dunbar*], Britannia Theatre, 10 February 1864.
Taylor, Tom, *Henry Dunbar; or, A Daughter's Trial*, Olympic, 9 December 1865.

Sir Jasper's Tenant
Stirling, Edward, *Sir Jasper's Tenant*, Sadler's Wells, 1865.

John Marchmont's Legacy
Anon., *John Marchmont's Legacy*, Prince of Wales Theatre, Birmingham, 23 April 1866.

The Trail of the Serpent
Holt, May [Fairbairn], *Jabez North* [*The Trail of the Serpent*], Oldham, 7 June 1881; Philharmonic, London, 11 March 1882 as *Dark Deeds*.

Like and Unlike
Braddon, Mary Elizabeth, *For Better for Worse* [*Like and Unlike*], Whitby, 1890; Brighton, 1891.

The Cloven Foot
Mouillot, Frederick and Janet Steer, *The Cloven Foot*, Blackburn, 27 January 1890; Pavilion, London, June 1890; Grand, 1 June 1891.

Bradley, Katherine Harris and Cooper, Edith Emma [pseud. 'Michael Field']
Accuser, The (London: Sidgwick & Jackson, 1911).
Anna Ruina (London: D. Nutt, 1899).
Attila, My Attila! (London: E. Matthews, 1896).
Brutus Ultor (London: George Bell & Sons, 1886).
Callirrhoë (London: G. Bell & Sons, 1884).
Canute the Great (London: George Bell & Sons, 1887).
Cup of Water, The (London: George Bell & Sons, 1887).
Fair Rosamund (London: G. Bell & Sons, 1884).
Father's Tragedy, The (London: George Bell & Sons, 1885).
Julia Domna, a Play (London: Hacon & Ricketts, 1903).
Long Ago (London: George Bell & Sons, 1889).
Loyalty or Love? (London: George Bell & Sons, 1885).
Messiah, A (London: Sidgwick & Jackson, 1911).
Noontide Branches (Oxford: H. Daniel, 1899).
Question of Memory, A, Independent Theatre Society at the Opera Comique, 27 October 1893.
Stephania (London: Mathews & Lane, 1892).
Tragic Mary, The (London: G. Bell, 1890).
Tristan de Léonois (London: Sidgwick & Jackson, 1911).
William Rufus (London: George Bell & Sons, 1885).
World at Auction, The (London: Ballantyne Press for Hacon & Ricketts, 1898).

Bradshaw, Mrs A.
Skyward Guide, The [with Mark Melford], 9 May 1895.

Bright, Eva
Love's Young Dream, Strand, 21 April 1890.
Tabitha's Courtship [with Florence Bright], Comedy, 18 February 1890.

Bright, Florence
Caught Out [trans. Pfahl, *Die Kunstreiterin*], St George's Hall, 17 July 1888.
Tabitha's Courtship [with Eva Bright], Comedy, 18 February 1890.

Bright, Kate C. Pitt [Mrs Augustus Bright]
Bracken Hollow, Alexandra, Sheffield, 27 November 1878.
Dane's Dyke, Theatre Royal, Sheffield, 22 August 1881.
Naomi's Sin; or, Where are You Going, My Pretty Maid?, Alexandra, Sheffield, 7 May 1879.
Noblesse Oblige, Exeter, 4 October 1878.
Not False but Fickle, Alexandra, Sheffield, 22 March 1878.

Browning, Elizabeth Barrett [Mrs Robert Browning]
Prometheus Bound [trans.], 1833.
Psyche Apocalypté [with Richard Hengist Horne].

Brunner, Madame
Our Lodgers, Lyceum, Sunderland, 26 June 1868.

Brunton, Annie [pseud. 'L. S. Dee']
Family Ghost, The, Hanley, 17 March 1881.
Queen of Diamonds, The, Coatbridge, 20 March 1882.
Won By Honours, Brighton, 21 April 1882.

Burleigh, Frances
Jones and Co., Myddleton Hall, Islington, 30 November 1893.

Burney, Estelle
County, The [with Arthur Benham], Terry's, 2 June 1892.
First Anniversary, The.
Greater Glory, The.
Idyll of the Closing Century, An, Lyceum, 2 December 1896.
Off the Cornish Coast.
Ordeal of the Honeymoon, The, Prince of Wales, 9 May 1899.
Settled Out of Court, Globe, 3 June 1897.
Wisdom of Lord Glynde, The.

Burton, Mrs
Repentance of King Aethelred the Unready [music by W. Hay], Shrewsbury, 31
    January 1887.

Byron, Medora Gordon
Zameo; or, The White Warrior, Royal Victoria Theatre, October 1834.

Cadogan, Lady
Caught At Last [adapted from Armand des Roseux, *La Souris*], Comedy, June
    1886.

Calvert, Adelaide Helen Biddles [Mrs Charles Calvert]
Amy Lawrence, the Freemason's Daughter [LCP title as A Tale of an Old Man's
    Love], Bower Saloon, 26 October 1851.
Can He Forgive Her? Comedy, Manchester, 18 September 1891.
Trotty Veck, Gaiety, 26 December 1872.

Cameron, Kate
Fatality, Eden, Bishop Auckland, 26 January 1898.

Campbell, Lady Archibald
Tamlin, Edinburgh, 27 November 1899.

Campbell, Lady Colin
Bud and Blossom, Terry's, 3 June 1893.

Campbell, Mrs Vere
King's Password, The, Shakespeare, Liverpool, 21 May 1900.
Maid of Yesterday, The, Queen's Gate Hall, South Kensington, 11 May 1896.
Mizpah Misery, Grand, Glasgow, 6 February 1894.

Carlyle, Rita
Falsely Accused, Pavilion, 5 July 1897.

Carr, Mrs J. Comyns
Butterfly, The, Gaiety, Glasgow, 12 September 1879.

Cassilis, Ina Leon
At Bay [with Charles Lander], Ladbroke Hall, 9 April 1888.
Cash for Coronets [with Frank Morland], North London Institute, Dalston, 14 June 1894.
Cheerful and Musical, St Peter's, Jersey, 14 August 1891.
Demon Darrell [with Frank Morland], Britannia, 20 June 1898.
Hearts or Diamonds, Steinway Hall, 12 May 1891.
Hidden Foe, A, Lecture Hall, Greenwich, 28 May 1892.
Light of Pengarth, The, Opera Comique, 17 December 1898.
Michael Dane's Grandson, Lyric, Hammersmith, 18 April 1896.
Noble Atonement, A, Opera Comique, 21 January 1892.
Those Landladies!
Two Misses Ibbetson, The.
Unfinished Story, The, St James's Hall, 22 June 1891.
Vida [with C. Lander], Ladbroke Hall, 12 October 1891.
Wrong Door, The, Comedy, 20 May 1890.

Caulfield, Frances Sally [Mrs Edwin Toby Caulfield]
Innocents, The, 1824.

Cavendish, Clara, Lady [pseud.]
Woman of the World, The, Queen's, 13 November 1858.

Chambers, Marianne
Ourselves, Lyceum, 2 March 1811.
School for Friends, The, Drury Lane, 10 December 1805.

Chandler, B.
Powder and Shot, Drill Hall, Basingstoke, 2 January 1896.

Chandos, Alice [pseud. 'A. V. Livondais']
Jealous of the Past, New Cross Hall, 17 September 1885.
Philanthropy, Princess's, 3 September 1888.

Chapin, Alice
Dresden China [with E. H. Oliphant], Vaudeville, 21 July 1892.
Shame [with E. H. Oliphant], Vaudeville, 21 July 1892.
Wrong Legs, The, Ilkeston, 14 September 1896.
Sorrowful Satan; or, Lucifer's Match [music by P. Rex], Stanley Hall, Kentish Town, 27 October 1897.
Woman's Sacrifice, A [adapted from Victor Hugo], St George's Hall, 3 June 1899.

Chapman, Jane Frances
King René's Daughter [trans. Henrik Hertx], 1845.
Axel and Valborg [trans. A. G. Oehlenschläger], 1851.

Chatterton, Henrietta Georgiana Marcia Iremonger [Mrs Lascelles, Lady Georgiana]
Oswald of Deira, 1867.

Childe-Pemberton, Harriet Louisa
Backward Child, A (London: T. H. Lacy, 1850).
Carmela, a Poetic Drama (London: Elkin Matthews, 1903).
Dead Letters and Other Narrative and Dramatic Pieces (London: Ward, Lock & Co., 1896), including *Chatterboxes, Nicknames, Shattered Nerves, Sunbeams at Home, a Fairy Play.*

He, She and the Poker: A Duologue, and Other Dramatic Pieces (London: Griffith,
    Farran & Co., 1900).
Her Own Enemy (London: John Long, 1904).

Chippendale, Mary Jane
Mamma, Gaiety, Dublin, 8 May 1876.

Clarke, Clara Saville [Savile-Clark, Clara]
Choosing a Ball Dress, in Crawfurd, Oswald, *Dialogues of the Day* (London:
    Chapman & Hall, 1895).
Human Sacrifice, A, in Crawfurd, Oswald, *Dialogues of the Day* (London: Chapman &
    Hall, 1895).
Point of Honour, A, in Crawfurd, Oswald, *Dialogues of the Day* (London: Chapman &
    Hall, 1895).
Woman's Vengeance, A, St George's Hall, 19 December 1892.

Clarke, Olivia, Lady
Irishwoman, The, Crow-street, Dublin 1819.

Clayton, Eliza
Red Lamp, The; or, the Dark Dens of the City, Grecian, June 1893.

Cleaver, Mary
Erl King's Daughter, The; or, The Fairy Reformed, 30 September 1851.
Ballybaggerty Bequest, The, Adelphi, Edinburgh, 14 June 1852.

Clevedon, Alice
Worship of Plutus, The; or, Poses, Ladbroke Hall, 6 July 1888.

Clifford, Lucy Lane [Mrs William Kingdon Clifford]
Hamilton's Second Marriage, Court, 29 October 1907.
Honeymoon Tragedy, A, Comedy, 12 March 1896.
Interlude, An [with Walter Pollock], Terry's, 3 June 1893.
Latch, The, Kingsway, 19 May 1908.
Likeness of the Night, The (London: Duckworth, 1912).
Long Duel, A, Garrick, August 1901.
Modern Way, The, in *Plays* (London: Duckworth, 1909).
Searchlight, The, Gaiety, Manchester.
Supreme Moment, A, Royal Court, 30 August 1899.
Thomas and the Princess, in *Plays* (London: Duckworth, 1909).
Woman Alone, A (London: Duckworth & Co., 1915).

Cobbold, Elizabeth Knipe [Mrs John Cobbold, formerly Mrs William Clarke]
Cassandra.
Roman Mutiny, The; an Historical Drama for the Performance of Children [fragment],
    in *Dramatic Fragments* (Ipswich: J. Raw, 1825).
Brave's Task, The [fragment], in *Dramatic Fragments* (Ipswich: J. Raw, 1825).

Cockburn, Mrs T.
Princess Verita [music by F. J. Smith], Art Gallery, Newcastle, 7 October 1896.

Coffin, Emily
My Jack, Princess's, 6 October 1887.
No Credit, Strand, 11 April 1892.
Run Wild, Strand, 30 June 1888.

Collette, Mary
Cousin's Courtship, Lyric, 24 September 1892.

Collins, Mabel
Suggestion; or, The Hypnotist, Lyric, Hammersmith, 21 November 1891.
Modern Hypatia, The; or, A Drama of Today, Bijou, 22 February 1894.

Compton, Mrs Charles G.
Vacant Place, A, Terry's, 23 June 1899.

Conquest, Mrs George
Flora and Zephyr, Grecian, 31 March 1852.
L'Union des Nations, Grecian, 22 November 1852.
La Fille mal Gardée, Grecian, 13 September 1858.

Cooke, Eliza [Mrs T. P. Cooke]
Forced Marriage, The; or, The Return from Siberia, Surrey, 5 December 1842.

Coquelicot, Madame
Song of the River, The, St George's Hall August 1900.

Corbett, Elizabeth Burgoyne [Mrs George Corbett]
On the Threshold.
War Correspondent, The [with W. Boyne], Surrey, 28 November 1898.
Bit of Human Nature, A, Terry's, 27 June 1899.

Corder, Henrietta Louisa Walford [Mrs Frederick Corder]
Lohengrin [with Frederick Corder, trans. Richard Wagner].
Mastersingers of Nuremberg, The [with Frederick Corder, trans. Richard Wagner].
Parsifal [with Frederick Corder, trans. Richard Wagner].
Rhine Gold, The [with Frederick Corder, trans. Richard Wagner].
Siegfried [with Frederick Corder, trans. Richard Wagner].
Sisyphus, King of Ephyra [with Frederick Corder].
Valkyrie, The [with Frederick Corder, trans. Richard Wagner].
Tristan and Isolda [with Frederick Corder, trans. Richard Wagner], Munich, 10 June 1865.
Storm in a Teacup, A, Aquarium, Brighton, 18 February 1882.
Noble Savage, The [with Frederick Corder], Aquarium, Brighton, 3 October 1885.
Dusk of the Gods [with Frederick Corder, trans. Richard Wagner].

Corner, Julia
Puss in Boots, in *Little Plays for Little Actors* (London: Dean and Son, 1865).

Corrie, Jessie Elizabeth
Obstinate Woman, An (London: Samuel French, 1903).

Costello, Miss
Plebeian, The, Vaudeville, 28 July 1891.
Bad Quarter of an Hour, A, Queens, Dublin, 31 August 1896.

Courtenay, Judith
Sisters, Jubilee Hall, Addlestone, 28 December 1893.

Cowen, Henrietta
Quiet Pipe, A [with S. M. Samuel], Folly, 7 March 1880.
Neither of Them.

Cox, Mrs Douglas
Pink Letter, The, Maidenhead, 27 January 1898.

Crackenthorpe, Blanche Alethea Elizabeth Holt [Mrs Hubert Montague Crackenthorpe]
Other People's Shoes, in Crawfurd, Oswald, *Dialogues of the Day* (London: Chapman & Hall, 1895).

Craigie, Pearl Mary Teresa Richards [Mrs Reginald Walpole, pseud. 'John Oliver Hobbes']
Ambassador, The, St James's, 2 June 1898.
Journeys End in Lovers Meeting [with George Moore], Daly's, 5 June 1894.
Osbern and Ursyne, 1899.
Repentance, A, St James's, 28 February 1899.
School for Saints, A, Lyceum, 30 March 1896.
The Flute of Pan. A Comedy in Four Acts (London: T. Fisher Unwin, 1904).
Wisdom of the Wise, The, St James's, November 1900.

Crauford, Mrs W. R.
Paul the Showman; or, The Dead Mother's Letter, Britannia, 16 April 1864.

Cresswell, Mrs G.
King's Banner, The, Dublin, 6 December 1872.

Crewe, Annabel
The Next Generation: A Farce (London: Provost & Co., 1879).

Crosland, Camilla Dufour Toulmin [Mrs Newton Crosland]
Hernani [trans. Victor Hugo], 1867.
Ruy Blas [trans. Victor Hugo], 1887.

Crowe, Catherine Stevens
Aristodemus (London: Simpkin Marshall & Co., 1838).
Cruel Kindness, The, Haymarket, 8 June 1853.

Cuthell, Edith
Wrong Envelope, The, Strand, 19 July 1887.

Dacre, Barbarina Ogle, Lady [later Mrs Thomas Wilmot and Baroness Brand]
Frogs and Bulls; A Lilliputian Piece in Three Acts, 1838.
Gonsalvo of Cordova [1810], in *Dramas, Transactions, and Occasional Poems* (1821, privately printed).
Ina, Drury Lane, 22 April 1815.
Pedrarias [1811], in *Dramas, Transactions, and Occasional Poems* (1821, privately printed).
Xarifa, in *Dramas, Transactions, and Occasional Poems* (1821, privately printed).

Dalrymple, Lina
Tricked.

Daly, Julia
In and Out of Place (Leeds, 1873).

Darling, Isabella Fleming
Woman's Rights.

Davidson, Frances A.
Giralda; or, Which is My Husband? Grecian, 25 October 1850.
Gustavus III [trans.] (London: G. H. Davidson, 1850[?]).

Davies, Blanche
Octavia; or, the Bride of St. Agnes (Doncaster: Brooke & Co., 1832).

Davis, Helen
Life Policy, A [adapted from her novel *For So Little*], Terry's, July 1894.

Davis, Lillie
Aunt Madge (Manchester: Abel Heywood, [1896]).
Bumps (Manchester: Abel Heywood, 1900).
Difficult to Please (Manchester: Abel Heywood, [1896]).
Don't Jump at Conclusions (Manchester: Abel Heywood, 1894).
Dorothy's Victory (Manchester: Abel Heywood).
Two Georges, The (Manchester: Abel Heywood, 1895).
Which Got the Best of It? (Manchester: Abel Heywood).

Davis, Mrs Maxwell
Pamela's Prejudice (London: Samuel French, 1890[?]).

de Burgh, Beatrice
Loyal Traitor, A, St James's, May 1900.

de la Pasture, Elizabeth Lydia [Mrs Henry de la Pasture]
Deborah of Tod's (London: Amalgamated Press, 1908).
Her Grace, the Reformer, 1907.
Little Squire, The (London, 1894).
Lonely Millionaires, The, 1906.
Modern Craze, The, St George's Hall, 2 November 1899.
Peter's Mother, in *The Dramatic Works of Mrs Henry de la Pasture* (London: Samuel French, 1910).
Poverty, Brighton n.d.

de Lacy, Mrs
My Lord Adam, Royalty, January 1901.

de Latour, Mademoiselle
Change of Fortune is the Lot of Life, Bath, 10 November 1874.

de Naucaze, Anna
Peruvian, The, Opera Comique, 12 November 1891.

de Rohan, Daphne
Oh! My Wife!, Lyric Ealing, 30 August 1897.

de Smart, Mrs A.
Purely Platonic, Kilburn, 26 April 1898.

de Vere, Florence
Bungles [with H. Morphew], Lyric, Ealing, 18 December 1892.

de Witt, Emilie
Guilty Shadows, The, Imperial, 6 February 1885.

Dening, Christina
Awful Experience, An, Somerville Club, 21 February 1893.
Justice, Town Hall, Westminster, 12 May 1893.

Mistakes, Pioneer Club, 19 October 1893.
Olympus, Somerville Club, 21 February 1893.
Training a Husband, Somerville Club, 21 February 1893.

Denvil, Mrs
Ada, the Betrayed; or, The Murder at the Old Smithy (London: Purkess's Pictorial Penny Plays, n.d.).
Alerame, the Knight of the Lion; or, The Hut of Sarona, Royal Pavilion, 4 February 1833.
Blue Beard; or, The Sepulchre of Death (London: Purkess's Pictorial Penny Plays, n.d.).
Bottle, The; or, The Drunkard's Doom (London: Purkess's Pictorial Penny Plays, n.d.).
Dred: Drama in Two Acts [adapted from H. B. Stowe, *Dred*], Pettingell Collection [held at Templeman Library, University of Kent at Canterbury].
Emily Fitzormond, Royal Pavilion, September 1841.
Fashion and Famine, Britannia Saloon.
Faust and Marguerite [adapted from Michel Carré], Princess's, April 1854.
Ivanhoe; or, The Jew's daughter: A Romantic Melodrama (London: Purkess's Pictorial Penny Plays, n.d.).
Kenilworth: An Historical Drama, in Two Acts (London: Purkess's Pictorial Penny Plays, n.d.).
Poisoner and His Victim, The; or Revenge, Crime and Retribution, Royal Pavilion, 10 February 1845.
Pride and Crime [altered from *The Wife's Tragedy or the Mystery of Twenty Years*], Effingham Saloon, 5 October 1846.
Susan Hapley; or, The Servant Girl's Dream: A Domestic Drama [adapted from Catherine Crowe, *Susan Hopley*], Royal Pavilion, September 1841.
Wealth and Poverty, Royal Pavilion, October 1841.

Dickens, Fanny
Living Lie, A; or, Sowing and Reaping, Royal, Blackburn, 18 June 1883.

Dickinson, Anna
Anna Boleyn, 1877.
Mary Tudor, 1876.

Dietz, Linda
Lessons in Harmony, St George's Hall, 26 June 1875.
Wild Love; or, Eagle Wally, Bristol, 18 April 1881.

Dillon, Clara
His Own Enemy, Aldershot, 13 December 1898.

Dixey, Kate
Girl's Freak, A, St George's Hall, 6 February 1899.

Dolaro, Selina
In the Fashion, Ladbroke Hall, 28 December 1887.

Donnay, Louise Maurice
Doloreaux, La, Lyric, June 1897.

Dorisi, Lisa
Japanese Lamp, A, Drill Hall, Tiverton, 22 May 1897.
Preciosita, St George's Hall, 4 July 1893.

Douglas, Dulcie
Librarian, The, Athenæum, Limerick, 22 May 1885.

Douglas, Miss Johnstone
Pamela, Falkirk, 7 November 1898.

Dowling, Mildred
Dangerfield '95, Garrick, 26 May 1898.
Lorna Doone [adapted from novel by R. D. Blackmore], Royalty, June 1901.

Downshire, Dowager Marchioness of
Ferry Girl, The [music by Lady Arthur Hill], Savoy, 13 May 1890.

Dufferin, Helen Selina Sheridan Blackwood, Lady [Countess of Giffard]
Finesse; or, A Busy Day in Messina, Haymarket, 16 May 1863.

Dunlop, Mrs
Female Cavaliers, The, Fitzroy, 17 February 1834.

Durant, Héloise
Dante, a Dramatic Poem (London: Lamley & Co., 1892).
Our Family Motto; or, Noblesse Oblige, Queen's Gate Hall, 27 February 1889.

Ebsworth, Mary Emma Fairbrother [Mrs Joseph Ebsworth]
Ass's Skin.
Payable at Sight; or, The Chaste Salute (London: John Cumberland, 1828).
Sculptor of Florence, The.
Two Brothers of Pisa, The, Coburg, 21 January 1822.

Edgeworth, Maria
Love and Law, Lyceum, 23 November 1810.
Old Poz (London: T. H. Lacy, n.d.).
Organ Grinder, The (London: T. H. Lacy, n.d.).
Rose, Thistle, and Shamrock, in *Comic Dramas* (London: Hunter and Baldwin, 1817).
Two Guardians, The, in *Comic Dramas* (London: Hunter and Baldwin, 1817).

Edwards, Mrs
Ought We to Visit Her? [with W. S. Gilbert], Royalty, January 1874.

Eliot, George
Armgart, 1874.
Spanish Gypsy, The, 1868.

Elliot, Silvia Fogg
Doubly Sold, in Crawfurd, Oswald, *Dialogues of the Day* (London: Chapman & Hall, 1895).

Elliott, Charlotte
One Fault, Wigan, 9 October 1885.

Ellis, Mrs R.
Last of the Latouches, The, Croydon, 3 December 1877.

Evans, Rose
Disinherited; or, Left to Her Fate, Great Yarmouth, 1 June 1874.
Quite Alone, Great Yarmouth, 25 May 1874.

Evelyn, Miss J.
Crown For Love, A, Princess, Edinburgh, 17 June 1874.
Life's Race, A, Royal Alfred, Marylebone, 19 February 1872.

Fairfax, Mrs
Best People, The, Globe, 14 July 1890.

Lamb, Mary Montgomerie [pseud. 'Violet Fane,' later Mrs Singleton then
    Lady Currie]
Anthony Babington (London: Chapman & Hall, 1877).

Farjeon, Eleanor
Floretta, St George's Hall, 17 July 1899.

Faucit, Mrs J. S.
Alfred the Great, Norwich, 11, 1811.

Fawcett, Mrs
At the Ferry, Kilburn, 26 April 1897.

Feltheimer, Lillian
Girl's Freak, A [with K. Dixey], St George's Hall, 6 February 1899.

Fiddes, Josephine
Deadly Foes, Belfast, 20 November 1868.

Field, Kate
Extremes Meet, St James's, 12 March 1877.
Eyes Right, Gaiety, 13 May 1878.

Field, Miss
Parricide, The [with Lucy Allen], Bath, 7 June 1824.

Fielding, Mary
John Wharton; or, The Wife of a Liverpool Mechanic, Queen's, Manchester,
    5 October 1868.

Field, Michael [see Bradley, Katherine, and Cooper, Emily]

Filippi, Rosina [Mrs H. M. Dowson]
Bennetts, The [adapted from Jane Austen, *Pride and Prejudice*], Court, May 1901.
*Duologues and Scenes from the Novels of Jane Austen Arranged and Adapted for
    Drawing-Room Performance* (London, 1895).
Flower Children, The, in *Three Japanese Plays for Children* (Oxford: H. Daniel, 1897).
Idyll of New Year's Eve, An.
Idyll of Seven Dials, An [music by Amy E. Horrocks], Town Hall, Chelsea, 31
    January 1890.
In the Italian Quarter, Vaudeville, 30 November 1863.
Little Goody Two Shoe [music by A. Levey], Court, 26 December 1888.
Mirror, The, in *Three Japanese Plays for Children* (Oxford: H. Daniel, 1897).
Night of a Hundred Years, The, in *Three Japanese Plays for Children* (Oxford: H. Daniel, 1897).

Fitzsimon, Ellen [Fitz-Simon, Ellen]
Bay of Normandy, The, in *Darrynane in Eighteen Hundred and Thirty-Two and other
    Poems* (Dublin: W. B. Kelly, 1863).

Fletcher, Julia Constance [pseud. 'George Fleming']
Canary, The, Prince of Wales, 13 November 1899.
Fantasticks, The [trans. Edmund Rostand] (London: Heinemann, 1900).
Mrs Lessingham, Garrick, 7 April 1894.

Florance, Mrs B. E.
Bohemian Bandit, The; or, The Shrine of St Margaret's, Olympic, 6 April 1843.

Fogerty, Elsie
Love Laughs at Locksmiths, West, Albert Hall, 13 May 1899.

Forbes, Hon. Mrs
All Hallow's Eve [with J. W. Whitbread], Queen's Dublin, 20 April 1891.

Ford, Mary
Lorna Doone [with Leonard Rayne; adapted from R. D. Blackmore, *Lorna Doone*],
    Princess's, December 1901.

Forrest, Amy
Out of Evil, Queen's Battersea, 4 December 1893.
Trick for Trick, Stratford, 16 December 1889.

Forrester, Stephanie
Black But Comely [adapted from Whyte-Melville], Gaiety, 16 September 1882.
My General, Ryde, 13 November 1890.

Fraser Julia Agnes
Barrington's Busby; or, Weathering the Admiral, Devonport, 4 October 1883.
Court Lovers; or, The Sentinel of the King's Guard (Plymouth: Trend & Co., 1891 [?]).
Dermot O'Donoghue; or, The Stranger from Belfast, Victoria, Strathaven, 24 July
    1872.
Hubert's Pride, Victoria, Strathaven, 8 July 1872.
Idle Words; or, Death and Glory, Opera House, Edinburgh, 21 December 1896.
Pat of Mullingar; or, An Irish Lothario (Greenock: Greenock Advertiser Office, [1879]).
Patrick's Vow, Victoria, Strathaven, 23 May 1873.
Shrilrick (London and Sydney: Remington and Company, 1894).
Slight Mistake, A, Victoria, Strathaven, 6 May 1873.
Star-Spangled Banner, The; or, The Far West.

Freake, Mrs
Deeds, Cromwell House, South Kensington, 25 February 1879.

Freund-Lloyd, Mabel [Mabel Freund Lloyd]
Breach of Promise, A, Opera Comique, 1 December 1891.
For Claudia's Sake, Vaudeville, 2 July 1891.
Sacrificed, Vaudeville, 2 July 1891.

Fry, Betsey
Area Sylph, The; or, A Foot-boy's Dream (London: J. Pattie, n.d.).

Fullerton, Georgiana Charlotte Leveson Gower [Mrs Alexander George Fullerton,
    Lady Georgiana Fullerton]
Fire of London, The; or, Which is Which [*Which is Which?; or, The Fire of London*], 1882.

Ganthony, Nellie
In Want of an Engagement, Vaudeville, 3 June 1891.

Last on the Programme, Lyric, Ealing, 24 September 1892.
Outward Bound, Terry's, 21 March 1896.

Garnett, Constance
Convert, The [trans. Sergius Stepniak], Avenue, 14 June 1898.

Garraway, Agnes J.
Marble Arch, The [written with Edward Rose] (London: Samuel French, 1882).

Garthwaite, Fanny
Leah; or, The Jewish Wanderer [adapted from Salomon Mosenthal, *Deborah*], Sadler's
  Wells, August 1866.

Gaskell, Mrs Penn
Run In, Constitutional Hall, Harlesden, 12 January 1899.

Gathercole, Mrs
Trick for Trick, Dewsbury, 16 February 1877.

Gibbons, Alice
Daughters of Eve (London: Dicks Standard Plays).
Haunted Room, The (London: Dicks Standard Plays).
Lilliput (London: John Dicks, n.d.).

Gibbons, Anne
Mary Stuart [trans. Schiller], Devonport, 1838.

Gibson, Miss C.
Chamois Hunter, The, Queen's, 13 September 1852.

Gilbert-Gilmer, Julia
Life's Parting Ways, Parkhurst, 9 September 1893.

Gillington, May Clarissa [later Mrs G. F. Byron]
Jewel Maiden, The (London: Joseph Williams, 1898).

Giraud, Mrs
Dear Jack, Colchester, 30 May 1892.

Glen, Ida
Woman's Error, A; or, The Stolen Diamonds, Shrewsbury, 1 May 1876.

Glinittzka, Marie von
Harold [trans. Ernst von Wildenbruch] (Hanover: Carl Schussler, 1884).

Glyn, Alice Coralie
Drama in Dregs, A: A Life Study (London: Simpkin & Marshall, 1897).

Goddard, Kate
Mistaken Identity (London and New York: Samuel French, n.d.).
Who Won? (London and New York: Samuel French, n.d.).

Goldschmidt, Anna
On Strike [music by Julia Goldschmidt], Mechanics Hall, Nottingham, 15
  November 1894.

Goldsmith, Mary
She Lives! or, The Generous Brother, Haymarket, 7 March 1803.
Angelina [*Walcot Castle*], Provinces, 1804.

Gore, Catherine Grace Frances Moody [Mrs Charles Gore]
Bond, The [a dramatic poem], 1824.
Dacre of the South; or, The Olden Time, 1840.
Don John of Austria, Covent Garden, 16 April 1836.
Good Night's Rest, A; or, Two in the Morning!, Strand, July 1839.
King O'Neil; or, The Irish Brigade, Covent Garden, 9 December 1835.
King's Seal, The, Drury Lane, 10 January 1835.
Lords and Commons, Drury Lane, 20 December 1831.
Maid of Croissy, The; or, Theresa's Vow [altered subtitle *The Return From Russia*], Haymarket, June 1837.
Minister and the Mercer, The, Drury Lane, 10 February 1834.
Modern Honour; or, The Sharper of High Life, Covent Garden, 3 December 1834.
Queen's Champion, The [altered title *Salvoisy*], Haymarket, 10 September 1834.
Quid Pro Quo; or, The Day of Dupes, Haymarket, June 1844.
School for Coquettes, The, Haymarket, 14 July 1831.
Tale of a Tub, Haymarket, July 1837.

Gowing, Emilia Julia Blake [Mrs William Aylmer Gowing]
Boadicea, in Aylmer Gowing, *Boadicea, a Play in Four Acts and Poems for Recitation* (London: K. Paul, Trench, Trübner, 1899).

Grahame, Mrs Cunningham
Don Juan's Last Wager [adapted from José Zorilla], Prince of Wales, 2, 1900.

Grand, Sarah [pseud. for Frances McFall]
Fear of Robert Clive, The [with Haldane McFall], Lyceum, 14 July 1896.

Gratienne, Mademoiselle
Only an Actress, Mont Dore Hall, Bournemouth, 12 January 1898.

Graves, Clotilde Inez Mary [Clo Graves, Clotilda Graves, pseud. 'Richard Dehan']
Bishop's Eye, The, Vaudeville, 2, 1900.
Bond of Ninon, The, Savoy Theatre, 19 April 1906.
Death and Rachel [altered title *Rachel*], Haymarket, 7 May 1890.
Dr and Mrs Neill, Manchester, 28 September 1894.
Florentine Wooing, A, Avenue, 6 July 1898.
General's Past, The (London: 'The Stage' Play Publishing Bureau, 1925), Royal Court, 3 January 1909.
Katharine Kavanagh, 30 September 1891.
Maker of Comedies, A, Shaftesbury, 9 February 1903.
Match-Maker, A [with Gertrude Kingston], Shaftesbury, 9 May 1896.
Mother of Three, A, Comedy, 8 May 1896.
Nitocris, Drury Lane, 2 November 1887.
Nurse, Globe, March 1900.
Princess Tarakanoff; or, The Northern Night, Prince of Wales, 29 July 1897.
Puss in Boots, Drury, Lane 1888.
She [with Edward Rose], Novelty, 10 May 1888.
Skeleton, The [with Y. Stephens], Vaudeville, 27 May 1887.

St Martin's Summer [with Lady Colin Campbell], Royal, Brighton, 7 February 1902.

Gray, Louisa
Between Two Stools, Glendower Mansions, South Kensington, 30 July 1886.
Tricks and Honours, West, Albert Hall, 7 May 1897.

Green, Katherine
What's In a Name?, Queen's Hall, 9 February 1895.

Greene, Louisa Lilias Plunket [Mrs Richard Jonas Greene, Baroness Greene]
Prince Croesus in Search of a Wife, William Gorman Wills, *Drawing Room Drama*.
'Nettle Coats; or, The Silent Princess' [with F. M. S.], in William Gorman Wills,
    Drawing Room Drama.

Greet, Dora Victoire [Mrs William Greet]
Elsie's Rival, Strand, 9 May 1888.
Flying Visit, A, Criterion, 6 November 1889.
Folded Page, A, Steinway Hall, 12 May 1891.
Jackson's Boy, Her Majesty's, Carlisle, 28 March 1891.
Little Squire, The [with H. Sedger], Lyric, 5 May 1894.
Real Prince, A, Bijou, 27 January 1894.
Thrown Together (London: Samuel French, 1893).
To the Rescue, Prince of Wales, 13 June 1889.

Greeven, Alice
Happy Nook, A [adapted from Sudermann, *Das Glück in Winkel* with J. T. Grein],
    Court, June 1901.

Gregory, H. G. Miss
Fate, Middlesbrough, 9 March 1874.

Greville, Beatrice Violet Graham, Lady
Old Friends, St James's, 26 June 1890.
Baby; or A Warning to Mesmerists, Brighton, 31 October 1890.
Aristocratic Alliance, An, Criterion, 31 March 1894.
Nadia [adapted from novel by H. Greville, *Les Epreuves de Raissa*], Lyric, 3 May
    1892.
Moth and the Candle, The [with Mark Ambient], Brighton, December 1901.

Griffiths, Cherry
All For Gold, Britannia, September 1878.

Grove, Florence Craufurd
Forget-Me-Not [with Herman Charles Merivale], Lyceum, 21 August 1879.

Guion, Nellie
Modern Judas, A, Vaudeville, 25 February 1892.

Hale, Mrs Challow
For the King's Sake, Albany Club, Kingston, 9 January 1897.

Hall, Anna Maria Fielding [Mrs Samuel Carter Hall]
St Pierre, the Refugee, French Refugee, The, St James's, February 1837.
Who's Who? [lost play, mentioned in S. C. Hall, *Retrospect of a Long Life: From
    1815 to 1883* (London: Richard Bentley, 1883), Vol. 2, p. 252].

Mabel's Curse! [music by Mrs G. A. A'Beckett], St James's Theatre, 27 March 1837.
Groves of Blarney, The, Adelphi, 16 April 1838.
Chester Fair, Queens, 27 May 1844.

Hall, Caroline
Will and the Way, The, City of London, 16 May 1853.

Hallett, Mrs
Nobodies at Home: Somebodies Abroad, A Farce in Two Acts, with Historical Reference to the Poet Churchill, Olympic Theatre & Queen's Theatre, n.d. given (London: W. S. Johnson, 1847).
Woman's Whims, or Who's to Win Her? Sadler's Wells, 7 August 1837.
Juniper Jack; or, My Aunt's Hobby, Queens, 16 June 1845.

Hamilton, Cicely
Diana of Dobson's, Kingsway Theatre, 12 February 1908.

Hamilton, Sarah
Alfred the Great, 1829.

Harbon, W. J.
Little Billie Carlyle; or, The Bell and the Hare [burlesque of *East Lynne*], 'Prince of Wales,' Wolverhampton, 18 April 1881.

Harkness, Mrs A. Lawson
The Man with the Camera [1890].

Harrison, Constance Cary
Short Comedies for Amateur Players [1892].

Harrison, Eva
Chaperoned, Assembly Rooms, Cheltenham, 3 June 1887.

Harvey, Margaret
Raymond de Percy; or, The Tenant of the Tomb, Sunderland, 1822.

Harwood, Isabella [pseud. 'Ross Neil']
Andrea the Painter, in *Plays* (London: Ellis & White, 1883).
Angel King, The, Westwood House, Sydenham, 17 July 1884.
Arabella Stuart, St George's Hall, 11 June 1877. *Plays* (London: Ellis & White, 1879).
Cid, The, in *Plays* (London: Ellis & White, 1874).
Claudia's Choice, in *Plays* (London: Ellis & White, 1883).
Duke for a Day; or, The Tailor of Brussels, in *Plays* (London: Ellis & White, 1874).
Eglantine (London: Ellis & White, n.d.).
Elfinella; or, Home from Fairyland, Princess, Edinburgh, 15 October 1875, in *Elfinella* (London: Ellis & White, 1876).
Heir of Lynne, The, in *Plays* (London: Ellis & White, 1879).
Inez; or, The Bride of Portugal, in *Lady Jane Grey* (London: Ellis Green, 1871).
King and the Angel, The, in *Plays* (London: Ellis & White, 1874).
Lady Jane Grey, in *Lady Jane Grey* (London: Ellis Green, 1871).
Lord and Lady Russell, in *Elfinella* (London: Ellis & White, 1876).
Loyal Love, Gaiety, 13 August 1887.

Orestes, in *Plays* (London: Ellis & White, 1883).
Paul and Virginia, Gaiety, Dublin, 23 September 1881.
Tasso, in *Plays* (London: Ellis & White, 1879).

Hatton, Bessie
Village of Youth, The, Rectory Grounds, Radstock, 12 July 1899.

Hawkins, Mrs P. L.
Ciceley's Secret, Bijou, 15 January 1895.

Hawthorn, May
Day Dreams, Park Hall, Camden Town, 23 May 1888.

Haydon, Florence
Jack of All Trades [with Henry Neville], Olympic, 26 December 1861.

Hayes, Maria Ximena
Jean Buscalle [trans. Valnay] (London: J. McDowell, 1879).
Paul and Virginia [trans. Jules Barbier & Michel Carré] (Paris: International Agency of Authors and Composers, 1878).

Hazlewood, Miss
Kevin's Choice [music by T. A. Wallworth] (London: Metzler & Co., 1882).
Maid of Glendalough, St George's Hall, 2 December 1867.

Hemans, Felicia Dorothea Browne [Mrs Alfred Browne]
De Chatillon; or, The Crusaders, in *Dramatic Works* (Edinburgh and London: Blackwood, 1850).
Sebastian of Portugal, in *Dramatic Works* (Edinburgh and London: Blackwood, 1850).
Siege of Valencia, The, in *Dramatic Works* (Edinburgh and London: Blackwood, 1850).
Vespers of Palermo, The, Covent Garden, 12 December 1823.

Henderson, Edith
Mischief Maker, The, Globe, 12 June 1891.

Henderson, Ettie
Almost a Life, Court, Liverpool, 6 November 1882.

Henry, Mrs Re
Going on the Stage, Corn Exchange, Blandford, 18 February 1895.

Herbert, Miss
Up the Ladder, Limerick, 1 December 1876.

Heron, Matilda [later Mrs Robert Stoepel]
Camille; or, The Fate of a Coquette (London and New York: Samuel French, 1856).
Medea [trans. Legouvé], Drury Lane, 5 November 1861.
Phaedra (Cincinnati: Wrightson, 1858).

Heyne, Mary
Rose and the Ring, The [music by Elena Norton], Dublin, 23 March 1878.

Hill, Isabel
Brian the Probationer; or, The Red Hand (London: W. R. Sams, Royal Library, 1842).
First of May, The; or, A Royal Love-Match, Covent Garden, 10 October 1829.

My Own Twin Brother, English Opera House, 9 September 1834.
Poet's Child, The, 1820.
West Country Wooing [lost script?].

Hills, Mrs Hammond
Lost Eden, A, Novelty, 1 June 1897.

Hilton, Hilda
Princess Caro's Plot, Novelty, 31 January 1887.

Hoare, Florence
Snow White [music by Madame Mely], St George's Hall, 3 May 1899.

Hobbes, John Oliver [see Craigie, Pearl]

Hodgson Burnett, Frances
Editha's Burglar [with Stephen Townsend], Bijou, Neath, 3 January, 1890.
Lady of Quality, A [adapted with Stephen Townsend from Burnett's novel], Ladbrooke Hall, 7 March 1896.
Real Little Lord Fauntleroy, The [adapted from her novel], Terry's, 14 May 1888 (London: Samuel French, 1889).
Nixie [with Stephen Townsend], Terry's, 7 April 1890.
Phyllis, Globe, 1 July 1889.
Showman's Daughter, The, Worcester, 12 October 1891.
Young Folk's Ways, Madison Square, New York [as *Esmerelda*], 29 October 1881, St James's, 20 October 1883.

Hodgson, Agatha
Captain's Daughter, The [with Archibald Hodgson], Drill Hall, Southampton, 3 December 1890.
Clerk of the Weather, The [with K. Osborne], Opera House, Torquay, 11 June 1892.
Doomed [with Archibald Hodgson], Philharmonic Hall, Southampton, 8 February 1890.
Gamekeeper's Wife, The [with Archibald Hodgson], Philharmonic Hall, Southampton, 22 September 1890.
In Olden Days [with Archibald Hodgson], Philharmonic Hall, Southampton, 8 February 1890.
On Zephyr's Wings [with Archibald Hodgson], Town Hall, Teddington, 30 July 1891.
Watching and Waiting [with Archibald Hodgson], Prince of Wales, Southampton, 15 January 1891.

Hodson, Emily
Another, Vaudeville, 14 December 1885.

Holcroft, Fanny
Baron, The [trans. Celenio], in *The Theatrical Recorder* (1805).
Emilia Galotti [trans. Lessing], in *The Theatrical Recorder* (1805).
Fortune Mends [trans. Calderon], in *The Theatrical Recorder* (1805).
From Bad to Worse [trans. Calderon], in *The Theatrical Recorder* (1805).
Goldsmith, The, Haymarket, 23 August 1827.
Minna von Barnhelm [trans. Lessing], in *The Theatrical Recorder* (1805).
Philip the Second [trans. Alfieri], in *The Theatrical Recorder* (1805).
Rosamond [trans. Weisse], in *The Theatrical Recorder* (1805).

Holford, Margaret
Marie de Courcelles; or, A Republican Marriage, Olympic, 9 November 1878.

Holt, May [Mrs R. Fairbairn, May Holt Fairbairn]
Dark Deeds [adapted from Mary Braddon's novel *The Trail of the Serpent*, licensed
   as *Jabez North*], Oldham, 7 June 1881.
Every Man for Himself, Aquarium, Great Yarmouth, 22 June 1885.
False Pride, Norwich, 24 September 1883.
High Art, licensed for October–November 1883.
Men and Women, Surrey, 17 July 1882.
Sweetheart, Goodbye, Scarborough, 10 October 1881.
Waiting Consent, Folly, 11 June 1881.

Holton, Florence
His Hidden Revenge, Public Hall, Upton Park, 10 October 1887.
From the Vanished Past, Public Hall, Upton Park, 30 April 1888.

Hope, Naomi
Armourer, The, Whitehaven, 20 September 1894.
Forgive Us Our Trespasses, Gaiety, Brighton, 1 June 1896.

Hughes, Annie
Husband's Humiliation, A, Criterion, 25 June 1896.

Humboldt, Charlotte de
Corinth, in *Corinth: A Tragedy, and Other Poems* (London: Longman, Orme,
   Brown, Green, & Longmans, 1838).

Hungerford, Mrs
Donna [with Mrs N. Phillips], Ladbroke Hall, 11 March 1892.

Hunt, Margaret Raine
Girls He Left Behind Him, The, in Crawfurd, Oswald, *Dialogues of the Day* (London:
   Chapman & Hall, 1895).

Hunt, Violet
End of the Beginning, The, in Crawfurd, Oswald, *Dialogues of the Day* (London:
   Chapman & Hall, 1895).
Hour and the Man, The, in Crawfurd, Oswald, *Dialogues of the Day* (London:
   Chapman & Hall, 1895).
Way to Keep Her, The, in Crawfurd, Oswald, *Dialogues of the Day* (London:
   Chapman & Hall, 1895).

Hunter, Mrs Talbot
Lost to the World, Lyceum, Crewe, 15 February 1892.

Irish, Annie
Across Her Path [adapted from novel by Annie Swan], Terry's, 21 January 1890.

Irvine, Mary Catherine
Heart Repose: A Dramatic Poem in Three Acts (London, 1867).

Isaacson, Beatrice
Day of Reckoning, The, Surrey, December 1900.

Isdell, Sarah
Cavern, The [with music by Sir John Stevenson], Hawkins, St Dublin, 1825.
Poor Gentlewoman, The, Crow, St Dublin, 4 March 1811.

James, Ada
Arts and Crafts [with Dudley James], Ladbroke Hall, 9 March 1897.

Jameson, Anna Brownell Murphy
Country Cousin, The [trans. Amalie, Princess of Saxony], in *Social Life in Germany* (London: George Routledge, 1847).
Falsehood and Truth [trans. Amalie, Princess of Saxony], in *Social Life in Germany* (London: George Routledge, 1847).
Princely Bride, The [trans. Amalie, Princess of Saxony], in *Social Life in Germany* (London: George Routledge, 1847).
Uncle, The [trans. Amalie, Princess of Saxony], in *Social Life in Germany* (London: George Routledge, 1847).
Young Ward, The [trans. Amalie, Princess of Saxony], in *Social Life in Germany* (London: George Routledge, 1847).

Jameson, Mrs
Odds are Even, The, Northampton, 22 June 1893.

Jay, Harriet [pseud. 'Charles Marlowe']
Alone in London [with Robert Buchanan], Olympic, 2 November 1885.
Fascination [with Robert Buchanan], Novelty, 6 October 1887.
Mariners of England, The [with Robert Buchanan], Olympic, March 1897.
New Don Quixote, The [with Robert Buchanan], Royalty, 19 February 1896.
Queen of the Connaught, The [with Robert Buchanan], Olympic, 15 January 1877.
Romance of the Shopwalker, The [with Robert Buchanan], Colchester, 24 February 1896.
Strange Adventures of Miss Brown, The [with Robert Buchanan], Vaudeville, 26 June 1895.
Two Little Maids from School [with Robert Buchanan], Metropolitan, Camberwell, 21 November 1898.
Wanderer from Venus, The [with Robert Buchanan], Grand, Canyon, 8 June 1896.

Jenner, Annabel
My Lady Fanciful, Tivoli Gardens, Margate, 15 August 1899.

Johnson, Ellen
My Aunt Grumble, Brighton, 21 April 1877.

Johnson, S. A.
Caleb; or, The Curse, Terry's, 6 June 1893.

Johnstone, Annie Lewis
On the Frontier, Shakespeare, Liverpool, 30 March 1891.

Jopling, Louise Goode [Mrs Joseph Middleton Jopling, later Mrs Rowe]
Affinities [with Rosa Praed], 1885.

Keating, Eliza H.
Aladdin; or, The Very Wonderful Lamp!, in *Fairy Plays for Home Performance*, No. 6 (London: Thomas Hailes Lacy, n.d.).

Ali Baba – or, A New Duo-(Decimal) Edition of the Forty Thieves!, in *Fairy Plays for Home Performance*, No. 10 (London: Samuel French, n.d.).

Beauty and the Beast, in *Fairy Plays for Home Performance*, No. 1 (London and New York: Samuel French, n.d.).

Blue Beard; or, Female Curiosity! and Male Atrocity! (London: Thomas Hailes Lacy, n.d [1869]).

Cinderella (London and New York: Samuel French, n.d.).

Gosling the Great; or, Harlequin Prince Bluebell; or, Baa Baa Black Sheep and the Fairy of Spring, Birmingham, 10 December 1860.

Home Plays for Ladies, 3rd Part (London: Samuel French, n.d.).

Home Plays for Ladies, 4th Part (London: Samuel French, n.d.).

House that Jack Built, ye Lord Lovell and ye Nancy Belle, The, Brighton, 27 December 1859.

Little Bo Peep, Brighton, 24 October 1860.

Little Red Riding Hood; or, The Wolf, the Wooer, and the Wizard!, in *Fairy Plays for Home Performance*, No. 8 (London: Thomas Hailes Lacy, n.d.). Birmingham, 9 December 1858.

Puss in Boots; or, The Marquis, the Miller, and the Mouser!, in *Fairy and Home Plays for Home Performance*, No. 7 (London and New York: Samuel French, n.d.).

Sleeping Beauty, The; or, One Hundred and Eighteen Years in as Many Minutes, in *Fairy and Home Plays for Home Performance*, No. 9 (London and New York: Samuel French, n.d.).

White Cat, The (London: Thomas Hailes Lacy, n.d.).

Yellow Dwarf, The, in *Fairy and Home Plays for Home Performance*, No. 5 (London: Thomas Hailes Lacy, n.d.).

Keeble, Mrs
Baronet's Wager, The, Drill Hall, Peterborough, 25 June 1869.

Kemble, Frances Ann [later Mrs Pierce Butler]
Mary Stuart [trans. Schiller], in *Plays* (London: Longman, Green, Longman, Roberts, & Green, 1863).

Francis the First (London: John Murray, 1832), Covent Garden, 15 March 1832.

Star of Seville, The (New York: Saunders Otley, 1837).

Mademoiselle de Belle Isle [trans. Dumas], in *Plays* (London: Longman, Green, Longman, Roberts, & Green, 1863). Haymarket, 3 October 1864.

English Tragedy, An, in *Plays* (London: Longman, Green, Longman, Roberts, & Green, 1863).

Kendal, Mrs Mark
Half Seas Over, St George's Hall, June 1882.

Kennion, Mrs
Nina; or, The Story of a Heart [dram Zola, *Nana* & Dumas fils, *La Dame aux Camélias*], Wigan, 13 April 1885.

Kimberley, Mrs F. G.
Eastern Nights, Grand Theatre Brighton, August 1919.

Five Play Season: A Spy in the Ranks; The Woman Who Didn't Wait; Was She to Blame?; Father; & Eastern Nights, Elephant & Castle, July, 1919.

Her Life of Pleasure, Elephant & Castle, October 1919.

Pride of the Regiment, Elephant & Castle Theatre, 11 March 1918.
Ruined Lives, Grand Theatre, Brighton, 2 September 1918.
Sister's Sin, A, Elephant & Castle, August 1901.
Soldier's Divorce, A, Theatre Royal, Wolverhampton, 11 September 1918.
That Little Old Mother of Mine, Elephant & Castle Theatre, 24 November 1919.
That Parson Chap, Grand Theatre, Wolverhampton, 24 May 1913.

Kingston, Gertrude
Bear and the Lady, The, in Crawfurd, Oswald, *Dialogues of the Day* (London: Chapman & Hall, 1895).
Match-Maker, A [with Clotilde Graves], Shaftesbury, 9 May 1896.

Kummer, Clare
Captain Kidd; or, The Buccaneers, Duke of York's, 11 July 1898.

Lacy, Katherine
My Aunt's Heiress (New York: Fitzgerald, n.d.).
Wonderful Cure, A (Boston: Walter H. Baker, n.d.).

Lancaster-Wallis, Ellen [Ellen Wallis, pseud. 'Florence Lancaster']
Amateur Wife, An, Criterion, April 1897.
Cissy's Engagement, Steinway Hall, 19 November 1895.
Cupid in Ermine, Princess, West Kennington, 27 March 1899.
For Wife and State [with J. W. Boulding], Lyceum, Edinburgh, 19 October 1883.
Little Miss Muffet (London and New York: Samuel French, n.d.).
My Son and I, Steinway Hall, 25 May 1894.
Pharisee, The [with T. Malcolm Watson], Shaftesbury, 17 November 1890.
Prior Claim, The (London and New York: Samuel French, n.d.).
Summer Clouds, Grand, Wolverhampton, 15 April 1899.
Wand of Wedlock, The [with H. Macpherson], Grand, Cardiff, 13 April 1896.

Landon, Letitia Elizabeth [Mrs George MacLean]
Triumph of Lucca, The, in *Life and Literary Remains of L.E.L.* (London: H. Colburn, 1841).

Lane, Sara
Albert de Rosen, Britannia, 30 August 1875.
Cobbler's Daughter, The, Britannia, 23 March 1878.
Devotion; or, a Priceless Wife, Britannia, 14 March 1881.
Dolores, Britannia, 6 April 1874.
Faithless Wife, The, Britannia, 15 April 1876.
Red Josephine; or, Woman's Vengeance, Britannia, 5 November 1880.
St. Bartholomew; or, a Queen's Love, Britannia, 21 May 1877.
Taken From Memory, Britannia, 10 November 1873.

Lane-Fox, Florence
Jew's Eye, The, Victoria Hall, Bayswater, 4 June 1889.

Langdale, Dorothy
Moths, British Library, Add. Mss. 53288i, Lord Chamberlain's Collection of Plays.

Latham, Grace
Florian [music by I. Walter], Novelty, 14 July 1886.
Beside a Cradle, Willis Rooms, 18 April 1888.

Latimer, K. M.
Cousin Charlie, Devonshire Park, Eastbourne, 9 February 1889.

Laurend, Madame
Truand Chief!, The; or, The Provost of Paris (London: John Duncombe, 1837[?]).

Lawrence, Eweretta
On 'Change; or, The Professor's Venture [adapted from G. von Moser, *Ultimo*], Strand, 1 July 1885.
Isobel, Ipswich, 2 February 1887.
Jess [adapted with J. J. Bisgood from novel by H. Rider Haggard], Adelphi, 25 December 1890.

Le Fanu, Alicia Sheridan
Sons of Erin, The; or, Modern Sentiment, Lyceum, 11 April 1812.

Le Thiere, Mademoiselle
Roma Guillon, All For Money, Haymarket, July 1869.

Leadbeater, Mary Shakleton
Cottage Dialogues among the Irish Peasantry (Dublin: Hibernia Press, 1813).

Lee, Eliza Buckminster
Correggio [trans. Öhlenschlager], in *Correggio* (Boston: Phillips & Sampson, 1846).
Sappho [trans. Grillparzer], in *Correggio* (Boston: Phillips & Sampson, 1846).

Leigh, Agnes
Contradictions (London and New York: Samuel French, n.d.).
Lady in Search of an Heiress, A (London and New York: Samuel French, n.d.).
Lunatic, The (London and New York: Samuel French, n.d.).
Number Seventeen (London and New York: Samuel French, n.d.).
Rainy Day, A (London and New York: Samuel French, n.d.).
Short Plays and Interludes (London: Samuel French, 1899).

Leigh, Norma
Auld Lang Syne, Ladbroke Hall, 19 June 1891.

Leightner, Frances
Queen Elizabeth; or, at the Queen's Command, Vaudeville, September 1901.

Leighton, Dorothy
Thyrza Fleming, Independent Theatre Society at Terry's, 4 January 1895.

Lemore, Clara
Crooked Mile, A, Comedy, Manchester, 23 January 1885.

Leonard, Martha
Lion Hunter, The [with J. T. Grein], Terry's, March 1901.

Leterrier, Jennie
My Courier, Comedy, Manchester, 23 August 1886.

Leverson, Ada [Mrs Ernest Leverson]
All For the Best, in Crawfurd, Oswald, *Dialogues of the Day* (London: Chapman & Hall, 1895).
Engaged, in Crawfurd, Oswald, *Dialogues of the Day* (London: Chapman & Hall, 1895).

Lewis, Catherine
Cupid's Odds and Ends, Parkhurst, 1 June 1895.
My Missis [with Donald Robertson], Opera Comique, 18 October 1886.

Lindley, Henrietta
For England's Sake, Haymarket, 10 July 1889.
Henrietta, Tangled Chain, A [adapted from Mrs Panton's novel], Prince of Wales,
    March 1888.
Her Dearest Foe [adapted from Mrs Alexander's novel], Criterion, 2 May 1894.
Power of Love, The [adapted from Michael Connelly's novel], Prince of Wales,
    6 March 1888.

Lonergan, E. Argent
Betwixt the Cup and the Lip, Mortley Hall, Hackney, 28 November 1896.
Love Letter, A, Strand, May 1894.
Love Versus Science, South West London Polytechnic, 9 May 1896.
To Be or Not To Be, National Hall, Hornsey, 24 November 1894.

Lord, Henrietta Frances
Nora; or, A Doll's House [trans. Ibsen], School of Dramatic Art, 25 March 1885,
    (London: Griffith, Farran, Okeden, & Welsh, 1890).

Lovell, Maria Anne Lacy [Mrs George William Lovell]
Beginning and the End, The, Haymarket, 27 October 1855.
Ingomar, the Barbarian, Drury Lane, 9 June 1851.

Lowther, Aimée
Dream Flower, The, Comedy, 30 June 1898.

Lyall, Edna
In Spite of All, Comedy, 2, 1900.

Lynch, Hannah
Folly or Saintliness [trans. Jose Echegaray], in *The Great Galeoto* (London: John
    Lane, 1895).
Great Galeoto, The [trans. Jose Echegaray], in *The Great Galeoto* (London: John
    Lane, 1895).

Maberley, Mrs
Day Near Turin, A, English Opera House, 6 May 1841.

Macauley, Elizabeth Wright
Marmion (Cork: John Connor, 1811).
Mary Stuart (London, 1823).

MacDonnell, Cicely [Mrs A. J. MacDonnell]
For Good or Evil, Royalty, 18 June 1894.
Life's Sarcasm, 6 May 1898.

MacFarren, Natalia
Barber of Seville, The [trans. libretto] (New York: G. Schirmer, n.d.).
Bride of Lammermoor [trans. libretto] (New York: G. Schirmer, 1898).
Dumb Girl of Portici, The [trans. libretto] (London: Novello, Ewer; Simpkin,
    Marshall, n.d.).

Lohengrin [trans. libretto] (London: Novello, Ewer, n.d.).
Tannhauser and the Tournament of Song at Wartburg [trans. libretto] (London: Novello, Ewer; Simpson, Marshall, n.d.).
William Tell [trans. libretto] (London: Novello, Ewer, n.d.).

Mark, Mrs
Half Seas Over, St George's, Kendal, 24 June 1882.

Marriott, Fanny
Capers [with A. K. Matthews], Vestry Hall, Hampstead, 18 March 1899.

Marryat, Florence [Mrs Francis Lean, later Mrs Ross Church]
Woman Against Woman [ts; reprinted in *English and American Drama of the Nineteenth Century*, Readex Corporation].
Miss Chester [with Young, Charles Lawrence, Sir], Holborn, 10 May 1872.
Her World Against a Lie [with G. F. Neville], Alhambra, Barrow-in-Furness, 24 May 1880.
Her Own Enemy [adapted from her novel], Gaiety, March 1884.
Gamekeeper, The [with Herbert MacPherson], Aquarium, Brighton, 16 May 1898.

Mars, Ann
Never Again [adapted from Maurice Desvallières & Ann Mars' novel], Vaudeville, October 1898.

Martin, Mrs
Repraffon; or, The Savoyards (London: John Nichols & Son, 1823).

Marx, Eleanor [Eleanor Marx Aveling]
Doll's House, A [trans. Ibsen], 1886.
Doll's House Repaired, A [with Israel Zangwill], 1891.
Enemy of Society, An [trans. Ibsen].
Lady from the Sea, The [trans. Ibsen], Terry's, 11 May 1891.

Masters, Julia C.
Scarlet Dye, The, St George's Hall, May 1888.
Scellés, Les, St George's Hall, 25 May 1888.

Maynard, Mary
Shakespeare's Dream; or, A Night in Fairy Land [trans. Tieck, music by B. Gilbert], Surrey, 7 September 1861.

McFall, Frances, see 'GRAND, Sarah'

McNamara, Annie
Our Garden [music by C. Schäfer], Parkhurst, 15 December 1894.

Meadows, Alice Maud
Run Down to Brighton, A, St Martin's Town Hall, 24 July 1893.

Medd, Mabel S. [Mabel S. Mead]
Broken Idylls (London and New York: Samuel French, n.d.).
Imogen's New Cook, Ladbroke Hall, 26 April 1898.

Medina, Rose
Ernest Maltravers, Britannia, 28 September 1874.

Meller, Rose
Light of Other Days, The, Middlesex County Asylum, 14 November 1889.
Summer's Dream, A, Avenue, 14 July 1891.

Mellon, Margaret
Jewess, The, British Library, Add. Mss. 42974, ff. 386–452, 472–506, Lord
    Chamberlain's Collection of Plays.

Merivale, Mrs Herman Charles
Butler, The [with Herman Merivale], Manchester, 24 November 1886.
Don, The [with Herman Merivale], Toole's, 7 March 1888.
Our Joan [with Herman Merivale], Prince of Wales, Birmingham, 22 August 1887.

Milligan, Alice L.
Last Feast of the Flanna, The (London: David Nutt, 1900).

Minton, Ann
Wife to Be Lent, A; or, The Miser Cured (London: A. Seale, 1802).

Mitford, Mary Russell
Alice, in *Dramatic Scenes* (London: George B. Whittaker, 1827).
Bridal Eve, The, in *Dramatic Scenes* (London: George B. Whittaker, 1827).
Captive, The, in *Dramatic Scenes* (London: George B. Whittaker, 1827).
Charles the First, Victoria, 2 July 1834.
Cunigunda's Vow, in *Dramatic Scenes* (London: George B. Whittaker, 1827).
Emily, in *Dramatic Scenes* (London: George B. Whittaker, 1827).
Fair Rosamond, in *Dramatic Scenes* (London: George B. Whittaker, 1827).
Fawn, The, in *Dramatic Scenes* (London: George B. Whittaker, 1827).
Foscari, Covent Garden, 4 November 1826.
Gaston de Blondeville, in *Dramatic Works* (London: Hurst & Blackett, 1854).
Henry Talbot, in *Dramatic Scenes* (London: George B. Whittaker, 1827).
Inez de Castro, City of London, 28 February 1841.
Julian, Covent Garden, 15 March 1823.
Masque of the Seasons, The, in *Dramatic Scenes* (London: George B. Whittaker,
    1827).
Otto of Wittlesbach, in *Dramatic Works* (London: Hurst & Blackett, 1854).
Painter's Daughter, The, in *Dramatic Scenes* (London: George B. Whittaker,
    1827).
Rienzi, Drury Lane, 9 October 1828.
Sadak and Kalasrade; or, The Waters of Oblivion [music by Packer], English Opera
    House, 20 April 1835.
Siege, The, in *Dramatic Scenes* (London: George B. Whittaker, 1827).
Wedding Ring, The, in *Dramatic Scenes* (London: George B. Whittaker, 1827).

Molini, Miss
William Tell [trans. Schiller], 1846.

Monckton, Lady
Countess, The, Sir Percy Shelley's Theatre, 2 June 1882.
Tobacco Jars, St George's Hall, 12 June 1869.

Moore, Ada
Sneaking Regard, A, Surrey, 16 April 1870.

Morgan, Sydney Owenson [Mrs Thomas Charles Morgan, Lady Morgan]
Cavern, The; or, The Outlaws [music by Sir John Stevenson], Dublin, 22 April 1825.
Easter Recess, The; or, The Tapestry Workers, in *Dramatic Scenes from Real Life* (New York: J. & J. Harper, 1833).
Manor Sackville, in *Dramatic Scenes from Real Life* (New York: J. & J. Harper, 1833).
Temper, in *Dramatic Scenes from Real Life* (New York: J. & J. Harper, 1833).

Morland, Charlotte E.
Matrimonial Agency, The, Victoria Hall, Bayswater, 15 November 1888.
Quicksands [adapted from Lovett Cameron, *The Devout Lover*], Comedy, 18 February 1890.
Shower of Kisses, A, Lyric Hammersmith, 27 June 1893.

Morrison, Mary [May Morrison, Mary Morison]
Jenson Family, The [trans. Edward Höyer], Criterion, April 1901.
Lonely Lives [trans. Hauptmann, *Einsame Menschen*], Strand, April 1901 (London: William Heinemann, 1898).
Weavers, The [trans. Hauptmann, *Die Weber*] (London: William Heinemann, 1899).

Mortimer, Rose
Ballet Girl's Revenge, The [with Frederick Marchant], Grecian, September 1865.

Morton, Martha
Bachelor's Romance, A, Gaiety, 11 September 1897.
Sleeping Partner, The, Criterion, 17 August 1897.

Moubrey, Lilian [Lillian Mowbray]
King and Artist [with Walter Herries Pollock], Strand, 30 June 1897.
Were-Wolf, The [with Walter Herries Pollock], Avenue, 15 February 1898.

Mowatt, Anna Cora [Mrs Ritchie]
Armand; or, The Peer and the Peasant [licensed in Britain as *Armand; or, The Days of Louis the XV*], Park Theatre, New York, 27 September 1847.
Fashion; or, Life in New York, Olympic, 9 January 1850.

Muir, Jessie
Beyond Human Power [trans. Bjornstjerne Bjornson], Royalty, November 1901.

Musgrave, Mrs H.
Cerise & Co, Prince of Wales, 17 April 1890.
Dick Wilder, Vaudeville, 20 June 1891.
Our Flat, Winter Gardens, Southport, 10 April 1889.

Nesbit, E.
Family Novelette, A [with O. Barron], Public Hall, New Cross, 21 February 1894.

Newman, Ethel L.
Wally and the Widow (London and New York: Samuel French, 1905).

Nordon, Julia B.
Misunderstood, Steinway Hall, 6 May 1899.

Novello, Mary Sabilla Hehl [Mrs Vincent Novello]
Turandot: The Chinese Sphinx (London: Samuel French, 1872).

O'Connell, Alice
All Jackson's Fault, Athenæum Hall, Tottenham Court Road, 27 November 1889.

Openshaw, Mary
My First Client (London and New York: Samuel French, 1903).

Osborne, Kate
Clerk of the Weather, The, Opera House, Torquay, 11 June 1892.

Overbeck, Miss E.
Round the Links, Albert Hall, 9 May 1895.
Sonia, Albert Hall, 9 May 1895.

Pacheco, Mrs R.
Tom, Dick, and Harry, Manchester, 24 August 1893.

Palmer, Mrs Bandmann
Catherine Howard; or, The Tomb, the Throne, and the Scaffold, Weymouth, 2 January 1892.

Pardoe, Julia
Agnes St. Aubin, the Wife of Two Husbands, Adelphi, 21 January 1841.
Breach of Promise of Marriage, The, Adelphi, 21 February 1842.
Louise de Lignerolles; or, A Lesson for Husbands, Adelphi, 5 November 1838.

Parker, Lottie Blair
Red Roses, Duke of York's, 12 November 1898.

Parker, Nella
Tom's Wife, Assembly Rooms, Worthing, 7 April 1896.

Payn, Dorothea
Midnight Shriek, A, Gaiety, Dublin, 5 January 1896.

Peard, Frances Mary
Pins and Needles (Torquay: Standard Printing, Publishing, & Newspaper Co., n.d.).

Penn, Rachel [Mrs E. S. Willard]
Lucky Bag, The [music by L. N. Parker], Savoy, 6 June 1893.
Merry Piper of Nuremburg, The, Savoy, 8 June 1893.
Punch and Judy [with M. E. Jones, music by E. Jones], Savoy, 8 June 1893.
Tommy, Olympic, 9 February 1891.

Perry, Mrs
Our Last Rehearsal [music by A. Oake], Pleasure Gardens, Folkestone, 25 April 1893.

Pfeiffer, Emily Jane Daub
Wynnes of Wynhavod, The, in *Under the Aspens* (London: Kegan Paul, Trench, 1882).

Phelps, Sydney
Lady Volunteers, The, Parkhurst, 13 July 1896.

Phillips, Elizabeth [Mrs Alfred Phillips]
Bachelor's Vow, The [altered title *Prejudice; or, A Bachelor's Vow*], Strand, 27 November 1848.
Caught in His Own Trap, Olympic, 13 October 1851.

Cupid in Brighton, Brighton, 9 February 1848.
First Love; or, Uncle's Letter [with A. S. Wigan], Brighton, 16 January 1839.
Katty From Connaught, Strand, 27 August 1849.
King's Choice, Strand, 27 November 1848.
Life in Australia, from Our Own Correspondent, Olympic, 21 February 1853.
Master Passion, The, Olympic, 1 September 1852.
My Husband's Will, Olympic, 19 September 1853.
Organic Affection, An, Olympic, 15 January 1852.
Original Bloomers, The, Olympic, 10 November 1851.
Uncle Crotchet, Olympic, 18 April 1853.

Phillips, Mrs Newton
All a Mistake, Ladbroke Hall, 28 January 1890.
Alpine Tourists, Ladbroke Hall, 24 January 1888.
Broken Off, Ladbroke Hall, 24 May 1892.
Charlotte Maria [with F. McRae], Ladbroke Hall, 24 May 1892.
Donna [with H. Hungerford], Ladbroke Hall, 11 March 1892.
Some Day [with John Tresahar], St George's Hall, 13 May 1889.

Pineo, Mabel [pseud. 'Max Pireau']
Double Deception, The [with Lois Royd], Bijou, 25 October 1897.

Planché, Elizabeth St George [Mrs James Robinson Planché]
Folly and Friendship, Olympic, 23 January 1837.
Handsome Husband, A, Olympic, 15 February 1836.
Hasty Conclusion, A, Olympic, 19 April 1838.
Ivan Daniloff; or, The Sledge Driver [altered title *Ivan Daniloff; or, The Russian Mandate*], Haymarket, 19 June 1834.
Pleasant Neighbour, A, Olympic, 20 October 1836.
Ransom, The: An Anecdote of Montesquieu, Haymarket, 9 June 1836.
Reflection, An Interlude, 9 December 1834.
Vision of Venus, A; or, A Midsummer-Night's Nightmare (London: John Dicks, n.d.).
Welsh Girl, The, Olympic Theatre, 16 December 1833.

Plowden, Dorothea Phillips [Mrs. Francis Plowden]
Virginia [music by S. J. Arnold], Drury Lane, 30 October 1800.

Polack, Elizabeth
Esther, the Royal Jewess; or, The Death of Haman!, Royal Pavilion, 9 March 1835.
St. Clare of the Isles; or, The Outlaw of Barra, Victoria, 16 April 1838.

Pollock, Ellen [pseud. 'St John Harley,' Mrs Julius Pollock]
Eunice (London: Tinsley Brothers, 1877).
Judael, Olympic, 14 May 1885.
Violent Passion, 1880.

Porter, Anna Maria
Switzerland, Drury Lane, 15 February 1819.
Fugitives, The [music by Busby], Covent Garden, 16 May 1803.

Porter, Helen Tracy Lowe
Three Heron's Feathers, The [trans. Hermann Sudermann], in *Poet-Lore*, New Series IV (April–June 1900).

Potter, Mary
Bag of Tricks, A, Brighton, 18 May 1896.

Praed, Rosa [Caroline Murray-Prior, Mrs Campbell Praed]
Affinities [with Louise Jopling] (London: Richard Bentley, 1885).
Ariane [with R. Lee], Opera Comique, 8 February 1888.
Binbian Mine, The [with Justin McCarthy], Margate, 6 October 1888.
Marked Man, A [with J. J. Hewson], Pavilion, September 1901.

Praeger, Nita
Outwitted, Meistersingers' Club, 20 June 1890.

Prevost, Constance M. [pseud. 'Terra Cotta']
Meadowsweet, Vaudeville, 5 March 1890.
Silence of a Chatterbox, The [from a story by Miss Wilford], Terry's, 30 October 1899.

Price, Florence Alice [pseud. 'Gertrude Warden,' afterwards Mrs James]
Cruel City, The; or, London By Night [with John Wilton Jones], Surrey, 5 October 1896.
Miss Cinderella, Strand, May 1900.
Woman's Proper Place [with John Wilton Jones], St James's, 29 June 1896.

Prinsep, Val
Cousin Dick, Court, 1 March 1879.
Monsieur le Duc, Princess's, Manchester, 28 August 1879.

Pritchard, Joanna
Auramania; or, Diamond's Daughter, Alfred, 4 September 1871.

Purvis, Mrs Herbert
After Long Years [with A. Law], Torquay, 20 October 1886.

Rae, Josephine
Bars of Gold [with Thomas Sidney], St Leonards, 6 June 1892.
Interviewed [with Thomas Sidney], West Pier, Brighton, 1 September 1896.
Love, the Magician [with Thomas Sidney], Shaftesbury, 7 July 1892.
My Little Red Riding Hood [with Thomas Sidney], Pavilion, St Leonards, 16 October 1895.
Pretty Mollie Barrington [with Thomas Sidney], St Leonards, 6 June 1892.
Ruby Heart, The [with Thomas Sidney], St Leonards, 6 June 1892.

Ramsay, Alicia
As a Man Sows [with Rudolph de Cordova], Grand, 22 August 1898.
Executioner's Daughter, The [with Rudolph de Cordova], Gaiety, Hastings, 6 April 1896.
Gaffer Jarge, Comedy, 11 January 1896.
Mandarin, The [with Rudolph de Cordova], Grand, April 1901.
Monsieur de Paris [with Rudolph de Cordova], Royalty, April 1896.

Randford, Maud
Harvest of Crime, A, Brierly Hill, 27 May 1897.
Streaks of Gold, Sunderland, 14 March 1878.

Ransome, Edith
Scenes from the Life of 'Goody Two-Shoes.' A Little Play for Little Actors (London: Griffith & Farran, 1882).

Rawson, Mrs Stepney
Love Snare, A, British Library, Add. Mss. 1902/14C, Lord Chamberlain's Collection of Plays.

Ray, Catherine
Emperor and Galilean [trans. Ibsen] (London: Tinsley, 1876).

Ray, Eileen
Caroona, Torquay, 20 January 1899.

Raymond, Catherine [Kate] Frances Malone
Devil's Share, The, Liverpool, 1843.
Mariette; or, The Reward, Liverpool, 24 October 1843.
Two Sisters, The; or, The Godfather's Legacy, Liverpool, 28 September 1843.
Waifs of New York, The, Liverpool, 13 September 1875.

Reade, Gertrude
Minkalay, The [with A. Leeds], Metropolitan, Devonport, 19 December 1896.

Reid, Bessie
Desperation [with G. Roy], West Bromwich, 10 June 1887.
Colonel's Wife, The [with L. Smith], Coventry, 6 February 1888.

Revell, Lilian
From Shadow to Sunshine [with Hawley Francks], Elephant & Castle, July 1901.

Richardson, Sarah Watts
Gertrude (London: C. Lowndes, n.d.).
Ethelred (London: Lowndes & Hobbs, 1810).

Righton, Mary
Cupid and Psyche, Bijou, 20 April 1895.
Dear Friends/Our Friends, Ladbroke Hall, 16 March 1888.
Little Nobody, Vaudeville, 24 July 1890.

Riley, Catherine
On and Off [adapted from Alexandre Bisson, *Le Contrôleur des Wagons-Lits*], Vaudeville, December 1898.

Robertson, Jessie
Dan, the Outlaw, Novelty, May 1892.

Robertson, Mrs
Ellinda; or, The Abbey of St Aubert, Newark, 1800.

Robins, Elizabeth
Alan's Wife [with Florence Bell], Independent Theatre [Club], at Terry's, 2 May 1893.
Votes for Women, Court Theatre, 1907.

Robinson, Emma
Revolt of Flanders, The (London: 1848).
Richelieu in Love; or, The Youth of Charles I, Haymarket, 30 October 1852.

Rogers, Maud M.
When the Wheels Run Down, St George's Hall, 29 April 1899.

Rose, Ada
At Cross Purposes (London: Samuel French, n.d.).
Man of Ideas, A (London: Samuel French, 1901).

Rouse, Miss T.
Naomi (London: Hamilton, Adams; Norwich: Jarrold & Sons, n.d.).

Rouse, Miss E.
Buy-em-dears, alias Bay-a-deres, Strand, 12 October 1838.

Rowsell, Mary
Friend of the People, The [with H. A. Saintsbury], Haymarket, 12 February 1898.
Richard's Play [with J. J. Dilley], Ladbroke Hall, 14 January 1891.
Whips of Steel [with J. J. Dilley], St George's Hall, 7 May 1889.

Royd, Lois
Double Deception, The [with M. Pineo], Bijou, 25 October 1897.

Rumsey, Mary C.
Midsummer Night, The; or, Shakespeare and the Fairies [trans. L. Tieck, *Die Sommer-nacht*], 1854.

Rund, Katherine
Golden Prospect, The; or, A Forlorn Hope, Pavilion, June 1891.

Russell, Georgiana Adelaide Peel [Lady]
Dewdrop and Glorio; or, The Sleeping Beauty in the Wood [with Russell, Victoria, Lady] (London: Charles Westerton, n.d.).

Ryley, Madeleine Lucette
Altar of Friendship, The; An Original Comedy in Four Acts, Hollis Street Theatre, Boston, USA, 9 September 1901.
American Citizen, An, Duke of York's, 19 June 1899.
American Invasion, An, Ford's Theatre, Baltimore, USA, 6 October 1902.
Coat of Many Colours, A, West London, 22 July 1897.
Grass Widow, The, An Original Farce in Three Acts, Shaftesbury Theatre, 3 June 1902.
Jedbury Junior, Empire, New York, 23 September 1895.
Lady Paramount, The; A Comedy In a Prologue and Three Acts, Alcazar Theatre, San Francisco, 10 April 1905.
Mice and Men, Theatre Royal Manchester, 27 November 1901.
Mrs Grundy: A Play in Four Acts, Scala Theatre, 16 November 1905.
My Lady Dainty, A Domestic Comedy in Four Acts, Theatre Royal, Brighton, 2 July 1900.
Mysterious Mr Bugle, The, Strand, 29 May 1900.
Realism, Garrick, October 1900.
Richard Savage, Historical Drama in Five Acts, Lyceum Theatre, New York, 4 February 1901.
Sugar Bowl, The, A Comedy in Four Acts, Queen's, 9 October 1907.
The Great Conspiracy, A Play in Three Acts, Duke of York's, 4 March 1907.

The Voyagers, A Comedy in Four Acts, Grand Opera House, Chicago, 10 October 1989.
Vanishing Husband, The, Stockton-on-Tees, 29 January 1897.

Sadlier, Mrs J.
Secret, The, A Drama (London: R. Washbourne, 1880).

Saint Aubyn, Daisy
Dark Hour, The, St George's Hall, 1 April 1885.

Saint Ruth, Abbey
Key to King Solomon's Riches, Limited, The, Opera Comique, 24 December 1896.

Salmon, Mrs
Jephtha (London: George C. Caines, 1846).

Sandbach, Margaret Roscoe
Giuliano de' Medici, in *Giullano de' Medici with Other Poems* (London: William Pickering, 1842).

Sandford, Edith
Firefly, Surrey, 17 May 1869.
Flamma; or, The Child of the Fire [with F. Hay], Britannia, 6 June 1870.

Santley, Kate
Vetah, Portsmouth, 30 August 1886.

Saull, J. A.
Prince Pedrillo; or, Who's the Heir?, Central Hall, Nottingham, 21 November 1893.

Saville, E. F.
Deserted Village, The, Swansea, 5 October 1835.

Schiff, Emma
Countess, The; or, A Sister's Love, Alfred, 21 February 1870.
On the Brink, Amphitheatre, Liverpool, 23 October 1875.
Rights of Woman, The, Globe, 9 January 1870.
Twin Sisters, The, Charing Cross, 18 April 1870.

Scott, Jane M.
Animated Effigy, The, Sans Pareil, 12 February 1811.
Asgard, the Demon Hunter; or, Le Diable à la Chasse, Sans Pareil, 17 November 1812.
Forest Knight, The; or, The King Bewildered, Sans Pareil, 14 February 1813.
Il Giorno Felice; or, The Happy Day, Sans Pareil, 27 February 1812.
Inscription, The; or, The Indian Hunters, Sans Pareil, 26 February 1814.
Mary the Maid of the Inn; or, the Bough of Yew, Sans Pareil, 27 December 1809.
Old Oak Chest The; or, The Smuggler's Son and Robber's Daughter, Sans Pareil, 5 February 1816.
Raykisnah the Outcast; or, The Hollow Tree, Sans Pareil, 22 November 1813.
Red Robber, The; or, The Statue in the Wood, Sans Pareil, 3 December 1808.
Row of Ballynavogue, The; or, The Lily of Lismore, Sans Pareil, 27 November 1817.
Two Spanish Valets, The; or, Lie Upon Lie!, Sans Pareil, 2 November 1818.
Ulthona the Sorceress, Sans Pareil, November 1807.

Vizier's Son, the Merchant's Daughter and the Ugly Woman, The; or, The Maid of Bagdad, Sans Pareil, 16 November 1811.
Whackham and Windham; or, The Wrangling Lawyers, Sans Pareil, 25 January 1814.

Scott, Mary Affleck
Tarantula, The, Haymarket, 4 September 1897.

Scotti, Sophie [Mme C Scotte]
Happier Days, Ladbroke Hall, 17 June 1886.
Peaceful War [adapted with Leopold Wagner from G. von Moser & Franz Schönthan, *Krieg im Frieden*], Prince of Wales, 24 May 1887.
Resemblance, Vaudeville, 10 December 1885.

Seaton, Rose
Andromeda, Vaudeville, 24 March 1890.
Mr. Donnithorpe's Rent, Opera House, Chatham, 9 June 1890.
Music at Home, Opera House, Chatham, 9 June 1890.

Seawall, Miss Elliot
Sprightly Romance of Marsac, The, Ladbroke Hall, 2 February 1898.

Serle, Mrs Walter
Outwitted, Aquarium, Scarborough, 26 April 1889.

Serres, Olivia [Olive Wilmot]
Castle of Avola, The (London, 1805).

Seymour, Mary
Daughter-in-Law, A, in *Home Plays for Ladies*, Part 9 (London and New York: Samuel French, n.d.).
Heiress, The, in *Home Plays for Ladies*, Part 7 (London and New York: Samuel French, n.d.).
Only a Jest, in *Home Plays for Ladies*, Part 7 (London and New York: Samuel French, n.d.).
Ten Years Hence, in *Home Plays for Ladies*, Part 9 (London and New York: Samuel French, n.d.).

Shannon, Mrs F. S.
Mountain Sylph, The (London: Thomas Hailes Lacy, [1834]).
Jealousy [with Charles Shannon], Covent Garden, 20 October 1838.

Shore, Louisa Catherine
Hannibal (London: Grant Richards, 1898).

Sim, Mrs Charles
Love and Be Silent, Garrick, May 1901.

Simpson, Ella Graham
Demon Spider, The; or, The Catcher Caught [music by W. E. Lawson] (London and Newcastle-on-Tyne: Andrew Reid, n.d.).

Simpson, Kate
Elfiana; or, The Witch of the Woodlands [music by W. M. Wood], Olympia, Newcastle, 30 September 1895.
Nanette [music by E. Lorence], Assembly Rooms, Newcastle, 12 November 1895.

Sinclair, Kate
Broken Sixpence, A [with Mrs G. Thompson], Ladbroke Hall, 11 April 1889.
Duskie [with Mrs G. Thompson], Ladbroke Hall, 17 June 1890.
Mademoiselle de Lira [with Mrs G. Thompson], Comedy, 7 January 1890.
Plucky Nancy [with Mrs G. Thompson], Town Hall, Kilburn, 16 March 1889.
Pounds, Shillings, and Pence [with Mrs G. Thompson], Town Hall, Kilburn, 18 January 1892.
Saint Angela [with Mrs G. Thompson], Town Hall, Kilburn, 18 January 1892.

Smale, Edith C.
Baffled Spinster, The (London and New York: Samuel French, 1901).
Bravado, Strand, 3 July 1889.
Compromising Case, A, Haymarket, 26 May 1889.
Forty Winks, 1896.
Old Spoons, Vestry Hall, Turnham Green, 2 February 1899.

Smedley, Constance
Mrs Jordan; or, On the Road to Inglefield, Royalty, February 1900.

Smith, Lita
Bridget's Blunders, Devonshire Park, Eastbourne, 5 August 1892.
Colonel's Wife, The [with B. Reid], Coventry, 6 February 1888.
Domestic Medicine, Grantham, 2 June 1887.
Mistress Peg, Vaudeville, 23 February 1892.
Mr. and Mrs. Muffett; or, A Domestic Experiment, Gaiety, Hastings, 6 June 1892.
My Friend Gomez [music by E. Stanley], Assembly Rooms, Preston, 28 May 1896.

Smith, Miss A.
Rainy Day, A [music by Virginia Gabriel], Gallery of Music, 23 May 1868.

Snowe, Lucy
Bondage, in *Two Stage Plays* (London: R. B. Johnson, 1900).
Croesus, in *Carpet Plays* (London: R. Brimley Johnson, 1903).
Denzill Herbert's Atonement, in *Two Stage Plays* (London: R. B. Johnson, 1900).
Paying Guest, The, in *Carpet Plays* (London: R. Brimley Johnson, 1903).

Southam, Gertrude
Archibald Danvers, M. D. [with E. Armitage], Pavilion, Southport, 20 October 1893.

St Clair Stobart, Mrs
Meringues: A Drawing-Room Duologue, Prince's Skating Rink, 25 May 1909.

Staples, Edith Blair
Was It a Dream? Mechanics' Institute, Stockport, 23 January 1896.

Steele, Anna Caroline Wood
Red Republican, A (Witham: W. R. King, 1874).
Under False Colours, St George's Hall, 9 February 1869.

Steer, Janet
Cloven Foot, The [with Frederick Mouillot, adapted from M. E. Braddon's novel, *Like and Unlike*], Blackburn, 27 January 1890.
Idols of the Heart, Shakespeare, Liverpool, 21 February 1890.

Steinberg, Amy [Mrs John Douglass]
My Mother, Toole's, 20 May 1890.
My Uncle, Terry's, 16 July 1899.

Stewart, Katherine
Episode, An, Pleasure Gardens, Folkestone, 17 May 1895.

Stewart, E. M.
Rival Knights, The, City of London, 21 August 1866.

Stirling, Mrs
Night of Suspense, A (London: Samuel French, 1843).

Stockton, Ella
Madcap Violet [dramatized from novel by Black], Sadler's Wells, 18 March 1882.

Stuart, Adeline
In Search of a Father, Grand, Derby, 1 August 1898.

Stuart, Mary
Out of the Shadow-Land, Bijou, 17 June 1899.

Swan, Myra
Her First Engagement, Middlesbrough, 5 March 1894.

Swanwick, Anna
Agamemnon, The [trans. Aeschylus] (Cambridge: University Press, 1900).
Dramas of Aeschylus [trans.] (London: G. Bell, 1881).
Faust [trans. Goethe] (London: Henry G. Bohn & John Mitchell, n.d.).
Maid of Orleans, The [trans. Schiller], in *Works of Frederick Schiller* (London: G. Bell
    & Sons, 1881).
Richard Coeur de Lion (London: Women's Printing Society, n.d.).
Talisman, The (London: H. K. Lewis, 1864).

Symonds, Emily [George Paston]
Parent's Progress, The (New York and London, 1910).

Syrett, Netta [Janet]
Fairy Doll and Other Plays for Children, The (London: John Lane The Bodley Head,
    1922), including *The Fairy Doll, Christmas in the Forest, The Christening of Rosalys,
    A Pastoral Play for Grown-Up Children, The Enchanted Garden, The Strange Boy.*
Finding of Nancy, The, St James's Theatre, May 1902.
Robin Goodfellow and Other Fairy Plays for Children (London: John Lane, 1918),
    including *Robin Goodfellow, Princess Fragoletta, The Old Toys, Venus and Cupid: A
    Sketch for a Ballet, The Dryad's Awakening: A Sketch for a Ballet, Queen Flora's
    Court: A Masque.*
Two Domestics (London and New York: Samuel French, 1922).
Two Elizabeths (London: 'The Stage' Play Publishing Bureau, 1924).

Taylor, Mrs Frank
Newmarket, Princess's, Manchester, 22 June 1896.
No Credit, Strand, 12 July 1898.

Temple, Grace
Ocean Waif, The [with H. M. le Blonde], St James, Wrexham, 16 May 1893.

Thomas, Jane Penhorn [Mrs Edward Thomas]
Merchant's Daughter of Toulon, The, Standard, 10 March 1856.
Wife's Tragedy, The, Standard, 10 December 1870.

Thomas, Berte W.
Joe the Miner, Margate, 12 June 1893.
Weather Hen, The [with H. G. Barker], Terry's, 26 June 1899.

Thompson, Helen
My Maggie [altered title *Darkest London*], Sefton, Liverpool, 22 October 1884.
Myra; or, Will the Fisherman (Maidstone: Burgiss-Brown, 1888).
Rex Cann, the Whipper-In, Sefton, Liverpool, 20 October 1884.
Shades, The, Sefton, Liverpool, 21 October 1884.

Thompson, Mary Anne
O'Shaughan; or, The Fatal Secret, Birmingham, 23 October 1850.

Thompson, A.
Woman's Freak, A, Memorial Hall, Chester, 15 December 1882.

Thompson, Mrs G.
Broken Sixpence, A [with Kate Sinclair], Ladbroke Hall, 11 April 1889.
Duskie [with Kate Sinclair], Ladbroke Hall, 17 June 1890.
Mademoiselle de Lira [with Kate Sinclair], Comedy, 7 January 1890.
Plucky Nancy [with Kate Sinclair], Town Hall, Kilburn, 16 March 1889.
Pounds, Shillings and Pence [with Kate Sinclair], Town Hall, Kilburn, 18 January 1892.
Saint Angela [with Kate Sinclair], Town Hall, Kilburn, 18 January 1892.

Thompson, Mrs Noel
Myra, Her Majesty's, Richmond, 27 September 1880.

Thomson, Augusta
Sunshine and Shadow, Marylebone, 25 March 1867.
Violet's Playthings, Marylebone, 1 April 1867.

Thorne, Eliza
Bleak House; or, Poor Jo the Crossing Sweeper, Alexandra, Opera House, Sheffield, 28
   April 1876.

Tinsley, Lily
Cinders (London and New York: Samuel French, 1899).
Devil's Luck; or, the Man She Loved [with George Conquest], Adelphi, Liverpool,
   August 1885, Surrey.

Trelawny, Anne [Anne Gibbons]
Mary Stuart [trans. Schiller] (Devonport: W. Byers, 1838).

Tudor, Catherine
Aunt Minena (London and New York: Samuel French, n.d.).

Tullock, Augusta
Web of Fate, The, Lecture Hall, Braintree, 9 October 1899.

van de Velde, Madame
Lena, Lyceum, 9 July 1889.
Bijou Residence to Let, A, Nottingham, 18 September 1889.

Vandenhoff, Miss
Woman's Heart, Haymarket, 11 February 1852.

Vasey, Grace
Man Who Did His Bit, The, Palace, Newton, Alfreton, 3 December 1917.

Vaughan, Virginia
New Era, The (London: Chapman & Hall, 1880).

Vaughan, Mrs
Mated, Criterion, 28 June 1879.
Monsieur Alphonse, Amphitheatre, Liverpool, 16 June 1875.
Outwitted, St George's Hall, 14 July 1871.

Vernier, Isabella
Barber and the Bravo, The; or, The Princess with the Raven Locks, Surrey, 31 August 1846.

Vokes, Victoria
In Camp, Prince of Wales, Liverpool, 24 September 1883.

Votieri, Adeline [Adelene Voteere]
Fool's Trick, A, St George's Hall, 20 June 1891.
Prudes and Pros, St George's Hall, 20 June 1891.
Syndicate, The, St George's Hall, 16 June 1897.
That Charming Mrs Spencer, Lyceum, Ipswich, 18 November 1897.
Unknown Quantity, An [music by D. Harrison], Bijou, 29 February 1897.

Vynne, Nora
Aftermath, Bijou, 22 June 1893.
Andrew Paterson [with St John E. C. Hankin], Bijou, 22 June 1893.

Wade, Florence
Madge, St George's Hall, 10 March 1891.

Walcot, Maria Grace
Cup and the Lip, The, Olympic, 21 October 1886.

Walford, H. L.
Ambition, Gallery of Illustration, 4 December 1870.
Edwin and Angelina; or, The Children of Mystery, Gallery of Illustration, 6 May 1871.
Impeached, Gallery of Illustration, 24 May 1873.
Lord Fitzharris, Gallery of Illustration, 24 May 1873.
Lost Life, A, Gallery of Illustration, 24 November 1870.
Veiled Prophet of Korassan; or, The Maniac, the Mystery and the Malediction, Gallery of Illustration, 24 November 1870.
Weeds, Gallery of Illustration, 6 May 1871.

Wallace, Margaret
Tiger Lily, St George's Hall, 16 January 1892.

Walton, Kate
Drop by Drop; or, Old England's Curse, Adelphi, Liverpool, 24 March 1884.

Warden, Florence [Mrs James]
Guinea Pigs, The, Princess of Wales, Kennington, 24 July 1899.
House on the Marsh, The [adapted from her novel], Nottingham, 2 March 1885.
In the Lion's Mouth, Bath, 25 September 1885.
Patched-Up Affair, A, St James's, March 1900.
Uncle Mike, Terry's, 8 December 1892.

Warden, Gertrude Alice, see Price, Florence

Webster, Augusta Davies
Prometheus Bound [trans. Aeschylus] (London and Cambridge: Macmillan, 1866).
Medea [trans. Euripides] (London and Cambridge: Macmillan, 1867).
Disguises, 1879.
Sentence, The (London: T. Fisher Unwin, 1887).
In a Day, Terry's, 30 May 1890.
Auspicious Day, The, Terry's, May 1890.

Webster, Miss [Margaret] Davies
Mine Hostess, Bijou, 12 June 1899.

Weldon, Georgina
Not Alone [with George Lander], Grand, Birmingham, 12 October 1885.

White, E.
Ambitious Mrs Moresby, The, Comedy, 22 April 1898.

Whitehead, Lucy
Block on the Line, A (Manchester: Abel Heywood and Son, 1896).
Granny (Manchester: Abel Heywood, 1890).

Wilde, Lilla
East Lynne, Cradley Heath, 19 December 1898.

Willard, Mrs E. S., see Penn, Rachel

Williams, Maria Josephine
Helpless Couple, A (London and New York: Samuel French, 1905).

Williams, Mrs Barney
Irish Assurance and Yankee Modesty, Adelphi, August 1856.

Wilson, Margaret Harries [Mrs Cornwell Baron Wilson]
Hussars, The, Sadler's Wells, December 1844.
Maid of Switzerland, The [altered title *Genevieve, the Maid of Switzerland*], English
    Opera House, 3 November 1834.
Venus in Arms; or, The Petticoat Colonel, Strand, June 1836.
Where Is She Gone? Strand, 17 September 1832.

Wilton, Kate
Pearl Darrell, Sefton, Liverpool, 17 September 1883.

Wilton, Jessie H.
Mrs Brown, Britannia, 11 May 1874.

Wilton, Mrs
Study of Two Women, A, Brompton Hospital, 15 February 1898.

Wishaw, Mrs Bernard [Mrs Bernard Whishaw]
Statue of Albemarle, The [music by F. Whishaw], Trafalgar, 16 November 1892.
Two or One, Avenue, 3 March 1891, Princess's, 28 May 1892, as *Will He Come Home Again?*
Zephyr, Avenue, March 1891.

Woodrooffe, Sophia
Buondelmonte, in *Four Dramatic Poems*, ed. G. S. Faber (London: Seeley, Burnside, & Seeley, 1824).
Cleanthes, in *Four Dramatic Poems*, ed. G. S. Faber (London: Seeley, Burnside, & Seeley, 1824).
Court of Flora, The, in *Four Dramatic Poems*, ed. G. S. Faber (London: Seeley, Burnside, & Seeley, 1824).
Sovereign Remedy, A, Princess's, 1 July 1847.
Zingari, The, in *Four Dramatic Poems*, ed. G. S. Faber (London: Seeley, Burnside, & Seeley, 1824).

Woodruffe, Adelaide
Braving the Storm, Drury Lane, 24 February 1871, Sadler's Wells, October 1871.

Wortley, Emmeline Charlotte Elizabeth Manners Stuart [Mrs Charles Stuart-Wortley, Lady Stuart Wortley]
Angiolina del'Albano; or, Truth and Treachery: A Play, in Five Acts (London: How & Parsons, 1841).
Ernest Mountjoy, A Comedietta (London: Moyes & Barclay, 1844).
Eva; or, The Error (London: Joseph Rickerby, 1840).
Jairah, a Dramatic Mystery (London: Joseph Rickerby, 1840).
Moonshine, Haymarket, 3 August 1843.
Alphonzo Algarves (London: Joseph Rickerby, 1841).

Wurm, Josephine
Princess Liza's Fairy [music by Marie Wurm], Prince of Wales, Southampton, 3 June 1893.

Wycombe, Magdeline
Cloris; or, Plots and Plans [with V. Shael, music by C. F. Hayward], Wolverhampton, 17 April 1885.

Wylde, Mrs Henry
Her Oath, Princess's, 26 November 1891.
Little Sunbeam, Lyric, 30 June 1892.
Mason and the Locksmith, The [trans. Scribe] (London: A. S. Mallett, 1879). Libretto.

Yabsley, Ada G.
Lively Hal [music by Mrs Brooks], District Hall, Plymouth, 11 April 1893.

Yarnold, Mrs Edwin
Marie Antoinette; or, The Queen's Lover, Royal Kent Theatre, Kensington, September 1834.

Yorke, Elizabeth Lindsey [Countess of Hardwicke]
Court of Oberon, The; or, The Three Wishes (London: Thomas Hailes Lacy, n.d.).

Young, Margaret
Honesty – A Cottage Flower, Avenue, 29 November 1897.
Trooper Blake, Gaiety, Dublin, 12 August 1896.
Variations, Garrick, 18 May 1899.

Young, Melinda [Mrs H. Young]
Bertha Gray, the Pauper Child; or, The Death Fetch, Victoria, 4 November 1862.
Catherine Hayes the Murderess, Effingham, 29 July 1864.
Dark Woman, The, Effingham, 17 May 1861.
Fair Lilias; or, The Three Lives, Effingham, 22 May 1865.
Fatal Shadow, The; or, The Man with the Iron Heart, Effingham, 16 February 1861.
Gipsy's Bride, The, Pavilion, 16 November 1863.
Jenny Vernon; or, A Barmaid's Career, Victoria, 17 November 1862.
Jessie Ashton; or, The Adventures of a Barmaid, Effingham, 18 April 1862.
Jonathan Wild; or, The Storm on the Thames, East London, 13 July 1868.
Left Alone, Effingham, 30 November 1864.
Life and Adventures of George Barrington, The, Effingham, 2 August 1862.
Light of Love, The; or, The Diamond and the Snowdrop, Effingham, 25 February 1867.
String of Pearls, The; or, The Life and Death of Sweeny Tod, Effingham, 11 July 1862.
Twenty Straws, Effingham, 17 March 1865.

Young, Mrs W. S.
Black Band, The; or, The Mysteries of Midnight, Pavilion, 25 September 1861.

Zalenska, Wanda
Marishka, Great Grimsby, 4 August 1890, Sadler's Wells, 4 May 1891.

Zech, Marie [Mrs C. Robinson]
It is Justice, Bury St Edmonds, 26 December 1890.

Zimmern Helen
Comedies of Carlo Goldoni [trans. Goldoni] (London: David Stott, 1892).

Zoblinsky, Madame
Annie of Tharau [trans. *Ännchen von Tharau*], Hamburg, 6 November 1878, Princess, Edinburgh, 12 April 1880.

Notes

Introduction: Framing the Victorian woman playwright

1. See, for example, the debates around Joan Scott's book, *Gender and the Politics of History* (New York: Columbia University Press, 1988), and particularly the exchange between Scott and Laura Lee Downs following its publication. Laura Lee Downs, 'If "Woman" is Just an Empty Category, Then Why am I Afraid to Walk Alone at Night? Identity Politics Meets the Postmodern Subject,' *Comparative Studies in Society and History*, 35: 2 (April 1993), 414–37, and Scott's somewhat exasperated response, 'The Tip of the Volcano,' *Comparative Studies in Society and History*, 35: 2 (April 1993), 438–43.
2. See Scott, *Gender and the Politics of History*.
3. See particularly, Michel Foucault, 'What is an Author?' (1969), reprinted in Paul Rabinow (ed.), *The Foucault Reader* (New York: Pantheon Books, 1984).
4. Agnes Heller, 'Death of the Subject?,' in Anthony Giddens, David Held, Don Hubert, Debbie Seymour, and John Thompson (eds), *The Polity Reader in Social Theory* (Cambridge: Polity Press, 1994), 247.
5. Catherine Burroughs, *Closet Stages: Joanna Baillie and the Theater Theory of British Romantic Women Writers* (Philadelphia: University of Pennsylvania Press, 1997), 23.
6. Misty Anderson, *Female Playwrights and Eighteenth-Century Comedy: Negotiating Marriage on the London Stage* (Basingstoke: Palgrave, 2002), 204–5.
7. Tracy C. Davis, 'The Sociable Playwright and Representative Citizen,' in Tracy C. Davis and Ellen Donkin (eds), *Women and Playwriting in Nineteenth-Century Britain* (Cambridge: Cambridge University Press, 1999), 30.
8. *Times*, 27 April 1914.
9. Brotherton Library, University of Leeds, Special Collections, BC Gosse correspondence, from Webster, Julia Augusta (Mrs Thomas Webster, pseud. Cecil Home) to Gosse, Edmund, 19 May 1876.
10. James Robinson Planché, *Recollections and Reflections, A Professional Autobiography* (London: Tinsley Brothers, 1872), Vol. 2, 98. See my discussion of Emma Robinson's attempts to negotiate the gap between her position as an educated gentlewoman and her professional career as a writer in ' "From a Female Pen": The Proper Lady as Playwright in the West End Theatre, 1823–1844,' in Tracy C. Davis and Ellen Donkin (eds), *Women and Playwriting in Nineteenth-Century Britain* (Cambridge: Cambridge University Press, 1999), 206–7.
11. Ellen Donkin, *Getting into the Act: Women Playwrights in London, 1776–1829* (London and New York: Routledge, 1995), 185.
12. See particularly Catherine Burroughs, *Closet Stages: Joanna Baillie and the Theater Theory of British Romantic Women Writers* (Philadelphia: University of Pennsylvania Press, 1997), and Thomas Crochunis (ed.), *Joanna Baillie, Romantic Dramatist: Critical Essays* (London and New York: Routledge, 2004).

13. For the best recent discussion of Baillie's 'self-fashioning' as a playwright, see Thomas Crochunis, 'Authorial Performances in the Criticism and Theory of Romantic Women Playwrights,' in Catherine Burroughs (ed.), *Women in British Romantic Theatre* (Cambridge: Cambridge University Press, 2000), 223–54.
14. Peter Bailey, 'Theatres of Entertainment/Spaces of Modernity: Rethinking the British Popular Stage 1890–1914,' *Nineteenth Century Theatre*, 26: 1 (Summer 1998), 5–24.
15. Helen Day, 'Female Daredevils,' in Viv Gardner and Susan Rutherford (eds), *The New Woman and Her Sisters: Feminism and Theatre 1850–1914* (London: Harvester Wheatsheaf, 1992), 137.
16. Jane Moody, *Illegitimate Theatre in London, 1770–1840* (Cambridge: Cambridge University Press, 2000), 244.
17. Angela Leighton, *Victorian Women Poets: Writing Against the Heart* (Charlottesville and London: University Press of Virginia, 1992), 203.
18. E. Warwick Slinn, *Victorian Poetry as Cultural Critique* (Charlottesville and London: University of Virginia Press, 2003), 28.
19. Sally Ledger, *Henrik Ibsen* (Plymouth: Northcote House Publishers, 1999), 3.
20. Hilary Fraser, Stephanie Green and Judith Johnston, *Gender and the Victorian Periodical* (Cambridge: Cambridge University Press, 2003), 100.

1 Rescuing the stage

1. *The Oracle*, 3 July 1793.
2. *The Works of Hannah More* (London: T. Caddell, 1830), Vol. 2, 125–6.
3. *The Theatrical Examiner*, 7 November 1826.
4. D.——G. [George Daniels], 'Remarks' in Mary Russell Mitford, *Rienzi* (London: Davidson, n.d.).
5. Ellen Donkin, *Getting Into the Act* (London and New York: Routledge, 1995), 185.
6. Mary Poovey, *The Proper Lady and the Woman Writer: The Ideology of Style in Mary Wollstonecraft, Jane Austen, and Mary Shelley* (Chicago: University of Chicago Press, 1984).
7. Greg Kucich, 'Reviewing Women in British Romantic Theatre,' in Catherine Burroughs (ed.), *Women in British Romantic Theatre: Drama, Performance, and Society, 1790–1840* (Cambridge: Cambridge University Press, 2000), 49.
8. Donkin, *Getting Into the Act*, 185.
9. See, for example, 'M. R.'s' letter to the *Times*, 27 August 1829. For a brief account of the complex financial arrangements of proprietorship and management at Covent Garden, see Tracy C. Davis, *The Economics of the British Stage, 1800–1914* (Cambridge: Cambridge University Press, 2000), 260.
10. Benson Earle Hill, 'Memoir of the Authoress,' in Isabel Hill (ed.), *Brian the Probationer: or, The Red Hand. A Tragedy in Five Acts* (London: W. R. Sams, Royal Library, 1842), 88–9.
11. Ibid., 87.
12. *The First of May, A Petite Comedy in Two Acts*, British Library, Add. Mss. 42897 ff. 229–256, Lord Chamberlain's Collection of Plays. All further references are to this manuscript.

13. 'The Drama. Covent Garden,' *The Athenæum*, 14 October 1829, 649.

14. Anderson, *Female Playwrights and Eighteenth-Century Comedy*, 204.

15. 'Theatrical Examiner. Covent Garden,' *The Examiner*, 18 October 1829, 663.

16. *The Times*, 12 October 1829.

17. 'The Drama. Covent Garden,' *The Athenæum*, 14 October 1829, 649.

18. Angela Leighton, *Victorian Women Poets: Writing Against the Heart* (Charlottesville and London: University Press of Virginia, 1992), 3.

19. Hill, 'An Indefinite Article,' *Holiday Dreams; or, Light Reading, in Poetry and Prose* (London: Thomas Cadell, and Blackwood, Edinburgh, 1829), 4.

20. Sherry Simon, *Gender in Translation: Cultural Identity and the Politics of Transmission* (London and New York: Routledge, 1996), 61.

21. Hill, 'Translator's Preface' to Madame de Staël, *Corinne* (London: Richard Bentley, 1833), v.

22. Ellen Moers, *Literary Women* (London: Women's Press, 1978; 1963), 173.

23. [3 May 1838], Benson Hill to Edward S. Morgan, British Library Add. Mss. 46649, Bentley Papers, Vol. XC, f. 280.

24. [3 May 1838] and 5 May 1838, British Library, Add. Mss. 46649, Bentley Papers, Vol. XC, ff. 280, 283. Compare with other translators' rates of up to a guinea a page, Add. Mss. 46649, Bentley Papers, Vol. XC, ff. 74, 75, f. 79.

25. *West-Country Wooing* was written for Harriet Waylett; for details of Waylett's career as actress and manager, see J. S. Bratton, 'Working in the Margin: Women in Theatre History,' *New Theatre Quarterly*, X: 38 (May 1994), 128.

26. Hill, *Playing About*, 2 vols (London: W. Sams, 1840), Vol. 2, 254.

27. Isabel Hill, *Brother Tragedians, a Novel, in Three Volumes* (London: Saunders and Otley, 1834, 87–8.

28. The financial difficulties of Covent Garden were reported almost daily in the *Times* from 25 August until 5 September, when the *Times* announced: 'We have, already, at a considerable sacrifice of valuable space, given insertion to a variety of letters from different correspondents on the pecuniary difficulties of the above-mentioned establishment, their reputed causes, and their proposed remedies. To-day we insert three or four more, and here the correspondence must [. . .] close.' However, on 10 September, the *Times* reported on another public meeting of performers, creditors and patrons of Covent Garden, on 14 September, it published a list of all subscribers to a fund to help pay off the theatre's creditors, and on 21 September, the *Times* carried a report of another share-holders' meeting.

29. Catherine Burroughs, *Closet Stages: Joanna Baillie and the Theater Theory of British Romantic Women Writers* (Philadelphia: University of Pennsylvania Press, 1997), 87.

30. *Playing About*, Vol. 1, 38, Vol. 2, 100.

31. Ibid., Vol. 1, 5–6.

32. Ibid., Vol. 1, 141–2.

33. Ibid., Vol. 1, 83.

34. Frances Anne Kemble, *Record of a Girlhood*, 3 vols (London: Richard Bentley & Son, 1878), Vol. 2, 5, 7–8, 59–60. All further references are to this edition.

35. Alison Booth comments on the power of Kemble's autobiographical writing in influencing subsequent biographies, 'From Miranda to Prospero: The Works of Fanny Kemble,' *Victorian Studies*, 38: 2 (Winter 1995), 227.

36. Mary Jean Corbett, *Representing Femininity: Middle-Class Subjectivity in Victorian and Edwardian Women's Autobiographies* (New York and Oxford: Oxford University Press, 1992), 110–11.

37. Ibid., 117.

38. Cited in Linda Peterson, *Traditions of Victorian Women's Autobiography: The Poetics and Politics of Life Writing* (Charlottesville and London: University Press of Virginia, 1999), 229.

39. Jacky Bratton, *New Readings in Theatre History* (Cambridge: Cambridge University Press, 2003), 180.

40. Ibid., 185.

41. Fanny Kemble Manuscript Letters, Harvard Theatre Collection, Houghton Library, bMS Thr 357 (71), Friday 16th (no month or year). From its content, it appears that the letter was written during her first Covent Garden season, 1829–30.

42. Valerie Sanders, *The Private Lives of Victorian Women: Autobiography in Nineteenth-Century England* (London: Harvester Wheatsheaf, 1989), 112.

43. Sanders, *The Private Lives of Victorian Women*, 113–14. Other critics have noted Kemble's ambivalence; see Elizabeth Fox-Genovese, 'Foreword' to Monica Gough (ed.), *Fanny Kemble: Journal of a Young Actress* (New York: Columbia University Press, 1990), xv.

44. Faye E. Dudden, *Women in the American Theatre: Actresses and Audiences, 1790–1870* (New Haven and London: Yale University Press, 1994), 27.

45. Dorothy Marshall, *Fanny Kemble* (London: Weidenfeld & Nicolson, 1977), 59–60 and Eleanor Ransome (intro. and ed.), *The Terrific Kemble: A Victorian Self-Portrait from the Writings of Fanny Kemble* (London: Hamish Hamilton, 1978), 35–8.

46. Sanders quotes Charles Greville's belief that Kemble quickly compared her unhappy marriage to Pierce Butler with her triumphant stage career, *The Private Lives of Victorian Women*, 114; certainly Kemble exults over the 30 guineas a week she earned as Juliet.

47. See Chapter 1 of Davis, *The Economics of the British Stage*.

48. J. S. Bratton, 'Miss Scott and Miss Macaulay: "Genius Cometh in All Disguises",' *Theatre Survey*, 37: 1 (May 1996), 59. See also Bratton, *New Readings in Theatre History*, Chapters 4 and 6.

49. See the *Report from the Select Committee appointed to Inquire into the Laws Affecting Dramatic Literature, with the Minutes of Evidence* (Parliamentary Papers, 1831–32, vii), Julia Swindells, 'Behold the Swelling Scene! Shakespeare and the 1832 Select Committee,' in Gail Marshall and Adrian Poole (eds), *Victorian Shakespeare, Volume 1, Theatre, Drama and Performance* (Basingstoke: Palgrave, 2003), 29–46, and Katherine Newey, 'Reform on the London Stage,' Joanna Innes and Arthur Burns (eds), *Rethinking the Age of Reform* (Cambridge: Cambridge University Press, 2003), 238–53.

50. Susan Carlson and Kerry Powell, 'Reimagining the Theatre: Women Playwrights of the Victorian and Edwardian Period,' in Kerry Powell (ed.), *The Cambridge Companion to Victorian and Edwardian Theatre* (Cambridge: Cambridge University Press, 2004), 254.

51. ' "The Era" Play Competition,' *The Era*, 14 June 1913, 17.

52. *The Era*, 21 June 1913, 17.

53. *Spectator*, 10 June 1843, 537.

54. For detailed accounts of the 1843 competition see Ellen Donkin, 'Mrs. Gore gives Tit for Tat,' and Katherine Newey, ' "From a Female Pen": The Proper Lady as Playwright in the West End Theatre, 1823–1844,' in Tracy C. Davis and Ellen Donkin (eds), *Nineteenth-Century British Women Playwrights* (Cambridge: Cambridge University Press, 1999), John Franceschina (ed.), *Gore on Stage: The Plays of Catherine Gore* (New York and London: Garland Publishing, 1999), 25–7, and Katherine Newey (intro. and ed.), Catherine Gore's *Quid Pro Quo* in Thomas Crochunis and Michael Eberle-Sinatra (eds), *The Broadview Anthology of Women Playwrights Around 1800* (Peterborough: Broadview Press, 2006).

55. Donkin, 'Mrs. Gore Gives Tit for Tat,' 56.

56. *Spectator*, 10 June 1843, 537.

57. *Athenæum*, 3 February 1844, 116.

58. Julia Swindells, *Victorian Writing and Working Women: The Other Side of Silence* (Oxford: Polity Press, 1985), 91.

59. G. H. L. [George Henry Lewes], 'The Prize Comedy and the Prize Committee,' *Westminster Review*, 42: 1 (September 1844), 106.

60. Brian E. Maidment, 'Victorian Periodicals and Academic Discourse,' in Laurel Brake, Aled Jones and Michael Madden (eds), *Investigating Victorian Journalism* (Basingstoke: Macmillan, 1990), 150.

61. Catherine Gore, 'Preface,' *Quid Pro Quo; or, the Day of the Dupes* (London: National Acting Drama Office, n.d.), v. See Donkin, 'Mrs. Gore Gives Tit for Tat' for a discussion of Gore's location of herself in a female playwriting tradition, 60.

62. *The Finding of Nancy*, BL LCP, Add. Mss. 1902/14, f. 7. All further references are to this manuscript.

63. Netta Syrett, *The Sheltering Tree* (London: Geoffrey Bles, 1939), 120.

64. Syrett recounts that Lady Alexander watched a rehearsal and commented 'What's the matter with this play? [. . .] I think it's charming.' *The Sheltering Tree*, 122.

65. Syrett, *The Sheltering Tree*, 124. There is a problem of record here. Syrett refers to Scott's *Daily Telegraph* review but gives no details of publication. Kerry Powell's account of critical reaction to the play discusses Scott's 'almost hysterical' critique of the play's immorality, but does not give a citation for Scott's review, *Women and the Victorian Theatre* (Cambridge: Cambridge University Press, 1997), 80–1. The only mention of *The Finding of Nancy* in the *Daily Telegraph* I have found is an unsigned full column review, in parts complimentary, of the play, from which I cite, 'The Finding of Nancy: The Playgoers Prize Play at St. James's Theatre,' *Daily Telegraph*, 9 May 1902, 10.

66. 'Miss Syrett's Play,' *Saturday Review*, 17 May 1902, reprinted in Max Beerbohm, *More Theatres* (London: Rupert Hart-Davis, 1969), 463–7.

67. *The Sheltering Tree*, 126.

68. 'St. James's Theatre,' *The Times*, 9 May 1902, 8.

69. Ann L. Ardis, *Modernism and Cultural Conflict, 1880–1922* (Cambridge: Cambridge University Press, 2002), 120.

70. Viv Gardner, 'The Invisible Spectatrice: Gender, Geography and Theatrical Space,' in Maggie B. Gale and Viv Gardner (eds), *Women, Theatre, and Performance* (Manchester: Manchester University Press, 2000), 40–1.

71. Ardis, *Modernism and Cultural Conflict*, 119.
72. *The Sheltering Tree*, 5–6.
73. Ibid., 90.
74. Ann L. Ardis, 'Netta Syrett's Aestheticization of Everyday Life,' in Talia Schaffer and Kathy A. Psomiades (eds), *Women and British Aestheticism* (Charlottesville: University Press of Virginia, 1999), 245–6.
75. *The Sheltering Tree*, Chapter XIX. See the announcement of the scheme in 'The Children's Theatre,' *The Times*, 27 October 1913, 12.
76. Pierre Bourdieu, *The Field of Cultural Production: Essays on Art and Literature*, Randal Johnson (ed. and trans.) (Cambridge: Polity Press, 1993), 42.
77. Donkin, *Getting Into the Act*, 185–6. For a sustained counter-argument to Donkin with respect to the position of Joanna Baillie, see Jeffrey Cox, 'Baillie, Siddons, Larpent: Gender, Power, and Politics in the Theatre of Romanticism,' in Burroughs (ed.), *Women in British Romantic Theatre*, 28–9.
78. My models here are Elizabeth Inchbald and Joanna Baillie. Of course, my discussion of this pattern is a generalization, and I am aware of more detailed accounts of the professional obstacles and ambivalent reception of both women's work.
79. Thomas C. Crochunis, 'Joanna Baillie's Ambivalent Dramaturgy,' *Joanna Baillie, Romantic Dramatist: Critical Essays* (London and New York: Routledge, 2004), 170.
80. Marc Baer, *Theatre and Disorder in Late Georgian London* (Oxford: Oxford University Press, 1992), Gillian Russell, The *Theatres of War: Performance, Politics, and Society, 1793–1815* (Oxford: Oxford University Press, 1995), and Elaine Hadley, *Melodramatic Tactics: Theatricalized Dissent in the English Marketplace, 1800–1885* (Stanford: Stanford University Press, 1995).
81. Davis, *The Economics of the British Stage*, Part I, 'Competition: Theatre and Laissez Faire.'
82. Jon Klancher, *The Making of English Reading Audiences, 1790–1832* (Madison: University of Wisconsin Press, 1987), 76, 97.
83. See also Iain McCalman, *Radical Underworld: Prophets, Revolutionaries and Pornographers in London, 1795–1840* (Cambridge: Cambridge University Press, 1988), 181–2, Ian Haywood, *The Revolution in Popular Literature: Print, Politics and the People, 1790–1860* (Cambridge: Cambridge University Press, 2004), Chapter 4, 'The Palladium of Liberty: Radical Journalism and Repression in the Postwar Era,' and Kevin Gilmartin, *Print Politics: The Press and Radical Opposition in Early Nineteenth-Century England* (Cambridge: Cambridge University Press, 1996), 'Introduction: Locating a Plebeian Counterpublic Sphere.'
84. Haywood, *The Revolution in Popular Literature*, 101.
85. Donkin, *Getting Into the Act*, 175.
86. Leonore Davidoff and Catherine Hall, *Family Fortunes*: *Men and Women of the English Middle Class, 1780–1850* (London: Hutchinson, 1987), 13.
87. Alison Sulloway, *Jane Austen and the Province of Womanhood* (Philadelphia: University of Pennsylvania Press, 1989), 4.
88. Mary Poovey, *Uneven Developments: The Ideological Work of Gender in Mid-Victorian Britain* (London: Virago Press, 1989), 10.
89. Moody, *Illegitimate Theatre in London*, 12.

90. Gaye Tuchman with Nina E. Fortin, *Edging Women Out: Victorian Novelists, Publishers, and Social Change* (London: Routledge, 1989), Chapter 3, 'Novel Writing as an Empty Field.'

91. Reproduced in William E. Fredeman (ed.), *The Victorian Poets The Biocritical Introductions to the Victorian Poets from A.H. Miles's* The Poets and Poetry of the Nineteenth Century (New York and London: Garland, 1986), 143–4.

2 Legitimacy

1. Letter to Charles Boner, 5 September 1854, in Charles Boner, *Memoirs and Letters of Charles Boner, with Letters of Mary Russell Mitford* (London: Richard Bentley and Son, 1871, 2 vols), Vol. 1, 282.

2. Crochunis, 'Joanna Baillie's Ambivalent Dramaturgy,' in Crochunis (ed.), *Joanna Baillie*, 169.

3. Jane Moody, ' "Fine Word, Legitimate!": Toward a Theatrical History of Romanticism,' *Texas Studies in Literature and Language*, 38: 3/4 (Fall/Winter 1996), 232. See also Newey, 'Reform on the London Stage,' in Innes and Burns (eds), *Rethinking the Age of Reform*, 238–53.

4. Pierre Bourdieu, *Distinction: A Social Critique of the Judgement of Taste* (London: Routledge, 1989), 466.

5. For the best discussion of the politics of theatrical legitimacy and illegitimacy, see Moody, *Illegitimate Theatre in London*.

6. See Maggie B. Gale for a short summary of the move towards 'non-profit-oriented theatre' in the late nineteenth century, *West End Women: Women and the London Stage, 1918–1962* (London and New York: Routledge, 1996), 6–8.

7. Emily Pfeiffer, *Under the Aspens: Lyrical and Dramatic* (London: Kegan Paul, Trench, and Co., 1882), vii.

8. *New DNB*, www.oxforddnb.com.

9. Gary Kelly states that Hemans was the 'most widely read woman poet in the nineteenth-century English-speaking world.' 'Introduction,' Gary Kelly (ed.), *Felicia Hemans: Selected Poems, Prose, and Letters* (Peterborough: Broadview Press, 2002), 15.

10. Stuart Curran, 'Romantic Poetry: The I Altered,' in A. Mellor (ed.), *Romanticism and Feminism* (Bloomington and Indianapolis: Indiana University Press, 1988), 188, Angela Leighton, *Victorian Women Poets*, 20–1.

11. Jeffrey N. Cox and Michael Gamer (eds), *The Broadview Anthology of Romantic Drama* (Peterborough: Broadview Press, 2003), ix.

12. Anthony B. Dawson, 'Performance and Participation: Desdemona, Foucault, and the Actor's Body,' in J. C. Bulman (ed. and intro.), *Shakespeare, Theory and Performance* (London: Routledge, 1996), 30.

13. Henry Chorley (ed.), *Letters of Mary Russell Mitford*, Second series, 2 vols, (London: Richard Bentley and Son, 1872), Vol. 1, 123.

14. Chorley, *Letters of Mary Russell Mitford*, 213.

15. To Thomas Noon Talfourd, Letter 24, Eng. Mss. 665, John Rylands Library, Manchester. Mitford's letters are reproduced in the microfilm series, *Elizabeth Gaskell and Nineteenth Century Literature: Manuscripts from the John Rylands University Library, Manchester* (Reading: Research Publications, 1989).

16. W. A. Coles, 'Mary Russell Mitford: The Inauguration of a Literary Career,' *Bulletin of the John Rylands Library, Manchester*, 40 (1957–8), 36.
17. Ibid., 36.
18. Norma Clarke, *Ambitious Heights: Writing, Friendship, Love – The Jewsbury Sisters, Felicia Hemans, and Jane Welsh Carlyle* (London and New York: Routledge, 1990), 51.
19. Catherine Burroughs, 'The English Romantic Closet: Women Theatre Artists, Joanna Baillie, and *Basil*,' *Nineteenth-Century Contexts*, 19 (1995), 130.
20. Donkin, *Getting into the Act*, 136.
21. Caroline Duncan-Jones, *Miss Mitford and Mr Harness: Records of a Friendship* (London: S. C. K., 1955), 46.
22. Duncan-Jones, *Miss Mitford and Mr Harness*, 47.
23. William Harness was thought to be its author, but Duncan-Jones argues that the evidence of his unpublished diary refutes this, *Miss Mitford and Mr Harness*, 47.
24. William Charles Macready, *The Diaries of William Charles Macready, 1833–1851*, edited by William Toynbee, 2 vols (London: Chapman Hall, 1912), Vol. 1, 323 (2 June 1836).
25. Famously so, in the case of the Victoria Theatre's production in 1834 of the banned play *Charles I*; for accounts of the censorship of Mitford's play, see Dominic Shellard and Stephen Nicholson, with Miriam Handley, *The Lord Chamberlain Regrets . . . A History of British Theatre Censorship* (London: British Library, 2004), 31–4, and my 'Women and History on the Romantic Stage: More, Yearsley, Burney, and Mitford,' in Burroughs (ed.), *Women in British Romantic Theatre*, 94–6.
26. Leighton, *Victorian Women Poets*, 19, Clarke, *Ambitious Heights*, 32, and Isobel Armstrong, *Victorian Poetry: Poetry, Poetics, and Politics* (London and New York: Routledge, 1993), 329, 332.
27. [Harriett Hughes], *Memoir of the Life and Writings of Mrs. Hemans, by Her Sister* (no publication details), 92–3.
28. Marlon Ross, *The Contours of Masculine Desire: Romanticism and the Rise of Women's Poetry* (New York and Oxford: Oxford University Press, 1989), 300; *Memoir of the Life and Writings of Mrs. Hemans*, 93. For discussion of the press reaction to *The Vespers of Palermo*, see Newey, ' "From a female pen",' in Davis and Donkin (eds), *Nineteenth-Century British Women Playwrights*, 195–6.
29. Ross, *The Contours of Masculine Desire*, 301.
30. Henry Chorley, *Memorials of Mrs. Hemans with Illustrations of Her Literary Character from Her Private Correspondence*, 2 vols (London: Sanders and Otley, 1836), Vol. 1, 93.
31. Ibid., Vol. 1, 76.
32. Diego Saglia, ' "Freedom's Charter'd Air": The Voices of Liberalism in Felicia Hemans's *The Vespers of Palermo*,' *Nineteenth-Century Literature*, 58: 3 (2003), 344–6.
33. Sarah Josepha Hale, *Woman's Record; or, Sketches of All Distinguished Women* (New York: Harper and Brothers, 1855), 745.
34. Virginia Blain, 'Period Pains: The Changing Body of Victorian Poetry,' *Victorian Poetry*, 42: 1 (Spring 2004), 75.
35. Shou-Ren Wang, *The Theatre of the Mind: A Study of the Unacted Drama in Nineteenth-Century England* (London: Macmillan, 1990), 203.

36. Kelly, 'Introduction,' in Kelly (ed.), *Felicia Hemans*, 15, 84–5, and Kelly, 'Death and the Matron: Felicia Hemans, Romantic Death, and the Founding of the Modern Liberal State,' in Julie Melnyk and Nanora Sweet (eds), *Felicia Hemans: Reimagining Poetry in the Nineteenth Century* (Basingstoke: Palgrave, 2001), 197–9, notwithstanding Jeffrey Cox's characterization of Hemans, together with Hannah More as 'powerful, conservative women,' 'Baillie, Siddons, Larpent: Gender, Power, and Politics in the Theatre of Romanticism,' in Burroughs (ed.), *Women in British Romantic Theatre*, 24. See also Nanora Sweet, 'Felicia Hemans' "A Tale of the Secret Tribunal": Gothic Empire in the Age of Jeremy Bentham and Walter Scott,' *European Journal of English Studies*, 6: 2 (2002), 164.

37. Saglia, ' "Freedom's Charter'd Air", ' 326–7.

38. Susan Wolfson and Elizabeth Fay (eds), 'Introduction,' *Felicia Hemans: The Siege of Valencia: A Parallel Text Edition* (Peterborough: Broadview Press, 2002), 8.

39. Simon Bainbridge, *British Poetry and the Revolutionary and Napoleonic Wars: Visions of Conflict* (Oxford: Oxford University Press, 2003), 200.

40. Kelly, 'Introduction,' in Kelly (ed.), *Felicia Hemans*, 36, Ross, *The Contours of Masculine Desire*, 278–85, Wolfson and Fay (eds), *Felicia Hemans: The Siege of Valencia*, 23.

41. 'Covent-Garden Theatre,' *The Times*, 17 March 1823, 3.

42. Felicia Hemans, *Vespers of Palermo*, in William Michael Rossetti (ed.), *The Poetical Works of Mrs. Felicia Hemans* (London: Ward, Lock, and Co., n.d.), Act I, scene I, 531. All further references are to this edition.

43. Catherine Clément [trans. Betsy Wing], *Opera, or the Undoing of Women* (Minneapolis: University of Minnesota Press, 1988), particularly Chapter 2, 'Dead Women.'

44. Mary Russell Mitford, *Foscari, A Tragedy*, in *The Dramatic Works of Mary Russell Mitford*, 2 vols (London: Hurst & Blackett, 1854), Vol. 1, 83. All further references are to this edition and indicated in the text.

45. A. G. L'Estrange (ed.), *The Life and Letters of Mary Russell Mitford, Related in a Selection from Her Letters to Her Friends*, 3 vols (London: Richard Bentley, 1870), Vol. 2, 161. Letter to Sir William Elford, 25 April 1823.

46. 'Drama,' *The Literary Gazette, and Journal of Belles Lettres*, 11 November 1826, 718.

47. Samuel Carter Hall, *Book of Memories of Great Men and Women of the Age, From Personal Acquaintance* (London: Virtue and Co., 1871), 438.

48. *New Monthly Magazine*, New Series, 2; 12 (December, 1826), 659.

49. 'Covent Garden,' *The Literary Gazette, and Journal of the Belles Lettres*, 11 November 1826, 718.

50. Leighton, *Victorian Women Poets*, 3.

51. 'Covent-Garden Theatre,' *The Times*, 6 November 1826, 2.

52. Mary Russell Mitford, *Rienzi*, in *The Dramatic Works of Mary Russell Mitford*, 2 vols (London: Hurst & Blackett, 1854), Vol. 1. All further references are to this edition.

53. D.——G. [George Daniel], 'Remarks,' in Mary Russell Mitford (ed.), *Rienzi: A Tragedy, In Five Acts* (London: Davidson, n.d. [1828?]), 8.

54. Kelly, 'Introduction,' in Gary Kelly (ed.), *Felicia Hemans*, 15–16.

55. 'The Drama,' *New Monthly Magazine*, December 1826, 499.

3 Money

1. Moers, *Literary Women*, 76–7, 83.
2. Outside my scope here is the movement of women into the early film industry in Britain. See my 'Women, Theatre and Film: Finding a Screen of Her Own,' in Sarah Street and Linda Fitzsimmons (eds), *Moving Performance* (Trowbridge: Flicks Books, 2000).
3. See Peter Duthie's account of the 'rumour and speculation' about the authorship of *Plays on the Passions*, in Joanna Baillie, *Plays on the Passions* (1798 edition), edited by Peter Duthie (Peterborough: Broadview Press, 2001), 17, n1.
4. This figure is a guide only, and is based on Allardyce Nicoll's 'Handlists' for 1800–1850 and 1850–1900 in *A History of English Drama, 1660–1900*, Vol. IV, *Early Nineteenth Century Drama, 1800–1850*, and Vol. V, *Late Nineteenth Century Drama, 1850–1900* (Cambridge: Cambridge University Press, 1970).
5. John Russell Stephens, *The Profession of the Playwright* (Cambridge: Cambridge University Press, 1992), 3.
6. See Tracy C. Davis on the theatre as a central constituent of the mass media of the nineteenth century, 'The Sociable Playwright and Representative Citizen,' in Davis and Donkin (eds), *Women and Playwriting in Nineteenth-Century Britain*, 19.
7. See Douglas Jerrold's evidence in House of Commons, Parliamentary Papers, *Report from the Select Committee appointed to Inquire into the Laws Affecting Dramatic Literature, with the Minutes of Evidence*, 1831–32, vii, Edward Fitzball's *Thirty-Five Years of a Dramatic Author's Life* (London: T. C. Newby, 1859), and G. H. Lewes' novel, *Ranthorpe* (London: Chapman & Hall, 1847). Stephens, *Profession of the Playwright*, Chapter 2, 'A Devil of a Trade,' offers an overview.
8. Bourdieu, *Distinction*, 261–3.
9. Morag Shiach, *Discourse on Popular Culture: Class, Gender and History in Cultural Analysis, 1730 to the Present* (London: Polity Press, 1989), 16.
10. Stephens discusses the 'bohemianism' of dramatic authorship and makes a survey of the professions from which (male) playwrights entered the theatre, and to which they usually needed to resort when faced with lack of success or meagre performance fees, *Profession of the Playwright*, 10, 13–19. See also John Sutherland, *Victorian Fiction: Writers, Publishers, Readers* (London: Macmillan, 1995), for a quantitative analysis showing that of a sample of 878 Victorian novelists only just over 10 per cent of male writers did *not* have a prior or alternative activity, whereas only 10.3 per cent of women *did*, 163.
11. A. Richardson, 'Review of Anne Mellor, *Mothers of the Nation*,' *Modern Language Quarterly* (June 2002), 267.
12. Amanda Vickery, 'Golden Age to Separate Spheres? A Review of the Categories and Chronology of English Women's History,' *The Historical Journal*, 36: 2 (1993), 383–414, provides an overview of the scholarship and an argument for care in the use of these concepts.
13. Jim Davis and Victor Emeljanow, *Reflecting the Audience, London Theatre-going, 1840–1890* (Iowa City: University of Iowa Press, 2001), 167.
14. See Nicoll, 'Appendix A, The Theatres, 1800–1850,' in *A History of English Drama, 1660–1900*, Vol. IV, *Early Nineteenth Century Drama, 1800–1850*.

15. This is a brief summary of the situation up to the 1843 Theatres Regulation act; for more detailed discussions of the legal and economic issues around the regulation and development of theatre in London, see Davis, *The Economics of the British Stage*, particularly Chapter 1, 'Monopoly and free trade,' Moody, *Illegitimate Theatre in London*, and Dewey Ganzel, 'Patent Wrongs and Patent Theatres: Drama and Law in the Early Nineteenth Century,' *Publications of the Modern Language Association* (1961, Lxxvi). For overviews of the situation in the theatres to 1843 see Michael R. Booth, *Theatre in the Victorian Age* (Cambridge: Cambridge University Press, 1991), Watson Nicholson, *The Struggle for a Free Stage in London* (1906; New York: Benjamin Blom, 1966), and George Rowell, *The Victorian Theatre, 1792–191: A Survey* (1956; Cambridge: Cambridge University Press, 1978).

16. Davis and Emeljanow, *Reflecting the Audience*, 167.

17. See David Worrall, 'Artisan Melodrama and the Plebeian Public Sphere: The Political Culture of Drury Lane and its Environs, 1797–1830,' *Studies in Romanticism*, 39: 2 (Summer 2000), for accounts of political activity around the Adelphi, and also Bratton, *New Readings in Theatre History*, on Adelphi audiences generally, 52, and for *Tom and Jerry*, 166.

18. In 1843, on marking William Macready's retirement from management of Drury Lane, the *Illustrated London News*' encomium included the comment that 'he sought, in a word, to make Drury-Lane a family theatre [...]. The eye of purity – of fair delicacy – of young womanly innocence – was never offended there by scenes which once brought blushes to every modest cheek [...] and fathers, husbands, and brothers did not dread for their fair charges a rude, insulting contact with the flaunting insolence of vulgar and shameless morality.' 17 June 1843, 421.

19. See Gwenn Davis and Beverly A. Joyce (com), *Drama by Women to 1900: A Bibliography of American and British Writers* (London: Mansell, 1992), and David Mann and Susan Garland Mann with Camille Garnier, *Women Playwrights in England, Ireland, and Scotland, 1660–1823* (Bloomington: Indiana University Press, 1996) on the preponderance of women playwrights from theatrical families. Dudden, *Women in the American Theatre*, argues that acting in America was also 'a familial business,' 12. For a preliminary discussion of historiographical implications of this pattern, see Tracy C. Davis, 'Questions for a Feminist Methodology in Theatre History,' in Thomas Postlewait and Bruce McConachie (eds), *Interpreting the Theatrical Past: Essays in the Historiography of Performance* (Iowa: University of Iowa Press, 1989), 70–1.

20. Bratton, *New Readings in Theatre History*, 183, and 'Miss Scott and Miss Macaulay,' 59–74.

21. *The Examiner*, 7 October 1827, 630.

22. *New DNB*, http://via.oxforddnb.com. This is an improvement on the first edition of the *DNB*, which acknowledged Caroline's existence as 'another (a daughter) inherited a facility for play-writing' (II, 741).

23. *New DNB*, http://via.oxforddnb.com.

24. Elizabeth Kowaleski-Wallace, *Their Fathers' Daughters: Hannah More, Maria Edgeworth, and Patriarchal Complicity* (New York and Oxford: Oxford University Press, 1991), 12, her emphasis.

25. On the importance of the domestic in Victorian farce, see Michael R. Booth, 'Comedy and Farce,' in Powell (ed.), *The Cambridge Companion to Victorian and Edwardian Theatre*, 131.

26. 'Haymarket Theatre,' *The Literary Gazette; and Journal of the Belles Lettres*, 19 September 1829, 621.

27. 'Theatrical Examiner: Haymarket,' *The Examiner*, 20 September 1829, 597.

28. 'Haymarket Theatre,' *The Times*, 2 September 1829, 2, and 3 September 1829, 2, my emphasis.

29. 'Theatricals: Haymarket Theatre,' *The Athenæum*, 14 July 1832, 460; 'The Drama,' *The New Monthly Magazine*, August 1832, 348, my emphasis.

30. D.——G. [George Daniels], 'Remarks,' *Fatality: A Drama, in One Act* (London: John Cumberland, n.d.), 7. First performed 2 September 1829, Haymarket Theatre.

31. 'Theatrical Examiner. Haymarket,' *The Examiner*, 6 September 1829, 564.

32. See Newey, ' "From a Female Pen",' in Davis and Donkin (eds), *Women and Playwriting in Nineteenth-Century Britain*, 206–7.

33. D.——G. [George Daniels], 'Remarks,' *The First of April; A Farce in Two Acts* (London: John Cumberland, n.d.), 5. First performed Haymarket Theatre, 31 August 1830.

34. 'Haymarket Theatre,' *The Times*, 12 September 1829, 2. *William Thompson* was first performed at the Haymarket Theatre, 11 September 1829.

35. See Jim Davis, *John Liston, Comedian* (London: Society for Theatre Research, 1985), 59–60 for an account of the success of the 1825 season.

36. Anderson, *Female Playwrights and Eighteenth-Century Comedy*, 203.

37. For an illustration of this role, see Davis, *John Liston Comedian*, plate 28a, 82–3.

38. Respectively, 'The Theatres,' *The Times*, 3 September 1883, and 'The Playhouses,' *The Illustrated London News*, 8 September 1883, 231.

39. Maria Lovell, *The Beginning and the End, a Domestic Drama in Four Acts* (London: G. H. Davidson, [1855]), 4.

40. James Robinson Planché, *Recollections and Reflections, A Professional Autobiography* (London: Tinsley Brothers, 1872), Vol. 2, 20.

41. For details, see my 'From a Female Pen,' in Davis and Donkin (eds), *Women and Playwriting in Nineteenth-Century Britain*, 200.

42. *Folly and Friendship*, Lord Chamberlain's Collection of Plays, British Library, Add. Mss. 42490, f. 324 (licensed for 18 January 1837).

43. *The Welsh Girl* (London: John Miller, 1834), 21.

44. *A Handsome Husband* (London: Thomas Hailes Lacy, n.d.), 3.

45. 'Music and the Drama,' *The Athenæum*, 20 February 1836, 148.

46. 'Theatricals,' *The Athenæum*, 21 December 1833, 321.

47. 'Drury-Lane Theatre,' *The Times*, 15 December 1834, 2 and 'Haymarket Theatre,' *The Times*, 20 June 1834, 3.

48. Frances Fleetwood, *Conquest: The Story of a Theatre Family* (London: W. H. Allen, 1953), 88, 104. Fleetwood lists the third generation of Conquests who were the main constituents of George Conquest's company at the Surrey from 1881 until 1901, 171.

49. Bratton, *New Readings in Theatre History*, 196.

50. Bratton, *New Readings in Theatre History*, 172–3.

51. Mary Ebsworth, *The Two Brothers of Pisa* (Edinburgh: Joseph Ebsworth and S. G. Fairbrother, 1828), 6.

52. 'New Strand Theatre,' *The Times*, 20 August 1839, 5.

53. *Caught in His Own Trap An Original Comedietta* (London: Hailes Lacy, n.d.), first performed at the Olympic Theatre, 13 October 1851.

54. For a more detailed discussion of this play, see my 'Women and the Theatre,' in Joanne Shattock (ed.), *Women and Literature in Britain, 1800–1900* (Cambridge: Cambridge University Press, 2001), 198–9.

55. *Katty from Connaught, A Comedietta*, British Library, Add. Mss. 43020, Lord Chamberlain's Collection of Plays, licensed for New Strand Theatre 27 August 1849.

56. 'New Strand Theatre,' *The Theatrical Mirror and Playgoers' Companion*, 3 September 1849, 1.

57. 'New Strand,' *The Athenæum*, 1 September 1849.

58. Davis and Emeljanow, *Reflecting the Audience*, 46.

59. Heidi J. Holder, 'The "lady playwrights" and the "wild tribes of the East": Female Dramatists in the East End Theatre, 1860–1880,' 174, and Jim Davis, 'Sarah Lane: Questions of Authorship,' in Davis and Donkin (eds), *Women and Playwriting in Nineteenth-Century Britain*, 125–47.

60. 'Theatricals. Royal Kent Theatre,' *Athenaeum*, 27 September 1834, 716. For further information about this theatre, see Errol Sherson, *London's Lost Theatres of the Nineteenth Century* (London: Bodley Head, 1925), 320.

61. Planché, *Recollections and Reflections*, Vol. I, 213–14.

62. 'Theatricals. Drury Lane,' *The Athenaeum*, 11 October 1834, 753.

63. 'Drury-Lane Theatre,' *The Times*, 7 October 1834, 2.

64. The Times, 4 February 1847, 6.

65. The Times, 12 January 1849, 6.

66. http://library.kent.ac.uk/library/special/html/specoll/petting.htm.

67. Mrs Denvil, *The Poisoner and His Victim; or, Revenge Crime and Retribution*, Lord Chamberlain's Collection of Plays, British Library, Add. Mss. 42982, f. 722.

68. Jerrold is supposed to have said of the domestic drama 'A poor thing, but my own,' Walter Jerrold, *Douglas Jerrold, Dramatist and Wit* (London: Hodder & Stoughton, n.d.) Vol. I, 211.

69. A term Catherine Gore uses in a letter to the Duke of Devonshire to describe the mixture of writers and members of the urban-based upper classes with whom she mixed at Knebworth. Devonshire Mss., Chatsworth, 2nd ser. 384.16, Dec 12th [1850?].

70. Reprinted in Richard W. Schoch (ed.), *Victorian Theatrical Burlesques* (Aldershot: Ashgate, 2003), 53–94.

71. For records of the plays' performances, see *Playbills and Programmes from London Theatres 1801–1900 in the Theatre Museum, London* (Cambridge: Chadwyck-Healey, 1983). See Frederick Wilton's use of the plays to fill out the Britannia's bills, Jim Davis (ed.), *The Britannia Diaries*; for the performance history of *East Lynne*, see Katherine Newey and Veronica Kelly (eds and intro.) *Ellen Wood's* East Lynne (St Lucia, Qld: Australasian Drama Studies Association, 1994). For an index of early film versions, see Denis Gifford, *Books and Plays in Films, 1896–1915: Literary, Theatrical and Artistic Sources of the First Twenty Years of Motion Pictures* (London and New York: Mansell, 1991). The most recent adaptation of *Lady Audley's Secret*, adapted by Douglas Hounam, was broadcast in the United Kingdom on ITV, 17 May 2000.

72. Robert Lee Wolff, 'Devoted Disciple: The Letters of Mary Elizabeth Braddon to Sir Edward Bulwer-Lytton, 1862–1873,' *Harvard Library Bulletin*, XXII: 1 (January 1974), 12.
73. 'Musical and Dramatic Gossip,' *Athenæum*, 89.
74. Davis (ed.), *Britannia Diaries*, 140.
75. Henry Morley, *The Journal of a London Playgoer*, ed. and intro. Michael R. Booth (Leicester: Leicester University Press, 1974), 244.
76. See Lyn Pykett's discussion of the class-based reception of *The Doctor's Wife*, 'Introduction,' Mary Elizabeth Braddon, *The Doctor's Wife* (Oxford: Oxford University Press, 1998; Oxford World's Classics), xx–xxi.
77. Patrick Brantlinger, *The Reading Lesson: The Threat of Mass Literacy in Nineteenth-Century British Fiction* (Bloomington and Indianapolis: Indiana University Press, 1998), 143.
78. Robert Lee Wolff, 'Devoted Disciple: The Letters of Mary Elizabeth Braddon to Sir Edward Bulwer-Lytton, 1862–1873,' *Harvard Library Bulletin*, XXII: 1 (January, 1974), 15.
79. 'St James's,' *Athenæum*, 7 March 1863, 338.
80. 'The Theatres,' *Illustrated London News*, 7 March 1863, 255.
81. 'St James's Theatre,' *Times*, 2 March 1863.
82. 'St James's Theatre,' *Daily Telegraph*, 2 March 1863.
83. 'Princess's Theatre,' *The Times*, 12 March 1863.
84. 'Princess's,' *The Athenæum*, 21 March 1863.
85. 'Princess's Theatre,' *Daily Telegraph*, 12 March 1863.
86. 'Adelphi Theatre,' *The Times*, 20 March 1863.
87. 'Princess's,' *The Athenæum*, 21 March 1863.
88. 'Princess's Theatre,' *The Times*, 12 March 1863.
89. 'Adelphi Theatre', *Daily Telegraph*, 19 March 1863.
90. Anne Cvetkovich, *Mixed Feelings: Feminism, Mass Culture, and Victorian Sensationalism* (New Brunswick, NJ: Rutgers University Press, 1992).
91. Cvetkovich, *Mixed Feelings*, 14–15.
92. Lyn Pykett, *The 'Improper' Feminine: The Women's Sensation Novel and the New Woman Writing* (London and New York: Routledge, 1992), 50–1.
93. Kate Flint, *The Woman Reader, 1837–1914* (Oxford: Clarendon Press, 1993), 276.
94. Michael R. Booth, *Victorian Spectacular Theatre, 1850–1910* (London: Routledge & Kegan Paul, 1981), 64.
95. Pykett, *The 'Improper' Feminine*, 97.
96. Cvetkovich, *Mixed Feelings*, 13.
97. Andrew King, *The London Journal, 1845–83: Periodicals, Production and Gender* (Aldershot: Ashgate, 2004), 195–6, Lilian Nayder, 'Rebellious Sepoys and Bigamous Wives: The Indian Mutiny and Marriage Law Reform in *Lady Audley's Secret*,' in Marlene Tromp, Pamela K. Gilbert, and Aeron Haynie (eds), *Beyond Sensation: Mary Elizabeth Braddon in Context* (Albany: State University of New York Press, 2000), 32, and Pykett, *The 'Improper' Feminine*, 80–81.
98. Pykett, *The Improper Feminine*, 134.
99. Gifford, *Books and Plays in Films*.
100. Powell, *Women and the Victorian Theatre*, 101.
101. Pykett, *The 'Improper' Feminine*, 51.

102. Flint, *The Woman Reader*, 294.
103. Nicola Diane Thompson (ed.), 'Responding to the Woman Questions: Rereading Noncanonical Victorian Women Novelists,' in *Victorian Women Writers and the Woman Question* (Cambridge: Cambridge University Press, 1999), 8. See also Jane Tompkins, *Sensational Designs: The Cultural Work of American Fiction 1790–1860* (New York and Oxford: Oxford University Press, 1985), 123.
104. Ardis, *Modernism and Cultural Conflict*, 6.
105. Andreas Huyssen, *After the Great Divide: Modernism, Mass Culture, Postmodernism* (Bloomington and Indianapolis: Indiana University Press, 1986), 53.
106. Lynne Hapgood, 'Transforming the Victorian,' in Lynne Hapgood and Nancy L. Paxton (eds), *Outside Modernism: In Pursuit of the English Novel, 1900–30* (Houndmills: Macmillan, 2000), 23.
107. For a discussion of the theoretical foundations of the association of mass culture with women, see Huyssen, *After the Great Divide*, 47–53. For an account of the contemporary debates over the feminization of *fin de siècle* culture, see Sally Ledger, *The New Woman: Fiction and Feminism at the* Fin de Siècle (Manchester: Manchester University Press, 1997), Chapter 7, 'The New Woman, Modernism and Mass Culture.'
108. Catherine Wiley, 'Staging Infanticide: The Refusal of Representation in Elizabeth Robins's *Alan's Wife*,' *Theatre Journal*, 42: 4 (1990), and Susan Torrey Barstow, ' "Hedda is All of Us": Late-Victorian Women at the Matinee,' *Victorian Studies*, 43: 3 (Spring 2001).
109. 'Foreign Actors and the English Drama,' *Cornhill Magazine*, 8 (1863), 172.
110. 'A Word on the Drama in England and France,' *Macmillan's Magazine*, 20 (1869), 70.
111. 'The Present State of the English Stage,' *Temple Bar*, 33 (1871), 458.
112. G. H. Lewes, 'Shakespeare in France,' *Cornhill Magazine*, 11 (1865), 35.
113. Henry Arthur Jones, *The Renascence of the English Drama* (London: Macmillan, 1895), vii.
114. Henry Arthur Jones, *The Foundations of a National Drama* (London: Chapman & Hall, n.d.), 37–38.
115. Jones, *The Renascence of the English Drama*, 15.
116. See Regenia Gagnier on Arnold's 'aesthetic of evaluation,' which, she argues, was 'historically linked with the idea of national cultures and races,' in 'Productive Bodies, Pleasured Bodies: On Victorian Aesthetics,' in Talia Schaffer and Kathy Psomiades (eds), *Women and British Aestheticism* (Charlottesville and London: University Press of Virginia, 1999), 273.
117. See also Thomas Postlewait, 'From Melodrama to Realism: The Suspect History of American Drama,' in Michael Hays and Anastasia Nikolopoulou (ed.), *Melodrama: The Cultural Emergence of a Genre* (London: Macmillan, 1996), 50.
118. Clement Scott, *The Drama of Yesterday and Today*, 2 vols (London: Macmillan, 1899), Vol. 1, 471.
119. William Archer, *The Old Drama and the New* (London: William Heinemann, 1923), 338.
120. William Archer, *English Dramatists of To-Day* (London: Sampson Low, Marston, Searle, & Rivington, 1882), 7.

121. George Bernard Shaw, *Our Theatres in the Nineties* (London: Constable and Co., 1948), Vol. 3, 58.

122. Martin Meisel, *Shaw and the Nineteenth-Century Theatre* (1963; New York: Limelight Editions, 1984), 72.

123. Huyssen, *After the Great Divide*, 50.

124. Powell, *Women and the Victorian Theatre*, especially Chapter 6, 'Victorian Plays by Women,' 122–46, Carlson, 'Conflicted Politics and Circumspect Comedy: Women's Comic Playwriting in the 1890s,' in Davis and Donkin (eds), *Women and Playwriting in Nineteenth-Century Britain*, 256–76, and Carlson and Powell, 'Reimagining the Theatre: Women Playwrights of the Victorian and Edwardian Period,' in Powell (ed.), *The Cambridge Companion to Victorian and Edwardian Theatre*, 237–56.

125. Ryley Plays, English Manuscripts, John Rylands Library, University of Manchester.

126. See William B. Todd, 'Dehan's *Dop Doctor*: A Forgotten Bestseller,' *The Library Chronicle of the University of Texas*, VII: 3 (Summer 1963), 17–26.

127. *Who Was Who in the Theatre* (Detroit: Gale Research, 1978), 2100–1.

128. Adrienne Scullion (ed.), 'Introduction,' *Female Playwrights of the Nineteenth Century* (London: Everyman, 1996), lxvii–lxviii.

129. For a brief discussion of the international dimension of the popular theatre, and a demonstration of the way mixed nationality could make women playwrights disappear, see my 'When is an Australian Playwright Not an Australian Playwright? The Case of May Holt,' in Susan Bradley Smith and Elizabeth Schafer (eds), *Playing Australia* (Amsterdam: Rodopi, 2003), 93–107. For further discussion of the transnational dimension of the popular entertainment industry at turn of the century, see Veronica Kelly, 'Hybridity and Performance in Colonial Australian Theatre: *The Currency Lass*,' in Helen Gilbert (ed.) *(Post) Colonial Stages: Critical and Creative Views on Drama, Theatre and Performance* (Hebden Bridge: Dangaroo Press, 1999), 40–54.

130. *Who Was Who in the Theatre*, 985.

131. Katharine Cockin, *Women and Theatre in the Age of Suffrage: The Pioneer Players, 1911–1925* (Houndmills: Palgrave Macmillan, 2001), 80.

132. David Mayer, 'Encountering Melodrama,' in Powell (ed.), *The Cambridge Companion to Victorian and Edwardian Theatre*, 160.

133. Julie Holledge, *Innocent Flowers: Women in the Edwardian Theatre* (London: Virago Press, 1981), 24–7. See also Marysa Demoor on literary hostesses' 'At Homes' as important links in female professional networks, *Their Fair Share: Women, Power and Criticism in the* Athenaeum, *from Millicent Garett Fawcett to Katherine Mansfield, 1870–1920* (Aldershot: Ashgate, 2000), 27, and Gail Marshall, *Actresses on the Victorian Stage: Feminine Performance and the Galatea Myth* (Cambridge: Cambridge University Press, 1998), 146.

134. I echo Wyndham Lewis' use of the word 'blasted' to describe the Victorians in setting up his journal *Blast*.

135. Johnston Forbes-Robertson, *A Player Under Three Reigns* (London: T. Fisher Unwin, 1925), 204–5. *Mice and Men* (London: Samuel French, 1903).

136. 'Drama,' *The Athenæum*, 1 February 1902, 156.

137. 'Lyric Theatre,' *The Times*, 28 January 1902.

138. 'Mice and Men,' *The Era*, 1 February 1902.

139. 'Terry's Theatre,' *The Times*, 15 February 1896.

140. 'Terry's,' *The Era*, 22 February 1896.

141. 'Drama,' *The Athenæum*, 22 February 1896, 259.

142. 'At the Play,' *The Theatre*, 1 March 1896, 162.

143. Carlson, 'Conflicted Politics,' in Davis and Donkin (eds), *Nineteenth-Century British Women Playwrights*, 262.

144. Powell, *Women and the Victorian Theatre*, 83–4.

145. *A Mother of Three* (London: Samuel French, n.d.), first performed 8 April 1896, Comedy Theatre. *A Matchmaker*, British Library, Add. Mss. 53594, Lord Chamberlain's Collection of Plays, first performed 9 May 1896, Shaftesbury Theatre.

146. 'The Comedy,' *The Era*, 11 April 1896.

147. 'A Mother of Three,' *The Theatre*, 1 May 1896, 289.

148. Shaw, *Our Theatres in the Nineties*, Vol. 2, 96–7.

149. 'A Matchmaker,' *The Theatre*, 1 June 1896, 349.

150. 'The Shaftesbury,' *The Era*, 16 May 1896.

151. Shaw, *Our Theatres in the Nineties*, Vol. 2, 137.

152. Carlson and Powell, 'Reimagining the Theatre,' in Powell (ed.), *The Cambridge Companion to Victorian and Edwardian Theatre*, 254.

153. Newey, ' "From a Female Pen",' in Davis and Donkin (eds), *Women and Playwriting in Nineteenth-Century Britain*, 208.

154. Kathy Mezei, 'Contextualising Feminist Narratology,' in Mezei (ed.), *Ambiguous Discourse: Feminist Narratology and British Writers* (Chapel Hill: University of North Carolina Press, 1996), 1.

155. Marysa Demoor, *Their Fair Share: Women, Power and Criticism in the Athenaeum, from Millicent Garett Fawcett to Katherine Mansfield, 1870–1920* (Aldershot: Ashgate, 2000), 14, 22. At the time of writing, membership of the Garrick Club is still open only to men.

156. Lynda Nead, *Victorian Babylon: People, Streets and Images in Nineteenth-Century London* (New Haven and London: Yale University Press, 2000), 66–70, and Judith R. Walkowitz, *City of Dreadful Delight: Narratives of Sexual Danger in Late-Victorian London* (London: Virago Press, 1992), 50–2.

157. See Thomas Richards, *The Commodity Culture of Victorian England: Advertising and Spectacle, 1851–1914* (London and New York: Verso, 1990), 7, Fraser, Green and Johnston, *Gender and the Victorian Periodical*, and Joel Kaplan and Sheila Stowell, *Theatre and Fashion: Oscar Wilde to the Suffragettes* (Cambridge: Cambridge University Press, 1994).

158. Barstow, ' "Hedda is All of Us",' 387, Gardner, 'The Invisible Spectatrice,' in Gale and Gardner (eds), *Women, Theatre, and Performance*, 33–4, Davis and Emeljanow, *Reflecting the Audience*, 217.

159. By shifting here from female disadvantage to male advantage I am following the approach of sociologist Joan Eveline, who argues that a feminist focus on male advantage, rather than female disadvantage, would enable a new and clearer articulation of patriarchal and sexist structures, 'The Politics of Advantage,' *Australian Feminist Studies*, 19 (Autumn 1994).

160. See the transcript of Julie Holledge's interview with Jane Comfort, actress, suffragette (and niece of Madeleine Lucette Ryley), in *Innocent Flowers*, 51.

161. Mary Poovey, *Uneven Developments*, 3.

162. This argument has been more fully developed in feminist literary history and criticism of the novel. See, for example Tompkins' argument that 'the popular domestic [American] novel of the nineteenth century represents a monumental effort to reorganize culture from a woman's point of view;' *Sensational Designs*, 124; Nancy Armstrong writes that 'I regard fiction [. . .] both as the document and as the agency of cultural history. I believe it helped to formulate the ordered space we now recognize as the household, made that space totally functional, and used it as a context for representing normal behaviour,' *Desire and Domestic Fiction* (Oxford: Oxford University Press, 1987), 23; and Lyn Pykett's discussion of the fear of the 'feminisation and the proletarianisation of the public sphere' through the figure of the New Woman, in *The Improper Feminine*, 139–41.

4 Art

1. Susan Brown, 'Determined Heroes: George Eliot, Augusta Webster and Closet Drama,' *Victorian Poetry*, 33: 1 (Spring 1995), 104.
2. Leighton, *Victorian Women Poets*, 1.
3. Marjean Purinton, *Romantic Ideology Unmasked: The Mentally Constructed Tyrannies in Dramas of William Wordsworth, Lord Byron, Percy Shelley, and Joanna Baillie* (London and Toronto: Associated University Presses, 1994), 21.
4. Christine Sutphin notes that Webster persuaded her husband to move to London so that she could mix in literary circles, 'Introduction,' Augusta Webster, *Portraits and Other Poems*, ed. Christine Sutphin (Peterborough: Broadview Press, 2000), 11. Webster was also able to limit her family to one child, see Leighton, *Victorian Women Poets*, 165.
5. BC Gosse correspondence, 19 May 1876, Special Collections, Brotherton Library, University of Leeds.
6. Rosemarie Bodenheimer discusses Eliot's ambivalence slightly differently in 'Ambition and Its Audiences: George Eliot's Performing Figures,' *Victorian Studies*, 34: 1 (Autumn 1990), 9–10.
7. There is an extensive critical literature on Eliot's use of artist and performer figures, most prominently in *Daniel Deronda*. For some starting points into this, see Gillian Beer, ' "Coming Wonders": Uses of Theatre in the Victorian Novel,' Marie Axton and Raymond Williams (eds), *English Drama: Forms and Development* (Cambridge: Cambridge University Press, 1977), Joseph Litvak, *Caught in the Act: Theatricality in the Nineteenth-Century Novel*, especially Chapter 5, 'Poetry and Theatricality in *Daniel Deronda*' (Berkeley: University of California Press, 1992), Alison Byerley, *Realism, Representation, and the Arts in Nineteenth-Century Literature* (Cambridge: Cambridge University Press, 1997), 126–33, and Marshall, *Actresses on the Victorian Stage*, Chapter 3, 'George Eliot, *Daniel Deronda*, and the Sculptural Aesthetic.'
8. Gordon Haight reproduces the Lewes/Eliot 1863 sketches of a play *Savello*, *George Eliot: A Biography* (Oxford: Clarendon Press, 1968), 374–5.
9. Rosemarie Bodenheimer, *The Real Life of Mary Ann Evans: George Eliot, Her Letters and Her Fiction* (Ithaca and London: Cornell University Press, 1994), 174.

10. Brown, 'Determined Heroes,' 91.
11. Armstrong, *Victorian Poetry*, 370; Kathryn Hughes, *George Eliot: The Last Victorian* (London: Fourth Estate, 1999), writes of its 'laborious gestation,' 381.
12. Brown, 'Determined Heroines,' 91. Eliot records in her journal on 21 February 1865 '*George has taken my drama away from me.*' Margaret Harris and Judith Johnston (eds), *The Journals of George Eliot* (Cambridge: Cambridge University Press, 1998), 123, and Rosemary Ashton, *George Eliot: A Life* (London: Allen Lane, The Penguin Press, 1996), 278, and Haight, *George Eliot*, 379.
13. Armstrong, *Victorian Poetry*, 370.
14. Marshall, *Actresses on the Victorian Stage*, 76–7.
15. Hughes, *George Eliot: The Last Victorian*, 392.
16. Ashton, *George Eliot: A Life*, 311; see also Haight, *George Eliot*, 429; but see Bodenheimer, *The Real Life of Mary Ann Evans*, 179–83, for Bodenheimer's reading of *Armgart* as directly autobiographical.
17. Ashton, *George Eliot: A Life*, 311.
18. Rebecca A. Pope, 'The Diva Doesn't Die: George Eliot's *Armgart*,' in Leslie C. Dunn and Nancy A. Jones (eds), *Embodied Voices: Representing Female Vocality in Western Culture* (Cambridge: Cambridge University Press, 1994), 139–51, and Susan Brown, 'Determined Heroines,' 92.
19. Pope, 'The Diva Doesn't Die,' 151.
20. Kathleen Blake, '*Armgart* – George Eliot on the Woman Artist,' *Victorian Poetry*, 18: 3 (Autumn 1980), 80, and Kathleen Hickok, *Representations of Women: Nineteenth-Century British Women's Poetry* (Westport, Ct. and London: Greenwood Press, 1984), 140.
21. George Eliot, *Armgart*, in *The Legend of Jubal and Other Poems* (Edinburgh and London: William Blackwood & Sons, 1874; 2nd edition). All further references are to this edition and will be given in the text. There is a modern edition of Eliot's poems, L. Jenkins (ed. & intro.), *Collected Poems* (London: Skoob Books, 1989). See Pope for a discussion of the significance of Eliot's knowledge of the European performance history of the Berlioz-Viardot production of Gluck's *Orpheus*, 'The Diva Doesn't Die,' 145.
22. Bodenheimer, 'Ambition and Its Audiences: George Eliot's Performing Figures,' *Victorian Studies*, 34: 1 (Autumn 1990), 25.
23. See Bodenheimer on Eliot's use of melodramatic dramaturgy in *Armgart*, 'Ambition and Its Audiences,' 24.
24. Robert J. Nelson, *Play Within a Play* (New Haven: Yale University Press, 1958), 90.
25. Bodenheimer, 'Ambition and Its Audiences,' 8.
26. Bodenheimer, *The Real Life of Mary Ann Evans*, 179.
27. Leighton, *Victorian Women Poets*, 164.
28. Dorothy Mermin, *Godiva's Ride: Women of Letters in England, 1830–1880* (Bloomington and Indiana: Indiana University Press, 1993), 79–80.
29. See Patricia Rigg, 'Augusta Webster and the Lyric Muse: *The Athenaeum* and Webster's Poetics,' *Victorian Poetry*, 42: 2 (Summer 2004), 135–64, and Christine Sutphin, 'Introduction,' in Webster, *Portraits and Other Poems*, for summaries of scholarship on Webster in the last decade.
30. See W. M. Rossetti's comment that Webster's play *The Sentence* should 'be generally recognized – and this can scarcely fail to come – as one of the

masterpieces of European drama,' 'Introductory Note' to Augusta Webster, *Mother and Daughter: An Uncompleted Sonnet Sequence* (London: Macmillan, 1895), 13–14.

31. 'Dramatic Gossip,' *Athenæum*, 7 June 1890, 746.

32. Crochunis (ed.), 'Introduction,' *Joanna Baillie*, 1.

33. Leighton, *Victorian Women Poets*, 167.

34. Mermin, *Godiva's Ride*, 80.

35. David Mayer, *Playing Out the Empire: Ben Hur and Other Toga Plays and Films, 1883–1908. A Critical Anthology* (Oxford: Clarendon Press, 1994), 2. According to Mayer, the term was first coined in 1895–1896, in response to the success of *The Sign of the Cross*.

36. Shou-Ren Wang, *The Theatre of the Mind: A Study of the Unacted Drama in Nineteenth-Century England* (London: Macmillan, 1990), xvii.

37. Brown, 101. See also E. Warwick Slinn's discussion of Webster's dramatic monologue, 'The Outcast' for an analysis of Webster's use of a speaking voice from the margins to produce 'innovative social analysis,' *Victorian Poetry as Cultural Critique: The Politics of Performative Language* (Charlottesville and London: University of Virginia Press, 2003), 161.

38. Virginia Woolf, 'On Not Knowing Greek,' *Collected Essays* (London: Hogarth Press, 1980), Vol. I, 12 (from The Common Reader, Series 1, originally published 1925).

39. Mermin, *Godiva's Ride*, 53.

40. Augusta Webster, *The Prometheus Bound of Æschylus*, edited by Thomas Webster MA Late Fellow of Trinity College Cambridge (London and Cambridge: Macmillan & Co., 1866).

41. Augusta Webster, *In a Day* (London: Kegan Paul, Trench & Co., 1882), 4. All references are to this edition.

42. Armstrong, *Victorian Poetry*, 372.

43. See Viv Gardner and Susan Rutherford (eds), *The New Woman and Her Sisters* (New York and London: Harvester Wheatsheaf, 1992), Viv Gardner and Linda Fitzsimmons (eds), *The New Woman* (London: Methuen, 1991), Jean Chothia (ed.), *The New Woman* (Oxford: Oxford World's Classics, 1998), and Katherine Kelly (ed.), *Modern Drama by Women, 1880s–1930s: An International Anthology* (London and New York: Routledge, 1996). For the connections between New Woman drama and the suffrage movement, see Holledge, *Innocent Flowers*, and Sheila Stowell, *A Stage of Their Own: Feminist Playwrights of the Suffrage Era* (Manchester: Manchester University Press, 1992).

44. Although Eleanor Marx informed her friends in 1884 that she and Edward Aveling were living together as if married, and requested she be known as Eleanor Marx-Aveling or Mrs Aveling, after her suicide and the revelation of Aveling's dishonesty and infidelity towards her, a family friend, Wilhelm Liebknecht declared that she should now be known by her own name again; cited in Chushichi Tsuzuki, *The Life of Eleanor Marx, 1855–1898: A Socialist Tragedy* (Oxford: Clarendon Press, 1967), 325.

45. Reprinted in Michael Egan (ed.), *Ibsen: The Critical Heritage* (London and Boston: Routledge & Kegan Paul, 1972), 41–50.

46. Review from *Licensed Victuallers' Mirror*, 11 June 1889, reprinted in Egan (ed.), *Ibsen: The Critical Heritage*, 105.

47. Moody comments on the similar fate of Anne Plumptre's translations 'disappearing' into those of Sheridan's in the late eighteenth century, 'Suicide and Translation in the Dramaturgy of Elizabeth Inchbald and Anne Plumptre,' in Burroughs (ed.), *Women in British Romantic Theatre*, 272.

48. Alex Owen, *The Darkened Room: Women, Power, and Spiritualism in Late Victorian England* (London: Virago Press, 1989), 4. Not all historians see these connections: Ian Britain characterizes these as 'bizarre appropriations' of *A Doll's House* for Christian Science and karmic philosophies, 'A Transplanted Doll's House: Ibsenism, Feminism and Socialism in Late-Victorian and Edwardian England,' in Ian Donaldson (ed.), *Transformations in European Drama* (Macmillan: London, 1983), 15.

49. Catherine Ray, 'Introduction,' to Henrik Ibsen, *Emperor and Galilean*, trans. by Catherine Ray, reprinted in Egan (ed.), *Ibsen: The Critical Heritage* (London and Boston: Routledge & Kegan Paul, 1972), 51. All further references are to this edition.

50. Henrietta F. Lord, 'Preface,' to Henrik Ibsen, *The Doll's House*, trans. Henrietta F. Lord (New York: D. Appleton & Co., 1907), 4. All further references are to this edition.

51. Sally Ledger, 'Eleanor Marx and Henrik Ibsen,' in John Stokes (ed.), *Eleanor Marx (1855–1898): Life, Work, Contacts* (Aldershot: Ashgate, 2000), 54.

52. William Archer's review of Henrietta Lord, *Nora*, reprinted in Egan (ed.), *Ibsen: The Critical Heritage*, 61.

53. Henrietta Lord, *The Academy*, 13 January 1883, reprinted in Egan (ed.), *Ibsen: The Critical Heritage*, 63.

54. Simon Shepherd and Peter Womack, *English Drama: A Cultural History* (Oxford: Blackwell, 1996). See also Bratton, 'Miss Scott and Miss Macauley,' and *New Readings in Theatre History* for parallels with the 1820s and 1830s.

55. Lori Chamberlain, 'Gender and the Metaphorics of Translation,' *Signs: Journal of Women in Culture and Society*, 13: 3 (Spring 1988), 458.

56. Cited in Michael Meyer, *Ibsen* (Harmondsworth: Penguin Books, 1974), 570.

57. Yvonne Kapp, *Eleanor Marx*, Vol. II, *The Crowded Years: 1884–1898* (London: Virago, 1979), 105.

58. Gail Marshall, 'Eleanor Marx and Shakespeare,' in Stokes (ed.), *Eleanor Marx*, 69.

59. Christopher Kent, 'Helen Taylor's "Experimental Life" on the Stage: 1856–58,' *Nineteenth Century Theatre Research*, 5: 1 (Spring 1977), 45–54.

60. Kapp, *Eleanor Marx*, Vol. II, 105.

61. Kapp, *Eleanor Marx*, Vol. II, 103–6.

62. Quoted in Kapp, *Eleanor Marx*, Vol. II, 103.

63. Errol Durbach, 'A Century of Ibsen Criticism,' in James McFarlane (ed.), *The Cambridge Companion to Ibsen* (Cambridge: Cambridge University Press, 1994), 234. See also Ledger, 'Eleanor Marx and Henrik Ibsen,' 56.

64. Edward and Eleanor Marx Aveling, *The Woman Question* (London: Swan Sonnenschein, n.d.), 16.

65. Ronald Bush, 'James Joyce, Eleanor Marx, and the Future of Modernism,' in Hugh Witemeyer (ed.), *The Future of Modernism* (Ann Arbor: University of Michigan Press, 1997), 63.

66. Lawrence Irving, *Henry Irving: The Actor and His World* (London: Columbus Books, 1989; 1951), 535.

67. Ledger, 'Eleanor Marx and Henrik Ibsen,' 54, and R. Brandon, *The New Women and the Old Men: Love, Sex and the Woman Question* (London: Papermac, 2000; 1990), 96.

68. Sherry Simon, *Gender in Translation: Cultural Identity and the Politics of Transmission* (London and New York: Routledge, 1996), 68.

69. Durbach, 'A Century of Ibsen Criticism,' 235.

70. John Stokes, *Resistible Theatres: Enterprise and Experiment in the Late Nineteenth Century* (London: Paul Elek Books, 1972), 3, and see Ian Britain, *Fabianism and Culture: A Study in British Socialism and the Arts, c.1884–1918* (Cambridge: Cambridge University Press, 1982), for a broad study of the involvement of the Fabian Society in theatre.

71. See Kelly, 'Introduction,' in Kelly (ed.), *Felicia Hemans*, on translation as one of Hemans' 'acceptably feminine ways of consolidating her career,' 20.

72. Ledger, 'Eleanor Marx and Henrik Ibsen,' 65–7; Bush, 'James Joyce, Eleanor Marx, and the Future of Modernism,' 51–2.

5 Home and nation

1. Eliza Lynn Linton 'What is Woman's Work?' (1868), cited in Anthony Jenkins, *The Making of Victorian Drama* (Cambridge: Cambridge University Press, 1991), 94.

2. Linda Colley, *Britons: Forging the Nation, 1707–1837* (London: Pimlico, 1992), 250. See also 'No More Separate Spheres!' a special edition of *American Literature*, 70: 3 (September 1998).

3. Anne K. Mellor, *Mothers of the Nation: Women's Political Writing in England, 1780–1830* (Bloomington and Indianapolis: Indiana University Press, 2000), 2–3.

4. Amanda Vickery, 'Golden Age to Separate Spheres? A Review of the Categories and Chronologies of English Women's History,' *Historical Journal*, 36: 2 (June 1993), 383–414.

5. Poovey, *Uneven Developments*, 3.

6. Fraser, Green and Johnston, *Gender and the Victorian Periodical*, 199.

7. Michel Foucault, *Power/Knowledge: Selected Interviews and Other Writings* (Brighton: Harvester, 1980), 193.

8. Mary Poovey, *The Proper Lady and the Woman Writer*, x.

9. Clarke, *Ambitious Heights, Passim.*

10. Catherine Waters, 'Gender, Family, and Domestic Ideology,' in John O. Jordan (ed.), *The Cambridge Companion to Charles Dickens* (Cambridge: Cambridge University Press, 2001), 122.

11. Barbara Caine, *English Feminism, 1780–1980* (Oxford: Oxford University Press, 1997), 82.

12. Barbara Caine, *Victorian Feminists* (Oxford: Oxford University Press, 1992), 52–3.

13. Sarah Stickney Ellis, *The Mothers of England: Their Influence and Responsibility* (London: Fisher, Son & Co., 1843), 23.

14. Mellor, *Mothers of the Nation*, 11.

15. Caine, *English Feminism*, 86.

16. Studies referred to here are Mary Chapman, ' "Living Pictures": Women and *Tableaux Vivants* in Nineteenth-Century American Fiction and Culture,'

Wide Angle, 18: 3 (July 1996), Florence C. Smith, 'Introducing Parlor Theatricals to the American Home,' *Performing Arts Resources*, 14 (1989), and David Mayer, 'Parlour and Platform Melodrama,' in Michael Hays and Anastasia Nikolopoulou (eds), *Melodrama: The Cultural Emergence of a Genre* (London: Macmillan, 1996). See also my '*Home Plays for Ladies*: Women's Work in Home Theatricals,' *Nineteenth Century Theatre*, 26: 2 (Winter 1998).

17. Nicoll, *A History of English Drama, 1660–1900*, Vol. V, 442, 685, 801, 845.

18. J. S. Bratton, *The Victorian Popular Ballad* (London: Macmillan, 1975), 208.

19. David Mayer, *Harlequin in His Element: The English Pantomime, 1806–1836* (Cambridge, Mass.: Harvard University Press, 1969), 311.

20. Eliza Keating, *Aladdin; or, The Very Wonderful Lamp! A Fairy Extravaganza in Two Acts* (London: Thomas Hailes Lacy, n.d.), 12.

21. Louisa Greene, *Nettlecoats; or, The Silent Princess, in Drawing Room Dramas, by William Gorman Wills & the Honourable Mrs Greene* (Edinburgh and London: William Blackwood and Sons, 1873), 136.

22. Florence Bell, *Fairy Tale Plays and How to Act Them* (London: Longmans, Green & Co., 1899).

23. Elsie Fogerty, *Tennyson's* Princess. *Adapted and Arranged for Amateur Performance in Girls' Schools* (London: Swan Sonnenschein, 1907).

24. For a representative sample see *The Amateur's Guide* (London: Thomas Hailes Lacy, n.d.), *Plays for Amateur Actors [...] with Instructions for Amateur Theatricals* (London: C. Arthur Pearson, 1911), Albert Douglass, *The Amateurs' Handbook and Entertainers' Directory* (London: Potter Bros, 1897), and C. Lang Neil, *Amateur Theatricals. A Practical Guide* (London: C. Arthur Pearson, 1904).

25. E. C. F. Collier (ed.), *A Victorian Diarist: Extracts from the Journals of Mary, Lady Monkswell, 1873–1895*, 2 vols (London: John Murray, 1944), Vol. 1, 39.

26. Augustus Mayhew, 'Acting Charades,' *The Illustrated London News*, 24 December 1859, 621.

27. Neil, *Amateur Theatricals*, 19.

28. Walter Herries Pollock and Lady Pollock, *Amateur Theatricals* (London: Macmillan, 1879), 1.

29. David Mann and Susan Garland Mann, *Women Playwrights in England, Ireland and Scotland, 1660–1823* (Bloomington and Indianapolis: Indiana University Press, 1996), 4.

30. *The Illustrated London News*, 20 March 1858, 295.

31. Anne Bowman and other writers, *Acting Charades and Proverbs. Arranged for Representation in the Drawing Room* (London: George Routledge and Sons, 1891), 5.

32. J. V. Prichard, Tableaux Vivants *Arranged for Amateur Representation* (London and New York: Samuel French, n.d.), 7.

33. Bell, *Fairy Tale Plays*, xxi, xxiii.

34. Benedict Anderson, *Imagined Communities: Reflections on the Origin and Spread of Nationalism* (London and New York: Verso, 1991. Revised edition), 6.

35. Stuart Curran, 'Women Readers, Women Writers,' in Stuart Curran (ed.), *The Cambridge Companion to Romanticism* (Cambridge: Cambridge University Press, 1993), 190.

36. ' "From a Female Pen", ' in Davis and Donkin (eds), *Women and Playwriting in Nineteenth-Century Britain*, 203.

37. Richard Hengist Horne, *New Spirit of the Age* (New York: J. C. Riker, 1844), 138.
38. See Ellen Donkin, 'Mrs. Gore gives Tit for Tat' and Newey, ' "From a Female Pen", ' in Davis and Donkin (eds), *Women and Playwriting in Nineteenth-Century Britain*.
39. Kelly, 'Death and the Matron,' 198.
40. Barbara Leah Harman, *The Feminine Political Novel in Victorian England* (Charlottesville: University Press of Virginia, 1998), 11.
41. See Devonshire Mss., Chatsworth, 2nd ser.
42. Winifred Hughes, 'Mindless Millinery: Catherine Gore and the Silver Fork Heroine,' *Dickens Studies Annual*, 25 (1996), 160.
43. Winifred Hughes, 'Silver Fork Writers and Readers: Social Contexts of a Best Seller,' *Novel: A Forum on Fiction* (Spring 1992), 331, and Edward Lytton Bulwer, *England and the English* (London: George Routledge and Sons, 1874), 252.
44. For a discussion of an alternative approach in the popular theatre, see Newey, 'Reform on the London Stage,' in Burns and Innes (eds), *Rethinking the Age of Reform*, 238–53.
45. Julie Carlson, *In the Theatre of Romanticism: Coleridge, Nationalism, Women* (Cambridge: Cambridge University Press, 1994), and Betsy Bolton, *Women, Nationalism, and the Romantic Stage: Theatre and Politics in Britain, 1780–1800* (Cambridge: Cambridge University Press, 2001).
46. It is interesting to note Ian Haywood's comment that even in revisionist Romanticist studies, 'the wider issues of the connections between public politics and popular literary and cultural production [...] rarely enter into discussions of Romanticism.' *Revolution in Popular Literature*, 82.
47. McCalman, *Radical Underworld*, 181–2.
48. *The School for Coquettes*, British Library, Add. Mss. 42911, ff. 86–283, Lord Chamberlain's Collection of Plays. *Lords and Commons, A Comedy in Three Acts*, British Library, Add. Mss. 42913 ff. 512–66, Lord Chamberlain's Collection of Plays. All quotations are from these manuscripts. See also John Franceschina (ed.), *Gore on Stage: The Plays of Catherine Gore* (New York and London: Garland Publishing, 1999).
49. The season can be traced through advertisements in the *Times*, and Haymarket playbills.
50. *Spectator*, 16 July 1831, 690.
51. Evidence given by Captain John Forbes, *Report from the Select Committee Appointed to Inquire into the Laws Affecting Dramatic Literature, with the Minutes of Evidence* (Parliamentary Papers, 1831–32, vii), paras 2003–2007.
52. For the knowingness of London audiences, see Jacky Bratton's discussion of intertheatricality in *New Readings in Theatre History*, 52.
53. 'The Drama,' *The New Monthly Magazine*, January 1832, 23.
54. *Figaro in London*, 17 December 1831, 8.
55. 'Drama,' *The Literary Guardian*, 24 December 1831, 207.
56. *The Hamiltons, or The New Æra*, by the Author of "Mothers and Daughters" in Three Volumes (London: Saunders and Otley, 1834).
57. Catherine Gore, *Women as They Are; or, The Manners of the Day* (London: Henry Colburn and Richard Bentley, 1830; 2nd edition).
58. Catherine Gore, *The Woman of the World* (London: Henry Colburn, 1838).

59. K. D. Reynolds, *Aristocratic Women and Political Society in Victorian Britain* (Oxford: Clarendon Press, 1998), 154.

60. 'Theatricals: Drury Lane,' *The Athenæum*, 24 December 1831, 837.

61. Although I use the term 'suffragette' and focus on women's activist work as performance, of course the contemporary distinction between suffragists – a commitment to gaining the vote via constitutional and legislative change – and suffragettes – who advocated direct action – should be remembered. However, at its founding the Actresses' Franchise League made no commitment to either set of tactics, and the performance activities they sponsored used a number of techniques.

62. Lisa Tickner, *The Spectacle of Women: Imagery of the Suffrage Campaign, 1907–14* (London: Chatto and Windus, 1987), 14.

63. Martha Vicinus, *Independent Women: Work and Community for Single Women, 1850–1920* (Chicago and London: University of Chicago Press, 1985), 263.

64. Wendy Parkins, ' "The Epidemic of Purple, White and Green": Fashion and the Suffragette Movement in Britain 1908–14,' in Wendy Parkins (ed.), *Fashioning the Body Politic: Dress, Gender, Citizenship* (Oxford and New York: Berg, 2002), 99.

65. Barbara Green, *Spectacular Confessions: Autobiography, Performative Activism, and the Sites of Suffrage* (New York: St Martin's Press, 1997), 5.

66. There is still anecdotal knowledge of these guerilla tactics. While teaching an adult education class in Victorian women's writing for the Workers' Educational Association in Sydney in the 1990s, one of my students, Bridget, told the story of her aunt who as a young woman was involved in the Pankhursts' campaigns of direct action of brick throwing and window smashing. Before going into the city, Bridget's aunt was lined up with the other young women, to have her overall appearance approved as neat and respectable. A hammer or a brick could be hidden in the lady like pocket or handbag. Part of the shock of the acts of civil disobedience and political vandalism was the disjunction between the ladylike appearance of the women – their femininity – and the violent destructiveness of their actions. And what I learnt from this was never to underestimate the political awareness of comfortably off, retired women – the 'blue rinse set,' as they are often derogatorily called in Australia.

67. For example, Katharine Cockin, *Women and Theatre in the Age of Suffrage: The Pioneer Players, 1911–1925* (Houndmills: Palgrave Macmillan, 2001), 44, notes that the earliest examples Baz Kershaw gives of British propaganda theatre is the Worker's Theatre movement of the 1920s.

68. Penny Farfan, *Women, Modernism, and Performance* (Cambridge: Cambridge University Press, 2004), 32.

69. Elizabeth Robins, 'The Suffrage Camp Revisited,' in *Way Stations* (London: Hodder and Stoughton, 1913), 65.

70. Note Jan McDonald's approving citation of Jane Marcus' contention that 'it was Ibsen who created Elizabeth Robins, the feminist,' ' "The Second Act Was Glorious": The Staging of the Trafalgar Square Scene from *Votes for Women*! at the Court Theatre,' *Theatre History Studies*, 15 (June 1995), 141.

71. Stowell, *A Stage of Their Own*, 12.

72. Farfan, *Women, Modernism, and Performance*, 29.

73. Elizabeth Robins, '*Votes for Women!*' in Jean Chothia (ed.), *The New Woman and Other Emancipated Woman Plays* (Oxford: Oxford University Press, 1998), II, i, 173.
74. Vicinus, *Independent Women*, 249.
75. Katherine Kelly, 'The Actresses' Franchise League Prepares for War: Feminist Theatre in Camouflage,' *Theatre Survey*, 35: 1 (May 1994), 123.
76. Reprinted in Dale Spender and Carole Hayman (eds), *How the Vote Was Won, and Other Suffragette Plays* (London: Methuen, 1985). Further references are to this edition. *Miss Appleyard's Awakening* is also reprinted in Julie Holledge, *Innocent Flowers*, 189–201.
77. 'Actresses' Franchise League,' *The Era*, 28 May 1910, 15. Claire Hirshfield argues that the AFL 'represented the glamorous face of the movement,' 'The Actresses' Franchise League and the Campaign for Women's Suffrage 1908–1914,' *Theatre Research International*, 10: 2 (Summer 1985), 130.
78. 'Scala Theatre,' *The Times*, 13 November 1909, and 'Actresses' Franchise League,' *The Era*, 26 November 1910, 21.
79. Hirshfield notes that in 1912, over seventy performances were logged through the Play Department, 'The Actresses' Franchise League,' 132.
80. Julie Holledge, *Innocent Flowers*, 59–60, and Dale Spender, 'Introduction,' in Spender and Hayman (eds), *How the Vote Was Won*, 11–12.
81. Katharine Cockin, 'Women's Suffrage Drama,' in Maroula Joannou and June Purvis (eds), *The Women's Suffrage Movement: New Feminist Perspectives* (Manchester: Manchester University Press, 1998), 129.
82. See Holledge, *Innocent Flowers*, 59–61, for an account of the training in public speaking and recitation the AFL provided the suffrage movement.
83. Cockin, *Women and Theatre in the Age of Suffrage*, 91.
84. For Invisible Theatre, see Augusto Boal, *Theatre of the Oppressed*, trans. A. Charles and Maria-Odilia Leal McBride (London: Pluto Press, 1979), and for Forum Theatre, see Boal, *Games for Actors and Non-Actors*, trans. Adrian Jackson (London and New York: Routledge, 1992).
85. See Farfan, *Women, Modernism, and Performance*, 33.
86. Kelly, 'The Actresses' Franchise League Prepares for War,' 130.
87. Hirshfield, 'The Woman's Theatre in England: 1913–1918,' *Theatre History Studies*, 15 (June 1995), 134.
88. 'Actress, Authoress, Manageress,' *The Era*, 10 May 1913, 13.
89. Letter from Mrs Kimberley, 27 February 1934. Compton Mackenzie Collection, Harry Ransom Humanities Research Centre, University of Texas (Austin).
90. *The Pride of the Regiment*, British Library, Add. Mss. 1917/23, Lord Chamberlain's Collection of Plays, licensed for performance Theatre Royal, Wolverhampton, 10 December 1917; *A Spy in the Ranks*, British Library, Add. Mss. 1918/2, Lord Chamberlain's Collection of Plays, licensed for performance Theatre Royal, Wolverhampton, 13 May 1918; and *The Soldier's Divorce*, British Library, Add. Mss. 1918/1563, Lord Chamberlain's Collection of Plays, licensed for performance Theatre Royal, Wolverhampton, 11 September 1918.
91. *The Era*, 9 October 1918, 4.
92. *The Era*, 25 September 1918, 11.
93. *The Era*, 20 March 1918, 13.

94. Steve Nicholson, *The Censorship of British Drama, 1900–1968*, Vol. I, *1900–1932* (Exeter: University of Exeter Press, 2003), 141–2.

95. Michael R. Booth, *English Melodrama* (London: Herbert Jenkins, 1965), and Peter Brooks, *The Melodramatic Imagination: Balzac, James, and the Mode of Excess* (New Haven: Yale University Press, 1976).

96. As Martha Vicinus characterizes the working-class heroes and heroines of melodrama of the 1820s and 1830s, ' "Helpless and Unfriended": Nineteenth-Century Domestic Drama,' *New Literary History*, 13: 1 (1981), 127–43.

97. Michael R. Booth, 'Soldiers of the Queen: Drury Lane Imperialism,' in Michael Hays and Anastasia Nikolopoulou (eds), *Melodrama: The Cultural Emergence of a Genre* (London: Macmillan, 1996), 15.

98. Fraser, Green and Johnston, *Gender and the Victorian Periodical*, 100.

99. Armstrong, *Victorian Poetry*, 332.

100. Sheila Stowell, 'Rehabilitating Realism,' *Journal of Dramatic Theory and Criticism*, 6: 2 (Spring 1992), 81–8.

Conclusion: The playwright as woman of letters

1. Susan Croft, *She Also Wrote Plays: An International Guide to Women Playwrights from the 10th to the 21s Century* (London: Faber and Faber, 2001).

2. Tracy C. Davis, *Actresses as Working Women* (London and New York: Routledge, 1991), 10, and Tracy C. Davis, 'Laborers of the Nineteenth-Century Theater: The Economies of Gender and Theatrical Organization,' *Journal of British Studies*, 33: 1 (January 1994), 50–1.

3. Elizabeth Robins, *Theatre and Friendship: Some Henry James Letters with a Commentary* (London: Jonathan Cape, 1932), 17.

4. Florence Bell, 'Introduction,' *At the Works: A Study of a Manufacturing Town* (1907; New York: Augustus M. Kelley, 1969), x. For one of the few recent discussions of Bell's social investigation, see Deborah Epstein Nord, *Walking the Victorian Streets: Women, Representation, and the City* (Ithaca and London: Cornell University Press, 1995), 227–30.

5. Reprinted in Florence Bell, *Landmarks. A Reprint of some Essays and other Pieces Published Between the Year 1894 and 1922* (London: Ernest Benn, 1929).

6. Florence Bell, *The Way the Money Goes* (London: Sidgwick & Jackson, 1910).

7. *New DNB*, http://via.oxforddnb.com.

8. Florence Bell and Elizabeth Robins, *Alan's Wife* in Linda Fitzsimmons and Viv Gardner (eds), *New Woman Plays* (London: Methuen, 1991), 19.

9. *Alan's Wife*, 25.

10. Catherine Wiley, 'Staging Infanticide: The Refusal of Representation in Elizabeth Robins's *Alan's Wife*,' *Theatre Journal*, 42: 4 (1990), 433.

11. Wiley argues that 'Robins's character rejects this law, ruptures representation, and the male critic watching her cannot believe his eyes.' 'Staging Infanticide,' 432.

12. Elin Diamond, *Unmaking Mimesis* (London and New York: Routledge, 1997), 37.

13. Cited in Angela V. John, *Elizabeth Robins: Staging a Life, 1862–1952* (London and New York: Routledge, 1995), 89.
14. Wiley, 'Staging Infanticide,' 444 and Diamond, *Unmaking Mimesis*, 37.
15. *The Theatre*, 1 June 1893, 334–5.
16. *The Athenæum*, 6 May 1893, 581.
17. *The Times*, 1 May 1893.
18. *The Era*, 6 May 1893, 8.
19. Wiley, 'Staging Infanticide,' 438.
20. Nord, *Walking the Victorian Streets*, 230.
21. 11 May [c.1891], Elizabeth Robins Papers, Fales Library, New York University.
22. [1895], Elizabeth Robins Papers, Fales Library, New York University.
23. Thurs [30 April 1914], Elizabeth Robins Papers, Fales Library, New York University.
24. *The Era*, 13 May 1893, 11.
25. *The Theatre*, 1 December 1887, 331.
26. *Dramatic Notes*, November 1887, 120.
27. *New DNB*, http://via.oxforddnb.com.
28. *The Theatre*, 1 March 1893, 160–1.
29. Tess Cosslett, *Woman to Woman: Female Friendship in Victorian Fiction* (Brighton: Harvester Press, 1988).
30. See Kerry Powell, 'Elizabeth Robins, Oscar Wilde, and the "Theatre of the Future",' *Women and the Victoran Stage*.
31. Holledge, *Innocent Flowers*, 22–3, 41–2, 77.
32. Shaw, 'Municipal Theatres,' *Our Theatres in the Nineties*, Vol. 2, 73–4.
33. Barstow, ' "Hedda is All of Us", ' 387–8, and Viv Gardner, 'The Invisible Spectatrice: Gender, Geography and Theatrical Space,' in Gale and Gardner (eds), *Women, Theatre, and Performance*, 33.
34. Barstow, ' "Hedda is All of Us", ' 389.
35. Clo. Graves, B. L. Farjeon, Florence Marryat, G. Manville Fenn, Mrs Campbell Praed, Justin Huntly McCarthy, and Clement Scott, *The Fate of Fenella* (London: Hutchinson, 1892), and Clo. Graves, B. L. Farjeon, Florence Marryat, G. Manville Fenn, Mrs Campbell Praed, Justin Huntly McCarthy, and Clement Scott, *Seven Christmas Eves, Being the Romance of a Social Evolution* (London: Hutchinson and Co. [1893]).
36. David Hannay, *Life of Frederick Marryat* (London: Walter Scott, 1889), 12.
37. Helen C. Black, *Notable Women Authors of the Day* (Glasgow: David Bryce and Son, 1893), 87. See also the card catalogue for the Lord Chamberlain's Collection of Plays, British Library.
38. Black, *Notable Women Authors of the Day*, 90.
39. Black, *Notable Women Authors of the Day*, 90–1.
40. [Florence] Marryat, ms. Autobiographical Note, Camden Morrisby Collection, 52, Special Collections, Fisher Library, University of Sydney, ff. 4–5.
41. Talia Schaffer, *The Forgotten Female Aesthetes, Literary Culture in Late-Victorian England* (Charlottesville and London: University Press of Virginia, 2000), 41.
42. Florence Marryat with Sir Charles Young, *Miss Chester* (London: Samuel French, n.d.).
43. 'Holborn Theatre,' *The Athenæum*, 12 October 1872, 476; 'Holborn Theatre,' *The Era*, 13 October 1872; *Illustrated London News*, 12 October 1872; 'Holborn Theatre,' *The Daily Telegraph*, 7 October 1872.

44. Andrew Maunder, 'Introduction,' to Florence Marryat, *Love's Conflict* (1865; London: Pickering and Chatto, 2005). This is the best recent account of Marryat's life and writing.

45. Edward Clodd, *Memories* (London: Chapman & Hall, 1916), 37–9. See also Marysa Demoor and Monty Chisholm (eds), *'Bravest of women and finest of friends': Henry James's Letters to Lucy Clifford* (University of Victoria: English Literary Studies, 1999), 11–16.

46. Gordon S. Haight (ed.), *The George Eliot Letters*, Vol. VII (New Haven: Yale University Press, 1955), 123.

47. Demoor and Chisholm (ed.), *'Bravest of women and finest of friends,'* 14.

48. See correspondence in the Brotherton Library, Special Collections, University of Leeds, and the Harry Ransom Humanities Research Centre, University of Texas (Austin).

49. London: Richard Bentley, 1885; 2 vols.

50. Lucy Clifford, *The Likeness of the Night: A Modern Play in Four Acts* (London: Adam and Charles Black, 1900). The story is reprinted in Kate Flint (ed.), *Victorian Love Stories: An Oxford Anthology* (Oxford: Oxford University Press, 1996).

51. *Sheffield Daily Telegraph*, 20 May 1908.

52. *The Era*, 22 July 1914, 12.

53. Lucy Clifford, *The Searchlight* (London: Samuel French, 1904).

54. Lucy Clifford, *The Hamilton's Second Marriage*, in *Plays* (London: Duckworth, 1909), and *A Honeymoon Tragedy* (London: Samuel French, 1904).

55. 'The Likeness of the Night,' *The Era*, 2 November 1901.

56. Peter Bailey, 'Theatres of Entertainment/Spaces of Modernity,' 17.

57. Ardis, *Modernism and Cultural Conflict*, 4.

58. Mellor, *Romanticism and Gender* (New York and London: Routledge, 1993), 1.

59. Rita Felski, *The Gender of Modernity* (Cambridge, Mass.: Harvard University Press, 1995), 10.

60. Bailey, 'Theatres of Entertainment/Spaces of Modernity,' 17–18.

Index